CW00500245

TRYPTAM… PALACE

"With this book, Oroc has proved that the impossible can in fact be put into words. WOW indeed! A must-have for any serious psychonaut on (arguably) the most important subject matter of all time."

DIMITRI DJANBANI, MODERATOR OF HTTP://DMT.TRIBE.NET, A DMT DISCUSSION GROUP

"If DMT is the 'Spirit Molecule,' then 5-MeO-DMT certainly qualifies as the 'God Molecule' as illustrated in this highly significant contribution to entheogenic literature. The immediate opening to full God consciousness that 5-MeO-DMT occasions demands careful attention by all those interested in spiritual states of consciousness, entheogenic experience, and the true nature of reality. Oroc's book is a great beginning to the fascinating exploration that awaits us with 5-MeO-DMT."

MARTIN W. BALL, PH.D., AUTHOR OF *MUSHROOM WISDOM: HOW SHAMANS CULTIVATE SPIRITUAL CONSCIOUSNESS*

"A gripping account of a mind transformed by the powerful psychoactive 5-MeO-DMT struggling to understand its unexpected conversion from atheist to true believer. Oroc fuses hard data and engaging speculations to fire the imagination. *Tryptamine Palace* is 'Mr. Toad's Wild Ride' for entheogen aficionados, where the firsthand experience of God may be just a toke away."

JON HANNA, MINDSTATES.ORG

"*Tryptamine Palace* is destined to be the seminal study of 5-MeO-DMT, just as *The Spirit Molecule* personifies DMT and *My Problem Child* evokes LSD."

ANDREW SEWELL, M.D., LSD CLUSTER-HEADACHE RESEARCHER

TRYPTAMINE PALACE

5-MeO-DMT
and the Sonoran Desert Toad

JAMES OROC

Park Street Press
Rochester, Vermont

Park Street Press
One Park Street
Rochester, Vermont 05767
www.ParkStPress.com

Park Street Press is a division of Inner Traditions International

Library of Congress Cataloging-in-Publication Data

Oroc, James.
Tryptamine palace : 5-MeO-DMT and the Sonoran Desert Toad / James Oroc.
p. cm.
Includes bibliographical references and index.
Summary: "A journey from Burning Man to the Akashic Field that suggests how 5-MeO-DMT triggers the human capacity for higher knowledge through direct contact with the zero-point field"—Provided by publisher.
ISBN 978-1-59477-299-3
1. Hallucinogenic drugs and religious experience. I. Title.
BL65.D7O76 2009
154.4092—dc22
[B]

2009007864

Printed and bound in the United States

10 9 8 7 6 5

Text design and layout by Priscilla Baker
This book was typeset in Garamond Premier Pro with Gill Sans used as a display typeface

The author can be contacted at TryptaminePalace@hotmail.com.

Dedicated to the Fathers of Western entheogenic literature:

William James (1842–1910)
Aldous Huxley (1894–1963)
R. Gordon Wasson (1898–1986)
Albert Hofmann (1906–2008)
William S. Burroughs (1914–1997)
Ken Kesey (1935–2001)
Terence McKenna (1946–2000)

And to Alexander "Sasha" Shulgin, for continuing to stoke the fire.

But most of all, to my beautiful wife, for marrying a madman!

"You're assuming," said Dr. Robert, "that the brain produces consciousness. I'm assuming that it transmits consciousness. And my explanation is not more farfetched than yours. How on earth can a set of events belonging to one order be experienced as a set of events belonging to an entirely different and incommensurable order? Nobody has the faintest idea. All one can do is accept the facts and concoct hypotheses. And one hypothesis is just about as good, philosophically speaking, as another. You say that the moksha-meditation does something to the silent areas of the brain, which causes them to produce a set of subjective events to which people have given the name 'mystical experience.' I say that the moksha-medicine does something to the silent areas of the brain, which opens some kind of neurological sluice and so allows a larger volume of Mind with a large 'M' to flow in to your mind with a small 'm.' You can't demonstrate the truth of your hypothesis, and I can't demonstrate the truth of mine. And even if you could prove that I'm wrong, would it make any practical difference?"

ALDOUS HUXLEY, *ISLAND* (1962)

Use the light that dwells within you
To regain your natural clarity of sight.

LAO-TZU

Contents

Foreword

The mystical experience is the foundation of all world religions, whose ultimate purpose is to provide to the faithful an intimate encounter with God, Christ, Consciousness, Buddhamind, Primordial Awareness, Infinite Intelligence. . . . To claim that the divine can be accessed via the use of a material substance would be considered heresy by most traditional religions as well as by science in our postmodern culture. However, the question of whether entheogens can catalyze a full-blown mystical experience has been answered affirmatively and verified scientifically.

In an early Harvard study formulated by Walter Pahnke in 1962, thirty Harvard Divinity students were given a single dose of either psilocybin or nicotinic acid. The dosed students were brought to Marsh Chapel to attend a Good Friday service and later asked to answer criterion defining the categories of the mystical experience. Over 60 percent of the subjects who ingested psilocybin reported a primary religious experience—personal contact with the Divine.

The war on drugs has prevented further follow-up studies until recently when, in a related but even more tightly controlled and carefully prepared trial at Johns Hopkins University, Roland Griffiths and his team demonstrated a 65 percent success rate. How many religious institutions or traditions can offer a similar guarantee, subject to the rigors of scientific verification, that in one afternoon 65 percent of their practitioners will achieve a bona fide mystical experience, one of complete unity within and with the cosmos, transcendence of space and time, a sense of vastness, infinitude and blissful ineffitude? Because the substances are illegal and reviled by much of society, these results hover like a heretical miracle in a materialist and rationally reductionist world.

Does this mean that the "psychedelic movement" of the '60s and the continued exploration of entheogens by millions worldwide have in fact ignited the beginning of a new world religion? The answer is yes. The examination of the nature of God and religion has landed squarely in the lap of the entheogenic community. A few brave seekers are willing to speak to the mystical experience and higher levels of awareness that are the result of their exploration of altered states through ingesting sacramental substances.

A new voice in the evolving literature of experimental mysticism is heralded with the book you hold in your hands, *Tryptamine Palace.* James Oroc has built this book around his connection with the Divine through the unique properties of 5-MeO-DMT. This special substance catapults the consciousness of its user into the white-light vast expanse beyond all distractions from the physical and subtle visionary dimensions.

My personal interest is the author's willingness to champion the religious importance of entheogens as a tool for spiritual transformation at this critical time of human history. May the story of his awakening empower your own.

Alex and Allyson Grey

Along with the preternatural lights and colors, the gems and the ever-changing patterns, visitors to the mind's antipodes discover a world of sublimely beautiful landscapes, of living architecture and of heroic figures. The transporting power of many works of art is attributable to the fact that their creators have painted scenes, persons and objects which remind the beholder of what, consciously or unconsciously, he knows about the Other World at the back of his mind.

ALDOUS HUXLEY, *HEAVEN AND HELL,* 1956

. . . as I toured the cliff-side town of Positano on the Amalfi coast near Naples, where buildings grow like barnacles—from the tops of hills and down the sheer slope to the Gulf of Salerno. It suddenly hit me that behind every society was a hidden, elflike voice that whispered: "Build! Create! Build! Create!" Moreover, some of the intricate structures I had seen during my journey were reminiscent of the sparkling, ornate palaces revealed to people under the influence of the psychoactive compound DMT (dimethyltryptamine). It seems as if DMT frees the mind to see the blueprint—hardwired by the whispering elves—instructing us to create, create, create.

CLIFFORD A. PICKOVER, *SEX, DRUGS, EINSTEIN, & ELVES: SUSHI, PSYCHEDELICS, PARALLEL UNIVERSES, AND THE QUEST FOR TRANSCENDENCE,* 2005

Preface

The book you are holding in your hands is a much revised and expanded version of the original *Tryptamine Palace,* which in 2006 and 2007 I gifted to members of the Burning Man community in successive versions. Burning Man, for those of you who have not already heard of it, describes itself on its website as "an annual art event and temporary community based on radical self-expression and self-reliance in the Black Rock Desert of Nevada."[1] Which is a rather tame description of what is the greatest annual counter-culture gathering on the planet—a mad tent city of up to 50,000 people from all over the world that is filled with tremendous art, unfettered love, and frequent explosions, existing in its entirety for only a single week of the year. Burning Man is all about participation, and knowing that among its inhabitants I could find those who would be most interested in my experiences, I decided to contribute to the Burning Man art-movement by writing this book.

Both of these earlier versions were poorly edited, containing numerous typos, incomplete statements, and factual errors; in many ways I am embarrassed that I gave them away at all, since the complete and final version of *Tryptamine Palace* was far from finished. Yet all of my excitement and most of my basic theories were there (if somewhat obscured by the writing at times), and the reception I received from the Burning Man community was overwhelming. I would like to thank everyone who waded through those original versions for their encouragement and support.

One of the most difficult things about the tryptamine experience is that the more you believe in the veracity of your own experience, the more difficult so-called normal reality becomes. There have been many times when I have wondered why I was writing this book, when I have told myself, "To hell with it, just go back to writing fiction, the truth is too hard to believe anyway." But something would not let go of me; something has kept pushing this project along. As I explain within the chapters of this book, it became a matter of faith: a resolute belief that the events that had happened to me were important, that ultimately they did mean something, and that the message conveyed in this book was intended for a greater audience.

Terence McKenna used to say that he was simply a mouthpiece for the mushroom, and I can honestly say that I know what he meant, for in many ways this book wrote itself: I was merely a conduit, somehow channeling a steady, virtually uninterrupted stream of information—a bizarre experience for a seasoned writer who has known days of frustration at a keyboard. This is a book that was determined to be written, despite any weak moments that my ego-laden self might have had.

Early on I decided that the fastest way to get *Tryptamine Palace* to a wider audience would be to self-publish and sell the book on the Internet. The potential in this journey seemed like a grand adventure, and in many ways I was embracing the freedom of the self-publishing age. But the truth of the matter was that in the twenty-something years that I have actively considered myself "a writer," I have always hated the idea of submitting my manuscript to uncaring publishers who would then pass judgment on my hard-earned words. This fear of rejection has meant that my non-magazine work has either been self-published or left to languish in my bottom desk drawer.

"Time to toughen up," I told myself. After dragging my heels for months, I finally sent a couple of my precious printed Burning Man copies of *Tryptamine Palace* off to two publishers, one who had published a book I considered similar to my own and the other to Inner Traditions, one of the most respected metaphysical publishers in the world and the company that published Ervin Laszlo's most recent revolutionary work that I admire, as well as a host of other brilliant minds.

"Might as well shoot for the top," I told myself, but I never expected any reply other than a rejection letter, which the first publisher speedily sent me. You can imagine my great surprise when I received an e-mail from Jon Graham, Inner Traditions' acquisitions editor, telling me that they in fact *were* interested in publishing *Tryptamine Palace.*

This humbling opportunity has allowed this final reexamination and ultimate version of *Tryptamine Palace* to be born. It's now a work that has been both diligently checked and internally realized and provides the most complete summation of my theories and conclusions. Various people have told me that my attempt to verbalize the realms of the tryptamine experience has led to a reemergence or reassessment of their own experiences. Previously unable to find any words for what they had been through on 5-MeO-DMT (or DMT), these people had kept their experiences locked up inside. However, the ideas and possibilities presented in this book have apparently encouraged them to again attempt to better understand and express their own experiences. It is my hope that *Tryptamine Palace* stimulates discussion of the unique effects that smokable tryptamines can have on human consciousness and spirituality.

While becoming an Inner Traditions author is undoubtedly the most surprising honor I've been given, I can't say that it is the greatest personal honor that *Tryptamine Palace* has so far afforded me. For my proudest moment occurred when I unexpectedly met Alexander "Sasha" Shulgin and his wife Ann at Burning Man.

I had no idea that 2006 was the twentieth anniversary of the Multidisciplinary Association for Psychedelic Studies (MAPS) and that in honor of this occasion Entheon Village at Burning Man would be showcasing a series of speakers, culminating in the Shulgins themselves. For some reason they were the last people I would have expected to suffer the harsh desert climate of Black Rock City. Perhaps it was because—as prolific at creating new psychoactive chemicals as he is—I could barely imagine Sasha ever emerging from his infamous lab. Since Alexander Shulgin is one of the "fathers of Western entheogenic literature" to whom I have dedicated this book—and since my friends had been watching me process the ideas culminating in the book over the previous two years—the members of my tribe immediately declared that I had to take the Shulgins a copy of the book. In true Burning Man fashion, we loaded up a box of books on our bicycles and headed over to Entheon Village.

As soon as I walked around the massive Alex Grey dome and into Entheon, I saw Sasha Shulgin. A towering figure with a shock of white hair, he looks like the quintessential Russian scientist, and I knew upon spotting him that it couldn't be anybody else. Dr. Shulgin was just getting in line for food when I introduced myself to him by apologizing for the fact that I had ruthlessly plagiarized quotations from him throughout my own book. He was very genial, if not a little bemused. I should mention at this point that we were all in our finest Mardi Gras costumes for our annual camp party, and that I became acutely aware of the fact that I was dressed in a red-white-and-blue striped American flag leotard, which makes me look like a bald Mary Lou Retton on steroids.

My wife and other tribe members started handing out copies of the original version of *Tryptamine Palace* to the crowd that had gathered around us quite quickly. I gave one to Sasha, and explained that I had dedicated the book—in part—to him. He then put on his glasses, opened the cover, and said:

"You have spelled my name wrong."

Which indeed I had, spelling it as "Sascha" instead of "Sasha." Perhaps because I knew him as the father of DOM, 2C-B, 2C-T-7, and godfather of MDMA, all those letters had finally gotten the better of me!

Talk about slapping my ego back down to size. But at the same time, it was a perfect Burning Man moment—one that I will never forget, and reason enough alone to write this book and a good warning for any writer who wants to take himself too seriously. But still I hope this work resonates with the light that resides within you and that you join in this new mind revolution. For if a positive future is to be ours, we all have a lot of work to do.

INTRODUCTION

How This All Began

I placed 25 mg of 5-methoxy-DMT in a stainless steel one-quarter teaspoon and vaporized it over a cigarette lighter collecting the smoke in an upside-down funnel. All smoke was inhaled; the taste was mild—none of the plastic taste of DMT. About 10 seconds or so after inhaling the last of the smoke, it began with a fast-rising sense of excitement and wonder, with an undertone of "Now you've done it," but dominated by a sense of, "WOW, This Is IT!" There was a tremendous sense of speed and acceleration. In perhaps 10 more seconds these feelings built to an intensity I had never experienced before. The entire universe *imploded through my consciousness. It's as if the mind is capable of experiencing a very large number of objects, situations and feelings, but normally perceives them only one at a time. I felt that my mind was perceiving them all at once. There was no distance, no possibility of examining the experience. This was simply the most intense experience possible; a singularity, a white-out (as opposed to a black out). I have little memory of the state itself. I have no memory, for example, of whether my eyes were opened or closed. After some seconds or minutes, it started to fade and came to resemble a merely intense psychedelic state. Here I had the feeling, a visualization of being part of the universe of beings, all active in our daily, interwoven tasks, still moving at an incredible rate, and with a longing for a single group/organism awareness and transcendence. In a few more minutes it faded to an alert (+one) state with an additional sense of awe and wonder, relief, and a strong feeling of gratitude toward the universe in general, for the experience.*

Alexander and Ann Shulgin,
TIHKAL: The Continuation, 1997

In July of 2003, shortly before my thirty-sixth birthday, I smoked 5-methoxy-*N,N*-DMT (5-MeO-DMT) for the first time. Attaching no particular importance to the event, and approaching it with the same characteristic lack of caution that has accompanied many of my various adventures in life, I sat down on a mattress in a nondescript suburban home in Portland, Oregon, and drew the strange-tasting smoke down into my lungs. I remember looking at my friend whose house we were in and wondering when something would happen, before he reminded me to breathe out. When I did that my old world—and indeed my old life—magically evaporated.

Having read Terence McKenna's descriptions of smoking DMT and not knowing at the time that there was any difference between 5-MeO-DMT and its less potent cousin,* I was expecting the effect of the drug to be something of a cross between taking LSD and a bong hit, and I was sure that I had had sufficient prior experiences on other substances to prepare me for this event. However, I cannot describe the paradigm-shifting amazement that I experienced when I suddenly exited my "trip" more than thirty minutes later, standing in a corner of the room and moving my arms in perfect yoga sun salutations as I watched dragons and griffins flying in waves of red and gold along the wall.

This sense of unabated amazement continued to grow as I turned around and found my friend and his brother with their eyes wide and their jaws agape after having been stunned witnesses to the whole affair. Then, as I learned that at one point I had gotten to my feet and declared ecstatically: "It exists! It exists!" and "I am there," I could only wonder what had actually just happened to me, and what in fact I had just experienced. For in the half hour after I had exhaled from that pipe, I had come in contact with a force far greater than I had ever known possible—or even imagined existed—and I now felt as if I had blindly stuck my wet finger firmly into the cosmic socket and come away with my senses totally fried. Smoking 5-MeO-DMT

***N,N*-dimethyltryptamine

had suddenly gone from being a mere curiosity to becoming one of the most important events of my life.

From this very first experience, my view of reality was rearranged in a more comprehensive manner than I could have ever believed. I now consider 5-MeO-DMT to be the only true entheogen I have ever encountered, since before that day I was a hardened atheist who embraced an inherited cynical scientific material-reductionist* worldview, while now I inhabit a universe that is mystically inspired, and thus I'm indelibly aware of the existence of G/d. And it was this first 5-MeO-DMT "experience" was solely responsible for radically changing me into a spiritually inspired, and much more hopeful, human being.

Entheogens

Entheogen ("generating God within") is an ethnographic term used to describe a plant or drug that invokes a sense of the numinous or a mystical experience. While several other well-known compounds—such as DMT, psilocybin, mescaline, and LSD—are often included in this category, I have personally found 5-MeO-DMT to be unique in that it is the only compound that has allowed me to experience an out-of-body reality that is both 100 percent convincing and completely unlike any "known" reality. Other compounds such as DMT, ketamine, *Salvia divinorum,* and DIPT also have considerable reputations for producing out-of-body realities, but I have had little experience with them.

I can now state with unshakable "faith"—a word that used to make my skin crawl—that I believe in the existence of the transcendent, formless Godhead and in the individual human ability to realize that transcendent ideal. I also now believe in the continued existence of my Soul (or consciousness if you prefer) after my physical body passes away—two newly acquired

*"Materialism is the belief that reality consists solely of matter and energy, the things that can be measured in the laboratory or observed by a telescope. Everything else is illusion or imagination. Reductionism is the belief that complex things can be explained by examining the constituent pieces, such as the illusion of consciousness arising from elementary chemical processes in the brain."[1]

"leap-of-faith beliefs" that have provided me with an enormous sense of peace and well-being, as well as a complete lack of fear of dying. The words of the great Russian novelist Vladimir Nabokov express my newfound perspective on the possibilities of the afterlife perfectly when he writes, "Life is a great surprise. I do not see why death should not be an even greater one."[2]

This radical and personally astonishing change in my own ideology has resulted in the most spiritually rewarding, intellectually stimulating, and thoroughly enjoyable six years of my life. In writing down my thoughts on the reasons for this powerful philosophical transformation, I have decided that the best course of action is to try to clarify the 5-MeO-DMT experience ("5MDE") in a phenomenological manner. In the pages of this book I have therefore compiled all the things that I have learned and speculated about 5-MeO-DMT (and its more famous cousin DMT), as well as some of the realizations about the remarkable capabilities of the human soul that I have acquired while on this personal journey from the outer reaches of the human experience back to the core of myself.

Throughout this mostly linear narrative you'll find my search for answers to the true nature of the 5-MeO-DMT experience and how it was able to have such a profound effect on my own personality and spirituality. This diverse physical and philosophical adventure includes hunting for the marvelous Sonoran Desert toads, visiting the unique community of Burning Man, and exploring the paradox and sublime beauty of India and its religious philosophies. I will also examine the possibility of a quantum-mechanical basis for consciousness, contemplate the strange properties of light, and examine some of the startling philosophical implications of the recent scientific discovery of a vast underlying energy source in the universe that scientists are calling the "zero-point field." All in an attempt to propose a theory regarding the nature of the phenomena that I have experienced and to elucidate how this "minimum working hypothesis" might fit in with other modern and ancient schools of thought.

Finally, and most importantly, I will explain how I have come to believe that it is both possible and necessary for many of us to realize our own transcendent vision of G/d (see box), before our species' time on this planet runs out due to both our ingenuity and our stupidity. A fate that can only be avoided if our society can reconnect with the sacred and learn to live in balance again with the world and thus see powerful entheogens like 5-MeO-DMT recognized as important and remarkable tools for the continued survival of humanity.

Naming God

The use of the name "God" has presented numerous difficulties in this inquiry. Thus, I have created the formula of G (over) d to express the source of the universal energy that we collectively as a species have named God. I originally developed this formula in a clumsy attempt to distance myself from the Christian "God" and the prejudices that designation carries with it, but I have come to realize that this formula is actually accurate.

G = the absolute expression of the transcendent formless God

d = the individual human ability to realize the transcendent ideal of God

G (over) d = the (knowable) God(s) of humanity

Thus the God(s) and Goddess(es) we as a species are capable of knowing are in fact historically realized individual visions that represent a fraction of the transcendental Other. This formula is congruent with Aldous Huxley's "minimum working hypothesis,"* a distillation of tenets common to most major religions.

*"First: the phenomenal world of matter and of individualized consciousness—the world of things and animals and men and even gods—is a manifestation of a Divine Ground within which all partial realities have their being, and apart from which they would be nonexistent. Second: human beings are capable not merely of knowing *about* the Divine Ground by inference; they can also realize its existence by a direct intuition, superior to discursive reasoning. This immediate knowledge unites the knower with that which is known. Third: man possesses a double nature, a phenomenal ego and an eternal Self, which is the inner man, the spirit, the spark of divinity within the soul. It is possible for a man, if he so desires, to identify himself with the spirit and therefore with the Divine Ground, which is of the same or like nature with the spirit. Fourth: man's life on earth has only one end and purpose: to identify himself with his eternal Self and so come to unitive knowledge of the Divine Ground."[3]

But first, after a lifetime of actively seeking out powerful new experiences, let me now attempt to give words to the most complex and irrevocably life-changing event I have ever encountered. For as impossible a task that relating a transcendental experience may be, I will now begin by trying to describe exactly what happens when I smoke 5-MeO-DMT.

ONE

The 5-MeO-DMT Experience

Confined in the dark, narrow cage
of our own making which we take for
the whole universe,
very few of us can even begin to imagine
another dimension of reality.

Sogyal Rinpoche, *The Tibetan Book of Living and Dying*, 2002

By attempting to describe the impossibly intense and paradoxically fleeting 5MDE (5-MeO-DMT experience), I am now moving onto purely subjective ground. I must stress that the chronology I provide here is only *my* personal interpretation of 5-MeO-DMT, gleaned from my own experimentation. Therefore while the following information is taken from "the front lines," so to speak, it cannot be overstated that every individual's experience is unique—what happens to me when I smoke 5-MeO-DMT will not necessarily happen to you, should you choose to smoke it.

For myself, after six years of fairly regular use of 5-MeO-DMT in both its natural and synthetic (lab-produced) forms, the following consistent patterns have emerged:

1. I fully inhale the smoke, generally holding it in until my vision of my physical surroundings has begun to break into fractals, and then I exhale. Virtually immediately upon exhalation, my vision experiences a field of light-fractals. My mind then dissolves into this white light, until the external vision of my eyes is no longer relevant (or at least no longer recognizes my physical environment). This white light—that blazes with the focused intensity of a laser and is both whiter-than-white, yet also sparkling with brilliant color—may be the crux of the experience. The first time I smoked 5-MeO-DMT, the only instruction I was given by the friend who provided it to me was to stay in this light for as long as possible.
2. Next, a variety of inner phenomena can appear. Some people report seeing protector spirits (animals or angels), while others describe communicating directly with the light. In some of my early journeys, I walked across plains of stars and talked with a Goddess who appeared in a blend of changing forms, some familiar, some archetypical, and I remember she laughed and treated me like a child. Whoever is in charge in that dimension knows to keep it simple when we visit there; we are children compared to them, and they teach us things in the slow methodical way any good teacher does: one simple lesson at a time.

Stanislav Grof has described such encounters in his extensive road map of the transpersonal experience, *The Cosmic Game.*

> Immediately following the experience of total annihilation—"hitting cosmic bottom"—we are overwhelmed by visions of light that has a supernatural radiance and beauty and is usually perceived as sacred. This divine epiphany can be associated with displays of beautiful rainbows, diaphanous peacock designs, and visions of celestial realms with angelic beings or deities appearing in light. This is also the time when we can experience a profound encounter with the archetypal figure of the Great Mother Goddess or one of her many culture-bound forms."[1]

Early on in my experimentations, when I was hyper-excited by some of the strange and wonderful ideas I had encountered in Terence McKenna's wild book *The Archaic Revival,* I meditated with serious resolve on the question, "What are you? Can you let me know?" before I made my journey to that other dimension. After reading McKenna's book I was intoxicated with the idea of gods, aliens, and other-dimensional beings, and I was certain that this was the correct way of attempting to communicate with them: surely they would respect my intent. Then, as soon as I exhaled, the answer from the other side blasted me like a million volts of pure electricity threatening to fry me to my core.

Love. That is all you need to know. I am Love.

This answer is one of the oldest known to humanity and the center of many great religions; but it was not one that I had expected, nor one that I had been looking for. In fact, I would probably have never considered it as an option at all. But as an answer to a child who is making his first frightful steps into the unknown, it could not be paralleled for its effect. "*Do not fear,*" this other dimension declares, "*There is an ocean of love over here.*"

After that experience, I stopped asking questions.

3. In this realm of light I relive all the experiences from my life in an instant. My whole life flashes before me like the wave of a hand—the passage of time is like a game here. All the people I have known and loved surround me as I become a part of them and they become a part of me as I expand out of my form toward realization.

Everyone seems very happy and excited at this point, with a keen sense of humor attached to the fact that we have had the great secret-and-answer contained within us all along. The multitude of faces around me keep laughing and silently shouting at me, "You knew it all along! We knew it all along! It's all right! We all knew it all the time! You exist! This is real! This is it! Now just relax! And just . . . *Be.*"

Everything that has come before in my life seems to have led to this point, to this moment. There is no sense of time. I am somehow splitting, growing, spreading outward, and becoming a part of everything. I am pervading and connecting with the entire universe from within my very being. As I expand out and integrate into the happy multitudes and the universe beyond them, then my ego-identity begins to dissolve as the realization dawns that I am returning to the Source from where everything came. Looking around, in a dimension without time or space, I recognize everything and everyone as One, as the embodiment of all those beings I have managed to love the most unconditionally. There is a definite feeling that to go past this point, I have to relax, believe, and somehow let go. At this point I have also at times heard a sound—and this is another experience commonly reported by tryptamine smokers—that grows to become the most incredible, all-encompassing note, which somehow transcends all of creation and beyond. It is pure otherworldly angel music, which I can only describe with the word *Aum* (or *Om*): the primordial noise, the logos, or original sound of creation. This is a transcendental note into which I effortlessly dissolve.

4. As I let go I experience dissolution into an omniscient state of *Oneness,* a place where there is no difference between G/d, the physical universe, or me. We have ceased to exist as separate entities and now resonate as *One.* I resonate with the possession of a knowledge that radiates with the surest sense of Love—Love that is in everything and *is* everything, and is so much more. It is a conscious Love more intelligent than anything we have ever known, a Love so great that it defies the need for a physical form and yet paradoxically realizes itself in us and in all of creation. *Aum.* I become that Love and I know that everything is *One,* everything is: G/d

This infinite pulsating field of intelligent energy, from which all physical forms manifest and into which everything shall one day return, is the all-encompassing, brilliant bejeweled light of Love. The Godhead, the Supreme Mystery, the Conscious Infinity, the Pure Light, the Void that is a Plenum, Brahman, Yahweh—whatever you wish to call it. It is the Unnamable Name and the Creation Principle. I recognize It. I know that *It* is real, that I am a part of It, and that in this moment I am able to return to It, like the Sufi "moth to the flame."

Resonating as one with my G/d and now having ceased to exist other than as a part of that divinity, all I have to do is breathe to feel the waves of omniscient energy radiate in and out of my ocean of bliss. My friends, my lovers, my life, my species, my world—we are all One and we are all part of

G/d. *Atman* (individual consciousness) and *Brahman* (universal consciousness) are One. There is no way to differentiate between anything: I am lost in waves of an awestruck ecstasy that cannot be described, an egoless bliss. What Rudolf Otto called the *mysterium tremendum et fascinans*—the overpowering sense of awe that envelopes one who comes face-to-face with the Divine—is revealed within the singular realization of the true nature of my G/d: that G/d paradoxically resides both without and *within*.

Physically, I believe this is when I go into the quietest part of my journey. Generally, I'm peacefully lying down and saying nothing. I am only in this indescribable cosmic resonance for a few short minutes, ten or fifteen at the most, but it makes no difference to me since I no longer have any concept of time, and its passage could just as easily be considered infinite. For some, this is the period of an intense singularity: the white-out (as it is sometimes called), a total dissolution. It is my belief that during this state my consciousness exists in resonance with a realm that is actually *beyond* ordinary human comprehension. Freed of the matter of my body, my consciousness is able to function in a manner that it can't understand, or barely even remember, once it has returned to the limitations of its corporeal form.

I believe that what I have experienced is the universal state of consciousness before the knowledge of ego and self, a state of undifferentiated cosmic consciousness that historically William James described as "Absolute Consciousness" (a term coined by the Theosophical Society's founder, Helena Blavatsky) and Aldous Huxley called "Mind (with a capital M)." This state is now commonly described among today's entheogenic community as "God consciousness." Me, I just call it G/d for short, which is a very clinical way of describing what has historically proven to be the most important and awe-inspiring force in the development of humankind: our ability to achieve some kind of mystical resonance with this G/d; the subsequent realization that the source of this G/d lies within; and the energy and inspiration that this realization has subsequently released into our human society.

"I" have now ceased to exist; there is no knowledge or recognition of "myself." And yet my consciousness remains, clearly still thinking and experiencing, while seemingly knowing everything, with all knowledge and information within my grasp.

5. Suddenly (probably as the 5-MeO-DMT first starts to wear off) there is the taste of fear: "*This is all too much.*" At the apparent pinnacle of the experience, when time has ceased to exist and I have dissolved into this G/d consciousness and lost all sense of my own identity, then I find myself abruptly searching around wildly in this out-of-body dimension, surrounded by layers of information and understanding, struggling to remember how this has all been possible. I exist as pure formless consciousness without limitations, until "I" consciously realize this anomaly, asking myself: "How did this happen? How have I come so far?" And then finally the killer: "Who *am I?*"

"I" begin to think: "I have an identity, don't I? How long has this been going on? What is going on here? How is this possible? I must exist! Something really weird is happening here . . ." The moment that I start thinking *about* the experience instead of simply being *in* the experience, my ego-based identity begins to assert itself, and suddenly it is way, way, too much. I struggle to remember a beginning, a start to "my" own existence, and with this search comes the terror, followed by an abrupt departure from this indescribable state of grace.

6. "You have smoked 5-MeO-DMT," I usually hear a voice say. Then the remembering pours back in a tellurian wave as my being inexorably flows from a dimension without matter or time back into this physical one. My vision suddenly focuses—I can see bizarrely for a moment between the two worlds, seemingly vibrating in both of them at once—before I am suddenly dropped into an awe-struck heap on the floor. The time between remembering that I exist and then reentering my body is terrifyingly quick and very disorientating.
7. Now I am fully back in this reality and over-awed by the sheer *POWER* that I have just experienced, the remnants of which still pulsate through my trembling body. For the following ten or fifteen minutes I am technically still feeling the effects of the 5-MeO-DMT, but my descent to ground zero is quick. I am usually fairly ecstatic during this period, my eyes filled with wildfire, and I can laugh great

> whooping belly laughs, deeper than I have ever laughed before. It's a cosmic laughter at this on-going humor we call life and the unbelievable joke that I have been let in on. (When I heard the Dalai Lama laugh in person, I was reminded of the nature of my 5MDE laughter.) Although these days I prefer to smoke 5-MeO-DMT alone, in the past this period has been a good time for witnesses to ask what I saw and experienced. I then respond with great authority on a variety of subjects—as if channeling from some higher force—only to have no memory of my statements thirty to sixty minutes later. The overwhelming sensation that accompanies this phase, even now after years of use, is that I still have no clue of the depth and breadth of the power of the substance I am so blindly imbibing and that I should strive to treat the 5MDE with sacred respect.

Forty-five minutes to an hour later, I am completely "straight" (and usually looking for ice cream). All chemical traces of the tryptamine have disappeared from my brain, and I am physically free of its influence.* Except now, having experienced a full out-of-body mystical experience, my world and my paradigm can never be the same again.

At this point let me recap my interpretation of the series of events that generally occur when I smoke 5-MeO-DMT:

1. Dissolution into fractals of white light upon exhalation of the 5-MeO-DMT.
2. A sense of transportation via the brilliant white-light and the possible appearance of spirit guides and various manifestations.

*DMT is metabolized very quickly (and this is probably the case with 5-MeO-DMT as well). In a study conducted by Kaplan et al. in 1974, less than 1.8 percent of the DMT dose injected in human subjects could be found in the blood at any time after the dose had been given, and the maximum amount recovered from urine unchanged was 0.16 percent of the dose, with 0.069 percent of the dose as the mean for seven subjects. Kaplan's group opined that it would be unlikely that any DMT produced endogenously could be detected in the blood. However, a study proposed by the newly formed Cottonwood Research Foundation—the Endogenous Hallucinogen Assay project—has recently set the goal of developing novel ultra-sensitive technology in order to measure DMT, 5-MeO-DMT, and bufotenine, as well as their metabolites. For more information, see www.cottonwoodresearch.org.

3. The recognition of the unity of all and that love is the principle that organizes the universe. The intuition that my entire life has come to this one moment in time, and the need to "let go" of my own identity
4. Next is the complete disassociation with ego-identity and any concept of time, as I dissolve into resonance with the One, with G/d ("Absolute Consciousness").
5. The reassertion of identity causes a rapid and disorientating transition back into a restricted consciousness and the return of "my" ego.
6. An abrupt repossession of my physical body as the last effects of the 5-MeO-DMT dissipate.
7. A period of fading resonance between physical consciousness (consciousness with a small letter "c") and G/d consciousness (Mind with a capital "M"), as I return completely to my normal "baseline" state.

It is important to state once again that an infinite variety of experiences for any given individual are possible within the rudimentary framework that I have provided. The scenario I have described here is purely from my own voyages and the experience is open to other interpretations. It is possible that the order in which I have catalogued these events is completely incorrect, since no linear passage of time is evident within the experience. Rather, it is more like being "hard-wired" into another dimension, where you are somehow able to experience everything simultaneously while being channeled toward the "Core."

Some people remember great chunks and frequently report that they went to a dimension "outside of time," where they (paradoxically) felt as if they stayed for an immeasurably long period of time. Others recall nothing but a blinding white light and the extreme disorientation of their return to physicality, which is the least pleasant part of the experience. Those who experience this "white-out" generally think their experience lasted only a few minutes, even though most out-of-body experiences are between fifteen and twenty-five minutes in duration once consciousness is "released." (A percentage of people have prolonged negative experiences or side effects, see appendix 6.)

I think that the specific period between remembering that they exist and then rapidly reentering their body is often what people remember. This is especially the case the first time or if they have smoked too much (which can be easy to do). There is a razor-fine line between smoking enough 5-MeO-DMT to fully experience its out-of-body wonders and smoking too much, which results in the participant remembering little or nothing of the experience other than an often bizarrely terrifying "white hole."

The length of time a person can stay in levels 2, 3, and 4 seems to be the main variable. Some people return to their physical body quickly (i.e., within ten minutes) and then can remain in an obviously "high" state for up to forty-five minutes, going in and out of the experience, but clinging as much as they can to physical "reality." The sign of a true enthusiast is his or her ability to completely let go, with maximum immersion in the resonant out-of-body experience. This is then usually followed by a quick, awe-struck return to normality.

It is my belief that many people only actually experience levels 1, and then levels 5, 6, and 7, since levels 2, 3, and 4, which are the metaphysical crux of the entire experience, can easily be forgotten during the intensity of the experience, or simply may not necessarily be experienced by all people. It may be that every individual has a varying ability to "filter" the white light through the lens of their own human experience, thus allowing some of us to perceive far more in this realm of light than others. There could be a plethora of reasons for this, but I think a combination of philosophical preparedness (accidental or not) and dosage has a lot to do with it.

Every person has his or her own minimum effective dose, which will allow the greatest memory of the experience to be retained. It takes some experimentation to determine an individual's ideal dosage. (This will require owning a gem scale capable of measuring within plus or minus 2 mg to do so accurately.)

If you are of the rare breed that has the desire to smoke 5-MeO-DMT regularly, then I recommend that you consistently *reduce* your dosage until you find the minimum required for release, as this will give you the best chance of remembering the largest amount of the experience. Too much happens in too short a time for it to be really possible to remember it all, but some people do emerge with remarkably coherent accounts of their experiences.

Dosage

In the original Burning Man versions of this book, I recommended a specific dosage range for achieving what I call "an out-of-body release." Since then, it has come to my attention that a number of people within the entheogenic community think that my recommended dosage is too high and potentially dangerous. Appendix 6, Heaven and Hell, examines the possible lasting negative effects that a small percentage of 5-MeO-DMT smokers may experience. This danger is very real, and should not be ignored. 5-MeO-DMT should always be regarded as a possibly life-changing sacrament, and one to be used only with the utmost respect. Hard as it is to conceive, 5-MeO-DMT is truly not like any other drug.

I have also come to realize that there are numerous "recreational" 5-MeO-DMT users who enjoy the physical effects of what I consider "low doses" of 5-MeO-DMT. I have heard of kids snorting it at clubs, I have seen pressed 5 mg pills for sale on the Internet advertised as "legal acid," and—most astonishingly to me personally—when I recently put 5-MeO-DMT into the YouTube search engine, I found a clip of some southern redneck smoking it in a trailer while watching TV, with a fat girl in the background who keeps shouting, "Look at Billy Bob: he looks weird. Doesn't he look weird? Look at Billy Bob . . ." This is very close to my personal idea of hell and most definitely not the kind of the sacramental usage of 5-MeO-DMT that I am advocating.

Having stumbled into this tangled web, I want to preface my remarks on dosage with this fact for guidance: there are two very different 5-MeO-DMT "trips." One is very physical, somewhat psychedelic, in which your consciousness remains within your physical environment throughout; this occurs at what I categorize as "low dosages." Then, at a specific point—and this point will be different for everyone—your consciousness will leave the physical containment of your body, leaving just the shell of your ego behind. For me, this is a true 5MDE, and this transpersonal out-of-body phenomenon is the subject of my book.

Dosage can vary greatly for different people, but to achieve a full out-of-body experience, I would recommend a starting point around 12 mg.

Please be aware that this is a much smaller dose than is usually used when smoking DMT. The book *Some Simple Tryptamines* by Keeper of the Trout and Friends remarks that 5-MeO-DMT can be "distressing" if the optimal dosage is exceeded, and it suggests that the dosage is under 10 mg for most people, if it is taken all at once. A person's body weight does not seem to have an effect on what dose works; heavier people do not need more.

In their book *TIHKAL*, the Shulgins list a smoked-dose range of 6 to 20 mg for 5-MeO-DMT. While the Shulgins have been criticized as sometimes presenting conservative doses, it is also possible that different methods of vaporizing 5-MeO-DMT may more be more effective than the method I present. My suggested dose range specifically relates to the method of ingestion I describe below. Those vaporizing 5-MeO-DMT in "crack"-type pipes—particularly of a style that allows for little slipstream loss of vapor—should start out with lower doses than those I recommend. (For reports of intense experiences at lower doses, see pages 532–533 of *TIHKAL*.)

Those who are serious about smoking 5-MeO-DMT should purchase a scale that can measure accurately within 1–2 milligrams, since any variation larger than that can make a big difference! If a dose of 12 mg doesn't allow a release, slowly work your way up in 2 mg increments. *Amounts in excess of 25 mg are definitely not recommended*, since they can lead to unconsciousness, physical malfunction, and occasionally to vomiting. Serious long-lasting psychological effects have also been reported in some individuals with dosages as low as 15 mg.

I have found that 5-MeO-DMT tends to be very self-regulating. My personal dosage has *reduced* from my initial experiments to a lower mg range. Although this is now an amount that is too low to achieve full release for many people, it sends my 230-pound mass hurling further through hyperspace each time. People seem to end up taking only as much as they need. Sometimes they will cough it out and it hits them straight away; other times they will hold their breath until no smoke is exhaled, and yet they cruise through the experience like a dog dozing in the sun. The only thing for sure is that you can never tell. So if you are feeling the missionary fever after your initial experiences and are getting ready to turn on the world, a word of caution: Your friends who are the most experienced "heads," the ones you are *sure* are going to love it, might turn into blubbering babies or raving loonies. And the frail little hippie girl—who you weren't sure you wanted to turn on because you were afraid she might not be able to handle the trip—could be the one who makes the journey to the Promised Land and returns with the answer that might save us all.

You never know how people will react, and you have to be prepared for anything. I have been bitten, punched, and watched people unexpectedly vomit. One friend, who is a great fan of the juice, arches his back fully, with his head on the floor like he is in a yoga position, and howls at the top of his voice like a wolf for fifteen minutes. (It's best to smoke 5-MeO-DMT with him in a place with no neighbors!) I thought another friend was going to leap through a third-story window, and I had to pin him to a bed for over ten minutes while he thrashed around and punched wildly at invisible demons. He later remembered none of it, believing that he had been lying peacefully on the bed the whole time. This happened on the second occasion that he smoked 5-MeO-DMT; his first trip had been entirely peaceful and was a tremendously positive event in his life.

It should also be noted that different people experience different levels of entheogenic effect due to their own personal intellectual and spiritual development. Not everyone will have a full mystical experience from smoking 5-MeO-DMT.

Fragments of the 5-MeO-DMT experience may filter back over a period of hours, days, and weeks, in the form of startlingly vivid recollections. My conjecture is that our consciousness is able to travel (or simply return) to another dimension during the 5MDE. Because this is a dimension where time and reality do not exist as we know them, it is impossible to remember everything that we have seen and learned there in a linear fashion.

In photographic terms, it is as if we are used to looking through a narrow aperture to see the world and then suddenly that aperture is blown wide open; the subsequent quantity of light pouring through "burns out our negative," so to speak. The sheer volume of what we encounter overwhelms our cognitive mind and perceptions. However, the mind is a brilliant computer as well as a camera and is very persistent when it comes to solving problems. It stores the memory of that white light and then runs all that data through its full spectrum of filters to see if it can make anything out of it all. Eventually, like the memories from a mad dream, scattered scenes and images do return.

TWO

5-MeO-DMT

Science, Discovery, and the History of Human Use

We do not understand much of anything, from the episode we rather dismissively (and, I think, defensively) choose to call the "big bang," all the way down to the particles in the atoms of a bacterial cell.

We have a wilderness of mystery to make our way through in the centuries ahead.

LEWIS THOMAS, "THE ART OF TEACHING SCIENCE,"
NEW YORK TIMES, 1982

I want to know God's thoughts; the rest are mere details.

ATTRIBUTED TO ALBERT EINSTEIN

After my initial paradigm-changing encounter with 5-MeO-DMT, I was in a state something akin to intellectual shock, with the tatters of my old worldview lying shredded around me and a whole new universe of mystery to explore. To regain my equilibrium I knew I would need a new view of reality, since I now intuitively believed that I had experienced a different dimension of existence that I previously had not known existed, and I would have to incorporate this experience into my own understanding. Everything else seemed minor and uninteresting compared to that, and I would spend most of the following three years searching for possible clues or answers to what had happened to me during the thirty-plus minutes that I had been under the influence of 5-MeO-DMT. But when I went looking for information, I quickly realized that there was precious little written about this rare compound, and I would end up spending months in virtual seclusion searching through a mountain of volumes on ethnobotany, philosophy, quantum sciences, alchemy, shamanism, and everything that I could find that had been written about DMT for leads, since there has been very little written about 5-MeO-DMT itself. This lack of available information would eventually be part of the inspiration for the writing of this book and the numerous speculations contained within it. But in this chapter I will relate the few *facts* that are known about 5-MeO-DMT, as well as the role that tryptamines may have played in the development of spirituality in the ethnosphere.

What is 5-MeO-DMT?

trypt-amine \ *'trip-ta-,mēn* \ *n. [tryptophan fr. tryptic, fr. trypsin, fr. Gk. tryein, to wear down (from its occurrence in pancreatic juice as a proteolytic enzyme) + amine fr. NL ammonia] 1: A naturally occurring compound found in both the animal and plant kingdoms. It is an endogenous component of the human brain. 2: Any of a series of compounds containing the tryptamine skeleton, and modified by chemical constituents at appropriate positions in the molecule.*

Alexander and Ann Shulgin,
TIHKAL: The Continuation, 1997

5-methoxy-*N,N*-dimethyltryptamine (5-MeO-DMT) is a member of the *tryptamine* family—a group of compounds that all have a basic tryptamine indole ring structure (see figure 1) and are chemically related to the amino acid *tryptophan.*

The tryptamines are a particularly fascinating branch of chemistry for human research, since they include many biologically active compounds, including both *neurotransmitters* and *entheogens.* The neurotransmitters include serotonin (5-hydroxytryptamine or 5-HT) and the primary pineal hormone, melatonin (*N*-acetyl-5-methoxytryptamine), see figure 2. The

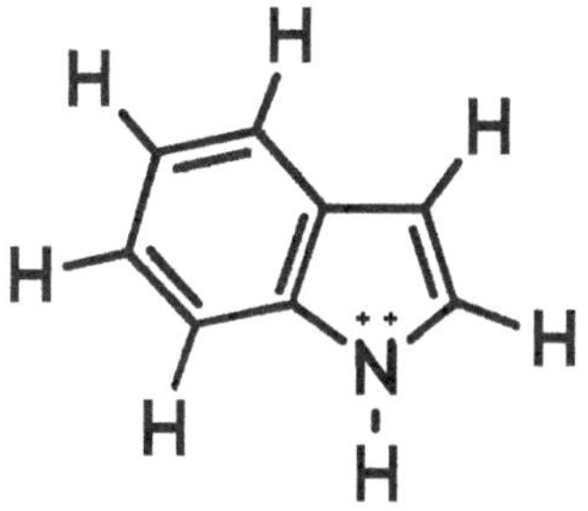

Figure 1. The basic indole ring structure that is the backbone for all compounds in the tryptamine family.

entheogens can be seen in figure 3 and include psilocybin (*O*-phosophoryl-4-HO-DMT)—the main active entheogen in "magic mushrooms"—as well as 5-MeO-DMT and its close relations bufotenine (5-HO-DMT) and DMT (dimethyltryptamine). The indole backbone can also be identified as part of the structure of more complex entheogens such as LSD and ibogaine.

Because these entheogens possess the same basic structure as neurotransmitters, they are able to cross the human blood-brain barrier, allowing them to have a dramatic effect upon consciousness. Unlike other

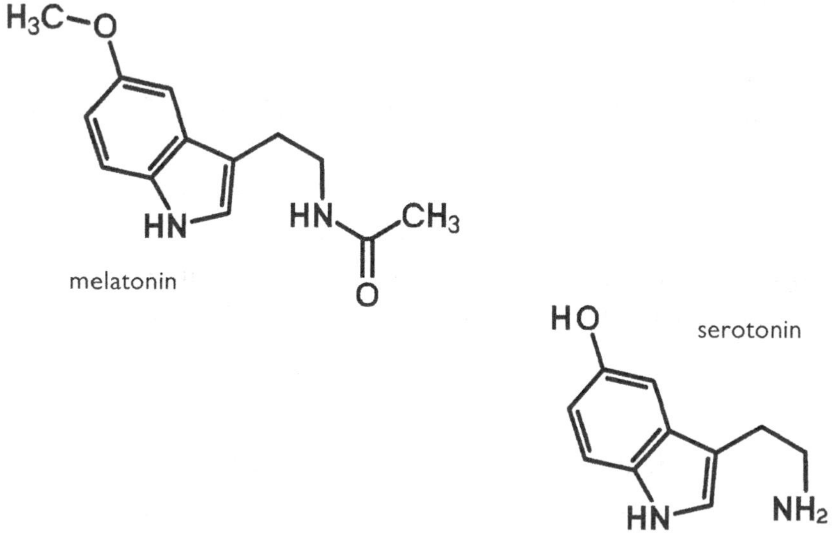

Figure 2. The tryptamine-based neurotransmitters, including melatonin and serotonin.

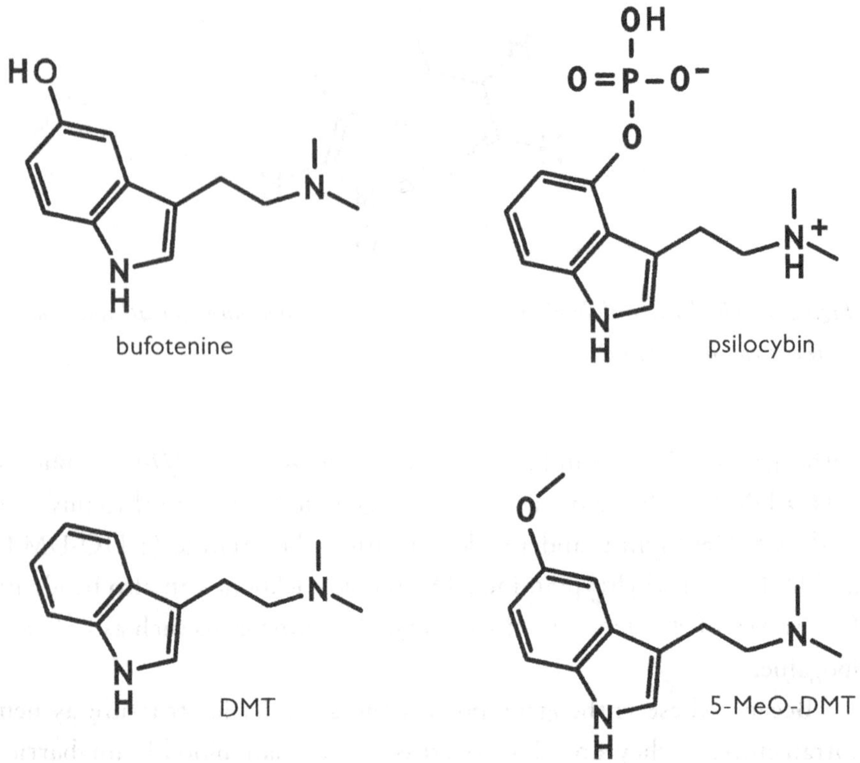

Figure 3. The tryptamine-based entheogens, including bufotenine, psilocybin, DMT, and 5-MeO-DMT.

known entheogens, however, 5-MeO-DMT, DMT, and bufotenine have all proven to be *endogenous* to the human body, which is to say they are produced naturally somewhere within us. Thus they can be defined not only as organic entheogens, but also (depending on your viewpoint) as "endogenous psychotoxins" or "natural neurotransmitters."[1] 5-MeO-DMT's closely related "cousin" DMT has also been described as a "brain hormone."[2]

Chronology of Scientific Discovery

DMT was first synthesized in 1931 by Richard Manske in the great wave of chemical experimentation that followed the discovery of mescaline at the end of the nineteenth century. It was then isolated independently from three different plant sources: *Mimosa hostilis* (= *M. teniflora*) in 1946 and *Piptadenia macrocarpa* (= *Anadenanthera colubrina* var. *Cebil*) and *P. peregrina* (= *A. peregrina*) in 1955.[3] DMT's psychedelic effect was first reported by Stephen Szára in 1956. After its introduction to the burgeoning psychedelic underground through the writings of Burroughs, Leary, and Metzner, it was made illegal in 1966. This halted scientific investigation into the compound in the United States until Rick Strassman's FDA-approved clinical trials of the early 1990s, which he describes in his 2001 book *DMT: The Spirit Molecule*.[4]

5-MeO-DMT was first synthesized in 1936.[5] It was then found in 1959 in a member of the Rue family of evergreen shrubs, *Dictyoloma incanesce*.[6] In 1963 it was isolated from *Anadenanthera peregina*[7] and consequently realized to be a major component in some South American snuffs.[8]

In 1965 5-MeO-DMT was discovered in the venom of the *Bufo alvarius* toad.[9] There are 485 species of *Bufo* toad worldwide,[10] and while the venom of many of these species contains trace amounts of bufotenine* (an alkaloid believed to have some psychoactive properties), the *Bufo alvarius* toad is the only creature in the world that is known to contain 5-MeO-DMT. The venom can contain up to 15 percent 5-MeO-DMT by volume in its dried cutaneous glands. The *Bufo alvarius* toad possesses a peculiar enzyme that methylates the common bufotenine into 5-MeO-DMT. This unique creature is the only known true entheogen-producing animal on earth.[11]

I have found no scientific speculation on why *Bufo alvarius* carries such a high percentage of a potent entheogen in its unique venom, nor have I found conclusive evidence to confirm the popular belief that Mesoamerindian shamans knew it was possible to collect, dry, and smoke the venom of this singularly potent and fascinating animal. Interesting speculations about the possibility of the shamanic use of *Bufo alvarius* venom do however exist, and I explore these further in chapter 7, which describes my own initiation into the strange world of toading.

---

*Bufotenine (5-HO-DMT) is also found in a variety of plants, mushrooms, and in human blood and urine. 5-MeO-DMT is the methyl ether version of bufotenine.

Smoking Tryptamines

Organic 5-MeO-DMT can be smoked by milking and then drying the venom of *Bufo alvarius*, the Sonoran Desert toad.* Smoking this venom can have a virtually identical effect to smoking laboratory-synthesized 5-MeO-DMT.

Contrary to the popular underground mythology that credits smoking toad venom as an ancient Native American pastime, it is quite possible that smoking toad venom is a completely modern invention. The first scientific paper to publicize the fact that *Bufo alvarius* is a walking 5-MeO-DMT factory appeared in 1965. This was at the height of the so-called psychedelic-revolution—a time when numerous young "anthropologists" were searching through scientific leads, looking for clues to "natural psychedelics" both new and old.

Although smoking tryptamine-containing seeds and plant extracts happened with some frequency in South America, these same botanicals were more often taken as snuffs or in potions. Smoking purified tryptamines is, in any case, an invention of our modern civilization. Nick Sand, the underground chemist who manufactured "Orange Sunshine" LSD, is credited as the first person to discover that synthetic DMT could be smoked. Prior to this the few "recreational users" of the modern period were following the lead of William S. Burroughs and injecting it.

*In 2006, a paper was published detailing findings and recommending taxonomic changes based on the largest phylogenetic analysis of living Amphibia accomplished to date. One result of the work described in this 370-pound tome, is that *Bufo alvarius* had its name changed to *Cranopsis alvaria*. Later that same year, the name was changed by implication to *Ollotis alvaria*. Then at the end of 2008, another name change was required, due to rules of seniority, with the (final?) accepted species name landing on *Incilius alvarius*. Because these name changes were so recent, and since virtually all of the sources I've cited herein use the older name, I have decided to retain the use of *Bufo alvarius* throughout my book in order to keep things simple. No one wants to have to look at "*Incilius alvarius* (= *Bufo alvarius*)" over and over again, right? For the same reason, I have retained the use of *Bufo marinus*, which—based on the paper's change—was switched to *Chaunus marinus*, and was later changed by implication in 2007 to *Rhinella marina*. For more related to these changes, see D. R. Frost et al., "The Amphibian Tree of Life," *Bulletin of the American Museum of Natural History* 297 (2006): 1–370, and D. Frost, *Amphibian Species of the World Online*, vers. 5.2 (2008), http://research.amnh.org/herpetology/amphibia/references.php?id=2893.

One astonishing discovery in the catalog of natural reservoirs of tryptaminesis is that DMT has been found in human blood, urine, and cerebrospinal fluid,[12] and 5-MeO-DMT has also been found in human cerebrospinal fluid.[13] In his book *DMT: The Spirit Molecule,* Strassman proposes that the pineal gland, which the Hindu religion associates with the "third eye" and which René Descartes believed was the seat of the soul, may be where endogenous DMT is produced. For more on this theory, please refer to appendix 3: Serotonin, Melatonin, 5-MeO-DMT, and the Pineal Gland.

A Chronology of Human Use

Human beings have used 5-MeO-DMT for at least two thousand years,[14] since 5-MeO-DMT is a component of various entheogenic snuffs used in the Amazon basin for at least this long, and probably a great deal longer. These include *yá-kee, yá-to,* and *yopo* in Colombia, *epéna* in Brazil and Venezuela, and *paricá* and *nyakwána* in Brazil.[15] These snuffs are derived from the seeds of *Anadenanthera* species and from various species of *Virola,* a genus of trees in the nutmeg family.[16] Traditionally, these snuffs are administered by forcefully blowing a mixture of powdered plant material up another person's nose, sometimes using the hollowed-out bone of a bird's leg. This rather painful method of delivery produces an out-of-body experience of approximately the same duration as smoking synthetic 5-MeO-DMT, during which the shaman takes a "journey."[17] While on this journey, the shaman undergoes a transformation that allows him or her to obtain significant knowledge from direct interaction with the gods.

5-MeO-DMT can also occasionally be found in plants used as admixtures in the preparation of *ayahuasca,* the principally DMT*-rich shaman's brew immortalized in William S. Burroughs *Yage Letters* to Allen Ginsberg and then popularized by the radical ethnobotanist Terence McKenna. The origins of ayahuasca, and indeed of the tryptamine snuffs themselves, may be much older than we can realize, as they appear to "predate written records,"[18] but there does seem to be some evidence that indicates that ayahuasca is the

*As an alkaloid from the *Psychotria viridis* plant, DMT is the main active entheogen in ayahuasca.

more recent invention. The first ethnographic reports of ayahuasca use come from 1855,[19] so we can be confident that it has been in use for a couple of hundred years at least. Archaeological evidence of the use of the 5-MeO-DMT snuffs reaches back further than the ethnographic evidence of ayahuasca use, but current speculation suggests that there could be an upper limit on detecting tryptamine alkaloids in archaeological artifacts of around 1,500 to 2,000 years.[20]

The more modern use of 5-MeO-DMT seems to date back less than 35 years. Although synthetic forms of 5-MeO-DMT may have been occasionally available, this compound doesn't appear to have been in popular use during the sixties by the counterculture, and this may be why it avoided being included—with DMT, LSD, mescaline, and other psychedelics—in the 1970 Controlled Substances Act's list of prohibited Schedule I drugs, which went into effect May 1, 1971.

On November 3, 1971, founder John Mann legally incorporated the Church of the Tree of Life in the state of California. This church was created in order to declare that those visionary plants and drugs that had not been scheduled were sacraments. The church hoped to shield members who used any of these stated sacraments by using a "freedom of religion" defense if the government tried to make these entheogens illegal in the future. In 1972, church staff produced *The First Book of Sacraments of the Church of the Tree of Life: A Guide for the Religious Use of Legal Mind Alterants.* The original edition of this book made no mention of 5-MeO-DMT. However, a 1973 booklet, *Legal Highs: A Concise Encyclopedia of Legal Herbs and Chemicals with Psychoactive Properties,* included 5-MeO-DMT, noting that "the Church of the Tree of Life has declared as its religious sacraments most substances in this book."[21] The *Legal Highs* booklet also listed Karma Kem Ko. in Yatesboro, Pennsylvania and Terrestrial Materials in San Francisco, California as suppliers of 5-MeO-DMT.

In a 1977 *Head* magazine article titled "DMT," authors Jeremy Bigwood and Jonathan Ott noted that 5-MeO-DMT "has been sold on the illicit market"; they also commented that it was not a controlled substance.[22] Nevertheless, Bigwood and Ott did little to promote the drug when they referred to a description of the effects of 5-MeO-DMT from M. V. Smith's 1976 book *Psychedelic Chemistry*: "The effects of 5-methoxy-DMT are unpleasant for most people (smoking it gives me nausea plus the feeling that I'm being sat on by an elephant)."[23] Bigwood and Ott concluded by stating that they felt the drug "has little recreational value."[24]

The 1978 *High Times Encyclopedia of Recreational Drugs* related that 5-MeO-DMT "has been synthesized and was occasionally available in the California underground market a few years ago. The effects are practically identical to laboratory DMT available in the sixties."[25]

In 1984, one of the true classics of underground entheogenic literature appeared, promoting the hallucinogenic value of the Sonoran Desert toad. Attributed to an author called Albert Most (probably not his real name) and published in Denton, Texas (by Venom Press), *Bufo Alvarius: The Psychedelic Toad of the Sonoran Desert* is an informative and practical how-to guide for finding this particular species of toad, for the purpose of collecting and smoking its venom. In this pamphlet, Most clearly identifies the active entheogen in *Bufo alvarius* venom as being 5-MeO-DMT (and not bufotenine). The enduring cult success of this publication is probably responsible for the culture of toad venom use that still exists in certain areas of the southwest today. (While Most and his followers advocated their Church of the Toad of Light, there is little evidence that this "church" was ever incorporated.)

By 1985, an updated edition of *The First Book of Sacraments of the Church of the Tree of Life* included mention of the fact that 5-MeO-DMT was available from Inner Center, Co., in Hermosa Beach, California. It is not clear when Inner Center first started offering 5-MeO-DMT for sale, but a 1994 post to Alt.drugs mentioned that Inner Center *used* to sell 5-MeO-DMT but that they didn't offer it any longer and may have stopped selling it around March of 1992. The edition of the booklet *Legal Highs* that came out in 1992 no longer included vendor listings for chemicals. Apparently the government had been targeting the companies that were included in earlier editions, pressuring them to stop selling to individuals who were not part of an established research laboratory. This may be why Inner Center stopped offering 5-MeO-DMT around that time.

Other than these references, there is scant mention of 5-MeO-DMT being extracted or synthesized for modern entheogenic consumption until the early 1990s. Interest in extracting DMT and 5-MeO-DMT was sparked through the publication in 1992 of *The Entheogen Review,* which frequently discussed various plant sources for ayahuasca analogues. Edited by Jim DeKorne, this quarterly journal acted as a "network newsletter" that shared brew prep and extraction techniques. In the winter 1993 issue, DeKorne published "Smokable DMT from Plants," describing a simple method of extracting "DMT" from *Phalaris* grasses. In the spring 1994 issue, DeKorne printed a correction, pointing out that the grass he had used primarily contained 5-MeO-DMT, and the description of the effects produced by the extract therefore reflected *that* tryptamine, not DMT. (In truth, some *Phalaris* grasses *do* contain DMT as their only or primary psychoactive alkaloid, while others contain only or primarily 5-MeO-DMT.) Further interest in plant sources of DMT and 5-MeO-DMT was sparked by the "Beta-Carbolines and Ayahuasca Potions" chapter in Jonathan Ott's 1993 book *Pharmacotheon: Entheogenic Drugs, Their Plant Sources and History* as well as his 1994 book *Ayahuasca Analogues: Pangæan Entheogens.*

Legality Issues

After about five-years' absence from the market, one specialty entheobotanical company—JLF Poisonous Non-Consumables—listed synthetic 5-MeO-DMT in their mail-order catalog in 1997. They appear to have been the first company to start offering it for sale again commercially. Then in a 1998 interview, Jonathan Ott mentioned his own incipient company Pharmacophilia, which planned to sell a product called Pharmahuasca—a two-pill combo of a Natural Herbal Relaxant (free-base harmaline) and a Natural Herbal Tonic (5-MeO-DMT).[26] Apparently Ott had changed his opinion on the value of 5-MeO-DMT since his article in *Head* some two decades earlier. Although a limited number of pressed Pharmahuasca pills were produced, and some research and development was done via human bioassays, Ott's Pharmacophilia company either never materialized as a commercial venture, was short-lived, or has remained an extremely "underground" and unpublicized venture.

For a brief window of time between 1997 and early 2004, 5-MeO-DMT became increasingly available for purchase via a number of web-based companies. These companies were offering a wide range of nonscheduled "research chemicals," primarily in the phenethylamine and tryptamine families, most of which whose psychoactive effects had been described in the Shulgins' books *PIHKAL* and *TIHKAL*. Yet under the Controlled Substances Analogue Act of 1986, many of these chemicals (including 5-MeO-DMT) could be considered to be analogues of illegal chemicals, and hence—under certain circumstances, constellated around their use as psychoactive drugs—they would also be illegal.

On September 7, 2001, police raided JLF Poisonous Non-Consumables, and on January 28, 2002, they arrested the owner, Mark Niemoeller, serving him with a 13-count federal grand jury indictment. The charges related to several specific chemicals that JLF sold. In order to get out of jail, Niemoeller made a deal with prosecutors not to sell any items mentioned in the indictment or in the search warrant, along with some additional items *not* mentioned, including 5-MeO-DMT and the skins of *Bufo marinus* toads. Niemoeller ended up spending a few years under house arrest.[27]

On July 22, 2004, the Drug Enforcement Administration (DEA) published an announcement describing their "Operation Web Tryp," which resulted in legal actions against five U.S. research chemical vendors. Charges were largely made on the basis of the Controlled Substances Analogue Act. Many of the companies selling research chemicals that were not busted responded to the DEA's announcement by closing their businesses.

These days, companies that sell research chemicals keep a much lower profile, and most of them cannot be easily located via web search engines. The days of easily obtainable synthetic 5-MeO-DMT seem to be behind us. I have provided a comprehensive list of the plants with higher amounts of 5-MeO-DMT and DMT in appendix 2, Tryptamine-Containing Plants, and various extraction methods are easy to find on the Internet. As far as I know, none of these plants are (as yet) specifically scheduled (except in Louisiana, when the intended use is consumption), although be aware that manufacture of controlled substances, which includes extractions from plant materials, is a crime that can result in fines and lengthy prison sentences in many countries. It is worth noting that while 5-MeO-DMT is not scheduled on the federal level, it is listed as Schedule I in Nebraska and South Dakota, and it is also restricted in some manner in Denmark, Germany, Greece, Japan, New Zealand, Sweden, Switzerland, and the United Kingdom. For current information related to 5-MeO-DMT law, see www.erowid.org/chemicals/5meo_dmt/5meo_dmt_law.shtml.

Strassman and the Scant Scientific Research on DMT

Due to the draconian governmental policies toward scientific investigation into the field of psychedelic drugs—resulting from reactions to the society-changing introduction of LSD to Western youth in the sixties (and the subsequent cultural fallout)—there have been few sanctioned studies of any psychoactive tryptamines since the late sixties and early seventies, when most psychedelics were placed into Schedule I. According to Jonathan Ott, there has been little information published on the human pharmacology of 5-MeO-DMT prior to his 2001 book *Shamanic Snuffs or Entheogenic Errhines,* which provided details related to his own intranasal, sublingual, and oral bioassays (both neat and with a concurrent dose of harmaline).[28]

The important exception to the lack of government approved studies was Dr. Rick Strassman's clinical investigation of DMT in New Mexico in 1990. Much of the scientific discourse in this chapter has been learned from the pioneering work Strassman describes in his book *DMT: The Spirit Molecule.* While his research involved DMT and not 5-MeO-DMT, these two closely related compounds have many similarities, allowing us to speculate that much of his information can be applied to both. Further, because DMT and 5-MeO-DMT are found endogenously in the human body, it would seem reasonable to assume that his theories on the role of one tryptamine could easily apply to the other. Indeed, some naturally occurring mind states, such as the near-death experience, much more closely resemble reports of 5-MeO-DMT trips than DMT trips.

Here is an outline of some of the important discoveries and speculations that have been made.

1. Once smoked, DMT (or 5-MeO-DMT) crosses the blood-brain barrier with astonishing speed. (5-MeO-DMT differs from DMT in that it has a methylated oxygen group attached to the DMT molecule; according to Alexander Shulgin, this results in an increase in potency.) The blood-brain barrier (BBB) is the most sophisticated defense system in the human body; it is far more impenetrable than the defenses surrounding the other organs, and it is incredibly selective in what it allows to cross over into the brain. For the most part

only simple sugar molecules like glucose (for energy) and certain amino acids are allowed across, transported by highly specialized "carrier molecules."

These same carrier molecules willingly transport DMT (or 5-MeO-DMT) molecules across the blood-brain barrier (BBB). The brain then consumes/metabolizes these tryptamines as quickly as possible, which is why a DMT trip is so short (and why you will always come out of it). Strassman has gone so far as to describe DMT as "brain food," and the same could be said about 5-MeO-DMT as well.

2. There has been some scientific speculation that DMT is produced within the body during the deepest part of REM sleep (and this may cause those heavily bizarre dreams that are difficult to remember). My own hunch is that Hindu saddhus and Buddhist monks can cause their bodies to produce DMT or 5-MeO-DMT during meditation after years of ascetic training. In Thailand today, the modern Qui Gong master Mantak Chia explains to his students that the visions they will experience during their arduous multiday "darkness meditation"[29] are caused by their pineal gland producing more DMT as its melatonin level drops. It is interesting to consider that many of the meditation traditions focus on visualizing dying and experiencing "emptiness," that Amazonian shamans believe that their spirit "dies" and is then "reborn" during their ayahuasca journeys, and that the 5-MeO-DMT experience bears a remarkable similarity to many near-death experience accounts.
3. In his book *DMT: The Spirit Molecule,* Strassman radically theorizes that the pineal gland may flood the human brain with DMT upon first forming in the fetus (at forty-nine days) and then again at death and that DMT is the chemical "vehicle" that allows the spirit (or the consciousness) to enter and leave the body. (This may be the bravest scientific speculation since Copernicus suggested that the Earth was not at the center of the universe!)

Strassman points out a fascinating corollary between human development and the Tibetan belief system. In development, the forty-nine days it takes for the pineal to appear corresponds to the same period it takes for a fetus to first display its gender and thus, one could argue, its identity or ego. This is exactly the same amount of days that the Tibetan Buddhists—who have by far the most sophisticated belief system with regard to the soul's passage after dying—believe elapse before the beginning of the "bardo of becoming." That is, it takes forty-nine days before a soul reincarnates into a new physical form if it failed to gain enlightenment, according to the *Bardo Thodol* (more commonly known as *The Tibetan Book of the Dead*).

Other potential corollaries can also be found between Dr. Strassmans' research and Tibetan Buddhism. The Tibetans also believe that at death our consciousness continues after all other signs of life in the body have ceased for the time "it takes to eat a meal," or approximately twenty minutes.[30] They regard this as the period during which the spontaneous nature of mind (*rigpa*) erupts, and we are either reunited with the universal mind (*dharmakaya*, the "clear luminosity," or "ground luminosity") or fall back into the bardos. This is the point when we have the greatest chance to obtain enlightenment and break the cycle of rebirth. If, as Strassman suggests, the brain is being flooded with potent tryptamines at death, then this twenty-minute period would correspond to approximately how long the effect of these tryptamines would last on our dying, matter-bound consciousness.

Entheogens and the Ancient Search for the Sacred

Dr. Strassman's modern research and theories on DMT can be regarded as a scientific continuation on one of the oldest themes in the history of humanity—the use of entheogens as a window to the sacred.

The consumption of entheogens has been at the core of humanity's search for the sacred since the earliest days of our societies, and examples are abundant. Some 3,500 years ago the ancient Hindus worshipped a lost entheogen called *Soma* as if it was a God and created their greatest legacy (the Vedas) in tribute to it. Mescaline-containing *Trichocereus* cacti were used by the Chavin culture of Peru as long as 3,000 years ago and continue to be used by northern Peruvian shamans today.[31] Psychoactive *kykeon* was drunk for the two thousand-year period of the Eleusinian Mysteries, which were considered to be the pinnacle of Greek civilization.* Tryptamine snuffs have been used in South America and the Caribbean for at least 2,000 years, although their origins, along with the origins of ayahuasca as well, now appear to be lost in the mists of time. Peyote has been used by Mexican Native Americans for the past 400 years,[32] and the *Amanita muscaria* in Siberia for perhaps the past 300 years.[33] A wide variety of many additional visionary plants—*Psilocybe* mushrooms, morning glory seeds, *Salvia divinorum, Cannabis,* tobacco, *Datura,* and so on—have been used ceremonially by other traditional peoples the world over.

The modern father of comparative religion Mircea Eliade credited *mysterium tremendum et fascinans*—instances of heightened awe—as the origin of spirituality among our human ancestors, possibly brought about by those moments when the caveman first saw lightning strike and create fire, or when the plains dweller first saw the mountains, or when the jungle dweller first saw the sea. Interestingly, though he popularized the term *shaman,* he was uncomfortable for most of his life with the idea that primitive societies used entheogenic plants to gain spiritual insights. In his pioneering work on the subject, *Shamanism: Archaic Techniques of Ecstasy,* he largely downplays the importance of entheogens, characterizing their use as being a decadent innovation rather than an integral component of the ecstatic experience. He even quotes the Russian anthropologist Åke Ohlmarks' assertion that

> in the Arctic the shamanic ecstasy is a spontaneous and organic phenomenon; and it is only in this zone that one can properly speak of a "great shamanizing," that is, of the ceremony that ends with a real cataleptic trance, during which the soul is supposed to have left the body and to be journeying in the sky or the underworld. But in the

---

*It has been theorized that the psychoactive component of kykeon came from ergot—the starting material for the semi-synthetic drug LSD—that grows on barley. This identification holds further weight since Demeter (who ordered the construction of the Eleusinian sanctuary and described how kykeon was to be made) is sometimes called *Erysibe*—a word that means "ergot"—and the symbol of the Mystery was an ear of grain. From R. G. Wasson et al., *The Road to Eleusis: Unveiling the Secret of the Mysteries* (New York: Harcourt Brace Javanovich, 1978), and J. Ott, *Pharmacotheon: Entheogenic Drugs, Their Plant Sources and History* (Kennewick, Wash.: Natural Products Co., 1993).

> sub-Arctic the shaman, no longer the victim of cosmic oppression, does not spontaneously obtain a real trance and is obliged to induce a semi trance with the help of narcotics or to mime the journey of the soul in dramatic form.[34]

Although it is true that some shamanic cultures relied on fasting, chanting, drumming, and other physical techniques to induce states of ecstasy, this was generally because no suitable visionary plants were readily available. The majority of shamanic societies around the world utilize a staggering number of different plant entheogens, and the most potent of these contain tryptamines: bufotenine (5-HO-DMT), DMT, 5-MeO-DMT, psilocin (4-HO-DMT), or psilocybin (*O*-phosophoryl-4-HO-DMT). Despite Ohlmark's remarks, few people would classify a tryptamine experience as a "semi trance" or describe the effects produced by psychoactive tryptamines as "[miming] the journey of the soul in dramatic form"! Eliade himself, in a conversation late in his life with the anthropologist Peter T. Furst, excused his dismissive attitude toward entheogens by noting that his seminal book first came out in France in 1951, and remarking, "What did we know in the early 1950s about these things?" At that time, for example, he was unaware of the antiquity of entheogen use in America.[35]

While it was suggested as early as the 1930s that the Greek and Hindu religions' first movement toward "dynamic religion" was associated with the "divine rapture" produced by intoxicating beverages,[36] it took other unconventional thinkers—the husband-and-wife amateur mycologist team of R. Gordon and Valentina Pavlovna Wasson—to suggest that some people likely first conceived of God after consuming psilocybin-containing mushrooms. The viewpoint that entheogenic plants were the source for most early religious ideation was later furthered by Robert Graves, Alan Watts, and Mary Barnard. R. Gordon Wasson, with Albert Hofmann and Richard Evans Schultes, went on to propose specific entheogenic plant sources for Soma and kykeon.[37] Sanskrit scholars acknowledge that the 114 verses of the ninth book of the ancient Hindu Rig Veda, which are dedicated to a mysterious god/elixir called Soma, surpass all other books of the Rig Veda in the awe of their tone.[38] And while the formula for that preparation has long been lost, some 3,500 years ago soma was the most precious thing known to humanity, because it ushered those who drank it into the presence of the Divine: "We have drunk Soma; we have become immortal; arrived at the light, we have found the Gods."[39] Yet, like Eliade, the majority of academics in the twentieth century rejected the idea that psychoactive plants have had any influence on humankind's discovery of God and spirituality. Although many continue to oppose this view today, acceptance of the impact of entheogens on the origins of religion has been steadily gaining ground in recent years.

Language, art, the controlled use of fire, and a realization of the Divine—these are unique to human evolution, and they form the cornerstones of civilization's foundation as we know it. All of these were invented or discovered within a relatively short period of each other, with the domestication of cattle following not long after. Such a genesis seems to beg the question: What, in fact, kick-started this radical transformation of human consciousness?

Naturally occurring entheogens seem to be the prime candidate for an easily obtainable psychological catalyst. Terence McKenna proposed in *Food of the Gods* that psilocybin-containing mushrooms would have been ubiquitous in the dung of the first domesticated cattle,[40] a suggestion that is particularly fascinating in light of the possibility that one very early religion was the Paleolithic cult of the Great Horned Goddess. Algerian cave paintings of the Goddess from this period, as well as paintings of the cattle she is clearly connected to, and other paintings of mushroom-headed people dancing while holding mushrooms appear to represent both the beginning of the artistic tradition and the shamanic use of entheogenic fungi.

The biggest challenge in the attempt to establish an accurate history of entheogenic practices is that the compounds themselves usually leave few traces; they are consumed. And the roots of many entheogenic practices lie in preliterate cultures. In cases when these practices survived into modern civilizations that *had* a written record (the Greek Eleusinian Mysteries, or the Vedic Soma ceremony, for example), they were kept secret, and assumed a cultlike status. The secrets of their preparation (and the primary psychoactive plants that were used) were apparently never committed to writing, but only passed along orally. Sadly, this has doomed such practices to extinction in our modern civilization, due to the eventual persecution of initiates by both invaders and more modern counter-philosophies eager for influence, and by the now overpowering effect of the written word upon our societies.

There is no physical trace left of Soma or kykeon. Unless some archaeologist discovers more specific written records or ceremonial vessels containing traces of psychoactive residues, these entheogens are effectively lost from human knowledge, destined to be a passing footnote of history at worst, or a launching point for endless speculations at best. Yet the Eleusinian Mysteries were considered the high point of Greek civilization—valid enough to last two thousand years. And, according to religious scholar Huston Smith, Alfred North Whitehead is reported to have remarked that Hindu Vedanta is the most impressive metaphysics the human mind has conceived and that, etymologically and otherwise, Vedanta is "the culmination of the Vedas." Smith feels that "the Vedas derive, more than from any other single identifiable source, from Soma."[41] But as important as Soma and kykeon may have been to the development of these two great spiritual societies whose combined philosophies have affected the entire world, we have no *true* knowledge of them anymore. All we have left are reports of their usage and their obvious entheogenic effect. We have no real way to recreate them or to say how they were discovered in the first place. Only those few cultures with surviving oral traditions retained a direct link with the sacred through the ingestion of natural entheogens.

The 5-MeO-DMT–containing snuffs, ayahuasca, and the *Trichocereus* cactus brews from South America can thus be regarded as the surviving *complex* entheogens from a human history that has had its equivalents in both the European (kykeon) and Asian (Soma) hemispheres. These sacraments are still widely used; both the tryptamine-containing snuffs and ayahuasca are still commonly employed (often now in urban mestizo communities) in Colombia, Peru, and Ecuador, while a version of ayahuasca known as *hoasca* is used in the government-sanctioned syncretic Brazilian churches of the União do Vegetal (UDV) and the Santo Daime.* The *Tricherocerusi* cactus, which has been in continuous use in Peru for 3,500 years and boasts the longest history of entheogen use that we know of, has also inspired a syncretic cult, where traditional Peruvian shamanism has

*On February 21, 2006, a unanimous Supreme Court decision regarding a preliminary injunction related to a UDV chapter in the United States granted that specific chapter the legal right to continue using and importing ayahuasca until a final decision is reached in their case against the government. While this decision does not create blanket legalization of ayahuasca for religious users, it is—at the least—a step in the right direction.

become mixed with primitive Christian beliefs, and which continues to be popular to this day.

I call these sacraments "complex entheogens" because they require the preparation of two or more plants that contain at least two different compounds to produce the desired result. (Clues seem to indicate that Soma and kykeon were also complex preparations that may have involved more than one ingredient. The secret of such preparations was kept within the priestly classes and was closely guarded.) While both DMT and 5-MeO-DMT are active when snuffed or smoked, DMT is not orally active (and 5-MeO-DMT is only very weakly orally active), due to these chemicals being neutralized by a stomach enzyme called monoamine oxidase (MAO).*

Ayahuasca, however, allows either tryptamine to become active when taken by mouth, because ayahuasca also contains another plant, *Banisteriopsis caapi,* which produces beta-carboline chemicals (such as harmine and harmaline) act as monoamine oxidase inhibitors (MAOI). The *Banisteriopsis caapi* vine is the principal ingredient used by all ayahuasca cultures. However it is the balance between the plants containing the tryptamines and the *Banisteriopsis caapi* vine containing the MAOI inhibitors that ultimately allows the full effects of the ayahuasca to be felt. This ancient discovery must be regarded as a significant feat of intrepid research from an area that contains as many possible plant combinations as the Amazon basin.

There is reasonable speculation that some *Tricherocerus* brews may have exploited this MAOI effect, and they sometimes employ additional psychoactive plants such as *Brugmansia* and tobacco.[42] There is also limited evidence that *Banisteriopsis caapi* is still used, combined with yopo, as a snuff

---

*Although there is one report that 5-MeO-DMT was not orally active at a 35 mg dose (Shulgin and Shulgin, 1997), and it is widely thought to be inactive orally, Jonathan Ott (2001) more recently found via personal bioassay that 30 mg of 5-MeO-DMT was orally active for him, producing a "threshold effect." Another underground psychonaut reported weak activity orally from using a dose of either 50 mg or 100 mg (unfortunately this person's memory of the dose used was not clear); the effects were more physical in nature, resembling only very mild smoked doses without any out-of-body effects. Oral doses in the 50 to 100 mg range represent at least two times (and possibly over three times) the quantity of material needed for a strong smoked dose. This is a waste of valuable sacrament, particularly since oral doses have not yet been reported to produce a "full" out-of-body 5MDE. Hence, I continue to regard 5-MeO-DMT as being essentially inactive orally without the concurrent use of MAO inhibitors.

today.[43] (Archaeological evidence supports this view, with an ancient Piaroa snuff sample testing positive for both bufotenine and harmine.)[44] The use of MAOI inhibitors in these preparations thus may have offered a clue to the eventual discovery of the formula for ayahuasca.

For me, the ancient discovery of the complex biochemistry of ayahuasca by the "primitive" shamans of the Amazon jungle stands out as one of the greatest puzzles of the entire tryptamine mystery. What kind of experimentation led to the discovery of this very specific interaction between the orally inactive tryptamines and the beta-carbolines that allow them to become active? This mystery deepens in light of the fact that there are estimated to be over seventy different ayahuasca cultures spread across the Amazon basin[45] that use different combinations of plants to provide variations on the same entheogenic effect, all for the specific purpose of traveling to the "other dimension," from where the shamans believe it is possible to return with significant new knowledge.

These shamans consider the *Banisteriopsis caapi* vine to be The Mother of All Plants and credit her direct intervention for all their botanical knowledge. While the ethnopharmacologist Jonathan Ott, who probably knows as much about the traditional use of 5-MeO-DMT as anyone else alive, has speculated that the South American shamans originally intuited the more complex formula for ayahuasca from their use of the much older 5-MeO-DMT–containing snuffs. Either way, the ritual use of both DMT and 5-MeO-DMT as entheogens by tribal shamans has been the primary method of guiding and maintaining these tribes' destinies, both as tools of prophecy via divine communication and as powerful healing agents. These tribal cultures—the caretakers of the last real "garden" on the planet—have lived with remarkable ecological sophistication in the Amazon for longer than any other society on Earth.

THREE

The Aftermath

Achieving genuine happiness may require bringing about a transformation in your outlook, your way of thinking, and this is not a simple matter . . .

His Holiness the 14th Dalai Lama,
The Art of Happiness: A Handbook for Living, 1998

Terence McKenna wrote that smoking "DMT is like an intellectual black hole in that once one knows about it, it is very hard for others to understand what one is talking about. One cannot be heard. The more one is able to articulate what it is, the less others are able to understand."[1] Terence was writing about DMT, but the same paradox applies equally to 5-MeO-DMT. You can really only begin to understand this book if you have experienced the disorienting effect of one the entheogenic tryptamines in any of the variety of their forms. This paradox applies even more so when trying to explain experiences as mystical as some of mine. But if you have been there, then you know, which seems to be the case with the handful of individuals I have met who have had experiences like mine, and who instantly comprehend. They all agree that a full 5MDE is very different from any other drug experience.

This point is well illustrated by the following e-mail that I received from Martin W. Ball, Ph.D., who had written books on both magic mushrooms (*Mushroom Wisdom: How Shamans Cultivate Spiritual Consciousness*) and *Salvia divinorum* (*Sage Spirit: Salvia Divinorum and the Entheogenic Experience*) prior to trying 5-MeO-DMT. Martin produces "The Entheogenic Evolution," a weekly podcast that discussed *Tryptamine Palace* and 5-MeO-DMT on one of his shows. While he was curious and polite in his discussion of my book, I could tell that he found some of my claims hard to swallow. Thus he could be considered an excellent example of an entheogenic practitioner who had a wide base of experiences that he could compare to his own eventual 5MDE. I received his e-mail the morning after his first 5-MeO-DMT experience.

> Greetings Oroc! Last night I went on a journey with 5-MeO-DMT . . . mixture of toad, phalaris, and psychotria . . . full and complete mystical union—no other way to describe it . . . the most beautiful and complete experience of my life. I think I can truly say that I now know exactly where you are coming from. WOW!!!

You are either outside of the experience, or you are in it. No description I can provide will really enlighten you. "The more one is able to articulate what it is, the less others are able to understand." While McKenna's observation struck me since the beginning of my quest as being one of the best descriptions of the DMT paradox, it has also occurred to me that the same could be said to equally apply to another of the great mysteries: the mystery of *faith*.

Prior to my use of 5-MeO-DMT, the word *faith* used to make my spine crawl, mostly because of my prejudice toward modern Christianity. Like most intellectuals, I associated the word with a form of mental weakness despite the numerous examples of great strength it has provided the world. Faith, in any creed or religion, is accepting that powers exist that are greater than we can ever hope to understand. In contemporary Western society, we are mostly taught that this viewpoint is archaic, since we are so infatuated with the Newtonian beliefs that have allowed our society's terrifyingly destructive Industrial Revolution. This modern viewpoint has attempted to deconstruct our universe into a simple machine in the belief that the expansion of physical knowledge will one day be able to create a world freed of ignorance and superstition.

This youthful and arrogant presumption that faith is merely a superstition and a weakness has largely killed off the belief in anything but a fundamentalist view of G/d, as well as any recognition or appreciation of the sacred in our society other than as ritualized forms of lip service. The focus on materialism at the expense of spirituality has disconnected our species so far from its natural environment that we now stand on the precipice of environmental destruction: a situation that the modern "intellectual" can logically understand, but feels inadequate and powerless to change. Our generation is one of the saddest in history; we are fatter, stupider, and unhealthier—in body, mind, and spirit—than any people before us. The only generations worse off will be the next ones to come.

I can say all this with honesty, because I have been one of the worst offenders. For twenty years I have lived off the fat of our decadent civilization, privileged in this incarnation as a white male first-world citizen. And yet I have spent most of my adult life poking and peering into the affairs of the peoples of many lands, too often with little real empathy—a life spent experiencing, entertaining, and occasionally enduring—and all the time believing that I was merely living out my days until they would eventually end. Life was without purpose: fascinating, but ultimately directionless and pointless. This was especially so because I have chosen to ignore the status quo, since family and career are the main providers of purpose in our lost society (as well as being the main tools by which our governments can control us).

My philosophy in life was largely hedonistic, politically anarchistic, and spiritually atheistic. I believed the religions of the world provided many useful rules of conduct to live by, but were ultimately hollow and meaningless in themselves. They were antiquated systems of societal control designed to keep the hungry masses stable and producing, an archaic system that has now been superseded by the societal use of prescription drugs and television.*

Prior to smoking 5-MeO-DMT, I believed that life was ultimately a riddle that I would have to try and solve on my own. The closest I came to any

*In a *Rolling Stone* magazine interview, William S. Burroughs pointed out that in the book *1984,* George Orwell predicted a draconian society where citizens would be forced to take drugs and then be indoctrinated via the use of a television screen. The frightening reality is that by the end of the twentieth century our society willingly accepted this method of brainwashing as one of the benefits of "freedom," and the military–industrial complex now controls its "citizens" in ways far more sophisticated than Orwell could have ever imagined.

kind of spirituality was through my regular connection with nature during my many years of living in the mountains and through an active appreciation of the world via skiing, climbing, cycling, and paragliding. As a mountain athlete, I found I could experience the same closeness to the wonder of nature through Zen-like dedication to "extreme"* sports that I did when I took LSD or magic mushrooms while out in the wilderness. Best of all was combining the two—skiing on acid, mountain biking on mushrooms—whereby I could really experience the phenomena that Zen describes as "action through non-action."

This is the rare feeling that jazz musicians in New Orleans call being "in the pocket," or what professional athletes describe as being "in the zone"—that place where all physical and mental creativity originates when you still the ego-mind and manage to just let things flow. All good athletes know that you don't *think* about the best things you do, you just *do* them—often after years of yogic discipline. *Think* about it, and you will fuck up.

Most of my spiritual and metaphysical leanings during the first thirty-five years of my life were devoted to a better understanding of this phenomena, eventually through yoga, the alpine environment, psychedelics, and a bit of philosophical reading on the side. Smoking 5-MeO-DMT changed all that, and I have effectively undergone a complete faith-based transformation—one that the majority of my close friends find as remarkable as I do. In the aftermath of my extraordinarily powerful initiation, I recognized what I had been through for exactly what it was (since I had spent years reading descriptions of it, while never thinking it might happen to me): a genuine mystical experience.

This is the spark of all forms of spirituality since the beginnings of humanity, which in my mind had been restricted to the shaman, the Sufi, the fevered saint. I had met the same knowledge that has inspired countless men and women throughout the mists of time. Some may argue that I have simply experienced a powerful, chemically induced hallucination, but my faith tells me something different. It tells me that I have experienced a deeper reality, contacting with a power greater than any I knew existed, and now my world will never be quite the same again.

*As a mountain-athlete of more than twenty years, I pathologically dislike this media-invented word—but its now common acceptance in the vernacular forces me to use it.

What are the most obvious changes? Where do I begin! Perhaps the most important change is that I have been instilled with a new sense of responsibility—a determination to work toward some positive end. Following my epiphany, I found I couldn't lie anymore (not even a little white lie), so I went around telling everyone exactly how I felt about everything, revealing my previous secrets and falsehoods. This process caused a great deal of confusion and upheaval in the beginning, but it has resulted in an almost total lack of friction in my private life, since everything is out in the open. This phenomenon fascinated an ex-heroin addict friend of mine, who—since kicking—had become a radical neo-Catholic. She said it was a classic sign of religious conversion.

While I have always been a voracious reader, my tryptamine experiences unleashed an unquenchable desire for knowledge. Since then, I have read more books, with a more thorough absorption of content, than in any other period of my life. One of the many ways that I often describe the effect that 5-MeO-DMT has had on me is by describing it as "the greatest intellectual adventure of my life." My worldview has been considerably enriched and enlarged, and I have become much more open to ideas that I would have previously found "unscientific" or "illogical." Since I have smoked 5-MeO-DMT, I have found myself far more tolerant, and even sympathetic, to the message of Christianity—although it is still hard to take seriously in most of its current forms.

When I initially experienced the realignment of my natural energies through the revelation of my first few experiences and the destruction of my old paradigm, I found that many boundaries had been removed. The occurrence of coincidences and synchronicities* in the rhythms of my life also became extraordinarily common, especially if the situation somehow involved tryptamines.

Take, for example, the day after I first smoked 5-MeO-DMT, which was obviously one of the most exciting and unsettling days of my life. As I confronted the astonishing fact that the core of my existence had been irreversibly altered, I drove to Hood River, Oregon, where I had an assignment to

*A marked increase in synchronicity is a common result of entheogenic revelation. Stanislav Grof devotes a full chapter of his book *When the Impossible Happens: Adventures in Non-ordinary Realities* to his own remarkable experiences with the phenomenon of synchronicity.

write a kite-surfing article for an English magazine. I parked my rented car on the main street and called my future wife on my cell phone while sitting on a park bench in the sun. As I described to her in great detail how excited my mind was at that point, I got up and started walking aimlessly down the main street. Talking to her as I walked, a jewelry store caught my eye, and I stopped and looked in the window at a psychedelic collection of hand-blown glass frogs and toads. I immediately went in and purchased one, which now sits proudly in my house shrine.

Upon returning home after the three-week trip to Oregon, I went to clear a pile of junk off the kitchen table and the first thing I found was a copy of *The Archaic Revival* by Terence McKenna. A friend had given me the book several months earlier when she had moved to Los Angeles, and though I had been keen to read it—having enjoyed *Food of the Gods* some ten years earlier—I had not even had a chance to look at it. I opened the book, and the first thing I read was that smoking "DMT is like an intellectual black hole . . ." which perfectly described the intense excitement and confusion I was experiencing as I struggled to try to explain to my friends what was going on in my mind during those days after my first 5-MeO-DMT experience. This book, by far McKenna's most radical, became for me both a lifeline and a rocket ship into intellectual hyperspace, as over the next few months, supplemented by regularly smoking 5-MeO-DMT, I gave full and open credence to the wildest rumblings of Terence's imagination.

Shortly after stumbling across that book, a random person turned up and gave me a jar of DMT. At that time, this was one of the most difficult drugs to find—I had been unsuccessfully searching for it for so many years that I had actually given up! Then, only a few months later, I met a mad Israeli in a Los Angeles taxicab who quickly insisted that he would take me to Mexico in search of the elusive *Bufo alvarius* toads.

For at least a year, I became somewhat obsessed with 5-MeO-DMT. After I first discovered the drug, I was fortunately living in a secluded house on a Caribbean island, where I had a steady diet of healthy food and exercise. Once I realized that I could smoke 5-MeO-DMT alone, the chance coincidence of my meditative surroundings allowed me to immerse myself fully in the 5-MeO-DMT experience in a stress- and paranoia-free environment. I therefore concentrated on getting as physically fit and healthy as I could for my tryptamine smoking.

During the first few months after my initial experience, I smoked 5-MeO-DMT two or three times a week. This regime, along with the voracious reading, triggered an avalanche of ideas that flowed constantly through my mind. My inner world became so all encompassing, both inside and outside of the experience, that I believe my mind and body began to separate. My body became more of a machine, and my consciousness became more of an independent entity, as I began to float through the world almost as a disembodied observer.

At the end of this period, which coincided with an unusually high popularity with both sexes (everybody seemed to want a piece of me, even complete strangers), I began to experience—for the first time in my life—a form of sexual impotency, as I found it difficult to concentrate on the physical act of lovemaking. (Paradoxically, my love for my partner during this period had substantially deepened and grown.) I was beginning to live in the ether, and while my physical reality remained healthy (my life was in as good a shape as it had ever been), my mind was ablaze with the world of possibilities that the tryptamines seemed to offer and by the spiritual evolution that I was rapidly undergoing. Fueled by a steady diet of radical reading, I found myself seriously considering the possibility of transcending completely out of concensus reality. So if anyone in my audience is undergoing a similar mental revolution, let me offer the same words of advice that Sogyal Rinpoche's master gave to calm him down as he observed his physical world dissolving after years of arduous meditation: "Don't get too excited. In the end, it's neither good nor bad."[2]

If it were not for the following two experiences, I might have continued smoking 5-MeO-DMT with the same carefree abandon that marked these first months of experimentation, continuing my light-headed ascent into the mental stratosphere until my physical form would have hardly mattered at all. But as fate would have it, the character of my 5-MeO-DMT experiences was about to change.

The first of these experiences is my most sacred tryptamine experience of all, and not one that I can easily relate. It challenges the last shreds of my worldview so soundly and touches a place so deep inside my soul that it is hard for me to share it with anyone. By relating my experience, I open this book up to ridicule (proof, some might say, of my own self-delusion), or even to charges of blatant fiction. But I can assure you that this is all true, described as it happened without embellishment. If you choose to take the experience at face value, then you must agree that the inexplicable nature of this 5MDE places it squarely within the realms of the occult and the Divine, and far outside of any "normal" drug experience. It is also one of the main reasons why I consider 5-MeO-DMT to be the only *true* entheogen that I have personally encountered.

This 5-MeO-DMT experience began at close to midnight on October 30th in New Orleans, in a neighborhood famous for its association with Haitian voodoo. I was with an old friend, Rene, a middle-aged Canadian woman long experienced in the ways of the counterculture, having spent many years in California and having worked as a photographer with the Grateful Dead for eight years. She had smoked 5-MeO-DMT once and was keen to do so again, but she was happy for me to lead the way. Rene doesn't smoke weed, had not been drinking, and thus was completely sober at the point when I inhaled the 5-MeO-DMT while sitting cross-legged on a couch opposite her.

On this occasion I sailed through the usual progression of steps, and I remember hitting the stage during which the enormity of the knowledge and the timeless nature of my environment usually would frighten me into a return to my physical form. I recall opening my eyes at that point, and in an unusual moment of physical clarity, I saw that Rene was sitting across from me meditating. I felt that everything was okay, sailed straight through that stage (which is usually my peak) and burst into a realm that can only be described as pure light. But this was not ordinary white light, nor even the white tunnel that I dissolve into when I exhale from a 5-MeO-DMT hit; instead, it was a fractal-filled prismatic light of indescribable radiance and beauty that pulsed with its own intelligence.

I remember this all with remarkable accuracy. I then felt a strong sense of the presence of my friend Brigid, who had died several years earlier. I had loved Brigid very much, yet I realized I had not thought about her in quite some time, perhaps because my thoughts had been overwhelmed by my fascination with my "new" world. But now she was clearly in my consciousness, and it was much more than a sense of simply remembering her. It was as if we were walking together, hand in hand, through towering shadowy trees on a field of stars, and she was laughing, her smile radiant. This was not a memory, but a feeling of actually being there with her.

The next thing I knew, I found myself back in normal reality, lying peacefully on the sofa and feeling totally calm and incredibly "straight," after what was my least tumultuous return from the Tryptamine Palace. All I said was, "I just remembered an old friend."

At this point Rene came over and sat down beside me where I lay and gripped my arm quite hard. I realized that her face was covered with tears. "There was a woman in the room," she said, as she wrung her hands with her eyes closed, seemingly occupying some place between two worlds. "She was young and beautiful. Oh, she seemed like she was so much fun. She was laughing. And she wanted to tell you that she was sorry she did not get a chance to say good-bye. And that she loves you. She is still here, but she's fading away." Rene went on to accurately describe my dead friend's appearance and personality, though she did not know her at all. She was obviously agitated and very emotional. It was as though *she* had taken some kind of a drug, and it took many hours before she completely "came down."

Rene's version of events went like this: After I exhaled the 5-MeO-DMT, she saw a beam of light the size of an American quarter come out of my chest.* When I split into two perfect copies of myself, sitting side-by-side on the couch, she found it hard to believe what she was seeing, being completely straight at the time. She said that even though she opened and closed her eyes, and rubbed them, the vision continued, apparently for a period of several minutes. After a while, she decided to close her eyes and meditate, since the whole affair was freaking her out a little. This is when the spirit of my dead friend suddenly appeared: an encounter Rene described in convincing detail.

Rene is a mother with a grown son, and she was completely sober during my trip. But if you had walked into the room while she was relating what had happened, you would have sworn that *she* had taken some kind of a drug and that I was the sober one. She has had considerable experience with people on all kinds of chemicals during her fifty-plus years on this planet, and yet it is safe to say that she had never experienced anything like *this* before. It is worth mentioning that Rene has lived in California for some

---

*In the second and third phases of the Tibetan bardo of *dharmata,* the "luminous" bardo of the after-death—very fine lights are said to spring from your heart, linking you with the various Buddhas and deities. According to Sogyal Rinpoche's *The Tibetan Book of Living and Dying,* ". . . the rays and beams of light are like lasers, piercing everything."

years, and she is receptive to various "New Age" concepts—far more so than I am! She has had other "channeling" experiences and comes from a long line of women known to possess fey powers. So she was later able to take the whole bizarre metaphysical occurrence somewhat in stride.

I, on the other hand, had no idea what to think, since I did not at this time believe in life after death, and certainly not in a form coherent enough to be able to wish me good-bye! Yet there was Rene, shaking and crying and describing Brigid—the same person I had just been walking with in another dimension—in fairly astonishing detail. To this day, I still do not know what to think or believe.

The veil between the worlds is thin in New Orleans—the most magic-believing city in North America—and people who really put stock in such things claim that around All Saints' Eve the veil barely exists at all. I had always felt that I had a strange karmic/telepathic bond with my beautiful friend, whom I had been with for the last time in New Orleans several years earlier. A few years later, I attended my first Mardi Gras. Early on its climactic final day—Fat Tuesday—I was standing on the street watching the Zulu parade when a sudden deep depression descended upon me, causing me to cry real tears for no apparent reason. My friends were concerned, but I managed to shake off this severe feeling and made it through the rest of the day with a general sense of unease—as if something *very* wrong had just happened in the world.

The following week I telephoned my homeland in the South Pacific to check on a pair of old friends who were expecting a baby (worried that this might have been the source of my concern). Upon hearing that their bouncing baby boy had been delivered premature but fine, I breathed a sigh of relief. Then I asked, for no real reason, if my friends had seen Brigid recently. Complete silence was the response on the end of the phone, before my friend told me that Brigid had died suddenly of a brain embolism. He had assumed that I had already heard. She had died on what had been, on the other side of the world in New Orleans, Mardi Gras Day.

Coincidences like these occur naturally enough in life and can easily be discredited by logical disbelievers. I certainly would not consider this a proof of any kind myself. But whatever happened between Rene and me (and who knows what other cosmic force) while I was under the influence of a brainfull of 5-MeO-DMT is a much harder experience to discredit. Did the spirit of my deceased friend enter the room? Or did my mind, supercharged from three months of regular 5-MeO-DMT smoking, project that image into the ether? And if this is so, then why is my recollection one of walking and laughing with Brigid, with no sense of her wishing to tell me anything? Yet Rene delivered a clear message that could only make sense to me, since she had no idea of Brigid's former existence.

All in all, this was a heavy experience, and I decided to take a break from tryptamine smoking for a while so that I could have adequate time to reflect on the variety of possibilities that this experience had opened up. Like I said, I still don't really know what I think—but this is the type of experience that places 5-MeO-DMT into a realm of its own as far as I am concerned. I don't consider 5-MeO-DMT to be a "drug." Rather, it is a sacrament of some kind, and it is best used and respected in such a context. Smoking 5-MeO-DMT up to this point had been mind-blowing good fun and spiritually enlightening enough to make me now believe in the existence of G/d. But after this experience in New Orleans, my interpretation and understanding of what was happening while I was under the influence of 5-MeO-DMT took on a deeper meaning. It's been several years now, since that night, and as I sit here writing these words, I still question what *really* happened that evening, as I have questioned it a thousand times before. Whose energy was at work in that room? What did Rene see while I lay there in the depths of my experience? Yet I know in my heart and in my mind that it all happened; it was, in Ludwig Wittgenstein's marvelous phrase, "true enough." And no amount of reading, tryptamine smoking, or sitting at Rinpoche's feet is likely to ever be able to explain it much better than the little I already know. It was the profoundest glimpse of an ancient unheralded reality that our contemporary society is now mostly too blind to see, an encounter that today we dismiss as myth, fantasy, or even schizophrenia, and one that cannot be easily classified by modern entheogenic lore. So after that experience, my spiritual and intellectual progress had no choice but to step away from the futuristic and the fantastic as my search moved on to both a careful examination of our sciences and to volumes that have been written by those men and women who have similarly drank from the mystic's cup throughout the ages.

If the 5-MeO-DMT experience grips you and really *moves* that mysterious energy inside of you that some call the Soul, then you will experience a period of intense excitement and disorientation, much like you have discovered an entirely new world. Looking around with the eyes of a child again, all that you have callously taken for granted now glows with fresh significance. And as exciting as this can be, it is also potentially terrifying. This experience can be quite different from individual to individual, and there is not—as of yet—a modern philosophy for those who taste a moment of entheogenic enlightenment. There are few saddhus, shamans, or sages to guide most of us. Few of us are prepared for a brush with the Divine, and talking of it leads us toward the occult* and toward ground that Western civilization largely abandoned centuries ago.

My experience that night in New Orleans produced the belief—still difficult to admit—that I had somehow communicated with a friend who had died several years before, and none of the wild and wooly imaginings of our New Age sages—their theories of aliens and insects, or parallel dimensions—had prepared me for *that.*

Over the first months of my experimentation with 5-MeO-DMT, I became a radically different human being, with a radically different way of viewing my world. My thirty-five years of only believing in modern scientific material reductionism had come to an end. This was both liberating and occasionally distressing at the same time. Had it had not been for three major "stabilizers," I believe I could have actually "lost my mind"—a possibility that I considered quite frequently as I moved into my new paradigm.

1. First, there were the obvious positive effects of my new worldview on my personality. I became notably more relaxed, happier, less likely to become angry, more compassionate, and my mental processes were thoroughly stimulated (and remain so to this day). Although I would not have described myself as tense, unhappy, easily angered, uncompassionate, or unintelligent before my 5-MeO-DMT experiences,

*Although some readers have been disturbed by my use of the word *occult,* which—primarily due to the excesses of Hollywood—is often regarded as implying witchcraft and dark forces, according to the *American Heritage Dictionary* it means: "1. Of, relating to, or dealing with supernatural influences, agencies, or phenomena. 2. Beyond the realm of human comprehension; inscrutable. 3. Available to only the initiate; secret: occult lore." If my New Orleans 5MDE doesn't fall into that category, then I don't know how else to classify it!

"the new me" knows that I have made significant progress in all these areas. I actually find it hard to remember what I was "like" before all this began. But I feel as if I have lost some of the "hard edge" of my personality, which resulted from many years of cynicism. I am now generally much more positive and hopeful.

2. My wife and close friends were (and have continued to be) supportive of my transformation, even though at times it has undoubtedly been concerning to them. They nevertheless seem to universally agree that I have been going through a powerfully positive experience. Those closest to me, and thus most affected by the changes in my personality, have all tried 5-MeO-DMT themselves, to varying effect. But all of them feel that it has had a profound impact in different ways on their lives, worldviews, and personalities.
3. After *The Archaic Revival* fell into my hands (about a week after my 5-MeO-DMT initiation) and I realized that I would be unable to locate conventional teachers in this matter, I went to the greatest body of sages I have ever known: the library, and its modern extension, the Internet.

A newfound lightness-of-intellect now seemed to accompany the lightness-of-consciousness that smoking 5-MeO-DMT had endowed upon me. This period marks the beginning of my greatest intellectual adventure since childhood, an era that has been defined by my newfound ability to grant even the craziest of New Age ideas at least a modicum of possibility and not immediately reject it because it was outside of my previously held worldview.

As I sit working on this treatise, it occurs to me that I am a bit like a DJ at times—a sort of literary mixologist—diving into the works and thoughts of various authors whose ideas are most fascinating to me, and whose worldviews have shed the most light on the peculiarities of my own radically altered reality. Scratch a little Terence McKenna in here, a little of David Bohm and the other physicists in there, Sogyal Rinpoche and the Tibetans to provide the heavy bass beat, throw in some Strassman and Shulgin for the technical details, some Joseph Campbell for a bit of magic, mythology, and historical transcendence. You get the picture. All these radical ideas floating around in the ether, visible to my mind and flashing like neon birds of paradise. While with my own plodding discourse, I try to make some sense out of what I have been through over the last few years.

At first, I was particularly interested in books such as those by McKenna, Strassman, and Shulgin, which directly shed light on the tryptamine experience. But these days, six years into this life-changing journey that blasted me to the far reaches of the universe, I am more likely to be reading Tibetan or Hindu cosmology, or the modern genius of Ervin Laszlo or Joseph Campbell, than any books specifically about entheogens.

There are two notable exceptions. First, I continue to be enthralled by the efforts of former LSD researcher and psychiatrist Stanislav Grof to map the transpersonal realms. I think that history will regard Grof's contributions to our understanding of the unconscious as important as those of Carl Jung or Sigmund Freud and that he will be seen as Jung's true heir. Grof's work has proven to be a grounding reaffirmation of my own extraordinary experiences and has thus helped keep me from going insane. It should not, therefore, be surprising that I will be making numerous references to a number of his books throughout this one.

The second exception is a fascinating book by Jeremy Narby, a Swiss/Canadian anthropologist, called *The Cosmic Serpent: DNA and the Origins of Knowledge,* which I like to periodically reread, since I find I resonate so much with Narby's own personal experience. Narby's world gets completely turned upside down when—after three years of living with various tribes in the Upper Amazon—he finally decides to try ayahuasca. After that single experience, Narby finds his reality and worldview split asunder. Then, with a somewhat delayed reaction, he embarks on a radical, tryptamine-inspired intellectual adventure of his own.

He begins with a reconsideration of the possibility that what the shamans had been telling him all along was literally true: that drinking ayahuasca opens the inner consciousness to a world of practical information and that the ayahuasca actually *tells* them things. Narby comes to regard the two giant fluorescent boa constrictors he hallucinated after drinking ayahuasca as, in fact, his own DNA talking to him. I'll leave the rest of the story for you to discover yourself, but can sum it up as the tale of a rigid material-reductionist who—when confronted by a reality greater than he had previously considered—finds himself knocked clean out of his intellectual box.

It is an excellent book: amusing, human, and very readable. Since Narby is a trained scientist, he presents a lot of fascinating facts on the way to his hypothesis that tryptamines allow us to tune in to a global wavelength of communication that is produced by DNA, which is the same in all living things, differing only in code, and has been unchanged on Earth since the existence of the first single-celled life forms almost four billion years ago. What is most interesting to me in this book, however, is how similar Narby's intellectual journey was to my own, in the sense that—through our tryptamine experiences—we were both flung to a point light-years away from our philosophical starting points.* There, our intellectual adventures became journeys back to ourselves and toward a heightened understanding of our own reality. Everything has changed in our worlds, but nothing has. Nothing has changed, but everything has. After having experienced this, both Jeremy Narby and myself have had to try and explain those experiences for our own elucidation. While reading *The Cosmic Serpent* I realized that one of the finest things you can hope to bring into this world is an idea.

Narby's book also contains some fascinating facts about consciousness. For example, did you know that when you look at this book, you are not really seeing it? Rather, you are seeing an internal 3D reproduction that is constructed by your brain. The photons of light reflected by the page strike the retinas in your eyes; they break it down into electrochemical information, and then send that on to your brain, where nerve cells separate the information into categories: form, color, movement, depth, and so on. Then the brain puts it all back together, virtually instantly, into a coherent image that forms the neurological basis of our consciousness—which is a complete mystery to science.

Now that's enough to keep anybody thinking for a while. But consider a corollary to these facts about our vision: this process requires the presence of light. *In the dark, we see nothing.* In the dark, all we can visually perceive is the lack of light. So the neurological basis of "hallucinations" (and dreams) is totally outside of the purview of current science. If we do not really understand how we see an actual object in front of us in broad daylight, then how can we hope to understand how we "see" something that is not externally even "there?"

*Dennis McKenna also appears to have taken a similar journey at La Chorrera, only more severely disorienting and with a correspondingly quicker return. For an account of that experience, see Terence McKenna's book *True Hallucinations* and the McKenna brothers' cult classic *The Invisible Landscape*.

Thus, there is currently no way to neurologically explain the fields of intense light that I "saw" just before I "saw" my dead friend Brigid that night in New Orleans, nor the tunnel of white light that is common to nearly every 5MDE that I have had, let alone the inner visual phenomena that I witness during the experience. Somehow, in the depths of a 5-MeO-DMT voyage, while my body still occupies the physical realm where light and darkness are "real" quantities (supposedly fixed and immutable), a tremendous light—brighter than any I have known—is produced from somewhere inside of my mind. And on that occasion in New Orleans, according to the testimony of a sober witness, some of this light apparently escaped my physical body as my Soul crossed between the boundaries of the living and the dead. Science would say such a thing is impossible, but in this case science admits that it cannot even begin to understand. Any way you look at it, this strange and mystical event confirmed for me—once and for all—that tryptamines provide a direct link to the sacred realm.

Up until this point, the vast majority of my 5-MeO-DMT experiences had involved an ecstatic aspect. And while they had been mind-blowing and awe-inspiring enough to ensure respect, they had also generally been enjoyable to the degree that I sometimes described the experience as a "cosmic orgasm." This joyful and loving aspect changed within the course of two experiences, the first of which was the All Saints Eve' experience.

The second experience that affected my ability to smoke 5-MeO-DMT, and the very nature of the 5MDE itself, was an accident that occurred a little over a month after All Saints' Eve. I decided to break my 5-MeO-DMT sabbatical to coincide with the visit of a good friend from Australia. He is a brilliant artist and an active seeker of curious things. With a lifetime of varied experiences behind him, I was keen to introduce him to 5-MeO-DMT, even though he himself appeared a little dubious. I had recently obtained a glass vial of 5-MeO-DMT that I was told was 99.5 percent pure, as had been all the samples I had seen from research chemical companies. However, this new batch of 5-MeO-DMT was an orange color, more like the extracted DMTs I had seen. And since all the 5-MeO-DMT I'd previously encountered had been totally white, I was curious to see if there would be any difference in effect with this orange material.

I had already become quite ritualistic about my 5-MeO-DMT use, and the sanctity of the 5MDE had been vitally reinforced by the All Saints' Eve visit of my dead friend. Around midnight, on an evening with no full moon, my Australian friend and I were joined by my regular 5-MeO-DMT partner, Captain Urquhart. He had never successfully "released" on 5-MeO-DMT, so he generally did not partake in smoking any longer himself, but he was very familiar with my behavior when I did.

I agreed to go first, and weighed out three large doses using an accurate scale. What happened next should be taken as a warning to all 5-MeO-DMT aficionados, and act as a reminder of the fact that we have absolutely no clue about the power of this substance once we inhale it.

I smoked the first dose in a glass pipe with a screen and a little bit of weed. Around this time, I had been studying the literature regarding DMT on Erowid (www.erowid.org), the best entheogenic information resource on the Internet. I had been reading a lot about not burning the DMT, but instead allowing it to vaporize. So I was trying to keep the flame of the lighter as far from the 5-MeO-DMT as I could while still volatizing it. I must have undershot due to this technique, and I had a mild experience during which I never really "released": my consciousness didn't leave my body or the room, despite the fact that I saw a variety of mild visual phenomena.

Methods for Smoking Tryptamines

After much experimentation I have settled on the following simple method for smoking 5-MeO-DMT. Using a long glass pipe (a bubbler works fine and cools the smoke) with a pipe screen, place a tiny amount of herb (mint, tobacco, whatever you prefer) into the bowl, with the 5-MeO-DMT on top. Torch it good, inhaling very slowly, and fill your lungs to their maximum capacity with the smoke. (Smaller initial dosages allow you to fill your lungs with all the available smoke without fear.) You should be on a bed or on the floor with cushions around you and any breakable objects placed out of reach. Retain the smoke as long as possible, until you can see the effects: your visual reality begins to dissolve into fractals. Then exhale.

If for some reason the hit apparently has no effect on the first attempt (though it always should if you follow this simple method), *do not increase the dosage*. Simply replace the screen with a clean one (very important, in order to avoid any unprocessed residue that would increase the dose) and try again. Other methods can also work (such as "chasing the dragon" on a piece of tinfoil), but I have found this simple approach to be best. A fully inhaled 15+ mg hit of 5-MeO-DMT is practically impossible for anyone to escape.

The first advice I was ever given about 5-MeO-DMT—by the brother who turned me on to it (and who was repeating the words that he had been told when he first smoked it)—remains the best guidance: "After you smoke it and breathe out, try to stay in the light. If you get out of the light, there will be all kinds of creatures and strange things that will want to distract you and talk to you. But if you stay in the light as long as you can, then it will take you all the way." This has certainly proven to be my experience, and I pass this advice on to every novice who asks me about 5-MeO-DMT.

I have found that it is best to smoke tryptamines three or four hours after a healthy light meal, one that doesn't contain meat. Apprentice ayahuasca shamans eat light meals of fish and plantains during their months of training. (Fish contains tryptophan and bananas contain vitamin B_6, both of which are required to produce serotonin.) A vegetarian meal is also a good option, but avoid fried foods.

Drinking large amounts of water, tea, or other liquids before smoking 5-MeO-DMT is not desirable, although it is a good idea to drink plenty of water earlier in the day. Alcohol should not have been consumed, and one's mind should be as clear and uncluttered as possible. 5-MeO-DMT should be experienced free of any other chemical distractions—smoking it while on acid or mushrooms is for souls braver than mine! Mixing with MDMA should be strictly avoided; this combination has resulted in negative experiences that appeared similar in character to overdoses of tryptamines alone. If during the 5MDE you think someone is having trouble breathing and looks like he or she might vomit, roll the person gently into the recovery position, and vomiting will happen if it needs to. Generally if the person does vomit, he or she will afterward relax into an easy experience, with the blockage—both physical and mental—now cleared.

Smoking 5-MeO-DMT at the dosages mentioned here is a heavy thing, and should not be taken casually. But it's best to avoid making too big of a deal out of it as well. This can be a real tightrope at times. If you are with those who have never smoked it before, it is natural to want to tell them that the experience they are about to undergo is sacred and amazing, but you should also note that the easiest way to get to the highest realms is by having no expectations. Maintain a dignified presence but, if at all possible, create an air of humor around the proceedings. Such a lack of tension, in my experience, leads to more loving and joyful journeys for the majority of participants involved.

After approximately five minutes, I was sufficiently recovered to remark about what tricky stuff tryptamines can be. Remembering the fact that the body's tolerance to DMT apparently builds rapidly—which means that the full effects from it are not obtained if it is smoked in too-frequent a succession—I wondered if this was also the case with 5-MeO-DMT. Disappointed with the mild results that the evening had so far provided, I decided that I might as well try another hit, something I had never done before.

Going back to the kitchen, I placed a fresh hit on top of the apparently completely burnt first hit, since there was still quite a bit of weed in the bowl (too much). Then I went back to the living room, where I repeated the same procedure of trying to vaporize the 5-MeO-DMT, this time receiving an even less effective sub-threshold hit. This appeared to confirm that the information about tolerance applied to both tryptamines, not just DMT. (This conjecture has since been disproved, however.*) Once that hit wore off, I was fairly convinced that I had been ripped off on this particular purchase of orange 5-MeO-DMT, since it seemed a lot weaker than the white 5-MeO-DMT I had previously encountered. I passed the

*Justin Case has reported that pyrolyzed doses of 5-MeO-DMT can be repeated at three to ten minute intervals (at least ten times in a row); even after three days following this approach, no tolerance built up. He actually found himself more sensitive to the per-dose effect once he was well into the evaluation (K. Trout, *Some Simple Tryptamines,* second edition [Austin, Tex.: MydriaticProductions, 2007]). Although tolerance or desensitization does build up rapidly with DMT (within three to five minutes), it also disappears fairly rapidly. Formal testing by Strassman using injected DMT has shown that any tolerance is entirely gone after thirty minutes (R. Strassman, *DMT: The Spirit Molecule. A Doctor's Revolutionary Research into the Biology of Near-Death and Mystical Experiences* [Rochester, Vt.: Park Street Press, 2001]), and it is clear, from the reports of multiple psychonauts, that smoked DMT is fully effective if one waits an hour between doses.

pipe to my smoking partner who confirmed that it appeared to be empty of any 5-MeO-DMT as I lay on the floor feeling mild effects that were far from entheogenic.

After a while I sat up, and the three of us smoked a joint of good weed and discussed again how tricky the 5-MeO-DMT could be. My friend from Australia was by then quite skeptical about all of the extraordinary things he had been hearing about the compound from me. My other friend remarked how there had been none of the distinct strong smell that he had experienced in other sessions: a warning that I should have recognized then and there.

The living room was darkly lit with lamps, so—perturbed by the "failure" of this new supply of 5-MeO-DMT—I picked up the pipe and went to the corner of room where I could better examine the remnants in the bowl under the light. In doing so, I noticed a dark little nugget of a crystal. Like the proverbial fool rushing in where angels fear to tread, I put the pipe to my lips and thoughtlessly torched the rock with the full force of the lighter. The room erupted in the distinctive overpowering smell that signifies 5-MeO-DMT and I immediately took in a tremendous hit that sent my senses reeling even though I had not yet breathed out.

"Shit, you've done it now haven't you?!" my Australian friend exclaimed, while Captain Urquhart just looked wide-eyed and flashed me a big grin as he took the pipe from my hands. The intense fractalization of the world had begun well before I exhaled, and I don't remember getting to the ground.

Some thirty-five minutes later (not that I had a clue of how much time had passed) I reentered this world and realized that I was propped up against the couch with wet towels draped around me and two worried-looking friends trying to get me to communicate with them.

"It's M.O.M.'s Ball," I shouted and laughed tremendously, feeling absolutely fantastic and totally energized in every cell of my body. "We knew it all the time! You knew it all the time! It's M.O.M.'s Ball!"

M.O.M.'s Ball

A few words of explanation are required at this point to see the connection between M.O.M.'s Ball and my 5-MeO-DMT experiences.

Mardi Gras is a centuries-old pre-Lenten carnival held in New

Orleans each year that is world famous for the revelry surrounding its parades and the accompanying balls. Each of the great parades is put on by a "Krewe," which usually goes by some mythological name like Bacchus, Rex, or Zulu. Many of these Krewes are like secret societies, and one needs to be a member in order to participate in their parade or attend their ball. Over the years, Krewe membership has become a political- and society-based situation (not unlike the Rotary Club or the Freemasons in other cities), with some Krewes being notably stiff and stuffy. As a reaction to this "uptown" stuffiness, some thirty years ago a group of the city's underground luminaries (bar owners, musicians, bikers, dope dealers, and so on) got together and decided that they would form their own Krewe, blow off the parade, and go straight to the party. This party is called the Mystics, Orphans, and Misfits' Ball but is more commonly called M.O.M.'s, and it has become a unique New Orleans Mardi Gras institution and an event like no other. On the Saturday night before Fat Tuesday (Mardi Gras Day) approximately twenty-five hundred freaks gather in their finest costumery for this over-the-top, invitation-only, often X-rated event, that is the hottest ticket for Mardi Gras, and arguably the world's greatest psychedelic costume party.

M.O.M.'s Ball is not for the light-hearted, since a lot of crazy shit can go down there. The crowd is mostly between their late twenties to late fifties. They are *serious* partiers who have come from all over America—with the best of whatever drugs they have—to enjoy this unique night. The party has an air of menace about it at times (an extreme good-time-with-an-edge, not unlike New Orleans itself), and this fact was taught to me in the most resounding manner when I attended my first M.O.M.'s Ball. Which, oddly, was the only M.O.M.'s Ball ever held outside of Mardi Gras—a special once-in-a-lifetime event on December 31, 1999—and a night that I will never forget.

The weirdness began around an exchange that occurred between myself and my girlfriend of the time and an older swinger couple that came up to tell us how gorgeous she looked. As the two women were talking, the husband quickly became a pain in my ear, bragging that he had backstage passes and a limo outside, while his jaw ground away. "Classic cocaine abuse," I thought to myself (I can't stand talkative cokeheads), and I quickly made a move to get away from this couple and back onto the dance floor. This resulted in a mildly combative exchange with the husband over the fact that we didn't want to "party" with them. Trying to be as polite as possible I gathered my girl away, after accepting a token drink as we departed. That should have been the end of the matter, except for the fact that some twenty minutes later all hell started to break loose inside of my head.

It started out fun enough, the massive rush of a large dose of good LSD, with the accompanying rippling waves of changing reality. A number of years previously, I had been a keen student of acid, almost a disciple you could say, and I had been lucky enough to be around enough high-quality acid (in foreign lands) to allow me the opportunity to explore my personal limits. Thus, I had taken what Terence McKenna would describe as "heroic doses" of both liquid and freshly dipped blotter.

Although I had consumed LSD in the 1000–1500 microgram range on numerous occasions, I had stopped taking what I considered "giant doses," having tired of journeys to where the entire world was made of blue electricity and I found myself dead-ended down some hopeless rat's alley, exhausted from the arduous experience. Even having willingly taken LSD in these large quantities, I was not prepared for the experience that I went through on what I presume must have been a *hell of a lot* of LSD (and who knows what else) contained within that spiked drink.

At first I felt as if I was becoming some kind of a god and that the passing of the millennium was allowing me to enter a new phase of cerebral development: I began to imagine that I was controlling the party with my mind. Deciding that I was now in control of how much fun could be had, I first considered summoning various friends from around the world, before I decided that instead I would change the musicians onstage—a white rock band called The Radiators who are the M.O.M.'s house band—into something more funky. Voila! Suddenly the Radiators turned black and grew afros, morphing into Bootsy Collins' Rubber Band or, at least in my mind, into something like it. I was experiencing what I regard as one of the classic differences between a synthetic psychedelic like LSD and the natural entheogens like psilocybin or DMT—the latter can help you find union-with-God, while too much of the former can make you think you *are* a god!* And while I thought I was the epitome of cool, I was apparently becoming increasingly physically out-of-control, and then (so I was later told) dropped my pants around my ankles in the middle of the dance floor and began to wave my large white-boy ass around in the air. It was only the fact that my best friend in the world was visiting from Europe that saved me, since he was one of a few people who could have controlled me in any shape or form at this point, and he and my girlfriend managed to get me outside and onto the levee banks by the Mississippi before the acid really took control.

That was only the beginning of what was by far the heaviest LSD trip I have ever been on and one of the heaviest experiences on any compound I have had, *before* I discovered 5-MeO-DMT. (The only experience comparable had occurred ten years earlier, also in New Orleans, when I accidently ate over 100 hits of Orange Sunshine acid in powdered form. On that occasion I had the only "true hallucinations" of my life, and came to in a hotel in Belize City some 36 hours later with no recollection of how I had gotten there.) My memories of this experience are vague at best, as I spent the following five hours virtually comatose, only occasionally coming in and out of "reality." But I do recall that there was an archetypal battle between Good and Evil going on in my head. In many ways I was on a classic shamanic voyage, traveling in other-dimensional worlds, as I experienced a form of psychospiritual death and rebirth.

It was a mythic LSD experience, my shamanic initiation on the cusp of the new millennium, and a journey far beyond any I had taken in nearly a decade. My few lucid moments corresponded with that peculiar rationality that one can get on acid—that sense that you know that the things you are seeing are not really happening. But in the other periods, when I was completely outside of myself, I was forced to abandon any attempts at rationality. And it was during those five hours that I came closest to the realms that I now access during a 5-MeO-DMT experience.

---

*Not all psychonauts share my views on the differences between natural and synthetic entheogens. On this topic, Sasha Shulgin himself once wryly quipped that he is, himself, a product of nature, and thus the compounds he creates are a product of nature.

M.O.M.'s and my 5MDEs

At first I thought that this was the obvious link to my 5-MeO-DMT experiences, since 95 percent of my 5MDE's end with me exiting through my own personal M.O.M.'s Ball as I am transported back from the wild other dimensions that 5-MeO-DMT allows me to access. I am "dropped back off" at my previous "high point" so to speak, and thus I can reoccupy this reality with a minimum of disorientation, with the heavy trip that I took on that New Year's Eve at M.O.M.'s Ball acting as some kind of preparation for my subsequent discovery of the tryptamine dimension. But I was puzzled that this phenomenon has continued despite my strong faith in the spiritual aspects of the 5-MeO-DMT experience, given that M.O.M.'s Ball is very hedonistic, and not exactly something one would ever call a spiritual affair, excepting perhaps in the Dionysian sense.

Now I have come to a different and more complex conclusion. There are two reasons why I currently discredit my original notion. First, I question why I would always "get dropped back" at M.O.M.'s Ball. I have undoubtedly been very high at other points in my life, such as my neo-mythical night on Orange Sunshine dust, and yet I have never been dropped off back at that night, nor at any of the other psychedelic places I have been (such as eating mushrooms at night on the pyramids in Tikal, or on my knees full-of-wonder in front of the Temple of Stars on the playa at Burning Man). So why is it always M.O.M.'s Ball? And not the comatose levee-stricken aspect of my new millennium M.O.M.'s Ball experience, but rather, a super-charged archetype of M.O.M.'s Ball, which seems more like some form of Paradise while I'm in there, with no obvious reminders of any real-world M.O.M.'s Ball that I have actually attended. The other reason that I now find it difficult to relate any more recent 5MDE to my first M.O.M.'s Ball acid trip is because LSD and 5-MeO-DMT produce such different effects.

5-MeO-DMT takes me over completely, transporting me to dimensions far stranger than anything in my imagination. Yet, because of this overpowering totality, what I experience seems so utterly real and convincing. Realer than reality, these are McKenna's "true hallucinations." Something about the experience feels inherently organic, natural, and holy—even if synthesized material is used. On the other hand, at the boundary limits of LSD, it always feels artificial, unreal, and "weird science," no matter how hard I trip, and my hallucinations are *recognized* as such. Consider, for example, the shattering hallucinations of my grand Orange Sunshine dust adventure. On that night, the billboards break-danced and talked to me, giant statues came down off their podiums (flashing in and out of the traffic), and, for a while, if I rested my eyes on anything it began to dissolve into molecules, then atoms, and beyond, so I had to constantly keep moving my head so I wouldn't see right through things. Yet as amazingly real as it all seemed—far more real than TV or any movie could ever be—my consciousness still hung on the fact that it was *not* real. As I moved toward those invisible boundaries between the worlds, my ego was still able to influence enough pull that I could never truly escape consensus reality, I could only warp it to the extreme. With 5-MeO-DMT, I am totally transported, and I cannot deny the supernatural reality that I encounter.

Grace Slick is said to have once remarked that dropping LSD was like being sucked up a straw, while smoking DMT was like being shot out of a cannon; this is a fairly accurate simile, even though she was talking about the gentler of the two naturally occurring tryptamines! It seems to me that DMT and 5-MeO-DMT—and to a lesser extent mushrooms, peyote, and San Pedro—can open you up to a natural place that is closer to the true center of existence. In contrast, the synthetic analogues that human beings have invented—LSD, DIPT, DOM, ketamine, and so on—can only reveal a crueler mirror-world of that reality—a place where ultimately our human frailties betray us.

We may have split the atom and escaped the atmosphere (in the vain hope of improving on what nature has already provided), but no laboratory will ever better the entheogenic perfection of 5-MeO-DMT: a product of G/d's nature, found in plants, animals, and possibly even nestled next to one's own brain within the pineal gland. For myself, it has been the most effective conduit to this sacred reality. This leads me to my "more complex" speculation as to why my 5-MeO-DMT experiences so often end at M.O.M.'s Ball.

Suppose that G/d wanted to talk to you in an indirect and yet totally effective way. Imagine that you are at your favorite party ever, a party that is *more* than just a party: a hedonic Garden of Eden, blissful Norse heaven of Valhalla, and the Islamic version of Paradise, all rolled into one. Everyone is there—your friends, your family, and those whom you love and admire, all present as magnificently costumed archetypal images. Now imagine that with each conversation you have that night, every interaction with friends and strangers alike, you are actually talking to G/d. Each being is a variation of the millions of possible permutations, themselves only a small fraction of the forms in which G/d can appear.

This idea is one of the cornerstones of mythology: the intervention of the Divine disguised within the physical workings of the mortal world. But can you imagine how effective such a strategy would be? G/d passing you a cold beer, G/d with a joint in his hand, G/d talking to you in a thousand loving voices, G/d dressed in silk, feathers, and lingerie—wiggling her tight little ass in your lap as she whispers eternal wisdoms in your ear . . .

This is now what I have decided is happening to me at the end of my 5MDE: my visible tryptamine gods have essentially become M.O.M.'s Ball, and M.O.M.'s Ball has become them, the Divine personified in that arena where I am the happiest and most free. Through M.O.M.'s Ball and its rainbow-plumed inhabitants, G/d talks to me. Teaches me. Loves me. Guides me.

Until I eventually have to go home.

My friend from Australia—who had attended M.O.M.'s Ball in New Orleans with me on several occasions—looked at me and said, "What the fuck are you talking about, Roc? This isn't M.O.M.'s Ball. You're in your bloody living room." But my other friend laughed and said that it was all right, since believing that I was at M.O.M.'s Ball was the way I often made my way out of my 5MDEs and that I looked like I would be okay. I remember exclaiming, "Okay?! I've never felt better in my life!"

Then, for the first and only time, I consciously reentered my 5MDE after coming out of it. Before I took leave of this world, I remember having the exquisite sensation of literally diving back into another dimension, into an apparently ongoing party in my mind, which is perhaps my own twisted idea of heaven: my own personal 5-MeO-DMT "M.O.M.'s Ball."

The next thing I remember was coming around again—apparently another ten minutes or so later—stretched out on the floor in my living room with a pair of now very concerned and somewhat pissed-off friends. My buddies had taken care of my catatonic body for close to forty minutes after I had first exhaled that gigantic hit of evidently perfectly fine 5-MeO-DMT, orange or not.

What had happened was that I had melted the two hits of 5-MeO-DMT into a single "rock" within the excess of weed in the bowl of the pipe. By trying to vaporize rather than burn the chemical, and by not changing the screen between attempts, I had created a single dose that was probably in excess of 40 mg—an amount that may have been strong enough to stop me from breathing (and possibly even kill me). My Australian friend—who has had a lot more experience with junkies, drug store cowboys, and the type of users likely to overdose than I have—was really upset, as he was convinced I had nearly checked out permanently. My vital signs had been weak and my breathing virtually non-existent. My two capable friends had been considering mouth-to-mouth at one point, before rolling me into the recovery position in case I needed to vomit. They had then hauled me up against the couch and draped me in wet towels, which had only momentarily interrupted my festivities at my private "M.O.M.'s Ball."

I could tell by the length of time of the whole trip—around 40 to 45 minutes, probably the longest trip I've ever taken—and the look of serious concern on my regular smoking partner's face that this really had been a close one and that I had been as physically non-responsive as they described. But, perversely, I felt unbelievable—better than I ever had in my life. I came out of my near overdose totally ecstatic from the experience! As close to physical death as I may have come, to me it had been nothing but pure rapture.

After these two journeys, my 5MDEs seem to have grown in sheer power, even though I have cut my dosage down by 25 percent or more. Now my visits to the Tryptamine Palace conclude in a sense of awe and wonder that feels far closer to terror than rapture. *Terror* is not actually the correct word. I am experiencing Rudolf Otto's *mysterium tremendum et fascinans:* the overpowering sense of awe that envelopes someone who confronts the Divine, an ancient timeless energy that is far greater than our existence or our imagination.

It is this sense of sacred awe at the tremendous power I experience that I now return with from my experiences. These days I often declare as I come out of the journey that, "I have no idea of the power of what I am dealing with," and that my friends should, "Under no circumstances, ever let me touch that stuff again!" It now takes every iota of my courage to return to travel further into that unfathomable zone. Those who have witnessed my experiences since the beginning say that in each trip I appear to be on a literal journey and that I pass many of the same mileposts along the way (such as when I declare, "I am there. It exists!" or "We knew it all along!"). But over time I have begun to reach each milepost faster (apparently better knowing the way) before quickly getting to the point where I can continue into the unknown, dissolving into that intense singularity. Most recently, I seem to have stopped "journeying" at all, and now I virtually immediately "drop in" to the resonant mystical state, with none of the signposts that used to mark my way. A friend offered the description that you are "a drop, which returns to the ocean"* on 5-MeO-DMT —an excellent metaphor in my opinion.

5-MeO-DMT has taught me *fear,* a powerful lesson for someone who has never feared authority, the ridicule of my peers, loneliness, or the possibility of physical injury. Yet now there is a force that I respect above all others, and one that I know I will never conquer. When I return from a 5MDE, I am blown away by the force I have encountered on the other side. One hundred percent completely, totally, and inconceivably, blown away. Period. The kid gloves are now apparently off; I have journeyed to that place too many times to expect any sympathy.

These days, when I knock on the doors of the Tryptamine Palace, I am no longer greeted with unconditional love, but instead, I am reminded of the *responsibility* that comes with ultimate knowledge: an undeniable responsibility to myself, to my tribe, to my species, to my planet. This is the terrifying responsibility that comes with such an awesome love. Every shaman knows it, Siddhartha Gautama knew it, Lao Tzu knew it, Christ knew it, St. Augustine knew it, and Krishnamurti, too—all knowledge comes with a price. Or as Hunter S. Thompson liked to put it, "Buy the ticket, take the ride."

*Attributed to the Dharma Punks.

FOUR

Welcome to the Power Zone

Ecstasy! . . . In common parlance . . . ecstasy is fun . . . But ecstasy is not fun. Your very soul is seized and shaken until it tingles. After all, who will choose to feel undiluted awe. . . ? The unknowing vulgar abuse the word, and we must recapture its full and terrifying sense. . . .

R. GORDON WASSON, "THE HALLUCINOGENIC FUNGI OF MEXICO: AN INQUIRY INTO THE ORIGINS OF THE RELIGIOUS IDEA AMONG PRIMITIVE PEOPLES," *BOTANICAL MUSEUM LEAFLETS HARVARD UNIVERSITY*, 1961

The strong man dares to be alone with God.

NATIVE AMERICAN PROVERB

Two months after my accidental overdose, I returned to my homeland in the South Pacific after an absence of several years. I was still full of 5-MeO-DMT fever, and greatly excited by the prospect of introducing my oldest and dearest friends to the universal truths one can learn by smoking tryptamines. But to my surprise and disappointment, I could not find anyone even willing to try it.

Everyone had kids, jobs, responsibilities, and the idea of a cosmic wake-up call that might jolt them out of their semi-comfortable reality did not seem to appeal. People these days want party drugs, happy drugs, horny drugs, keep-me-awake drugs, make-me-forget-about-my-job drugs, and not many are game for a "heroic dose" of a full-blown entheogen. Most of my friends just looked uncomfortable when I declared that smoking 5-MeO-DMT had caused me to find my G/d. A lot of people, I realized, just aren't ready for that.

I also went home determined to improve my rather tenuous relationship with my father—a result of the compassionate desire for reconciliation that a faith-based epiphany can release in an individual. Alas, that intention failed miserably, when a financial argument (my father's favorite kind) spiraled out of my control and resulted in me demanding that he appear at court to sign certain papers. After that, he ceremoniously disowned me, telling me never to come near him or my mom again. (He's since gotten over that, at least.)

Dispirited by the turn of affairs and disgusted by my own lack of self-control, I spent the night on the farm of two of my closest childhood friends. I again attempted, unsuccessfully, to convince them that they needed to try 5-MeO-DMT. Finally, I decided to smoke some myself—partially as a demonstration for my friends, and partially to dispel the bad mindset that had resulted from the negative dealings with my father. I didn't have a particularly accurate scale with me, so I made the dose on what I figured to be the small side—a precaution that probably made no difference, since this was the beginning of what I now refer to as my "power" experiences.

Simba is my best friend from high school, while I literally grew up with Charley, his wife, since our families were friends from before either of us was born. Both of them were in the adjoining kitchen when I smoked the 5-MeO-DMT while sitting on their living room floor in the company of Simba's older brother Johnny. Simba and Johnny are more like brothers to me than simply friends, since their family home was a constant refuge from my own while I was a troubled teen.

I took a solid hit on my long wooden pipe and felt the swirl of that other reality, even as I handed the pipe to John, and I remember seeing the twinkle in his eye as he watched the drug grip me. I exhaled, and the next thing I knew I was coming back wide-eyed and shouting, stretched out on the floor with all three of my friends on their knees—laughing with tears in their eyes as they held on to me, apparently by request.

"Roc," I heard Johnny bark, addressing me by my childhood name, "What's Mother's Ball?"

But I couldn't reply. I was too blown away by what I had just experienced. I remembered Terence McKenna saying that if he had to use one word to describe DMT and one word to describe 5-MeO-DMT, it would be "magic" for the former and "force" for the latter.* Well, now I knew exactly what he meant! All of my experiences up to this point had been so full of love and wonder that I had thought that he was being pedantic. But the power level had somehow been cranked up another few notches, and I felt as if I had just come within a hair's breadth of getting fried.

With eyes as wide as saucers and feeling extraordinarily happy to be alive, I ran out into the backyard of the farmhouse hooting and hollering, before flinging myself face down on the grass and embracing the earth. My friends, who continued to be amused, were quite impressed by the whole show. I think this was the first time I declared that someone should, "Bury that vial in the ground and never let me near it again." I remember the overwhelming sense that I had no idea of the force of this substance that I was toying with. My friends were quite sure that they didn't want to try the 5-MeO-DMT after watching my ride. Actually, it was my *reaction* to my inner experience that dissuaded them, as during the 5MDE I was sitting and lying down peacefully. (This has continued to be typical of my experiences with 5-MeO-DMT, which tend to be heavier than those of most others: only upon coming out of them do I become so mentally excited, physically agitated, and over-awed by the sheer power of what I have experienced. I have learned to go last in the circle so as not to dissuade others!) Eventually, everybody said their "goodnights" and went off to bed.

The next morning I rose around dawn and drove my rental car a hundred miles to the nearest international airport in order to fly back to my Caribbean home via the United States. I went through ticketing with a minimum of pleasantries, and then sat silent with my thoughts for the entire thirteen-hour flight to Los Angeles. My flight from LAX to Miami got bumped, so I called an old girlfriend who happened to live nearby in Venice Beach and arranged to take her out for lunch. (Coincidentally, she was the same person who had given me *The Archaic Revival.*) I found a cab—a big American van painted blue and yellow—and I jumped in with two other guys to share a ride, since

*McKenna professed a preference for DMT; he seemed to think that 5-MeO-DMT was just too intense.

we were heading in the same direction. One of the guys had a surfboard, and out of sheer boredom I struck up a conversation about surfing and mentioned that I now mostly "kite" surfed. The other occupant of the cab was a dark, brooding chap with a painful-looking pierced chin, who had remained completely silent throughout the entire exchange up to that point. But he now looked across at me and asked how I liked kite surfing, his English betraying an obvious Israeli accent. I replied that I liked it a lot.

"My wife just left me for a famous kite surfer," he replied, introducing himself as "Yaron." And from that potentially unpleasant beginning, we moved like lightning through a discussion that included various Caribbean islands, the blue rock called larimar, Atlantian pyramids under the sea, New Orleans and Mardi Gras, Dr. Albert Hofmann and his closest associates, some of their children, and then Yaron asked me if I was familiar with *PIHKAL* and *TIHKAL,* the Shulgins' unique contributions to the world of entheogenic literature. By then I figured that our conversation had gone so far, so fast, that I might as well just "throw it out there," so I made a statement to the effect that I was a lot less affected by the ongoing drought of quality liquid LSD in the world than I might have thought that I would have been, purely because I had discovered the wonders of smoking 5-MeO-DMT.

When I said that, my newfound friend Yaron looked at me and declared, "Brother, we have to talk. Each year I go down to Mexico and hunt for the toads." Enough said. We swapped e-mail addresses, shook hands, and the cab arrived at my destination in Venice Beach. Ultimately, that conversation—which took less than ten minutes—would lead me to the living source of organic 5-MeO-DMT. Once again, coincidence and synchronicity in the tryptamine universe came about with the same regularity as the tides, or the movement of the sun and the moon.

Six months after spending Christmas in my homeland, I was in Boca del Drago on an island in Panama near the border of Costa Rica, staying at a friend's house in the middle of nowhere. As so often occurs with tryptamine ceremonies, a stranger turned up with intimate connections and references, and it was decided that we would all dip into my tryptamine supplies that night. I only had a small amount of 5-MeO-DMT and DMT with me, so I decided to share the 5-MeO-DMT with the others, and try the DMT myself, as my experiences with 5-MeO-DMT had grown in power to such a degree that I could only approach doing it every few months.

Our session came close to not happening at all, since at one point the evening disintegrated into a fairly heavy verbal battle between my host's wife, Nina, and myself. Nina is a very intelligent, well-educated woman who works on massive AIDS projects in Africa; as she sat, drinking her way through a bottle of wine and listening to me talk, it became increasingly obvious that she could not handle the way I was liberally using words like "faith" and "G/d." Our "conversation" became more and more combative, and as we argued, her scientific-rationalist opposition struck me as being virtually identical to the kind of argument I would have used prior to my own initiation to 5-MeO-DMT. Finally, as her opposition to my claims and theories became outright hostile, I declared that everyone had to stop drinking and that we needed to sober up for an hour or two before we took to smoking the "mystery" in question.

Around midnight we all made our way up to the rooftop terrace where the ceremony was to take place. The night was a blanket of brilliant stars, and the house lay surrounded by thick native jungle, adding to the growing sense of expectation. Nathan (our mystery guest, who no one knew) volunteered to be the first to try the 5-MeO-DMT, and he proceeded to embark on one of the most peaceful, all-knowing, and remarkably coherent 5MDEs that I have ever been fortunate enough to witness. At one point during the experience he looked straight at me and asked in a voice filled with wonder, "Will this last forever?" I had to tell him that it wouldn't, and that he should hold onto it while he could. When he finally emerged from his journey, his countenance could only be described as beatific. He sat in a comfortable chair gazing out at the cosmos, like a man who had just seen the shining reality implicit in the nature of his own Soul.

Nina came next, obviously curious after seeing Nathan's taste of enlightenment. We moved into a small room just off the terrace to smoke the pipe, since the wind was playing havoc with our attempts outside. Nina took a short sharp hit and immediately coughed most of the smoke out, but she was already on her way. She didn't remember later that her husband and I had led her back out onto the terrace to lie down.

During her experience it was as if we were watching the astounded pleasure of a little kid who has just discovered the ocean for the first time.

There were touches of fear, but most obvious was pure wonder, excitement, and cries of delight. As she excitedly started to come out of the experience, she insisted that her husband and I join her on the mattress and hold onto her (much as I apparently had done while coming out on my friend's farm). She repeatedly apologized for being so hardheaded and combative. Later, as rationality slowly took hold again, she said she could remember hardly anything about the experience: she had a "white-out," and she wasn't sure that it had any meaning at all. In a white-out—a commonly related phenomena that I have seen on various occasions—the person, like Nina, comes out of their experience with clear recollections of some kind of an event, yet half an hour later can only recall dissolving into the white light and then nothing at all.

Nina's experience was particularly childlike compared to Nathan's, who remained calm throughout his experience, like a wise old man sitting on top of a mountain. And, in stark contrast to Nina, Nathan retained one of the most coherent memories of his experience that I have ever witnessed. The differences between these two experiences have caused me to theorize a possible mechanism for reincarnation based on the concepts of "polarity," or "creation by subtraction." These ideas, which in truth have circulated in Hindu and Buddhist philosophies for centuries, have their modern origin in theories proposed by Aldous Huxley, Peter Russell, and most lately, Bernard Haisch, regarding the idea that our consciousness is essentially a filter of a far greater universal consciousness.

Aldous Huxley proposed that our consciousness is a filtered version of "Mind at Large." Citing the work of Cambridge philosopher C. D. Broad, he came to the conclusion that our consciousness is literally unlimited, as indeed it would be if each of us is indeed a manifestation of an infinite consciousness. Huxley explained that it is the function of the brain to filter out virtually everything other than immediate consensual reality, until we are left with what he described as "a measly trickle of the kind of consciousness which will help us stay alive on the surface of this particular planet."[1]

A potential mechanism for this filtering is proposed by Bernard Haisch in his book, *The God Theory.* Naming this mechanism "creation by subtraction," Haisch proposes how these filters could progressively allow us to recognize more and more form out of the undiluted light of Mind:

> In optics, the process of creating something (the projected color slide) involves taking something away. White light may be bright and beautiful in its own right, but you can't depict anything using just white light alone. A world in which everything is precisely and perfectly white would effectively be an invisible world. By that I do not mean one that you would see through; rather I mean one that you could look at but still see nothing, because everything would be exactly the same, a fog of white. In optics you create by taking away. To create the sky blue, you have to take away the violet, indigo, green, yellow, orange, and red.
>
> The esoteric traditions tell us that creation by subtraction is one of the fundamental truths underlying reality. . . . [T]hese traditions teach that creation of the real (the manifest) involves subtraction from infinite potential . . . *By limiting the infinitely possible, you create the finitely real* . . . A replica of our real world can thus be created out of the unlimited potential of the white light through a process of intelligent subtraction carried out in space and time. A virtual reality is thus created out of formless possibility. In fact, motion pictures are a concrete example of how a filter, the film, by selectively subtracting from a formless potential, can generate a virtual reality.[2]

This filtering of the Undiluted Mind as Divine Light through our evolving consciousness is what creates the various form-bound deities; until ultimately we arrive at the unfiltered transcendental formless realization of our own divine nature when in union-with-G/d—the individual realization of Jesuit paleontologist Teilhard de Chardin's concept of "The Omega Point."* If 5-MeO-DMT really does free our consciousness from matter and gives us a glimpse of what it will be like when we return to the omniscient Mind, freed of what Alan Watts called our "skin-encapsulated ego,"[3] then it would make sense that some of us would be closer to making that final recognition of our true nature (due to the superior development of these necessary "consciousness filters") while others would be overwhelmed (and retain little memory), since they would not yet have developed a consciousness capable of

---

*Teilhard de Chardin proposed that the goal of evolution as a species was toward a final unity, a "coaxing of life forms toward future perfection."[4] He called this final perfect moment of realization, "The Omega Point." Chardin himself was a close friend of Sir Julian Huxley, Aldous Huxley's older brother.

an "unfiltered" recognition of the true nature of mind, being, and G/d.

It is likely that these more advanced filters are acquired through contemplation and other methods ascribed to mystical traditions; they may also come in the form of sudden spontaneous intuitions regarding of the true nature of reality. It may be that we develop more and more advanced consciousness filters through a series of births and rebirths. Perhaps some of us have undergone far more rebirths into this dimension, while others are like children at the beginning of their explorations in this earthly paradise of matter, with a long, discovery-filled path of many reincarnations ahead of them.

That night also revealed another mysterious dimension of the 5MDE. Strassman states that DMT is consumed by the brain quite quickly, and this is equally the case with 5-MeO-DMT. The brain eats tryptamines like food, and once that has happened, virtually no traces are left in the system. So by the time someone comes out of a 5MDE, after fifteen to thirty minutes (depending on how much was smoked) there is practically none of the 5-MeO-DMT left in his or her body.

That night under the stars, it was at least forty-five minutes and probably more after Nathan came out of his experience before Nina took the pipe. I always allow a participant some time to enjoy the afterglow of the experience. Then I try to get him or her to express what was seen or felt during the 5MDE, since this is the period when some people say incredibly interesting things, almost as if speaking from outside of themselves, most of which they will not recall when you ask them about their experience again an hour or so later. As I said before, Nathan had emerged with a remarkably coherent picture of his 5MDE, and I questioned him to get him to express as much of his experience as possible, due to my own interest in the matter. Then I prepared and administered the dosage to Nina, after providing her with instructions and describing the sort of effects she might experience, all of which takes time, and even more so because the wind was playing havoc on my preparations.

Thus it strikes me as being physically impossible that forty-five to sixty minutes after Nathan had come out of his experience there could have still been enough residual 5-MeO-DMT in his body to send him on another trip when Nina began her own. But during her 5MDE, he sat the whole time staring out at the stars and randomly shouting out loud exclamations like,

"Wow!" and, "How amazing!"—verbalizations that I thought were totally inappropriate, as Nina was in the depths of her own experience, and several times I told him to be quiet. When Nina came out of her experience she demanded a lot of attention from her husband and me, getting us to lie down on the mattress and hold her as she recounted what she could of her voyage.

After Nina had finally calmed down, Nathan shook his head and laughed while he looked at me and declared, "You didn't warn me about that!" He told me that as soon as Nina had fallen into her 5MDE, he had gone back into his own 5MDE without warning—in his own words, "Just as hard, if not harder than before." Through one of those strange resonant phenomena that add even more mystery to the 5MDE, he unquestionably had a second experience, effectively "piggy-backing" his way into a spontaneous 5MDE. Since then I have learned that such "contact highs" are not uncommon. I have witnessed them on several occasions with different participants who had no idea that it might happen, and I also have experienced the effect to varying degrees myself.

This piggy-backing anomaly should not be confused with a similar one that I have seen with old acid-heads, whereby a more experienced freak "sucks" the experience out of a novice tripper upon psychic contact and walks away high, while the person who actually took the LSD is left trying to figure out how they have suddenly "come down" (the infamous "acid succubus"). The 5MDE piggy-backing phenomenon that I am describing does not seem to have the inherent vampirism that happens with other substances, since the subject is apparently unaffected in terms of the strength of their own experience (although sometimes he or she seems to become calmer), while the second person involved (who is inevitably still recovering from his or her own 5MDE) embarks on another experience without warning. (You generally have to have very recently smoked 5-MeO-DMT in order to piggy-back, though spontaneous events can occur in some individuals if they have smoked 5-MeO-DMT in the past.)

It is my hypothesis that the organic tryptamines rearrange the patterns of consciousness, making it possible to step through a portal into another reality. Briefly, after returning to consensus reality, the person's consciousness remains connected to a pattern that it is still capable of glimpsing through a window into the Tryptamine Palace to observe the wonders inside. All it takes is the right suggestion, and consciousness willingly returns there. Shamans use this space between the two dimensions to heal, but in ceremonies they generally take ayahuasca (or peyote, or San Pedro) in doses well below what we would consider "entheogenic" or "visionary"—doses so small that they could almost be considered homeopathic. But the shaman has trained his or her sensitivity to that zone through years of journeying there at full-force, and thus can recontact the *manikari*—the healing spirits—with the slightest suggestion.

Shared or "group-mind" experiences are commonly reported with ayahuasca, an entheogen that is frequently taken in a group. One of the original names that chemists gave to harmine (a beta-carboline MAOI alkaloid contained in ayahuasca) when it was first isolated from *Banisteriopsis caapi* in the 1920s was "telepathine," due to the legendary reputation of the Amazonian brew even then. However, I believe that the piggy-backing phenomena is related to the apparently telepathic quality of the tryptamines in ayahuasca, rather than the harmala alkaloids.

I gave my last hit of 5-MeO-DMT to my friend Doug. Since he does not smoke pot or cigarettes, he coughed the whole thing up and did not achieve a release experience (even though it looked to me as if he had actually inhaled far more of the smoke than Nina had managed). He blamed his own high expectations on the apparent failure. But after having witnessed Nathan and Nina's solid experiences, I could only assume that Doug's mild response was due to his virgin inability to retain the 5-MeO-DMT and *Cannabis* smoke in his lungs.

Having now given away all my 5-MeO-DMT supply, I decided that I might as well try some of the conventional DMT that I had. I loaded my pipe with a dose at the high end of the range described in *TIHKAL,* which I realized was larger than anything I had previously tried. Substantially more DMT than 5-MeO-DMT is needed to achieve a release, as it is estimated by various sources to be three to five times weaker. Three "good tokes" seems to be the consensus on the appropriate dose. But the tiny amount of 5-MeO-DMT needed for release tends to make me wary of accidentally indulging in too much of any tryptamine!

Sitting cross-legged, I took a number of steady hits on the pipe. In the distance I began to hear a mechanical humming noise, which at first I took to be a distant generator until I realized the noise was building steadily in volume as I hit on the pipe and stared out into the darkness. In an instant, the veil was lifted and I saw the tryptamine world glowing as colorful as a cartoon on television. Suddenly all I could see were snakes—large, fluorescent, primitive-looking snakes covered in dots—and the whole scene reminded me of an Australian Aboriginal song-line painting.

"Damn these snakes," I thought. I was annoyed because Doug had told me earlier that day about Narby's book, *The Cosmic Serpent,* and how ayahuasca shamans commonly saw snakes, and I wondered if some kind of autosuggestion was at play. The field of snakes completely occupied my vision in the dark. I could not see the jungle behind it, but I was still aware that I was sitting on the balcony and that I was myself (although that "self" would have been incapable of taking another hit on the pipe at that point!). The hundreds of snakes in my vision wriggled this way and that, rapidly and unbelievably congealing into a clear representation of the Hindu elephant-headed god.

"Ganesha!" I remember thinking in surprise, "What are you doing here?!" The image seemed so out of place. Then my DMT trance shattered, almost as if it had been dashed to pieces by my surprise, and I found myself at baseline and back on the balcony, just a few minutes after I had inhaled the DMT. This was the most success I had personally had with smoking DMT up to that point.

I consider it more difficult to obtain a full experience with DMT than with 5-MeO-DMT, since the latter is easier to consume. There are other, qualitative differences between the two experiences as well. DMT is visually outrageous in the way you would expect from a psychedelic, while the visual impact of 5-MeO-DMT includes multiple layers, some of plain images (such as the faces of your loved ones or seeing yourself lying on the bed under the effect of the drug) while other layers contain ineffable visual elements that cannot be explained, since they are (presumably) projected from a realm language simply cannot describe. On 5-MeO-DMT, I have never seen snakes, foreign gods, UFOs, mechanical gnome insects, or any of the other weird things that people report seeing on DMT. What I have experienced is an infinite Void that is a Plenum that is ultimately both myself and G/d. But how do I begin to describe that?

Another difference was apparent in my experience that night: DMT's effects are somewhat fragile, difficult to get into, and easy to disturb. The "out-of-body" aspect of a DMT experience fluctuates; it has an ebb and flow. 5-MeO-DMT, on the other hand, at the correct dosage is virtually inescapable (except for certain rare cases). It instantaneously and completely sends you into another realm, which is essentially beyond imagery.

In his book, *The Essential Psychedelic Guide,* author D. M. Turner describes DMT as "sheer perfection" and 5-MeO-DMT as "sheer force." My own interpretation is that 5-MeO-DMT is more entheogenic, as it seems to transport me straight to a place of formless omniscience that I intuitively recognize as union with G/d. I suspect that if Dr. Strassman had focused on 5-MeO-DMT instead of DMT in his search for the "spirit molecule," he would have found results closer to the entheogenic effect he was looking for—more in line with a near-death experience, or the "faith-based" epiphany of recognizing the true nature of G/d—with less of the "extraterrestrial" visionary element that DMT supplies.

As far as I understand, the chemical and pharmacological difference between the two tryptamines is that 5-MeO-DMT has a methyl molecule and an oxygen molecule attached to the basic DMT ring, which allow it to cross the blood-brain barrier faster. This is presumably why it is more potent than DMT. With such a slight difference, it may be difficult to understand why there seems to be such an obvious difference between the effects of the two. In fact, I believe that there *isn't* that much difference in the effects of these two tryptamines, at least at higher doses. A number of hits of regular DMT are needed to achieve release, and, when you do, it generally doesn't last very long. To use the analogy of a rocket escaping the pull of Earth's gravity, it is as if DMT is only powerful enough (at regular doses) to send you out of the atmosphere, but then the gravity of your ego pulls you back in. 5-MeO-DMT, on the other hand, is an interstellar vessel—it blasts you out of the atmosphere before you can even put the pipe down, and if you can learn to use it right, it can take you straight back to the Mind of G/d.

A powerful dose of 5-MeO-DMT (in the 15 to 25 mg range, which can be taken in one solid hit) can arguably send you further than most other known substances—hence the entheogenic *force* and the comparative lack of the visual *magic* that DMT traditionally provides. This correlates with the Hindu and Tibetan traditions, which state that magical powers are obtainable through years of meditation, but that these powers themselves are a "lower effect" on the way to the ultimate goal of a transcendent reunification with G/d. Traditional shamanism also believes that those who are seduced by the magic of their craft will fall into black magic and become sorcerers—shamans who use magic for their *own* purposes rather than for the betterment of others. Such sorcerers are considered to have lost their way among the "lower powers" of the ayahuasca.

Even when compared to smoking DMT, the increased potency of 5-MeO-DMT allows human consciousness to access different and deeper dimensions; in fact, it allows the prepared consciousness the "unfiltered" experience of reality's ultimate nature. Once the normal filters of our matter-bound consciousness return (as the 5-MeO-DMT wears off), then there can be no "normal" understanding of that formless "unfiltered" experience, due to the physical limitations within which human consciousness is generally bound.

The physicist and philosopher Peter Russell has written a definitive overview of meditation using the same analogy of filtered white light flowing from a projector that we just examined with Bernard Haisch. In Russell's overview, the white light flowing from a projector indicates the four different states of consciousness identified by Hindu philosophy: the waking consciousness and the dreaming consciousness (states which "filter" the light of the projector); the "unconscious" state of deep sleep (where the plug from the projector has been pulled, and there is no white light); and a fourth state of consciousness that is the pure unfiltered white light of consciousness itself. This pure self-awareness of the "unfiltered" light is our ultimate consciousness, a state of peace and bliss—an awareness that the pure consciousness one experiences is but a concentrated point within a single universal consciousness.

DMT still "filters" the world of form through our "adjusted" consciousness, generating a magical myriad of visual worlds that John Perry Barlow once described to me as "God's video game." At its conventional dosages, DMT gives access to dimensions rooted in the collective experience of the human imagination: the sixth chakra, the domain of Jung's archetypes, the Tibetan bardos of beneficent Buddhas and their terrifying demonic counterparts, the Hindu pantheon with its countless gods and goddesses, the shamanic realms of god-like animals and protector spirits. But in the Tibetan model of the bardos, the Hindu concept of atman-Brahman (the oneness of individual and universal consciousness), and in virtually all of the mystical traditions throughout history, there is the belief that there is yet another realm of knowledge *above* these.

As Aldous Huxley wrote, "Visionary experience is not the same as mystical experience. Mystical experience is beyond the realm of opposites. Visionary experience is still within that realm. Heaven entails hell, and 'going to heaven' is no more liberation than is the descent into horror. Heaven is merely a vantage point, from which the divine Ground can be more clearly seen than on the level of ordinary individualized existence."[5] The mystical experience is the supreme realization that is *beyond* visualization—the supreme recognition of the true nature of self, the identification with Oneness, atman-Brahman, the total union with G/d, accompanied by the corresponding snuffing out of your own identity, which the Sufi mystic Jalal ad-Din Rumi described as being like "a moth caught in flame's allure."[6]

While 5-MeO-DMT commonly rockets the user to that unfiltered realm beyond both form and the human imagination, smoking DMT results in this transcendental resonance with Oneness much less frequently. This seems to be partially due to DMT's lower potency and partially to the trickier nature of delivering a high enough dose. During a 5-MeO-DMT experience, I am able to experience "consciousness without identity," and I neither remember smoking the 5-MeO-DMT, nor have any sense of who "I" am. The "I" in me ceases to exist, now a part of something greater. With DMT, I generally retain knowledge of who I am and what I have done. No other compound, at any dose, has ever been able to produce DMT or 5-MeO-DMT's liberating effect upon my consciousness.*

My theories on the essential difference between DMT and 5-MeO-DMT have proven to be unpopular with a number of people, especially those who are enamored with the visually exciting elements of the DMT experience. Some even seem somewhat threatened by my assertion that 5-MeO-DMT is the more "powerful" of the two tryptamines, and their general response is one of incredulity: How could I possibly consider 5-MeO-DMT to be more entheogenic? Yet, ironically, their arguments for the "superior entheogenic effect" of DMT actually support my beliefs. For example, DMT users

*Large doses of DMT can, however, achieve virtually the same "peak" effect as 5-MeO-DMT—that is, a transcendental point *past* imagery—it's just getting there that's harder, due to the amount required.

report fantastic visual worlds, which often contain weird elements like elves on bicycles or holographic floating Sony signs, whereas 5-MeO-DMT users experience a less visual, more tellurian experience of Oneness, which defies description.

DMT smokers usually retain and can describe their experiences in great detail, which generates its own potent mythology, while 5-MeO-DMT users often experience a "white-out" or singularity, which is all you might expect to be able to remember if your consciousness had experienced the universe "outside" of the normal five senses and your consciousness was not sufficiently open or prepared. As mentioned earlier, recollection of the 5MDE seems to be due to a different set of conditions (that is, the user's philosophical preparedness), rather than simply being a memory of the drug's visual dialogue.

Support for my view can be found in a somewhat unlikely source: a scientific paper on the *Bufo alvarius* toad by Wade Davis and Andrew Weil. When speculating on the reason why DMT was added as a Schedule I controlled substance in the late sixties, while 5-MeO-DMT wasn't, Davis and Weil proposed:

> The disparity in the law probably has to do with the different reputations of these two drugs. When smoked, DMT produces a very rapid, intense intoxication of short duration that is marked by vivid visual imagery. These effects made it popular among users of LSD, psilocybin, and other well-known psychedelic drugs, and thus drew the attention of authorities. By contrast, smoking of pure 5-MeO-DMT, a more potent tryptamine, produces an overwhelmingly powerful experience that can be unnerving. One user describes inhaling 5-MeO-DMT vapor as "a rocket ship into the Void." Another comments: "If most hallucinogens, including LSD, merely distort reality, however bizarrely, 5-MeO-DMT completely dissolves reality as we know it, leaving neither hallucinations nor anyone to watch them. The experience need not be negative, but it is not for a novice" (anonymous, personal communication, April 11, 1987). As a result, 5-MeO-DMT never gained the street popularity or notoriety of its chemical cousin. Over the years it has remained an obscure drug taken mostly by small groups of psychiatrists and explorers of consciousness.[7]

It may be that my theory only applies at what I will call "the release-level" of either compound, as reports from those who have taken *large* doses of DMT are strikingly similar to a 5-MeO-DMT experience, such as in this quote from *TIHKAL,* which describes a 100 mg smoked dose of DMT: "Up, up, out, out, eyes closed, I am at the speed of light, expanding, expanding, expanding, faster and faster until I have become so large that I no longer exist—my speed is so great that everything has come to a stop—here I gaze upon the entire universe."[8]

Arguing over which of these two tryptamines is the "most" entheogenic is probably pointless, since—at the right dosages—they clearly both are able to terrify and enlighten. They reveal layers of the same truth, which originates in the same arena, and the main difference between the two is the speed with which they cross the blood-brain barrier and deliver their "revelations."

My DMT trip in Boca del Drago might seem rather unremarkable compared to the entheogenic effect that 5-MeO-DMT has had on me, were it not for two interesting postscripts. The first of these relates to the miraculous aftereffect I experienced in the days following my brief meeting with Ganesha.

I awoke the next morning feeling better than I ever had before. After witnessing a sunrise that unexpectedly nearly bought me to tears with its sublime beauty, I began to realize that everything was glowing with an inner light and beauty and that I was enveloped in a blissful state. Feeling unbelievably alive and in balance, I climbed out of the rooftop perch where I had been sleeping, went down to the main house for some breakfast, and then decided to walk three miles to the small jungle research station where I was taking a course.

I felt as if I was walking six feet in the air, and everything continued to glow with the same inner light. I can only describe my mood as euphoric, an unbelievable state of inner bliss. It lasted for more than three days, during which I ate the same food each day from the single available restaurant and shared dormitory accommodations with a bunch of mostly American college students who were all about fifteen years younger than me—two variables that usually would have dampened my mood. Yet I was as happy as I could possibly be.

Filled with an indescribable sense of wonder and contentment, I went to sleep each night curious about whether the miracle would continue through to the next day. The rational observer inside of me could see that something remarkable was going on: it was as if I was eating a steady diet of that good, legal MDMA I once tried from Texas in the 1980s. It was better than that though, as I had the total euphoric feeling without any of the excess energy, sweating, and madness that can come from that love drug. I simply had a tremendous sense of satisfaction and inner happiness. Smoking the DMT and bumping into a snake-infested Ganesha somehow had triggered a deep-seated inner peace within me that touched upon the sublime.

During my brief university tenure as a student of the Phenomenology of Religion, I had written a paper on the subject of whether or not it was possible to obtain enlightenment while you were alive. I argued that the Buddhist faith asserted that it *was* possible and that in Gautama's time, according to the Buddhist texts, several hundred people had obtained enlightenment while they were alive by realizing nirvana through his teachings. It was one of the few papers that I ever received an "A" for, and I remembered being deeply impressed by the idea that we could strive for and obtain enlightenment in this lifetime. The whole concept seemed so positive when compared to contemporary Christianity's "you must accept Jesus to die pure and enter the Kingdom of Heaven" doom and gloom.

There in Panama—after dismissing my DMT encounter with fluorescent anacondas and Ganesha as "a minor effect"—I had somehow stumbled into a state of grace in which I couldn't feel a hint of malice toward anyone; it was a state of total euphoria and contentment, a living state—dare I say?—of nirvana. But I didn't believe that it could last. I almost felt as if I had to hold my breath to stop the bubble from bursting. Maybe that was my mistake: not believing that I could remain in that blissful state. When Nathan's eyes had shone with wonder and he asked me if he could stay that way forever, I told him that it wasn't possible, so he should hold on to it while he could. Maybe I was wrong. Maybe I shouldn't have told him that. Maybe, with enough believing, you really *can* retain nirvana.

Unfortunately for me, it came to an end after three incredible days, when all of us at the research station arose at dawn and made our way by boat, and then by bus, into the interior to visit the cloud forests in the mountains. During that bus journey, I felt my euphoric state gently fading. It slowly evaporated away, the change in scenery apparently enough to cancel the effect. Over the next twenty-four hours I returned to my normal self, somewhat saddened to lose that state of grace, but glad that I had been fortunate enough to experience it—to know that such ways of living are real and possible.

The second postscript related to this singularly remarkable DMT experience happened nine months later, when my time in India (and a heavy diet of Tibetan philosophy) reawakened my interest in Buddhism and Hinduism. In Hinduism—which may be the most tolerant and resilient religion in history—countless different gods have been venerated throughout the ages (with more being created all the time). In fact, the number of Hindu Gods is theoretically equal to the number of practicing Hindus! Yet out of that mass of possibility, a few—such as Krishna, Hanuman, Lakshmi, and so on—have achieved the highest status in the pantheon due to their popularity with practitioners. And out this of pantheon of gods, I discovered that the elephant-headed Ganesha is one of the gods most loved and venerated by all Indians, even by non-Hindus! His popularity is now a worldwide phenomenon: just look around the nearest hippy coffee shop or yoga studio!

Among his many attributes, including being the lord of writers and scribes, Ganesha is considered both "The Remover of Obstacles" and, paradoxically, "The Guardian of Gateways" or the Gate Keeper, and most homes in India have a picture of Ganesha above their doorway to prevent evil forces from entering the house. Since I believe that DMT is effectively a "gateway" to another dimension, I am now no longer so surprised at bumping into Ganesha that evening in Panama. Perhaps it was not my night to step through that door.

FIVE

Into the Quantum Realm

If we think we can picture what is going on in the quantum domain, that is one indication that we've got it wrong.

ATTRIBUTED TO ERWIN SCHRÖDINGER

May God us keep
From single vision & Newton's sleep!

WILLIAM BLAKE, FROM A LETTER TO
THOMAS BUTTS, NOVEMBER 22, 1802

What began as a studious attempt to understand what happens to me when I smoke 5-MeO-DMT has become—after six years of research—a comprehensive examination of the workings of human consciousness, perception, and ultimately, what the true nature of reality may be. Out of the myriad of extraordinary events that have occurred within the context of my own 5-MeO-DMT experiences, a more limited number of questions regarding the nature of the 5MDE have occupied a central position in my mind. They can be summed up as:

1. What is the source of the brilliant laser-like light that I encounter?
2. How can I feel as if I am occupying a reality outside of time?

3. How can this dimension outside of time seem to contain all possible permutations and information?
4. How can I exist as consciousness without ego or identity, and yet clearly still be me?
5. Why do I so firmly believe that this experience is a recognition and subsequent realization of both the true nature of G/d, and of myself?

My search for answers to these questions led inexorably to the world of quantum physics, a realm that I knew little about other than reading popular accounts, such as Gary Zukav's book *The Dancing Wu-Li Masters,* even though I generally found quantum physics intimidating due to my misconception that it involved a lot of applied mathematics. Like most people, I stopped studying math after getting out of high school, and I never had a strong grasp of calculus—my mind just doesn't work that way. Or perhaps it was simply because of the shifting complexity of the ideas quantum physics presents that I never really could grasp them. But as I followed the leads present in much of the DMT literature—from the McKenna brothers, to Jeremy Narby, to Rick Strassman, and beyond—I repeatedly found myself back in the quantum realm.

Slowly the collective ideas of a small group of scientific renegades—maverick thinkers such as David Bohm, Rupert Sheldrake, Roger Penrose, Hal Puthoff, Bernard Haisch, and Ervin Laszlo—have effectively helped me to construct a new worldview to replace the old paradigm that my 5-MeO-DMT experiences dissolved away. The obvious similarities between the emerging scientific view of reality and the possibilities implicit in the 5-MeO-DMT experience (and tryptamines in general) have allowed me to feel as if my metaphorical mental feet are returning to somewhat firmer philosophical ground.

We are *Homo sapiens,* "the knowing man," animals that prized psychological knowledge over the physical bounties of the Earth, and who—thanks to that same Promethean knowledge—now hold the fate of the planet in our hands. This unquenchable thirst for knowledge, combined with the ingenuity of our modern wonder-tools (such as the particle accelerator, the super computer, and the Hubble telescope), has allowed us over the last twenty years to probe the universe at levels—both great and small—that humanity never previously imagined possible. And the findings that today's most radical scientists are discovering with these incredible instruments are so strange and unbelievable that it is as if they have come from another dimension. (Which they well may have!) Most of what we were taught about "science" at high school is now turning out to be false; the model we were taught for the atom is as wrong as the model we held for our solar system before Copernicus; and the models we have for the mechanism of consciousness may well be equally as antiquated and naive.

The Trap of Material Realism

Our modern worldview is built on the physical model of the universe provided by Newtonian physics: the idea that all objects in the universe have mass and influence upon each other and that without the influence of this mass, all objects would remain at rest. A good visualization of this is balls on a pool table, which will remain at rest until another ball hits them and sets them in motion. This philosophy, known as material realism, asserts that all bodies in the universe—from pool balls to galaxies—move according to universal laws. This method of thinking laid the groundwork for the belief that *all* activity in the universe must be caused by knowable laws and formula, the most fundamental of which is Newton's $F = ma$ (force = mass × acceleration).

The belief that knowing these "universal laws" would enable us to understand all the workings of the universe (from the creation of stars all the way down to our own biological function), as if everything was a complex machine, has led to three centuries of scientific material deconstructionism: a process of breaking everything down to its most basic components in an attempt to prove that these laws were in themselves inescapable. In the process of reducing the mystery of the universe into simple action and reaction—and by ignoring its obvious complexity and interconnectedness—we embraced the belief that by mastering these laws, we could free the human species from the "bonds" of nature.

Ironically, our "faith" in this model of purely random action and reaction has resulted in the dominance of the philosophy that the universe is simply a complex machine, and that we are mere creations of blind chance. This leaves us with the philosophical conundrum that it shouldn't really make any difference whether we are here or not. And, even though we clearly *are* here, we are seen as only biological machines, slightly more than robots. Our consciousness is considered to be merely a strange side effect of purely chemical and electrical interactions. A hundred years after killing off God, we've concluded that we have no purpose other than "fighting to survive." We have taken the magic out of the world and reduced it to mere formula, thus allowing our "superior sciences" to deconstruct *ourselves*.

Modern civilization is built on the foundation of three theories that have become dogma, which we inherited from the three most influential thinkers of the pre-quantum age. From Newton's equation we concluded that the universe is nothing but a machine; from Darwin we accepted the gospel that man is a creature of chance that has to "fight to survive"; and Descartes convinced us that the physical world of the body and the mental inner world of the mind should be considered as separate entities.

Though they remain unproven, these three ideas are universally accepted. They have been responsible for spliting us off from our planet, from our biosphere, and ultimately from our true selves; embraceing these theories has resulted in the creation of a rabid culture that now threatens the ecological balance of the planet itself. For, as Alvin Toffler says in the introduction to Ilya Prigogine's *Order Out of Chaos* (1984) "One of the most highly developed skills in contemporary Western civilization is dissection: the split-up of problems into their smallest possible components. We are good at it. So good, we often forget to put the pieces back together again."[1]

Since the beginning of the Industrial Revolution we have increased the human population by over five times. We continue to tear the planet to pieces in search of resources that we cannot replenish, while we defile and pollute the rivers, oceans, and even the air we breathe, as we send tens of thousands of species of flora and fauna to extinction—a fate whose door we could soon be knocking on ourselves. The mechanical materialistic model of both humans and the universe as mere machines, has not only destroyed our belief in G/d. As the American philosopher Danah Zohar remarked, "Newton's vision tore us out from the fabric of the universe itself."[2]

This paradigm has only been around for the last few centuries, which—even compared to the minor span of human existence as a whole—is a miniscule amount of time. When compared to any kind of geological epoch, it is not even a blink in the eye of the universe. Yet even while and kings of industry race to further these Newtonian exce origin of these destructive simplifications—has moved on to s certain ground. This new paradigm of uncertainty and potential, lutionary human view of the universe, is called *quantum physics.*

A Quantum Reality

Ironically it was science's unquenchable thirst for breaking things into smaller and smaller pieces that ultimately bought the walls of Newtonian physics tumbling down. As our instruments grew more and more powerful, and we began to probe the subatomic realm—the supposed "building blocks" of the universe—scientists came to a staggering realization. In the realm of the very small, Newtonian physics did not hold. In fact, in the realm of the very small, nothing we believed in as solid reality turned out to be true. Solid reality, if we look deep enough, does not seem to exist at all!

To understand how this is possible, we have to comprehend a concept that is central to the ideas of quantum physics. It is called "nonlocality." It refers to the capacity of quantum particles (such as two electrons) that have once been in contact to retain a connection even when separated—the actions of one will always immediately influence the other, no matter how far apart they are. Today it is widely accepted that, in the subatomic realm, one quantum entity can influence another instantaneously, over any distance, despite there being no exchange of force or energy.

Physicists started moving toward this realization in 1935, when Einstein, along with Boris Podolsky and Nathan Rosen, published a paper—the so-called EPR thought experiment or EPR paradox—that showed that under certain circumstances, quantum mechanics predicted a breakdown of locality. According to this theory, a particle could be put in a measuring device in one location and, through that action alone, would instantly influence another particle an arbitrary distance away. Einstein, Podolsky, and Rosen themselves refused to believe this effect—which Einstein labeled "spooky action at a distance"—and viewed the experiment as evidence that quantum mechanics was incomplete. However, the EPR experiment set the basis for a potential scientific proof of the existence of nonlocality.

Almost thirty years later, J. S. Bell proved mathematically that the results predicted by quantum mechanics could not be explained by any theory that preserved locality. In the forty years that have followed, countless experiments using physical instrumentation have been performed to try to prove the EPR experiment. In the empirical experiments of French physicist Alain Aspect in the 1980s (subsequently replicated in laboratories all over the world), a bizarre thing took place. In the experiments, the correlation of spin state between two particles was maintained—instantaneously—irrespective of how far apart the particles were. (Theoretically this would apply if the two particles were on opposite sides of the universe.) In Aspect's original experiments, the speed of this transmission was estimated at less than one billionth of a second, about twenty times faster than the speed of light in empty space. In a subsequent experiment performed in 1997 by Nicolas Gisin, it proved to be 20,000 times faster than the speed of light.[3] Many consider these experiments as "proof" of nonlocality. These experiments also obviously put a dent in Einstein's special theory of relativity, which states that nothing can travel faster than light.

"Teleportation" experiments of the 1990s—where one electron has been "teleported" to another position—have also been cited as "experimental proof" of nonlocality.[4] And in 2004, two independent teams of physicists—one at the National Institute of Standards in Colorado, the other at University of Innsbruck, Austria—announced that they had "teleported" the quantum state of entire atoms.[5] While nonlocality still has its skeptics who state that "sufficient experimental proof" has not been offered, today the concept of nonlocality is assumed to be valid in quantum physics.

This realization was the deathblow for Newtonian physics as a model for the whole universe, since matter could no longer be considered to be individual and separate. Actions did not have to have an observable cause over an observable state. Nothing (at the quantum level) can be considered independent of anything else; all can only be understood in terms of their relationships to each other. The quantum model proposes that the universe exists as an interconnected web of relationships, forever indivisible, since nothing has any meaning by itself!

Our great instruments, which we had built to confirm the solidity of the universe and our concept of the world as a machine built of understandable and predictable parts, now reveal that at its most basic level, the universe is as ethereal and drifting as a dream and as solid as a mirage! *Nothing* is solid; nothing is real; the universe is a seething field of energy and potential. What is even more astonishing is the realization that we—the living consciousness that observes "reality"—may be the most essential ingredient in this indivisible and interconnected universe. The quantum physicists found something that could have as profound implications for the destiny of the human species as anything we have ever discovered. They found that: "the state of all possibilities of any quantum particle collapsed into a set entity as soon as it was observed or a measurement taken."[6]

To understand this we have to reexamine the model of the atom we were all taught at school, which is that of electrons orbiting the nucleus like planets going around the sun. This model has been proven to be completely incorrect. What physicists now believe is that a cloud of "potential," which can cause the electron to materialize in any position, surrounds the nucleus. To visualize this, imagine a race around a track where the runners "appear" at certain spots on the course for a second or two, then disappear and reappear a hundred meters further along—without having to physically cross the distance between the two points. This happens for no apparent reason, nor with any indication as to where they might disappear and appear again. Where this gets really weird, is that some physicists now believe that the "force" causing an electron to appear in some particular position—which is only a possibility and does not have to happen—is the fact that a living consciousness is observing it.

At the subatomic level, where everything is a pulsating sea of electrical charge and possibility, the universe takes physical form (which we call reality) only because we are here to observe it. The act of observation "forces" the electron to appear in *a* position out of that sea of possibility, and so by observing, we cause "reality" to happen. Just as the Australian Aboriginals believe that their ancestors sang up the world as they walked through the desert, it is possible that through perceiving, we create the universe and everything in it.

These are the main foundations of quantum physics: nonlocality, the fact that the observer cannot be removed from the equation, and that the observer may actually be the reason a particular event occurs at all. At its most basic level, the universe does not operate according to the laws of Newtonian physics; those laws only apply to a small window of the universe we choose to call "our reality." Once you look past that point, things get peculiar. Energy moves around without apparent rhyme or reason, possessing strange qualities like "charm" and "spin," while every electron in the universe appears to influence (and be influenced by) every other electron in the universe, through "spooky action at a distance."

Many of the early contributors to quantum physics—Niels Bohr, Werner Heisenberg, and especially Erwin Schrödinger—realized the profound philosophical implications that their work presented, and they consulted the Kabbalah and Eastern philosophy for help in understanding this new paradigm. But the modern industrial world is built on the foundations of Newton's physics, as well as the ideas of economic thinkers—such as Adam Smith and John Locke—who followed his mechanist philosophy. And while physics—the cutting-edge of scientific philosophy—moved into the quantum age more than eighty years ago, most other sciences have been moving far slower. Biological systems, for example, were presumed to be dependent on predictable Newtonian laws, and investigations into their quantum nature have only begun in earnest over the past twenty-five years.

As a result, our society has not really considered the profound implications of this totally different view of reality. Yoked to the needs of industry, mainstream science is good at clinging to ideas that it believes it *knows,* putting things it cannot understand aside for a later day. While we have utilized the breakthroughs that quantum mechanics fostered (such as the processor chip and atomic energy), we have largely ignored the philosophical implications.

Ninety-five percent of modern scientists are highly specialized technicians. They are good at performing a single function, much like a mechanic who can only fix transmissions and does not really know how the whole car operates. Those few scientists who venture outside of the conventions that industry-supported universities allow have often been branded as dangerous mavericks and have been aggressively disavowed (as seen in the fate of Nikola Tesla compared to that of Thomas Edison). Hence, the philosophical implications of quantum physics have mostly been ignored as we hold fast to the dying days of the Newtonian worldview, still treating our severely ailing planet like some kind of machine whose parts we can "fix" when they break down, instead of realizing the truth inherent in the quantum model, which asserts that all life on Earth is interdependent and impossible to regard as anything but a whole.

Only in the last couple of decades has the dominant Newtonian paradigm begun to erode in the sciences outside of physics, thanks to our incredible modern technology, which has produced both the instruments to achieve the results and the computers to crunch the enormous amount of data that has been provided. (More information will be produced by our society in the next twelve months then in the previous 5,000 years! And our technical knowledge is *doubling* every twelve months!)[7] Quantum relationships are now believed to regulate all processes in the universe, whether it is atoms, cells, galaxies, or even the ultimate human mystery of all: the source of our own consciousness. The most elemental level of living things can no longer be considered as chemical reactions, but as energy.

As Lynne McTaggart explains in her pioneering work *The Field*:

> [Scientists] also discovered that . . . [on] our most fundamental level, living beings, including human beings, were packets of quantum energy constantly exchanging information with [an] inexhaustible energy sea. Living things emitted a weak radiation, and this was the most crucial aspect of biological processes. Information about all aspects of life, from cellular communication to the vast array of controls of DNA, was relayed through an information exchange on the quantum level. Even our minds, that *other* supposedly so outside of the laws of matter, operated according to quantum processes. Thinking, feeling—every higher cognitive function—had to do with quantum information pulsing simultaneously through our brains and [bodies]. Human perception occurred because of interactions between the subatomic particles of our brains and the quantum energy sea. We literally resonated with our world.[8]

The Implicate Order

The first building blocks of a new philosophical paradigm that could incorporate my 5-MeO-DMT experiences came when I discovered the major works of the British physicist David Bohm. His complex theories of philosophy and physics, most famously expressed in his book *Wholeness and the Implicate Order,* have drawn praise from spiritual luminaries such as Jiddu Krishnamurti and the Dalai Lama (who called Bohm his "personal physicist").

Dr. Bohm proposed that mind and matter coexist in different dimensions, unfolding and enfolding upon each other. In principle, then, reality is one unbroken whole—an "implicate order" that includes the entire universe with all its fields and particles. True reality is thus an infinitely multilayered, multidimensional wholeness, while what we typically consider "reality" is only a fragment of the whole. It is more like a dream or an illusion (or even a hallucination), from which our consciousness may one day presumably awake.

This is an extreme simplification of a fully fleshed-out theory of physics by one of the greatest Western minds since Einstein. Bohm's idea would have been hard for me to even begin to understand if it were not for the fact that it was—up to this point—the best description I had found for what I experience at the peak of a 5MDE. During the peak, I become pure consciousness, with no concept of the normal boundaries of space or time. For that instant, I am a part of the integrated wholeness (where nevertheless *I* still exist, even though not a shred of my ego or identity remains).

Bohm's theory is also eerily similar to many Hindu and Buddhist concepts of the true form of the universe and its infinite manifestations. Hindu cosmology depicts the universe as having virtually incalculable size and age, ideas that used to be readily dismissed by Western scholars as deliberate gross exaggeration. However, thanks to instruments like the Hubble telescope, recent discoveries are proving that Hinduism is the only cosmology that is even close, while the Greeks, Christians, Arabs, and others had all massively underestimated.

According to David Bohm, matter is "condensed or frozen light."[9] Therefore, the entire physical world can be regarded as ordered forms of slow-moving light. This includes all organic life, whose existence and survival is entirely sustained by light energy from the sun. Life on this planet is a continuing process of light evolving itself into more complex forms of order: first into the simplest of atoms and molecules, then into increasingly complex forms of matter, then into exponentially more complex organic life forms (thanks to the wonders of DNA and RNA), and now—most recently, in our world at least—the latest evolution into conscious, questioning life forms.

The process of exponentially increasing complexity of order in a (supposedly) closed system (which should be increasing in disorder) is called *negentropy*. This process directly contradicts the second law of thermodynamics, which states that all isolated systems must move from a state of order toward a state of chaos (entropy). According to the Newtonian paradigm, this highly improbable complex ordering of light has been the result of purely random interactions. However, since the advent of the quantum sciences and the invention of the tremendous number-crunching computers of recent years, some scientists have begun to suspect that the mechanisms of "life, the universe, and everything" (with apologies to Douglas Adams!) are much too balanced and finely tuned to have been able to evolve by blind chance alone.

According to calculations by Roger Penrose, for example, the probability of the evolution of our particular universe by a random selection from among the alternative-universe possibilities is one in 10 to the power of 10 to the power of 123! This is an inconceivably large number, indicating an improbability of astronomical proportions![10] The universe is turning out to be *so* complicated, in fact, that—according to David Bohm's theories—it *requires* the existence of a superior or implicate order of organization that defines the physical principles of our universe and governs all known physical processes, including ourselves.

That led me to the more recent explorations of a vast field—analogous to David Bohm's higher dimension of mind—that fills the empty spaces between other particles in the universe and contains far more energy than all the energy in the known physical universe. This all-filling field goes by the mysterious name of "the zero-point field."

SIX

Enter the Zero-Point Field

"Bring me a fruit of that banyan tree."
"Here it is, venerable Sir."
"Break it."
"It is broken, venerable Sir."
"What do you see there?"
"These seeds, exceedingly small."
"Break one of them, my son."
"It is broken, venerable Sir."
"What do you see there?"
"Nothing at all, venerable Sir."
The father said: "That subtle essence, my dear,
which you do not perceive there—from that very
essence this great banyan arises. Believe me, my dear.
Now, that which is the subtle essence—in it all that
exists has its self. That is the True. That is the Self.
Thou art that, Svetaketu."

CHANDOGYA UPANISAD, CHAPTER TWELVE

One who is in harmony with emptiness
is in harmony with all things

NAGARJUNA

David Bohm's theories revived interest in an ancient concept that had been abandoned by the end of the nineteenth century called "the aether field," and predicted that such a field must exist. By the end of the twentieth century, numerous scientists working in different disciplines around the world had begun to come to the same conclusion—that a previously disregarded "field-of-fields" could explain many of the mysteries that quantum physics postulated. My own introduction to the growing recognition of this field of "zero-point energy" came from reading Lynne McTaggart's pioneering and tremendously readable book, *The Field: The Quest for the Secret Force of the Universe*. It was in her excellent layman's descriptions of the timeless coherent nature of the zero-point field that I would first find clear parallels to the strange dimensions of my own 5-MeO-DMT experiences.

The Aether Field

Although the zero-point field is a very recent idea, the concept of the existence of an invisible substance that fills the whole universe (called aether/ether) was first suggested in the West by Aristotle (384–322 BCE). Interest in this aether field reawakened in the seventeenth century, after English scientist Robert Hooke endorsed it in his work *Micrographia* (1665), the first treatise on microscopic principles and observation. Christiaan Huygens, one of the leading proponents of the wave theory of light, also endorsed the concept of the aether in his *Traité de la Lumière* (1690).

Numerous British physicists of the nineteenth century believed that ether was the medium through which forces were transmitted, and the modeling of ether was a major preoccupation.[1] Michael Faraday, William Thomson (later known as Lord Kelvin), and James Clerk Maxwell posited that ether was the propagating medium for electromagnetic forces.

Maxwell ultimately concluded that mechanical modeling of the ether was too imprecise to be useful, but an unexpected implication of his work was "that the velocity of electromagnetic waves propagated in the ether was found to be identical to the velocity of light, leading Maxwell to conclude that electromagnetic and luminiferous ethers were the same. In this electromagnetic theory of light, light was considered an electromagnetic vibration in the ether."[2]

The final and most elegant development of the classical nineteenth century ether theories is now known as the Lorentz ether theory, in which an abstract (undetectable) electromagnetic ether replaced the older mechanistic model. In his explanation Hendrik Lorentz introduced a strict separation between matter (electrons) and ether, whereby ether is completely motionless and cannot be set in motion by matter.

However, after the famous Michelson–Morley experiment (1888) failed to detect the motion of the earth through the ether, and Heinrich Hertz's experimental detection of electromagnetic waves (1888) was regarded as the definitive experimental confirmation of electromagnetism, the days of examining the so-called ether field were numbered. When the mathematics of Einstein's special theory of relativity (1905) were able to mirror the mathematics of the Lorentz ether theory without referring to ether at all, luminiferous ether fell to Occam's razor.[3]

By the beginning of the twentieth century, electrodynamics had replaced mechanics in providing the conceptual foundation of physics. Nikola Tesla, the great Serbian-American scientist who is the father of modern communication technologies, was the last major proponent of the ether field. As early as 1891, Tesla described the universe as a kinetic system, which could be harnessed from any location. When asked where electricity came from, he famously remarked, "from the ether around us," and Tesla spent a fortune trying to build a wireless electrical transmission system based on these principles.

Shortly before his death in 1943, Tesla announced he was working on a "dynamic theory of gravity" that presumed the existence of a luminiferous ether that filled all space. He claimed that at speeds near the speed of light the ether is thrown into infinitesimal whirls (micro helices) and becomes ponderable matter. Unfortunately Tesla died before he revealed his own unified field theory and the FBI confiscated all of his papers, which remain classified to this day. Most of the remainder of the twentieth century elapsed before the idea of a universal ether energy field was resurrected.

However, Einstein himself stated in a lecture he gave on May 5, 1920, titled "Aether and the Theory of Relativity" that "more careful reflection teaches, however, that the special theory of relativity does not compel us to deny aether," and "to deny the aether is ultimately to assume that empty space has no physical qualities at all."[4]

Heisenberg's Uncertainty Principle

The idea that empty space might not be truly empty resurfaced as a result of what is known as the "Heisenberg uncertainty principle," which "states that the values of certain pairs of conjugate variables (position and momentum, for instance) cannot both be known with arbitrary precision. That is, the more precisely one variable is known, the less precisely the other is known. This is not a statement about the limitations of a researcher's ability to measure particular quantities of a system, but rather about the nature of the system itself. . . . Heisenberg was trying to show that this was not a flaw in his theory; rather, it was a previously unknown truth—a deep, surprising aspect of the universe."[5]

This principle implies that no particle is ever completely at rest, but is always in motion due to a ground state field of energy that is constantly interacting with all subatomic matter. A *field* in this sense is a matrix or medium that connects two or more points in space, usually via a force like gravity or electromagnetism. Largely because of Einstein's theories, we now believe that

> [all] elementary particles interact with each other by exchanging energy through other quantum particles, which are believed to appear out of nowhere, combining and annihilating each other in less than an instant—10^{23} seconds, to be exact—causing random fluctuations of energy without any apparent cause. The fleeting particles generated during this brief moment are known as "virtual particles." They differ from real particles because they only exist during that exchange—the time of "uncertainty" allowed by the uncertainty principle.
>
> This subatomic tango, however brief, when added across the universe, gives rise to enormous energy, more than is contained in all the matter in all the world.[6]

Richard Feynman calculated that there is enough energy in one cubic meter of "empty" space to boil all the oceans in the world! And David Bohm calculated that the total field energy would exceed all energy in matter by a factor of 10 to the power of 40—that's a one with forty zeros after it![7] Astrophysicist Bernard Haisch explains why, even though the extent of this energy is enormous, the energy field that exists in the apparent emptiness of the universe is called the "zero-point field."

> "Zero-point" refers to the fact that, even though the extent of this energy is huge, it is at the lowest possible energy state. All other energy operates over and above the zero-point state. Take any volume of space and take away everything else—in other words create a vacuum—and what you are left with is the zero-point field full of zero-point energy. We can imagine a true vacuum, devoid of everything, but in the real world, a quantum vacuum is permeated by the zero-point field with its ceaseless electromagnetic waves.

An old adage states that nature abhors a vacuum. Actually nature has nothing to abhor. The vacuum as a condition of complete emptiness, as an absolute void, does not exist. Rather the laws of quantum mechanics posit the seat of the zero-point field as a state of both paradox and possibility—a seething sea of particle pairs, energy fluctuations, and force perturbations popping in and out of existence.[8]

In Lynne McTaggart's words, "What quantum calculations show is that we and our universe live and breathe in what amounts to a sea of motion—a quantum sea of light." What this means is that—whether it be stars and galaxies separated by billions of miles of nothingness (or vacuum), or electrons "orbiting" a nucleus with empty space in between—physicists now believe that these empty spaces are in fact far from empty and "that the basic substructure of the universe is a sea of quantum fields that cannot be eliminated by any known laws of physics."[9]

Hal Puthoff

Initially, even though zero-point energy was assumed to exist, it was considered both a mathematical by-product and an annoyance and was generally disregarded. It was assumed that zero-point energy cancelled itself out—and therefore mathematically could be regarded as a zero. This was the situation from 1926 until the mid-1970s when a physicist named Hal Puthoff started giving the zero-point field some consideration as a potential source of inexhaustible clean energy. His contribution to our understanding of the zero-point field (for which he undoubtedly deserves a Nobel Prize someday) was to figure out the mathematics of our reality. He tackled one of the oldest problems of quantum physics, which is the question of why atoms are stable, or why electrons "orbit" around a proton.

> In the solar system, gravity accounts for the stable orbit. But in the atomic world, any moving electron, which carries a charge, wouldn't be stable like an orbiting planet, but would eventually radiate away, or exhaust, its energy and then spiral into the nucleus, causing the entire atomic structure of the object to collapse.[10]

Niels Bohr provided an "explanation" by declaring that he wouldn't allow it. Bohr believed that electrons only lose energy when they jump from one orbit to another. (These are the structured "orbital shells" that folks my age were taught about in school.) But Bohr worked out the math to support his perspective. His ideas regarding static orbits sparked assumptions about matter and energy both having wave- and particle-like qualities, which eventually led to the birth of quantum physics.

But what Hal Puthoff did was to show mathematically that Bohr's dictum was no longer necessary if the zero-point field was taken into account.* Puthoff proved that electrons lose and gain energy constantly from the zero-point field, keeping them "in a dynamic equilibrium, balanced at exactly the right orbit. Electrons get their energy to keep going without slowing down because they are refueling by tapping in to these fluctuations of empty space. In other words, the Zero Point Field accounts for . . . the stability of all matter."[11] According to McTaggart:

---

*Puthoff's discovery was inspired by the earlier work of an English physicist named Timothy Boyer. A recent study of the hydrogen atom by Boston University professor Dan Cole showed that, if you let an electron lose energy—as it must according to the laws of electrodynamics—and simultaneously take into account the energy it picks up by constantly being buffeted by the fluctuations of the zero-point field, you can reproduce the complex quantum behavior of the electron in the ground state of hydrogen. This is a major extension of the earlier simple harmonic oscillator models of Boyer and of Puthoff, and does indeed suggest the possibility that the zero-point field provides the foundations for atomic stability; B. Haisch, *The God Theory: Universes, Zero-Point Fields, and What's Behind It All* (York Beach, Maine: Red Wheel/Weiser, 2006).

> This constant exchange [of energy] is an intrinsic property of particles, so that even "real" particles are nothing more than a little knot of energy which briefly emerges and disappears back into the underlying field. According to quantum field theory, the individual entity is transient and insubstantial. Particles cannot be separated from the empty space around them. Einstein himself recognized that matter itself was "extremely intense"—a disturbance, in a sense, of perfect randomness—and that the only fundamental reality was the underlying entity—the field itself. . . . The existence of the Zero Point Field implied that all matter in the universe was interconnected by waves, which are spread out through time and space and can carry on to infinity, tying one part of the universe to every other part. . . . Hal also showed by physics calculations that fluctuations of the Zero Point Field waves drive the motion of subatomic particles and that all the motion of all the particles of the universe in turn generates the Zero Point Field, a sort of self-generating feedback loop across the cosmos.[12]

After proposing that the zero-point field (ZPF) was the source for the stability of matter, Puthoff then began to consider what other mysteries might be solved by factoring in its existence. He took a fresh look at a radical hypothesis that physicist Andrei Sakharov had proposed in 1968. Sakharov suggested that gravity might merely be a side effect created due to the zero-point field becoming altered when it interacted with matter. This notion countered the common assumption that gravity resulted from matter interacting with other matter; Puthoff worked out Sakharov's idea mathematically and ultimately came up with a unified theory of physics that explained gravity (as well as nonlocality), via the zero-point field. According to McTaggart:

> Hal published his theory of gravity to polite and restrained applause. . . . [What] he'd been saying in these papers in essence unsettled the entire bedrock of twentieth-century physics. Quantum physics most famously claims that a particle can also simultaneously be a wave unless observed and then measured, when all its tentative possibilities collapse into a set entity. With Hal's theory, a particle is always a particle but its

> state just seems indeterminate because it is constantly interacting with this background energy field.[13]

Hal Puthoff turned out to be equally talented as an inventor as well as a theorist and went on to use his calculations based on the zero-point field in conjunction with condensed charge technology to develop electronics applications in very tiny spaces. In conjunction with a lab technician named Ken Shoulders, he invented

> a special device that could fit an X-ray device at the end of a hypodermic needle, enabling medics to take pictures of body parts in tiny crevices, and then a high-frequency signal generator radar device that would allow radar to be generated from a source no larger than a plastic credit card. They would also be among the first to design a flat-panel television, the width of a hanging picture. All their patents were accepted with the explanation that the ultimate source of energy "appears to be the zero-point radiation of the vacuum continuum." . . . [Along the way, the Pentagon] listed condensed-charge technology, as zero-point energy research was then termed, as number three on the National Critical Issue List, only after stealth bombers and optical computing. A year later, condensed charge-technology would move into the number two slot.[14]

Newton Meets the Zero Point Field

Hal Putthof's ideas would attract little attention for the following two decades until, in 1993, mathematician Alfonso Rueda was able to derive Newton's Law $F = ma$ (force = mass x acceleration) by using zero-point calculations in proving an idea proposed by colleague Bernard Haisch. Now to most of us, that statement means absolutely nothing. It's a shame that we live in an age where the first skateboard 1080 makes front page news worldwide, while the first radical reinterpretation of one of the most unassailable postulates of physics since 1687 passed by mostly unrecognized.

$F = ma$ is the second most famous law in physics, only recently superseded by Einstein's $E = mc^2$, and laws like this are not proven, they simply *are.* Yet Rueda's math "proved" that the property of inertia possessed by all objects in the physical universe was simply resistance to being accelerated through the zero-point field. This in turn implied that the hard stuff of matter was, in fact, illusory: an "effect" caused by the slowing down of light due to the resistance of the zero-point field. Here is Bernard Haisch's explanation of this radical redefinition of our physical reality.

> Esoteric traditions attribute primacy to light rather than to matter, which is intimately connected with space and time. Arguably, matter cannot exist apart from space and time, and is dependent upon them. Einstein's relativity theory also suggests that space and time are defined by the propagation of light. So the key to creation does seem to lead back to light, in the context of both ancient traditions and modern physics. . . .
>
> A beam of light, or the smallest quantum bundle of light called a photon, moves through space and time at a fixed pace of 186,000 miles per second—at least from your material perspective. From its own perspective, however, there is no space or time. Herein lies what I suspect is a profound connection between the basis of space and time, and light in the form of the zero-point radiation of the quantum vacuum. I propose that light may be the progenitor of an apparent universe of matter. In some sense, "slowing down" ever so minutely from that privileged, timeless, spaceless reference frame of light manifests a realm of space and time. In other words, space and time are created when you leave the reference frame of light.
>
> Einstein's special relativity theory tells us that light propagation defines the properties of space and time. I argue that light propagation may actually *create* space and time. The zero-point field inertia hypothesis implies that the most fundamental property of matter, namely mass, is also created by light.[15]

Rueda and Bernard Haisch then coauthored a paper with Hal Puthoff that presented this mathematical proof of Newton's Law. The paper was published in the journal *Physical Review* in 1994, and it was received in the same way that radical new ideas that rewrite our definition of reality are generally received: to considerable criticism from the scientific establishment, criticism that created a degree of professional notoriety—the journal *Science* called it "a grand claim based on obscure theory."* Undeturred, a year later Haisch received funding from NASA to support a three-year study on inertia. Rueda and Haisch then published two new papers that confirmed that the inertia of matter can be traced back to the zero-point field. In these two papers they achieved a completely different analysis that used Einsteinian relativistic physics instead of the classical Newtonian physics approach that they had used in their original proof.† Now, after four hundred years of Newtonian physics, the mystics and the ancient Egyptians have been proven mathematically correct. We are indeed all beings of light.

*Rueda had spent nearly two decades working with SED theory (stochastic electrodynamics). This little known and apparently frequently misunderstood field (B. Haisch, *The God Theory: Universes, Zero-Point Fields, and What's behind It All* [York Beach, Maine: Red Wheel/Weiser 2006]) accepts the existence of the zero-point field as real for all practical purposes, and uses ordinary electrodynamics to describe the field as equivalent to completely random electromagnetic waves. By using a combination of "ordinary" classical physics formula and zero-point energy fluctuation calculations, SED can explain certain bizarre quantum effects without becoming embroiled in complex quantum theory. According to Bernard Haisch, what is not understood is that to physicists like Rueda, SED is a useful tool, an analytical technique, and not an alternative physics. It was this approach that allowed the laws of inertia to be defined by SED mathematics.

†By deriving $F = ma$ using an entirely different set of mathematics, Rueda and Haisch fulfilled the orthodox scientific requirement of a mathematical "independent verification." This mathematics required a much more complicated "four-vector" version of this equation that is used in special relativity theory.[16]

SEVEN

Toading

Within thirty seconds, there will be an onset of almost overwhelming psychedelic effects. You will be completely absorbed in a complex chemical event characterized by an overload of thoughts and perception, brief collapse of the EGO, and loss of the space-time continuum. Relax, breathe regularly, and flow with the experience.

ALBERT MOST, *BUFO ALVARIUS: THE PSYCHEDELIC TOAD OF THE SONORAN DESERT*, 1984

Every time my quest has taken another twist or turn that appears to bring me closer to the core of the matter—to that place where what I *feel* is instinctively worth more than what I might *think*—then my focus tends to move from the outer limits of the modern psyche (alien species, impending end-times, quantum physics, and so on) back toward the sacred and ancient occult knowledge (communicating with departed souls, precognition, and belief in the mystical union with G/d).

So it is now, as this adventure turns from the theoretical imaginings of the modern physicist to the real-world entheogenic adventure I embarked on while investigating the interspecies relationship between human beings and the *Bufo alvarius* toad: the potentially shamanic pastime of smoking toad venom.

> *The* Bufo *toad (and related genera) has held a place in humanity's archaic consciousness since time immemorial. The earliest representations of* Bufo *toads (and toads generally) go back thousands of years. The appearance of toad-based artifacts is prehistoric and possibly protolinguistic, being portrayed in ancient pictographs, paintings and small sculpture . . . [Anthropologist Peter] Furst . . . places the uses of* Bufo *toad venom "all the way back to Neanderthal Man one hundred thousand years ago."*
>
> THOMAS LYTTLE, DAVID GOLDSTEIN, AND JOCHEN GARTZ, "BUFO TOADS AND BUFOTENINE: FACT AND FICTION SURROUNDING AN ALLEGED PSYCHEDELIC," *JOURNAL OF PSYCHOACTIVE DRUGS,* 1996

Humankind and toads have been in close contact with each other ever since the first *Homo sapiens* irrigated a field, and it has even been suggested that toad venoms might have inspired the first Indo-Uralic or "Ur" religions of the Stone Age.[1] Sculptures, pictographs, and, most tellingly, the skeletons of *Bufo* toads have been found in remarkable numbers at ancient grave sites in both Europe and the Americas.

The toad's amphibious nature clearly influenced the many different guises in which it has been depicted: "as a fertility symbol, chthonic symbol, symbol of transformation, and psychopomp."[2] The toad has also been viewed as the Great Earth Mother, "an image of transformation, death and regeneration, harbinger of the seasonal rains and protector of crops is a potent mythic complex found throughout the Americas."[3] To the superstitious early civilizations who cohabitated with the toad in the mud of their fields, its sudden appearance "out of nowhere" was deemed supernatural, giving the toad an exalted position in the magical shamanic realms.[4] Starting with Roman times, an abundance of European literature testifies to *Bufo* toads' reputation for use in poisons[5] and as part of "witches brews."[6] The Chinese have used preparations made from toxic toad secretions as medicines for centuries if not millennia.

An ancient and pervasive link also exists between Bufo toads and psychoactive mushrooms. Bufotenine (*N,N*-dimethyl-5-hydroxytryptamine or 5-HO-DMT), the first indolic base isolated from toad venoms, has also been found in half a dozen varieties of *Amanita mushrooms,* including *Amanita muscaria,*[7] the infamous Siberian entheogen. This curious correlation between toads and mushrooms can be found in many languages, such as the English word "toadstool." Mushrooms are named after toads in a number of other languages, including Welsh, Dutch, Norwegian, French, Ukrainian, Basque, and Chinese.*

The *Bufo* toad plays a substantial part in the mythology of the ancient Mesoamerican civilizations of the Olmec, Mayan, and Aztec, and can be found represented in these cultures' art as far back as 2000 BCE.[8] Large quantities of *Bufo* toad skeletons have been found at Olmec ceremonial sites. There is some debate over whether or not they were a food source, as certain toxins in their skin are deadly. Some anthropologists have proposed that these toads were used as an entheogen source, and "evidence" for this view comes from toad representations in Aztec art. Many of these depictions focus in detail on the toads' parotid glands, where the major supply of their venom lies.[9] These include a sculpture in Mexico City's incredible National Museum of Anthropology and a glyph at the palace in Palenque, in which three circles down the toad's back represent parotid glands.[10]

Originally, the large *Bufo marinus* toads common to the marshy regions of the Yucatan—the original homeland of the Olmecs and Mayans—were considered to be the toad represented in Mesoamerican mythology. Bufotenine had a significant reputation (from Europe) as a hallucinogen, and not one anthropologist seemed to doubt that eating *Bufo marinus* would provide the necessary "entheogenic" punch. Perhaps, these anthropologists suggested, the ancient Mesoamericans had a manner of preparing the *Bufo marinus* that removed the more deadly of their toxins, while retaining psychoactive effects. There is scant evidence of folk preparations among the Maya, where toads were steeped in fermented beverages to produce an extra kick.[11]

A smattering of unconvincing ideas was proposed on how the Mesoamericans might have mitigated the toads' toxicity. One graduate stu-

*Even the basic "distinctions" made between a frog and a toad and a mushroom and a toadstool are the same: there is no classifiable difference. The different terms are not based on toxicity as many people presume. They arise simply from attitude: whether or not a culture views the frog/mushroom positively or, as a toad/toadstool, negatively. This simple cultural anomaly was the initial inspiration for the Wassons' examination of mycology throughout the world.

dent in anthropology—Alison Bailey Kennedy (perhaps more well-known under the moniker Queen Mu, as the editor and publisher of *Mondo 2000* magazine)—even won a prize for her paper suggesting the highly speculative notion that the Mayans fed the toads to ducks, and then ate the ducks to get high.

Kennedy proposed that ducks, which have unusually efficient livers, could have "served as bio-processors or bio-mediators of the toad venom, rendering it both more potent and less toxic, by converting it into certain metabolites in their livers."[12] She even went so far as to feed fifteen young toads to some ducks at the San Antonio Zoo, but she stopped short of getting any definitive answer to her far-out proposal, as she did not test her hypothesis by actually butchering and eating the ducks.

There is one major problem with this widely speculated anthropological view. Licking a cane toad (as the *Bufo marinus* is commonly known) doesn't get you high. *Bufo marinus* venom doesn't contain any 5-MeO-DMT, or even any bufotenine apparently. It does contain the quaternary amine salt dehydrobufotenine.[13] The human pharmacology of this compound appears to be unknown, but potentially unpleasant: given subcutaneously, a lethal dose in mice is around 120 micrograms, and death occurs with clonic convulsions.[14] *Bufo marinus* venom also contains bufothionine in quantities ranging from 100–100 micrograms per gram of skin.[15] The activity of bufothionine isn't known and may be "doubtful."[16]

Apparently none of the anthropologists debating the methods cultures of old may have used to ingest *B. marinus* venom ever considered the idea that it might be smoked. While the safety of such a proposal is vastly unknown—and I certainly don't recommend that any of my readers *try* this—there has been a single report of smoked *B. marinus* venom "leading to psychotropic effects." Under no circumstances should anyone ever *lick* this or any other toxic toad! Licking, or even worse, eating *Bufo marinus* toads—or licking or eating any species of toad (or frog) for that matter—will only cause illness (at best) or death (at worst), due to the extreme toxicity of certain alkaloids in their venom.*

---

*Toad venom contains extremely powerful and highly toxic cardiac glycosides called bufogenin and bufotoxin; Meyer and Linde, 1971, as cited in W. Davis and A. Weil, "Identity of a New World Psychoactive Toad," *Ancient Mesoamerica* 3 (1) (1992): 51–59.

As pervasive and popular an urban myth as toad licking has become, there are no grounds for these reports. Those few unfortunate souls documented as trying it undoubtedly did so after hearing sensational reports from the mainstream media. As Alexander Shulgin put it, "Of course the [toad] licking myth is newspaper hype—it is the venom that is active, and it is smoked."[17] While hallucinations and convulsions could undoubtedly result from ingesting *Bufo marinus* toads—and might be taken to have some entheogenic force by onlookers—true poisons are rarely employed as entheogens, for the simple reason that they can be lethal.

In entheogen-rich Mexico—with a long history of ritual use of psilocybin-containing mushrooms, mescaline-containing cacti, lysergic acid amide–containing morning glory seeds, and *Salvia divinorum*—it seems unlikely that its culture would develop an affinity for the exceptionally unpleasant and potentially lethal venom of *Bufo marinus*.

According to Davis and Weil, over two hundred psychoactive plants have been identified, and "their significance to indigenous cultures has been justly celebrated," but "for ethnopharmacologists the discovery of a psychoactive toad would be astonishing, because it would be the first proven instance of the use of a hallucinogenic agent from the animal kingdom. To date, all known and deliberate human use of natural hallucinogens has involved derivatives of higher plants and fungi."[18] Davis and Weil do note a few reports in the ethnopharmacologic literature of other putative psychoactive animals—a moth larvae and some fish. There are also scattered reports of others that they don't mention: ants, salamanders, scorpions, snakes, and spiders. However it is doubtful that any of them produce an entheogen comparable in effect to 5-MeO-DMT.

In their paper, "Identity of a New World Psychoactive Toad," Davis and Weil propose that the toad so venerated in the Mesoamerican mythology and iconography might not be the *Bufo marinus* indigenous to the wet Mexican coastal-lowlands, but the physically similar *Bufo alvarius* whose habitat lies thousands of miles away, in the vast Sonoran Desert.[19] This is the creature of interest to us, since it is the only animal on earth that carries 5-MeO-DMT in its venom (and the only animal other than the human known to produce it). It resides in the Sonoran Desert of old Mexico, an area that runs into western Sonora, Mexico, up through southwestern Arizona and southeastern California to northwestern Baja, California.

Bufo alvarius is North America's largest toad; it can grow up to seven-and-a-half inches in length and weigh several pounds. Due to its large size, squat body, and flat broad head, the *B. alvarius* is reasonably easy to identify, with smooth and leathery skin that can range from a dark brown to olive or grayish green.[20] But by far its most distinguishing feature is the presence of the large parotid glands on its neck and limbs—the same glands that are so conspicuously represented in Mesoamerican art.

Unlike most toads, *Bufo alvarius* is semi-aquatic and needs a dependable water source to survive (a requirement that would seem detrimental to the survival of a species that resides in one of the driest places on Earth). The *B. alvarius* has thrived however, mostly within the drainage areas near the permanent rivers and streams of the Sonoran Desert. These toads also take advantage of a network of canals built by the ancient and mysterious Hohokam Indians over fifteen hundred years ago, which diverts water from the Gila River, irrigating more than 1.5 million acres of the desert.[21] The toad lies dormant in the mud of the desert from September through to April and then comes out in considerable numbers with the first monsoon rains of the summer, usually in June. *Bufo alvarius* is unique within its genus in that it possesses an unusual enzyme—O-methyl-transferase—that converts bufotenine into 5-MeO-DMT in the toad's parotid and tibial glands. This 5-MeO-DMT accumulates in the toad's venom, which contains up to 15 percent by volume.[22] The fact that the same lab-made compound that had been responsible for my spiritual epiphany was also available as a naturally produced venom fascinated me, and I was determined that I should experience it to see how similar the two really are. So it was the Sonoran Desert toad that I set out to find.

Do not be amazed by the true dragon.

Dogen Zenji, *Fukanzazengi*

How should I relate my experience of toading? Should I tell the whole mad tale of that supreme entheogenic adventure? The nonstop insanity that began the moment Yaron's olive-green bio-fuel bus screeched to a stop outside the terminal at LAX, and I stepped aboard and walked right past him at the wheel, since he had shaved off his beard and hair and I didn't recognized him from our ten minutes together in a Los Angeles taxicab eight months previously? Need I write about the hours we scoured the Sonoran Desert in a fruitless search, until we were forced to think like toads—become toads—lying for hours at night in the hot mineral springs of Paradise trying to decide where to search for our subterranean gods, then driving for miles each day in the searing hot sun on tips or Yaron's wild hunches?

Hunches that took us to places like the blind canyon where we drove up into some desert version of *Deliverance* and an ancient naked hippy—whom Yaron claimed to know—emerged from an animal-hide clad dome, his baggy skin brown as dirt from the sun. Who, even though he didn't seem to recognize Yaron, still took us down to visit his friend who knew about toads—an asexual crone of considerable size who had obviously suffered from a life of wear and tear.

She told us that the *Bufos* came out like flies when she watered the gardens in the morning. And that she had a pet toad who often lived under the very seat that I was sitting in, which she wouldn't have minded us milking, but he had disappeared a day or two before. Upon seeing the obvious disappointment in our faces, she then informed us that she had stopped smoking toad venom herself, on account of the fact that it made her want to do LSD, and there wasn't any more good LSD around—at least not in those parts. As if that might be some kind of a consolation.

I could tell you all about that first fruitless week of toad hunting: about living on the bus, about Paradise and the incredible complex of hot springs there. Or how I accidentally killed the first *Bufo* we found, hitting it on the road in a rental car at dusk while on our way to one of Yaron's "secret" toading sites. This event so completely freaked out the superstitious hippies I was with, who were convinced that I had doomed our expedition entirely, that we had to bury the giant toad unmilked, along with some of Yaron's most precious crystals.

But none of that story really belongs here. That all belongs in some other yet-to-be-written book, one that I tell friends will be called *The Lunatics I Have Known.* What I will relate is how we found our first big living *Bufo alvarius,* just minutes after I had declared that it didn't really matter if we found any toads at all—since the trip to Mexico on my Israeli host's bus had been crazed adventure enough for anyone—and that I no longer cared whether or not we found the living source of the most powerful entheogen known to humans.

Less than half an hour later, there he was—sitting right beside the giant hot pool that we had been swimming in every night—a fat green toad as big as a soup plate. After the days traversing the desert, we were shown that we hadn't needed to move inches, let alone a mile. He just sat there looking at us, at well past midnight, even though *Bufos* generally come out at dawn and at dusk. What this fellow was doing up so late, I will never know. Not fifty yards from where we had ceremoniously buried the toad I'd accidentally killed, this very living *Bufo* obligingly jumped between us, as Yaron and I shouted and laughed like the pair of naked fools we were until we finally managed to grab him.

Taking him straight back to the bus, we milked his venom over a pane of glass, pressing on the glands behind the head and on the legs until the milky white liquid spewed out as if we had popped a massive pimple. It formed puddles that dried by morning into a white crystal more synthetic looking than anything I had ever seen. Yet it was purely organic and contained up to 15 percent 5-MeO-DMT. We knew that we could carefully milk him twice within a twelve-hour period and then let him go (apparently after two milkings the glands are empty and require four to six weeks to refill fully).[23] Even after such treatment the bored ancient seemed utterly unperturbed by the whole affair, perhaps only thinking, "Here we go. Bloody humans again!"

Our first *Bufo alvarius* netted us half a gram of dried venom. From then on we would find a couple of toads a day until we left, by walking the perimeters of Paradise with a flashlight and a cooler at dusk and dawn. Eventually we had two or three grams of the crystallized venom—enough so that we could sit down by the pool and think about smoking something sacred, something that had not been bought from any dealer, nor isolated by any chemist, something sought after and hard-earned, one of the rarest treasures known to humanity. We had milked an ancient and carefully scraped up crystals more precious than diamonds: our alchemical white gold.

When the flame hit the venom in the pipe, we could smell that same unmistakable smell and experience that same unmistakable gateway, that same intense fractalization of reality; but somehow it was miraculously softer, smoother, and—dare I say it—more organic. Somewhere between my intake and my transportation to that other land, while I was holding my breath with the smoke tickling my lungs, with that transportation just a moment away, I realized—no, I *knew*—that I had reached the tip of the entheogenic iceberg.

It was as if I was being told: "You have followed the great road, and this is the reward for your diligence—these are the wonders you will be shown. Everything in your life has led up to this one moment. You are following the most sacred of paths, and if you are fortunate, you will realize a timeless truth—one that can only be *experienced,* not explained. Words just cheapen it, because it really just *is,* and you can become One-with-That. Now you must relax and let go—into the light. And that which can be so difficult on the rocketship of pure 5-MeO-DMT is as light and easy as a cloud on the grace of nature's gift from the venomous toad."

Aum . . . breathe.
Aum . . . be.
Aum . . . breathe.
Aum . . . be.
Aum . . .

What good is quantum physics compared to *that* you might ask? What good are all the works of genius, compared to going out into the desert and milking *Bufo alvarius* toads, sitting by a pond, and for a brief window in time experiencing a truly different dimension of reality—perhaps even marveling in the wonder of becoming one with G/d?

When you smoke the venom of the Sonoran Desert toad, you enter a realm beyond the limitations of any human language, a place where even the wildest ranting of an afflicted mystic or the maddest fantasies of a theoretical physicist both fall universes short of describing the knowledge implicit in that omniscient tryptamine zone. In this place, all the words in the world are like a desperate message in a solitary bottle, thrown into an endless sea.

Inspired by what I had found, I had intended to make this part of my literary adventure a D.I.Y. manual on practical toading, breaking the whole process down from start to finish, to help those readers who might want to search for the ultimate organic entheogenic prize. But I decided against this, since the relevant information about "how to toad" is readily available on the Internet (see appendix 1), and there is nothing more of much value I could really add. Just remember that the toads come out with the first good rain, and the window of opportunity to interact with them is very short.

After my experience in the Sonoran Desert, I was fascinated by the murky history of this craft. Who first thought of milking a *Bufo alvarius* toad to smoke its venom, and why? I was captivated by this seemingly unanswerable question. I started questioning whether it was possible that pre-Aztec Indian shamans had made this discovery and incorporated it as a significant part of their culture. Or was it a modern discovery, a by-product of the confluent emergence of the sixties' "psychedelic culture" and the coincidental discovery during that decade of 5-MeO-DMT in *B. alvarius* venom?

The written history related to toad venom smoking is nonexistent, and the archaeological history isn't much better. No toad-venom–containing vessels are left, nor pipes that have been shown to contain venom residue. With the lack of an identifiable physical record, it is impossible to accurately say when a practice might have first started, or even whether or not it is ancient in the first place.

Still, I wonder what knowledge was traded on the face of the Earth during the same era that the Greeks revered kykeon, the Vedas deified Soma, and the great southern shamans intuited the complex formula of ayahuasca and the idea of blowing entheogenic snuff up someone's nose with a hollowed-out bird leg bone? Vast stores of tryptamines have been unleashed into the minds of humans via Amazonian plants and seeds. Could toads have been used to similar effect? Indians in Peru use the venom of a certain species of tree frog to cause a psychoactive effect by burning their skin and then rubbing in the venom.

Neither the milking of toads (or tree frogs), nor the invention of a sophisticated brew such as ayahuasca, which utilizes the chemistry of one plant species to activate the chemistry of a totally different plant species, could be considered events that erupted spontaneously. It is possible to imagine accidentally eating a magic mushroom or two, as R. Gordon Wasson and Terence McKenna espouse, but how could someone "accidentally" milk an amphibian and then figure out how to safely ingest its venom, or spontaneously brew some pounded lengths of vine and a shrub's leaves for twelve hours? Or decide—just for the hell of it—to try blowing a bunch of ground bark or seeds up someone else's nose?

An oft-repeated refrain is that the shamans in South America claim that the plants told them. Perhaps all really *can* be known if you listen to the plants and your dreams. Alas, the great shamans of the north are long gone, leaving few traces behind other than the occasional marking on an ancient rock wall. And as much practical information as I could find on the Internet about toading, I could find virtually nothing about its history or origins. Like the origins of tree-frog poison use in the Amazon, or the invention of ayahuasca, its conception is almost as great a mystery as the state produced by the venom itself.

Mystery that it will remain, I personally like to believe that the archaic tribes of the Sonoran Desert first started the practice of smoking toad venom. Modern Huichol Indians represent the toad colorfully in both their cosmology and in their psychedelic beaded art. I have been unable to locate anything indicating that the Huichol of old knew about smoking toad venom, although it would not be surprising if such a tradition had been kept secret due to the relentless persecution of Amerindian cultures.

While there is no physical proof that the tribes of Mesoamerica knew that *Bufo alvarius* possesses venom that is psychoactive when smoked, there is some pertinent circumstantial speculation. From the wide diversity of entheogenic plants that these tribes used, it is clear that their shamans actively searched for such things, curiously experimenting with numerous natural substances, often at the risk of their own injury. According to Davis and Weil, "Many Indians regarded smoke as sacred essence, a vehicle to the spirit world. The use of tobacco established a pattern of consuming psychoactive drugs by smoking."[24] They also quote the anthropologist Peter Furst:

> The area to which *Bufo alvarius* is presently native was once inhabited by archaic desert cultures; it is also the putative homeland of the Uto-Aztecans, from which they expanded southward into Mexico as early as 1500 B.C. Was it the shamans of the pre-agricultural desert cultures who discovered the potent psychotomimetic effects of toad poison and whose ecstatic trance experiences gave rise to the now widespread beliefs in the toad as a transforming shamaness . . . ?[25]

The "archaic desert cultures" that Furst refers to are the Hohokam Indians, who are known to have traded with ancient Mesoamerican cultures to the south, and whose own culture—with ball courts, pyramidal mounds, and pottery decorations—reflects an influence from those southern contacts (including their probable cultivation of tobacco, the seeds of which likely came from Mesoamerica).[26] Davis and Weil point out that, like plant seeds, light-weight and durable toad venom would have been easy to transport over the well-documented, extensive trade routes that were available.[27] And the greater an entheogenic force that a substance provided, the greater its trade value would have been. Since it is only found in the Sonoran Desert area, this could have also added to its worth.

It seems easy enough to believe that the Indian tribes of the Sonoran Desert could have identified *Bufo alvarius* venom as a potent entheogen and traded it to their southern neighbors. Perhaps the possession of such a potent link with the Divine is what ultimately caused the Aztec nation to believe in its own manifest destiny, sparking their subsequent conquest of much of what we now call Mexico. Could this venom have been a sacred treasure from their homeland, whose mythical properties they celebrated repeatedly in their art and mythology, even going as far as to pointedly represent the *Bufo alvarius* toad's parotid glands in their sculpture and pictography?

We can never really know for sure. But consider this description of Tlaltecuhtli, the Aztec Toad "Owner (Guardian) of the Earth," in her monstrous, devouring form: "Tlaltecuhtli is of course not just a toad. . . . She is . . . an ideal image of the mediator, by which otherwise apparently disparate states are united—life and death, air and water, death and rebirth . . . at once impressively fertile and also cannibalistic . . . metaphor for the earth as the Great Mother who is at once giver and taker of life."[28]

While this couldn't be submitted as even speculative evidence, it sure sounds like the experience of smoking Sonoran Desert toad venom to me. And there is no doubt that at least one contemporary American Indian has learned about this practice and related it to the shamanic practices of his ancestors. The artist Cristobal González wrote about the vision he received from smoking *Bufo alvarius* toad venom:

> The symbol of brother toad and mushroom, which are Gods . . . to give wisdom of the shamanism, and how to study; how to be able

> to communicate and be able to receive direction. And encounter the sacred spaces that exist. Because not all (places) serve for that which one wants to know.
>
> For the Gods say in which place, one can ask for that; which a person "living in reality" wants to know. To be able to learn here, is when the shaman are in the sacred places with their candles, praying to wait for the hour when God arrives . . . to be able to communicate for their powers and ask for luck for their shamanism. And when that hour arrives, they see the candles surge . . . the life-force appears, as if it explodes . . . And from the sparks, the force which comes out is seen, and that is the way it is, where the transformation occurs. It is power which the brother toad and the mushroom have. Because in this way . . . the Gods speak.[29]

All I really know for certain is that going into the desert for days on end searching for toads, catching them, milking them, and seeing that thick venom turn into white crystal in the morning—and then ultimately experiencing actually smoking it—is a great deal different than hanging out with your bros and doing a bunch of random drugs that someone purchased from an anonymous dealer and whose origins you will never *really* know.

Legally produced and purportedly 99.5 percent pure synthetic 5-MeO-DMT was responsible for my true epiphany, my moment of clarity, during a rare window of opportunity in this repressed "drug war" culture. But toading closed a circle that began in a laboratory and ended out under an endless starry sky in the Sonoran wilderness. Voyaging to a timeless place of eternal knowledge—no different now than it was ten thousand years ago—granted exactly the same understanding to a modern seeker as it would have to the high-plains shaman of old: the knowledge of G/d generated within. Our society has spent so much time trying to quash the production and sale of LSD, yet all the while, sitting in the mud on the side of the road, there is a natural tryptamine that makes acid look like training wheels. The ghost of ancient shamanic knowledge moves across our times like a warm wind: calling up the past, calling up the future; trying to bring us back to the path, back to experiencing the true knowledge of G/d.

To close another circle, I took a small amount of the toad venom I had gathered to share with the friend who had originally turned me on to 5-MeO-DMT, and who had given me the instructions that initiated my first 5MDE. He is of northern Mexican Indian stock, so perhaps the blood of the original toad hunters runs in his veins. When he smoked the venom, he lay back and arched his back and howled like a wolf at the top of his lungs for at least ten minutes before beatifically coming out of the trip and declaring that it had been "the most peaceful thing in his life." The next morning I went into town to check out the bookstores. I saw a calendar of Alex Grey's artwork on display, and as I flipped through it I suddenly recognized with a shock one of the paintings, titled *Bardo,* from my own journey the night before. Of course I bought it and took it home. When my friend came home from work, he checked out the calendar I had left on the table. From where I was in the other room, I heard him excitedly shout out: "That was what I saw last night!"

A week later I was in London, England, on my way to India. I stopped into a shop called The Great Frog, located just off Carnaby Street, to check out the work of Paterson Riley, an infamous jeweler who has made rings for clients like Keith Richards, Billy Idol, Kate Moss, and the Harry Potter films. As soon as I saw it, I purchased a ring with a massive, silver bulging-eyed head that looks for all the world like an ancient, bored *Bufo alvarius.* It is without a doubt my favorite ring, and I rarely take it off. When people ask me about it, I tell them that it's how I found G/d. And the crazy thing is that it's true.

EIGHT

Burning Man

The Gnostic of today could no longer be a preacher of salvation, a holy man living a solitary existence on his mountain-top, nor some illuminated spirit living in a great city and devoting himself to his beloved ancient texts, but rather a perceptive man, his eyes turned towards the present and the future in the intuitive conviction that he possesses above all within himself *the keys to this future, a conviction he must hold steadfastly against all the reassuring mythologies, the so-called salvatory religions and disalienating ideologies which serve only to hinder his presence in the true reality. For the important thing today is not so much to discover new stars as to break down the new frontiers that constantly arise before us, or which are delineated within ourselves, so that we may cross over them, as into death, with our eyes wide open.*

JACQUES LACARRIÈRE, *THE GNOSTICS*, 1989

After our toading adventure ended, we headed north on the bus until we reached Black Rock Desert and Burning Man, the greatest counter-culture celebration of our times. The Burning Man festival is held each year over the week leading up to Labor Day weekend in the Black Rock Desert of Nevada, reputedly the flattest place on earth. I had been to Burning Man before in the nineties and reveled in its glorious anarchy then, but now I went with a purpose: to look for answers, fellow seekers, and a community of enlightened

5-MeO-DMT smokers whom I believed *must* exist. But all I found were shadows and rumors amid a culture of happy drugs and mood enhancers. Most people are too busy trying to have fun to want to look into the depths of their own souls, and no one (apart from our bus) appeared to possess any heavy tryptamines. While I was sure that there were pockets of 5-MeO-DMT aficionados scattered among the camps, I did not come across any of them.

DMT was on everyone's lips—everyone had their own DMT experiences, and I saw more than one copy of *The Spirit Molecule* being read—but no one apparently *had* any. No doubt there were some mature and sensible tryptamine heads who quietly smoked their sacrament in their private domes in the company of their tribe. But among the more hectic, public drug culture at Burning Man in 2004, there was no sign of DMT or 5-MeO-DMT.* If some had been available, it probably would have come our way, since we occupied a prominent psychedelic enclave somewhere between a group of original Pranksters turned fisherman and the Oregon Country Fair camp. (You know you're with the old school when Wavy Gravy and various Kesey kids are wandering around.) But there was even a dearth of decent LSD.† Rumor had it there were four vials in the whole of Burning Man, and at the time I wondered if acid might actually become "extinct." Maybe this was why 5-MeO-DMT had suddenly become so easily available (via the Internet): to replace LSD in its unique role of jolting the consciousness of the Western world.

I had gone to Burning Man looking for teachers, and I ended up putting on that mantle myself, which was probably the unconscious germination of this book. Over the following days, I had the opportunity to guide a number of people—both friends and strangers—through that gateway and into the

---

*Since then I have come to realize that both forms of DMT have been available on the playa since at least 1996 if you knew the right people. However, while popular post-hippie compounds like 2C-B were readily available through the psi-trance community, no smokable tryptamines were offered to me in 2004. I apparently wasn't hanging out with the right drug geeks. Both forms of DMT are apparently now available on the black market—thanks, no doubt, to a plethora of extraction recipes that are available on the Internet or published in journals like *The Entheogen Review*. See appendices for more information.

†This was at the height of the new-millennium LSD drought, a consequence of the now infamous 2000 Kansas missile-silo bust. The DEA claimed that the supply of blackmarket LSD in the United States dropped a staggering 95 percent after this single sting.

tunnel of light that marks the end of the searching and the beginning of something much more.

I have continued to learn about 5-MeO-DMT by witnessing the journeys of friends and strangers, but I have also come to realize—through the reactions of people who claimed to be "regular DMT smokers" and could wax eloquent about the chemical complexities of tryptamines—that very few people in modern times have experienced a full-blown 5MDE, no matter how often they may have sucked on a normal DMT pipe. Further confirmation of this belief was revealed by the inner workings of life on our bus, and how a timely dose of 5-MeO-DMT turned a near tragedy into a rare success.

By the time we settled into our camp at Burning Man and got rid of the inevitable stragglers who had caught a free ride on the bus, we were down to a crew of six: myself; Captain Urquhart, a close friend from New Orleans who had joined us on the bus for Burning Man; Mr. Burner, a psi-trance DJ from the West Coast; Millie, a seventeen-year-old English lass who seemed the most mature and wisest among us; Yaron; and Wisconsin, a big, good natured red-haired country hippie acting as Yaron's designated "bus boy." (This meant he had gotten a free ride in turn for being Yaron's indentured servant—an arrangement Wisconsin revolted against not long after camp was struck.)

Wisconsin had been with us through the entire toad escapade, and he and I had struck up a solid bond as I tried to defend him against the worst of Yaron's excesses. I could not help but think he would have been an immediate candidate for the original Prankster bus, with Cowboy Neal behind the wheel. Wisconsin was the prototypical Kesey farm hippie. He didn't hesitate to get his hands dirty—true Rainbow stock—and was exactly the kind of hard-working cat you want around your camp.

Mr. Burner and I had previously gotten to know each other over the course of a few random meetings, due to our fraternal interest in a long-gone band of fiends called Crash Worship. His dry wit and encyclopedic knowledge about the inner workings of the music scene at Burning Man made him another ideal camp mate.

Millie was new to us all. As soon as Wisconsin saw her, he was in love. She spent the following ten days torturing him, much to the amusement of the rest of us. ("She's tough, that one," Wisconsin confided in me with a shake of his hairy teenaged head.) She took everything that came her way so much in stride that it actually gave me hope for the latest generation. I just hope that there are more like Millie around. Having a couple of mature teenagers on the bus was bizarre, but rewarding, and somehow made us feel more like a family.

The only problem on the bus turned out to be Yaron, whose domineering thousand-mile-a-minute style tends to run right over people. The bus had encountered numerous problems with its fuel filters as we hauled our way through California, and at one point, I had driven for over forty hours, desperate to get to Reno. So I was already exhausted by the time we arrived in Black Rock City, and the nerves of everyone on the bus were strained and thin. Yaron managed to aggravate the situation with his habit of pulling groups of random acquaintances onto the bus for big puff sessions—while the rest of us were in the middle of trying to erect our structure and set up camp—and then screaming at us if we took a break ourselves. His shouting and general lack of calm threatened to ruin our time at Burning Man, and before long virtually everyone (and especially Wisconsin) was ready to kill him.

By the second evening, the work was finally done. Camp was erected and looked strong enough to stand up to the harsh desert winds. Yaron had mercifully disappeared with a group of followers on an art car, and he did not seem likely to return for some time. Peace reigned on the bus as we enjoyed the first true moments of relaxation since we had arrived on the playa. As conversation turned toward our plans for the evening, someone suggested that we kick off the week properly with a 5-MeO-DMT ceremony and I readily agreed. My friend Captain Urquhart had sat with me through more of my own 5-MeO-DMT sessions than anyone else and was well aware of the liberating effect it had had on my consciousness. However, the few times he had tried smoking it himself, he had seemed unwilling to really draw on the pipe and hold the smoke in and had only received lower-level effects. When I had mildly pressured him abut trying it again most recently, he had responded that he was "waiting to get to Burning Man," and now that we were on the playa, I was eager for him to finally experience a full 5-MeO-DMT release himself.

Everyone agreed it seemed like a fine idea, although Captain Urquhart expressed the concern that Yaron might return while one of us was entranced (so to speak). I assured him that Yaron seemed like he was gone for the night, and Wisconsin agreed to lead the way. The only problem was, by the time I got everything organized, Wisconsin was sound asleep after all his hard work, and it didn't seem that we could rouse him.

This put Captain Urquhart up next, so he slid into the astronaut's chair and took his first solid 5-MeO-DMT hit. I could tell that *this* was going to be the one that would send him. But as bad luck would have it, Yaron noisily returned with a group of strangers just a few minutes later, and walked straight through the ceremony we were holding beneath the considerable awning in front of the entrance to the bus—despite the fact I asked him to be quiet since Captain Urquhart was obviously deep into his journey! Five minutes later—just as Captain Urquhart was coming back, in a confused state from his experience—the whole group came traipsing out, straight through our ceremony once again, with Yaron loudly explaining to his friends that we were smoking 5-MeO-DMT. The group departed as abruptly as it had arrived, leaving only Yaron behind in the tattered remains of what had began as a peaceful and serious attempt at ritual.

Setting and Ceremony

The more I smoke 5-MeO-DMT, the more I realize the necessity of presenting this unique entheogen in a ceremonial setting. This is not only because this is a compound that can lead to the ultimate mystical realization and as such is sacred, but also because the ceremonial setting is the safest and most effective way for a person to experience a 5MDE. If you are surrounded by a protective circle of genuinely loving people who respect the seriousness of what you are doing, then you will experience the least fear and the greatest chance of achieving the highest result.

Other than that aspect, the nature of the setting is not as important as it is with other psychedelics, since—at the higher dosages—the 5MDE is a true out-of-body experience. However, it is good to be in quiet comfortable surroundings with enough room to lie down. Indoors is generally best. Soft instrumental music can be a good lifeline for people as they return from a 5-MeO-DMT journey. (I like Coltrane's *A Love Supreme*, or some Krishna Das.) Music can also help cover outside noises, if you are in an urban environment.

I usually turn the music on at a low level a few minutes into an individual's experience, especially if the person seems to be having any physical tension or difficulties. Tensing up during a trip is usually the first sign that someone may be having problems. If that happens to someone you are with, quietly and repeatedly tell him or her to relax and breathe, and, if it is not already playing, turn the music on. If the person looks really tense, it can be useful to touch his foot and talk to him. A small amount of physical human contact is one of the best ways to start bringing someone back toward this reality. It is very important to give people some time after they have "come down" from the peak of their 5MDE, since they are still receptive to the greater energies of the tryptamine universe. This is also the period where the participant can reveal extraordinary wisdoms to the circle, only to forget that they ever uttered them.

Generally, the smaller the number of participants, the better. The exception to this is in a larger ceremonial space, such as a specifically designated dome at Burning Man, with a group of participants who recognize the sacred nature of the quest. In such a setting, using the group for support, the circle can be as large as fifteen or twenty people (although less is better). Otherwise, five is my maximum number for a room, preferably with all the observers being participants at some point. I have found three people to be the ideal number for a ceremony, with one of the two people often being a close friend of mine, while the other is a stranger (usually a friend of my friend). One of the many anomalies of the 5MDE is that it is often this person—the stranger to me—who achieves the greatest entheogenic effect during the session.

Make sure all possible interruptions will be avoided, such as telephones, animals, or people suddenly coming in. If you are leading the ceremony, and the person about to smoke the 5-MeO-DMT has a significant other with him or her, then everyone must understand that you will be the guide for the person smoking, and that everyone else should resist getting involved or touching the participant during his or her journey—unless you ask them to. It is better to clarify things at the start, than to have a situation in the middle of an experience where the observers become freaked out because of the weird things that they are watching their loved one do. Watching a physically heavy 5MDE can be more stressful then actually going through it, since the person who is having the apparently "bad trip" often does not remember any of the difficult part at all, and sometimes thinks that he or she has had nothing but an amazingly loving and peaceful experience.

If you become experienced enough in smoking tryptamines you may start smoking them alone. A 5MDE becomes an intensely personal thing—it can be your dialogue with G/d—and I now have a hard time letting my friends—let alone strangers—see my fear and wonder when I come out of it. But when the 5MDE is presented as a sacred ceremony, such as some do within the billowing domes of Burning Man, it is one of the most powerful ways to help build unity within the tribe, because then all are common witnesses to something remarkable, and a group of minds can in some way "mesh," for both participant and nonparticipant alike. Smoking 5-MeO-DMT can be one of the most important events of your life, and, as is common with any life-changing event, those who accompany you on that journey can become as close to you as family, unified by the cosmic field of One Love. This is not something you quickly forget.

Captain Urquhart is one of the few people I know who believes that the 5-MeO-DMT experience was bad for him as he would suffer from what he believes to be lingering effects over the months to come. (See appendix 6.) He was very disoriented when he came out of his voyage, a situation only made worse when he discovered he was surrounded by curious strangers. As I witnessed my friend's obvious distress I became truly furious with Yaron, who as usual seemed oblivious to the damage he had just caused. Once Captain Urquhart had calmed down I went into the bus without saying anything and packed a massive 30 mg hit into the bowl, then took it back outside and handed it to him.

"What's this?" Yaron asked. I told him it was his introductory 5-MeO-DMT hit, and he immediately agreed to do it with the same lack of forethought that seems to accompany all of his actions.

Now—although my portrait of Yaron so far may seem less than kind—

he is, in his unique way, a remarkable cat who lives by his own peculiar set of rules. At this time, he was something of a West Coast counterculture fixture, on account of the uncompromising way he lives his life (and the fact that he once managed to start a full-blown riot). When I first met him, and then when his name came up again while talking to mutual underground friends, I had high hopes that he would be my introduction to the West Coast society of enlightened 5-MeO-DMT users that I was sure existed. (I had naively hoped that if I could just get in touch with this group, then all my questions could be answered.) Outwardly, Yaron initially had seemed like the ideal candidate: he was willing to take me toading, knew about the literature on tryptamines, and had established his own personal DMT mythology based on his apparently numerous experiences.

However, once I went to Mexico with him, I realized that Yaron's introduction to toading had been by chance, through a much older English underground chemist—a character who had lived in the desert for years and obviously had nothing to do with any "West Coast tryptamine society." In fact, Yaron actually knew only the barest basics about toading (all of which were readily available on the Internet), and our trip was his first fairly successful venture since the death of his mentor, who had been shot dead by the local police. He caused us to buy a lot of equipment that we did not need (making the venture unnecessarily expensive) and to drive all around the Mexican desert, before we realized we just had to pay more attention to where we already were. Still, he *was* able to identify the correct toads (there are a surprising number of different toads out there, once you start looking). And he had milked them of their venom before, which is as weird a specialized occupation as one can imagine (all you trimmers and fluffers bow down!).

But as much as he *talked* about DMT and 5-MeO-DMT, and as much as he knew about the drug culture in California, he did not know the one piece of information I had taken for granted would be common knowledge among the psychedelic community on the West Coast. That was the simple fact that 5-MeO-DMT was not a scheduled compound, and it was readily available (at that time) for purchase from several Internet-based vendors. Nor did anybody else that I discussed this with at Burning Man seem to know that this was the case. I began to realize that somehow I had fallen into the world of easily available 5-MeO-DMT fairly early and that at that point, due to my insatiable curiosity, I undoubtedly knew a lot more about the compound than most.

That evening at Burning Man, as I angrily handed Yaron a pipe packed with as high a dosage as I would dare give anyone, I acted as close to malice as I ever have with a tryptamine pipe. But I was determined to drive something into his hardened skull, and I was clinically curious what he would make of the experience. He sucked hard on the pipe while sitting cross-legged on the mattress we'd laid under the awning of the bus, then instantly coughed out a thick cloud of smoke and was out cold before he hit the ground. Managing to wrest the pipe from his hands as he fell back, I looked into the bowl with the flame of the lighter to assess how much he had taken in and saw that there was still a fair residue of the orange powder. So I took a hit, which I could immediately tell was going to be 100 percent effective. I then collapsed beside Yaron, who was lying there with his eyes wide open, but was obviously completely "gone."

After an unknown period of time and a full-blown 5MDE of my own, I came around with my head lying on Yaron's legs. The first thing I noticed was the thump of the generator and a faint smell of diesel in the air. I struggled to sit up and saw the stars through the entrance of the awning and then immediately suggested that we go outside to get some fresh air. Captain Urquhart put his hand on my arm, laughing, and told me to listen to what Yaron was saying. I suddenly remembered that Yaron had taken a hit of 5-MeO-DMT as well. I looked around confused, noticing that everybody looked like they had been laughing their heads off. Mr. Burner, Millie, and Captain Urquhart were all wide-eyed and smiling, and I realized that something special had been going on. Focusing my attention on Yaron, who was now sitting up beside me, I heard him say:

"If I say anything harsh this Burning Man or worry about anything—any bullshit, money, anything at all—I want you to take me out in the desert and shoot me. Just shoot me and bury me in a hole in the ground. 'Cause none of it means anything!"

He threw his hands up in the air and laughed. "It was a pleasure to die with you people," he exclaimed. "And this guy, this crazy fucking guy," he declared as he wrapped me up in a big ugly Israeli bear hug and kissed me on the cheek, "I love this fucking guy, and his crazy fucking DMT! I have smoked plenty of DMT before, but I have *never* experienced anything like that!"

So spoke one of the most hardened and jaded of West Coast heads, further supporting my supposition that it's all about the delivery and the dosage and that a lot of people who *think* they have experienced DMT or 5-MeO-DMT have only played around on the edges. The rest of the bus had tears streaming down their faces by now, and this shared experience would set the "ground state" of our camp for the next week and a half. We would all come and go, but we were a family because of what we shared that night, and the bond stayed strong between all of us. Yaron completely chilled out from that point on—at least as much as was possible for him—and seemed to actually try to show some respect for the rest of us living on the bus, which was a great relief to everyone.

Wednesday night at Burning Man, there is no better place to be in the counterculture world. Most of the hard work is done, camp is built, and the next night the gate is closed for the rest of the event. Tomorrow the "week-enders" will stream in, more than doubling the size of Black Rock City—these days to somewhere in the vicinity of 50,000 freaks. Wednesday night is the line, it could be argued, between the Community and the Curious, since the majority of the people who create Black Rock City come for at least ten days, while many of those who come only for only the weekend tend to treat the event like a glorified rave (my apologies to those true Burners with inflexible work schedules!).

That night, once Yaron and I had recovered sufficiently from our shared 5-MeO-DMT experiences (and Wisconsin had groggily awoken, after missing the whole show), we took our bicycles out onto the open playa—a gigantic horseshoe-shaped plain of pancake-flat desert outside of the camping area—which contains the Man, the Temple, and the majority of the art installations. Before we left the bus, Captain Urquhart and I had split three of "Dr. Hofmann's Sweet Tarts" that we had been gifted. As soon as we got out onto the playa, I felt the juice hit me like a ton of bricks—the lights blurring and streaming like a heavenly video game, as I began laughing and howling like a lunatic. Burning Man was on!

Our intention was to cruise around as a group, but now full fiendish madness had come down upon me and I found myself concentrating on every random event with increasing intensity. "Fuck," I thought to myself, "This is a hit-and-a-half? I haven't been this twisted in years!" Suddenly Mr. Burner's calm monotonic voice reeled me in, as we cycled past a sound system that looked vaguely like Stonehenge, the music pulsing out of it with the astonishing clarity of pure energy.

"Oh yeah, I forgot about these guys, their sound system is probably just as sweet as ours," I heard him say, and then the next thing I knew, I was standing in the center of Stonehenge, with the music lapping over me like waves of light, surrounded by new people and completely separated from my group of friends, whom I would not see for the rest of the night. So began one of the great psychedelic (as opposed to entheogenic) nights of my life, which reignited my personal love affair with Dr. Hofmann's "Problem Child."

The events of that night are far too long to entirely recount here, although I must mention having a neo-religious experience on my knees alone at the Temple of Stars, as somewhere deep within my soul I realized the genius and sheer beauty of that immaculate structure, and cried out in astonishment and disbelief that we would burn it down in four short nights. (Respect to the Temple builders!) But many hours later, after I had witnessed an indescribable sunrise with my family of thousands and then, unwilling to let such a magical night end, had dallied until it had grown too hot to be outside any more, I finally returned to the bus, still cackling away to myself.

"Here he is!" I heard Captain Urquhart shout, as I came around the front of the bus and found Mr. Burner waiting for me—his face in the early morning light looking extraordinarily serious and appearing entirely purple to my twisted eyes.

"I just want you to know," he said, "I think we can find some of the world's finest LSD today."

"Acid?!" I laughed, laughing down deep inside from the joy and wonder of the night I had just lived through and the sunrise I had just seen. "Who needs *that* stuff?!" Laughing like a madman, I bee-lined toward Captain Urquhart and the bong, leaving a somewhat confused Mr. Burner standing in my demented wake.

My point in all this is the fact that smoking the 5-MeO-DMT right before I took the "sweet tarts" produced an effect so powerful that it was almost as if I were trying them for the first time. Captain Urquhart's experience mirrored mine and caught him equally by surprise. Since we had eaten these particular "sweet tarts" numerous times before, we thought we knew what to expect! But the power of the experience that night was far greater than we would ever have expected from one-and-a-half hits apiece. It is generally accepted DMT lore that this effect works in reverse also—that is, taking even a very small dose of LSD or psilocybin can result in considerably amplified DMT (and 5-MeO-DMT experiences).

This experience was added to the others that ultimately sent me on a search into the quantum realm for explanations of what was truly taking place in my brain. Although at the time I had never heard of things such as "Bose–Einstein condensates" and knew little of the physics concept of coherence, it was in those terms that I believe I finally found a deeper understanding of what I was experiencing. At the time, however, I simply reveled in having had one of the great psychedelic nights of my life. It was also my personal night of commitment to becoming a bona fide member of the Burning Man community, which also inspired the production of this book. Its creation, construction, and continued distribution is both my act of "radical self-expression"* and my humble contribution to the community of this unique and necessary event, my gift to my Burner brothers and sisters. May our construction of the New Jerusalem continue unhindered and may the lessons we learn there—about art, love, G/d, and the strength of the tribe—spread out across our mad and dying world.

*Radical self-expression is one of the founding principles of the Burning Man community. For those of you who don't know it, Burning Man is a great deal more than just a party. See www.burningman.com for more information.

NINE

India

A wise man will not go out of his way for information.

HENRY DAVID THOREAU,
JOURNAL ENTRY, MARCH 18, 1852

As my fate would have it, I had a trip planned to India to realize a long-time dream of flying a paraglider in the Himalayas, and this seemed like the perfect place go after the mad adventures of toading, Yaron's bus, and Burning Man. The wisdom of this plan only seemed confirmed when I found out, to my surprise, that Bir—the small town in northern India where I would be staying—was the site of a significant Tibetan refugee population and the home of a famous teacher, Khyentse Rinpoche. Life seemed to be moving me in the correct direction without any discernible effort on my part (other than interpretation), and I was sure that this trip to India would open up new regions of both my mind and my soul for further exploration.

I had been to India once before, to attend the Maha Kumba Mela, the famous religious gathering that happens once every twelve years on the banks of Allahabad and is said to be the largest gathering of humanity in the world. On that occasion I had more interest in the spectacle as a photographer than I had in any sort of spiritual quest. Yet I had been undeniably moved by the intense religious belief I witnessed there and by the relevance of spirituality to the lives of the Indians themselves.

As the birthplace of Hinduism, Jainism, and Buddhism and the home to millions of Jews, Zoroastrians, Christians, Muslims, and just about every other religion you can possibly think of, India is the "DMT of spirituality." There is no other more amazing cauldron of religion, ritual, and philosophy than is contained within those borders, since India is, in itself, worlds upon worlds upon worlds. India and its religions are inseparable, just like the wave/particle phenomena of quantum physics; take one away from the other, and you have nothing left. India *is* religion, with all its divine blessings and all its glaring faults, and like many a naive and hopeful Westerner, I went there flying high on my discovery of G/d, fantasizing that among India's many philosophies I might find some answers to my own, only to have the sheer weight of India's history and its harsh modern reality send me crashing back down to the ground.

Before I even made it to India, I injured my back lifting a heavy bag in Heathrow airport. Then I got the worst case of food poisoning in my life within forty-eight hours of landing in Delhi. For over a week I lay in a dollar-a-night stone room in Bir, suffering the unseasonably cold weather, shitting and vomiting, and in severe pain every time I had to get off my cot and lurch into my (mercifully) private bathroom. Finally, thinking that I might actually die in this barren hotel if I didn't do something, I decided that a change of scenery might do me some good. So I took a taxi and a six-hour bus ride to Manali, where I found a pharmacy that sold me some pills that cured whatever was wrong with me. (The pharmacist took one look at me and immediately reached under the counter for the correct medicine—some kind of heavy antibiotic I presume.)

I spent a couple of days lying in a modern hotel room with an astonishing view of the mountains, since it had just snowed in the Kulu Valley, closing the pass north to Leh and Ladakh for the winter, and now all the peaks lay buried in white. I was incredibly weak from not being able to hold down any food, and my back was still so badly fucked-up that I had a hard time walking, but at least I was alive. Eventually I managed to haul myself out of bed and slowly made my way up to one of my favorite places in India: Jakhu Temple (also known as the monkey temple), just outside of Old Manali. The snow had melted off the ground down low, and I walked unsteadily along a trail between towering pine trees, with the whole lower valley a vibrant patch of living energy among the white sparkling fields of the Himalaya.

This Hindu temple is a beautiful carved wooden structure dedicated to Hanuman, the Monkey God, and locals claim it has existed since the times of the *Ramayana* epic (somewhere between 500 and 100 BCE), in which Hanuman plays a significant role. I sat outside the temple in the sun, grateful just to be there, and still too shy to the alien world of India to go inside, make my offering, and ring the temple bell.

I had come to India to fulfill a dream of paragliding in the greatest mountains in the world, and now I considered myself lucky to be able to accomplish a twenty-minute walk up a moderate hill in an hour and a half. Physically, I felt the weakest I had in years—maybe ever. While my mind was light and clear, it seemed as though I was waking up from a long dream (or a 5MDE) and was just discovering that I possessed a physical flesh-and-blood form. I realized that in the year and a half that had passed since I first smoked 5-MeO-DMT, I had forgotten about my body. I had been increasingly living in my mind and ignoring the obvious realities of my physical well-being. For example, I had stopped practicing yoga after a number of years—undoubtedly the root of the return of my back problems. My condition effectively hammered home to me that while I might be able to escape the boundaries of the physical world during a 5MDE, back in this world I was inextricably linked to my own flesh, blood, and bone, and the health and vitality of that body could not be maintained by the realm of the mind alone.

Body/mind, particle/wave, male/female, yin/yang—our limited view of reality asserts that we live in a world of opposites and totally misses the point: that one without the other is not whole. This is the quantum view, the only paradigm in the twenty-first century that has any hope of making a difference. And nowhere is it more obvious than within the living example of our own being. Whatever the meaning of life may actually be (and I don't believe that there is a concrete answer), it lies in the fact that there *is* life—that the balance between wave and particle, between mind and body, has found a way to exist. Space and time are purely products of that interface; one without the other would be only the void.

Evolution, termed "the arrow of time" by Ilya Prigogine, is the ongoing perfection of that process—the advancement of the capabilities of that interface. The only significant evolution of the human species over the last 40,000 years has been the advances of our consciousness, since we have changed very little physically over that time, other than the enlargement of the frontal lobe of the brain. As we are beginning to realize the true scale of the observable universe—our probing telescopes finding it larger and older than we had ever imagined—we have made ourselves smaller and smaller. The more we learn of the universe, the more we are taunted by the unbelievably brief span of our own existence and our (seemingly) unique* ability to question why. Stretching its growing muscles, mind keeps banging against the limitations of its physical form.

But mind cannot live without body—or at least not in this realm of space and time. One good bout of dysentery clears you of any fantasies about that, as the mind struggles with the fluctuations in the temperature and plumbing of its bodily function like a person drowning. India taught me that much at least, and over the next few months I struggled to regain my physical balance. My ill-health amplified India's faults and scabs and challenged my worldview and beliefs at every turn, while my ego was slowly chipped away.

India did not want to go easy on me. I guess there was a lesson I had to learn, perhaps simply one of humility. But it seemed that for every step I took forward over the next few months, I took two steps back. My general lack of health and lingering stomach and back problems meant it was some time before I was able to paraglide. When I finally did get in the air, I was still too sick to really enjoy it, so I ended up spending a lot of my time just hanging around the Tibetan village of Bir. (Bir is actually comprised of two villages—one Indian and one of Tibetan refugees and their Indian-born families.) Being in Bir wasn't necessarily a bad thing, but was rather frustrating for a person generally used to good health. Then, to make matters worse, I was involved in a head-on collision with a taxi while riding my rented Royal Enfield motorcycle, and still later had a heavy down-wind

*Cosmologists now estimate that that there could be anywhere from 100 million (Shapley) to 100 *billion* (Su-shu Hang) life-bearing planets within our cosmos. (Even larger estimates also exist [Brown]). And in 2003, the Hubble Telescope found the first planet in an ancient part of our own galaxy, with an estimated age of 13 billion years. In the last fifteen years, ninety extrasolar planets have been found from the scrutiny of twelve hundred stars in our vicinity, which are similar to our own sun. In 1979, Carl Sagan and colleagues elaborated upon an equation proposed by Frank Drake in 1960 to calculate the statistical probability of advanced civilizations in our galaxy; according to their computations, up to a million intelligent civilizations could exist in our galaxy. Statistically, the chance that we are all alone in the universe gets slimmer and slimmer every day.

landing with my paraglider, so I just kept piling on the bruises and injuries. Compared to the heady days of the previous summer, when the combination of voracious reading and my 5-MeO-DMT intake had me nearly convinced that there was some way to completely escape physicality, I was being brutally reminded of how necessary my "meat" really was.

My philosophical quest was not going much better. My reading had moved on by now, from McKenna, Shulgin, Strassman, and other tryptamine experts, to a heavy diet of Buddhist and Hindu philosophy that I had purchased in Delhi. (India is the third-largest publisher of books in English in the world, and the bookseller's alley in Delhi is a metaphysical book lover's dream.) As I learned more and more about the significance of the daily activities I was observing—the centuries of belief layered in the countless temples and monasteries with their constant ritual and ceremonies—I felt myself becoming increasingly entranced by India's intoxicating religious spell. But when confronted with the sheer enormity of the Hindu and Buddhist philosophies, my own ideas often seemed like shadows passing over the surface of the pond—so illusionary they might as well be useless. It became harder and harder for me to know *what* I really believed. I could see plenty of parallels between the Eastern philosophies and various aspects of the 5MDE, but in the end, what good did that really *do* for me? What truths unfolded? Nothing new at the time, that's for sure—just a deeper understanding of the values of compassion, tolerance, clear thought, and the importance of the search for meaning.

I didn't need texts or teachers to be reaffirmed of that, as the ordinary Tibetan people whose presence I was living among taught it to me daily. Their humility and humor was more impressive to me than the hordes of red-robed monks from the various neighboring monasteries. Time spent with Tibetans made me quickly realize how spoiled and ungrateful the rest of the world has become—how soft and dull and disinterested. The unflagging optimism and constant good nature of the Tibetan people challenges us to identify the source of our misery and discontent. Most of the time when we examine it, we realize we have little to be upset about at all. It is simply our lack of control over our own lives that causes us the majority of our own suffering. Attack the *real* root of the situation, and we can solve the problem. But any other action simply causes more problems.

Many of the lessons of Buddhism (in particular) can be described as "sensible philosophies"—practical methodologies for navigating our way through life. They make our own life, and the lives of those around us, easier and more fulfilled. The tenacity and optimism of Indian Tibetans is the ultimate proof of the solid value in their worldview, and the grounded nature of their beliefs seemed a million miles away from the wonders of smoking toad venom. It was only the esoteric, far reaches of their philosophy—among the demons and visions depicted in the tantric *thangka*s adorning monasteries' walls—and their commitment to the importance of the moment of dying, with the intricate descriptions they have of that "final" process, that seemed to have any relevance to the 5MDE. And these seemed unimportant, compared to the vitality of the everyday existence of the Tibetan people and their remarkable refugee story. But I also knew it was from their faith in the truth of their esoteric vision that the Tibetan people drew their great strength.

As I battled with the daily contradiction that is life in India, I tried to make some sense of the mess I had gotten myself into. Smoking 5-MeO-DMT had opened me up like nothing else ever before and shown me the wonder of G/d, and now India was making me realize the wonder of life again and how fortunate some of us really are. But recognizing the existence of G/d is completely different from making sense of the fact that G/d allows us to make such a mess of this world. Nowhere is that contradiction more evident than in India, the most religious, most populated, most polluted, and most terminally stone-crazy country on the planet.

When I called India the "DMT of spirituality" earlier in this chapter, I really could *see* that descriptively while I was there, what with the bizarre mélange of shapes, colors, smells, sights, smoke, and sounds that *is* religion in India. Thanks to my friendship with a remarkable Sanskrit scholar from England and his lovely wife, Jim and Claudia, I have been fortunate to experience India from a very "Indian" perspective. Jim is a tall thin English viscount with dreadlocks down to his ass. A Ph.D. in Sanskrit from Oxford, he speaks fluent "BBC" Hindi and has studied in India with a saddhu (Hindu holy teacher) for many years. Because Jim reads Sanskrit, something that most of the saddhus can no longer do, he is somewhat of a novelty and is well known and treated favorably by India's elite saddhu hierarchy. Common Indian people often treat him as if he is a saddhu, touching his feet and giving him money (which he then gives away again about ten feet down the road). A journey with them anywhere in India inevitably involves giving *puja* (offerings) at numerous interesting temples and smoking a lot of Parvati Valley hash with the astonishing variety of saddhus found along the way—most of whom claim to have met Jim at some Mela somewhere.

It was thanks to Jim and Claudia that I was able to experience the Maha Kumba Mela on my first trip to India, since they had invited me to camp with them and their saddhu, Sri Ram Balak Das, who is the leader of an ancient sect of Ram Baba (a monastic sect of saddhus devoted to the Hindu God Lord Rama, the great hero of the Ramayana epic). Due to the fact that we were with such a prestigious sect, we were allowed to march in the Royal Procession with the thousands of holy teachers and bathe in the Ganges on that most prestigious day in 144 years. Only a handful of Westerners were allowed this honor, while 15 million ordinary Indians watched and waited for their signal to bathe. Jim explained to me that by bathing at this particular moment it was possible to wash away 144 × 144 lifetimes worth of bad karma. Two years later, with my mystical connection to 5-MeO-DMT firmly established, I looked back on that day of bathing in the Ganges (an act I undertook in complete faith, since I figured 15 million people couldn't be *that* wrong) and wondered exactly what *did* get washed away that magical day.

Thanks to my friendship with this pair of informed and enthusiastic Hindiphiles and the places they took me where we never saw another white face, I was able to experience India at times at a virtually magical level—lost among the frenzied energy of religious devotion pulsing through the ancient temples of India with their vast throngs of fervent believers. Every temple carries with it a unique, palpable aura, a sense of being that is different in each location. A distinct identity that can only be realized once you step from the elevated vantage where you enjoyed a view of the architecture to that below, into the crush of daily life where you are lost, submerged in the sea of humanity—a press of bodies that push forward as One, deep into the bowels of the Mystery itself.

At the end of my time in India on this latest trip, I ventured alone to Balaji, Rajasthan, to visit a little-known temple that performs mass exorcisms—try and imagine a couple of thousand people all smoking 5-MeO-DMT at once and you kind of get the idea. After a lifetime of seeking out the unusual, this is probably the strangest place I have ever been. (Beating out the Rat Temple in Karnakata, India, where they have been feeding thousands of sacred rats for hundreds of years.) An Indian who was explaining the various bizarre goings-on to me pointed out the small temple that contained three painted rocks that had been venerated as gods for over three thousand years. There was a throng of people trying to get in to make offerings to them, and the Indian remarked, "See, this is why our religion is superior to yours. Here we can *see* our gods." This is the strength of religion in India: it is a tangible thing. You can touch it, smell it, taste it, and throw offerings into its flames. There are countless Hindu gods, with new ones being created every day, and India finds myriad ways to celebrate and honor each and every one of them. This is a kaleidoscopic, multifaceted vision of G/d that in its entirety resembles the visions I see in a 5-MeO-DMT experience.

But for every vision of heaven that they might represent, each of these gods looks down upon a living hell. It is no wonder the Buddha saw life as suffering. For in India, the sacred and the downright cruel walk down the street hand in hand. You see poverty and deformity that would sicken you if it were not for the strength of the smiles on the afflicted. India constantly does your head in, because you know that you are not as strong as these people; you know you have so little faith. There are days in India when life seems like the most vicious of jokes—yet a joke that somehow the Indians instinctively understand. Which is why they can always be laughing, mocking you for your lack of spine, for how easily you can come apart in a "meltdown" that is commonly known by foreign travelers as a "bad India day." Bare ideas seem like the flimsiest of constructs here, because they lack passion, commitment, faith. India feeds on ideas like wood feeds a fire: the flames may get a little higher, but the fuel is all used up and turned to a powdery ash in your hands that is impossible to grasp, leaving you struggling to find an answer among the rapidly cooling remains.

Consider, for example, my single strange meeting with the renowned Khyentse Rinpoche. Since I had been too ill to paraglide, I had spent my time taking a lot of photos. As I wandered around the village and monasteries, several people approached me to see if I would be interested in taking photographs at the dedication ceremony of a huge new university built by Khyentse Rinpoche, which had just been completed. The Dalai Lama was coming to open the school—which was going to be a very prestigious event—and the entire Tibetan population of the area was excited about the visit by His Holiness. I said that I would be honored to help out, and was told that I should visit the Rinpoche at his house just outside of Bir to offer up my much-needed services.

During this period I had been deeply moved by Sogyal Rinpoche's modern classic *The Tibetan Book of Living and Dying,* and I had started to read a number of other Buddhist texts. Repeatedly, I came across the immutable Indian belief that you cannot achieve enlightenment without a teacher, and I found myself wondering about Khyentse Rinpoche, who I knew had a reputation as a scholar and a filmmaker. He had been Bernardo Bertolucci's assistant director on *Little Buddha,* and had himself just finished directing and producing *Travelers and Magicians,* which would prove to be popular on the art-film circuit.

Everything I heard about the man was impressive, and I wondered if perhaps fate intended for me to be his student. Maybe this was why I had ended up in Bir without the stomach (literally) to fly. So I trekked down to a large house that was still being constructed and was told that the Rinpoche was in Europe and that I should come back in a week. The next time I went I was told that he was in the United States and that I should try again in a week, the next time that he was in Delhi, and that I should try . . . well, you get the picture.

Finally, on the fourth or fifth time that I went down, I walked in and saw a middle-aged man in a simple robe standing there. I had gotten used to speaking in simple clipped phrasings while trying to communicate with the Tibetan construction workers that I would find there and, without thinking, asked him in a sing-song pidgin English (something I almost never do) if the Rinpoche was around.

"I am the Rinpoche," he answered in perfect English, while coolly looking at me with quizzical eyes.

I heard a shriek of laughter, and realized that two twenty-something European girls were watching us. One of them came over and stuck a video camera in my face, recording my stammering efforts to explain to the Rinpoche about the request for a photographer. The woman with the camera was quite obtrusive, and the other girl clearly thought this was hilarious, while the Rinpoche said nothing and seemed to be gauging my reaction to this somewhat bizarre scenario.

"I don't think we need a photographer," he said. "We have plenty of photographers don't we?" he asked the girl with the camera. She answered back with a quick, "Yes, Rinpoche, we have plenty of photographers," all the while continuing her obtrusive filming, with her camera uncomfortably close to my face while the Rinpoche stood there smiling at me in silence. I stammered an apology and made my retreat, with the girls' laughter still echoing in my ears as I exited the driveway. Every other time I had come down to the house, I had been treated with the utmost respect and politeness: I generally was asked if I wanted a cup of tea and some biscuits and was thanked profusely for even offering my services. Thus the entire tenor of this last encounter with the Rinpoche himself was rather unsettling and odd.*

As I considered the possibility that this was a test of some kind (which I undoubtedly *felt* like it was), I remembered that a Rinpoche is different than a Lama, in that he does not have to take a vow of chastity. Rinpoches have been known to engage in numerous liaisons, sometimes with European women. I had already met a few European "followers" of the Rinpoche, all of whom seemed somewhat star-struck and needy. One follower, an intelligent psychiatrist from England, told me that "it was great to hang out with the Rinpoche in London, because he has an apartment there in the West End, but there is no center for him in London, so only his closest followers get to see him." (Along with Bernardo Bertolucci and assorted Hollywood types, I was guessing.)

Walking away from Khyentse Rinpoche's house, I decided that I wasn't sure what it was that he was teaching, but I was pretty sure I could do without it. Maybe he knew that as well, who could tell? And with that decision, it occurred to me that if there *had been* a test of some kind, I had just passed. The accomplishments of Khyentse Rinpoche left no doubt that he was indeed a remarkable man. Still, my path, it seemed, was truly my own:

---

*I did get the opportunity to photograph the Dalai Lama a few weeks later at the opening of the enormous university. This was due entirely to luck, since the Indian security wouldn't let me into the hall where he was going to speak but left me alone on the steps where His Holiness passed within a few feet of me. Khyentse Rinpoche's secretary—one of the people who had told me that they needed a photographer—then escorted me into the hall. I heard the Dalai Lama speak and, more importantly, laugh, which reminded me of my 5-MeO-DMT belly-rolls, a laughter that comes from somewhere deep within. Whatever one thinks of the Tibetan religion and philosophy, there is no doubt that their selection process found a remarkable leader for them at the time of their direst need. One can only wish that the rest of the world could find such enlightened leadership.

investigating a modern brand of mystical knowledge. Apparently no one other than myself was going to be able to help me understand it.

I smoked 5-MeO-DMT only once while I was in India. The experience is worth mentioning, mostly because of events that occurred a few weeks later, which by a strange twist of geology are linked even though they occurred in different countries. Because of this fateful linkage, I will quickly relate this particular 5MDE, and later on in this book, you will be able to see the connection.

We were in the Kangra Valley, a couple of hours from Dharamsala, visiting a small temple carved out of the side of a cliff that had a deep stone pool fed by a hot spring at the base of it. To get there we had hiked down a river for close to an hour before crossing it to arrive at the temple just outside of a small village. I went there with Jim, Claudia, and a couple of Italian paraglider pilots we knew from Bir. There had been some talk of smoking 5-MeO-DMT at this spot, and so I had prepared a few doses before we left, but by the time we finally got there it was nearly dark, and the pool was far more inviting. We soaked for a number of hours and then slept outside on a concrete pad underneath a giant banyan tree. Women came and went from the village to take water from the pool, but they never approached us. It was the only place in India I ever went where the people simply left us alone. (It's mighty hard to get a moment's peace in India.)

I awoke the next morning to an ethereal misty dawn punctuated by the temple keeper's ritual ringing of the bell as he performed the morning's opening prayers and offerings. There was a timeless, mystical quality to that dawn, which encapsulated everything I had come to India looking for—the magic lay like dew on the ground—and I remember lying in my sleeping bag wishing that the moment would never end. It passed in a few breaths, the sun rising an inch, the temperature climbing a degree or two . . . and then Kiko, one of the Italians, began packing the day's first chillum (smoking pipe) while putting on water for the first cup of chai.

We were all awake by then, some of us with blankets wrapped around our shoulders, some still in our sleeping bags. All of us huddled around the morning fire, waiting for our tea under the branches of a gigantic tree that you could easily imagine the Buddha sitting beneath. When drops of water began to fall off the leaves of the tree and the ground began to shake, the others looked up from the chillum and chai cups, unsure. But I had been through these in enough countries that after a second I recognized the tremor and named it out loud as the shaking picked up in force and tempo:

"Earthquake."

Everyone just sat there, waiting, as the thick concrete pad twisted and moved for thirty seconds or more. There was nothing else we could do. Finally the force of the tremors subsided, and the temple keeper's son ran up wide-eyed as everyone began to speak excitedly at once. It turned out that I was the only one who had ever experienced an earthquake before.

Another chillum was hastily packed, and another pot of water put on the fire for more tea. Jim went off to the edge of the stream to meditate, while the rest of us sat drinking chai and discussing how strange it is to feel the earth move. Then I remembered that I had brought my 5-MeO-DMT smoking kit with me, and it suddenly seemed like the perfect time to engage in a 5MDE.

One of the Italians took me up on the offer, the exotic setting undoubtedly an attraction, and he enjoyed a peaceful and harmonious introductory 5-MeO-DMT experience. No one else wanted to try it, so I loaded myself a pipe, and I remember the world dissolving away before I even exhaled. It was an exceedingly powerful experience, full of dark energy and turmoil. There seemed to be a clear message behind it: that I needed to stop smoking 5-MeO-DMT for a while, or maybe even forever. I couldn't tell.

I emerged in a state of shock from my heavy experience, sure that I must have been screaming at some point. But my friends told me that I had remained sitting cross-legged for most of the experience, which Kiko found very unusual, as he had never seen anyone who was able to remain seated after smoking DMT. Outwardly I was totally peaceful, and toward the end I had lain down without them noticing. At no time did I make a sound. Apparently I have learned how to leave my body behind with virtually no resistance, clinging to nothing as my mind flashes further and further away—deep into the void.

As peaceful as I may have appeared, I was shocked by the awesome power of what I had just experienced. I lay there on the concrete pad, looking at the myriad leaves fanning out above my head and hearing the sounds of women drawing water from the temple well, with the chants of the temple-keeper and his son behind them. I wondered about my compulsion to continue pushing into that unknown energy, searching for the power and coming back fried.

"Isn't this magic enough?" I asked myself. "What is it that I am hoping to learn?" As Alan Watts once said, "When you get the message, hang up the phone."[1] Now that I had actually felt the presence of G/d and really believed in it, did I *need* to keep going back there again and again? Or did I need to keep returning to keep on believing? Maybe I was becoming addicted to this feeling of getting my ass kicked? I felt closer to being terrified than I felt to being addicted, and in my heart I knew it would be many months before I got the courage to smoke the 5-MeO-DMT again. Nevertheless, I continued to question my motivation and compulsion to access those terrifying realms.

The strange thing is that if you start smoking tryptamines, then the whole world seems to become a tryptamine experience: you cannot tell when the changes began—identify the time before gnosis—nor can you draw a line around what changes were made. Perhaps it is the same as it is for the characters in the Peruvian novelist César Calvo's translucent novel *The Three Halves of Ino Moxo*—heading up the river to find a famous shaman, the world *is* an ayahuasca vision.[2] This is the revelation: life is a dream—an experience from which we will one day wake up, into another dream, another experience. Putting down a tryptamine pipe on the other side of the universe and trying to explain where it is we have been.

After the turmoil of this experience, I resolved to abstain from smoking any more 5-MeO-DMT until the world told me it was time to start again. I contemplated the possibility that perhaps my moment in the sun was over; maybe now I just had to hold on to the lessons I had learned. But it would not be long before it would be made dramatically obvious to me that the knowledge I had gained from visiting the Tryptamine Palace was responsible for guiding me in ways that I would never consciously know. It was having such a profound influence upon my path, my life, and perhaps even my destiny that I could hardly deny it. And over a period of time, many of my experiences in India—including this tumultuous 5-MeO-DMT experience—began to make more sense to me.

At that time, however, I prepared to leave India more confused than I had been when I arrived. After twenty years of travel experience, I can honestly say that I had never been so glad to be leaving a country behind. But as the Chinese say, "You cannot polish a diamond without roughness," and India definitely managed to polish my consciousness into some kind of a shine. And because of that—as hard as it can be—I hope that I will one day return there, to keep working on that shine.

As the paragliding season in the Himalayas drew to a close with the advent of the monsoons, I attempted to complete a Vipassana meditation course outside of Jaipur. But I found that my still-injured back couldn't endure the long hours of sitting (the silence was no problem), so I headed south to the holy town of Pushkar in the Rajasthan Desert to attend its annual Camel Fair, which is a photographer's wet dream. It was while walking the streets of Pushkar one night that I first conceived the idea of writing this book. I had been in India more than three months by then, and the culture had finally beaten me down to its pace.

The next weeks slid by, broken only by my daily yoga classes, but since I didn't have long left in India, I felt like I should go and see some other sights before I had to depart. I took a disastrous bus trip to Jaisalmer on the Pakistani border. The heavily overcrowded bus ran out of diesel in the middle of the desert at night and took an extra day to get there. I then spent a couple of dissolute days kicking around inside Jaisalmer's timeworn pink stone walls, before I booked myself a first-class train ticket back to Delhi. Then, on that train ride, something remarkable happened: for a handful of hours, my brain *really* began to work.

Maybe it was the virtually empty first-class carriage, or the maximum 30 mph of the train's speed. Or maybe it was the endless flat gray vista outside the window (Rajasthan is the most boring desert I have ever seen), the long hours of the journey, or the months I had already endured in India, which, when combined, finally slowed me down enough so that I could really think. Or maybe I had simply had the ego and the intellect beaten out of me. Whatever it was, something opened up in my mind on that train ride like a flower in bloom. And long before I had ever *heard* of the zero-point field or a quantum basis for consciousness, a steady stream of ideas about the true nature of reality as various forms of light flowed seamlessly through my mind. Ideas that seemed solid enough that I made the effort to find a pen and paper and write them down.

Now, several years later—with a great deal of reading on current ideas of quantum physics under my belt—I have come to realize those ideas correspond to the cutting-edge of modern science to an uncanny degree. I find this rather startling, since I did not know about any of the latest discoveries of quantum physics at the time. Whatever happened on that train ride, I know one thing for sure: my mind received a solid dose of *in-formation,* a fundamental factor in nature that has the capacity to "inform" the recipient. When I read how Rupert Sheldrake's revelatory intuitions about "morphic resonance" fields had occurred while he was staying at an ashram in India, I found it easy to understand. There are few places left in the world where a person can calm the hubris of modern life enough to fish through the waters of the still pond for divine answers. In the age of rapid-fire digital sensibilities, countries like India may be our last link to a past age of contemplation and revelation. For this reason alone, India will continue to attract foreign interlopers like myself, to crash and burn upon its fabled shores. India is where you discover that it's what you *make* of the shipwreck that ultimately teaches you the most. Some days, I think this is the most important lesson I have ever learned.

TEN

The High Priest

Timothy Leary and the Legacies of the Psychedelic Age

A botanist I know (who does not take recreational drugs) believes that 30 million Americans took drugs between the 1960s and the 1990s, and that the visions the drug users had while in that altered state account for the utterly new sea-change of attitude that we find today at the end of the century: a deep and reverent regard for our planet and for those others out in space, for our environment, for the rain forest and both wild and domestic animals, for the idea that the Earth itself—Gaia—is breathing, has consciousness, and that all living beings, all rocks and plants and sentient beings are inextricably entangled; that we humans are now evolving to a higher plane of divine consciousness.

SOPHY BURNHAM, *THE ECSTATIC JOURNEY: THE TRANSFORMING POWER OF MYSTICAL EXPERIENCE*, 1997

My time in India impressed upon me the timeless nature of many of Hindu philosophical concepts, whose parallels within the emerging paradigm of the quantum sciences were becoming increasingly obvious to me. The fact that these metaphysical beliefs that originated in the Indus Valley thousands of years ago could still circulate and seem relevant to our modern age seemed incredible to me, and I could only marvel at their staying power.

However, the fact that all real knowledge of the preparation of Soma—the Hindu entheogen of the Vedas—has apparently been lost in the mists of time, while the philosophies it birthed and encouraged have remained, caused me to question if the ideas themselves are not more powerful than the entheogens that create them. A paradox that also exists in Western Philosophy, since the Eleusinian Mysteries and the use and preparation of kykeon lasted 2,000 years, only to disappear as well, while the ideas of the Greek Philosophers who participated in these Mysteries still continue to influence us.

Clearly there was a shift in perspective in our more "modern" human societies that caused us to abandon the use of sacred entheogens. Words, prayers, and ultimately scripture replaced the first-hand experience of the Divine that Soma and kykeon had provided, as we turned the pursuit of spirituality over to the priests and their "holy books." It has only been in the last hundred years that our (Western) society has begun to turn back to entheogens in an attempt to experience the sacred first-hand again, perhaps as a polar reaction to our science's bold assertion that any belief in spirituality is nothing more than superstition.

A Psychedelic Movement?

After Aldous Huxley's book *The Doors of Perception* reintroduced to popular culture the possibilities inherent in the spiritual use of entheogens, the "acid generation" of the sixties and early seventies was the most obvious large-scale rediscovery of the ritualized use of such compounds, while the current, much smaller-scale interest in ayahuasca and shamanism is the latest attempt at reasserting the sacred role of entheogens within our own society.

However, as Huston Smith points out in his book *Cleansing the Doors of Perception,* modern "psychedelic theophanies" have lacked substantial staying power. The fleeting nature of the experience itself, as mystical as it may be, is not enough to create "a movement," since a moment of spiritual understanding is not necessarily enough to ignite "a religious life."

Due in part to the repressed urges of the American youth of the mid-twentieth century, contemporary "psychedelic movements" have been portrayed as more hedonistic or utopian than spiritual or philosophical. But in the midsixties, when mescaline and LSD were still legal and readily available, the modern Western consciousness threw open the doors to the unknown—to the infinite—and we jumped in. Deep inside that experience, we realized that we were now swimming in a dimension we had somehow forgotten—one with tremendous new possibility for the future of humanity. But these were far deeper waters than the "modern" Western mind had ever swum in before, perhaps deeper than we could handle. And I believe we flinched.

We flinched in the face of that psychedelic vision of the infinite unknown because the minds of *that* generation—who were born before television, who were children when the atomic bomb was dropped, and whose lives had mostly been lived in terms of black and white—were ill-prepared for exploring those realms of vivid realization. They had been deprived of a mystical history for too many generations. The psychedelic experience was a brutal shock to the generation born after World War I, less than a century after the horse and cart. In William S. Burroughs' letters to Allen Ginsberg, for example, which describe his yagé experiences in 1953—perhaps the real beginning of the "psychedelic age"—much of what you read is terror: sheer terror and bafflement at the extreme and vivid nature of his seething ayahuasca visions.

By the time Dr. Timothy Leary's "Harvard experiment" and his provocative brand of pedagogy came around, we were clearly on the cusp of a new era of technology that promised to have a profound impact on the future exploration of the capacities of human consciousness. Aldous Huxley realized that mescaline and LSD had a unique potential to be important tools in reshaping the way we *understand* our psyche and that if we used them correctly, we could explore higher forms of consciousness. Timothy Leary, unfortunately, popularized the belief that LSD would reshape the psyche itself, and save us the job of worrying about it.

To further clarify, Huxley felt that if you took LSD, you were more likely to understand the metaphysical content of, for example, *The Tibetan Book of the Dead*. Through the many paths of knowledge, meditation, and "psychodelics" (the more etymologically correct term that Huxley commonly used), you could progress toward the higher realms of consciousness and understanding. Leary, on the other hand, promoted that LSD and the *Tibetan Book of the Dead* were basically the same thing. You didn't have to really think, you just had to drop acid, and society would change itself overnight. This cultural "enlightenment" clearly does not appear to have occurred, despite the pockets of sixties idealism that remain. (Although with over forty years of hindsight, psychedelics clearly *have* had an important impact on society.)

In Zen terminology, Leary made the mistake of "forgetting that the finger that points at the moon is not the moon."[1] In a position to lead the advance of our knowledge of inner space like no man in history before him, Leary instead—like every religious conman—promised enlightenment in a bottle, and then latched his own social and political aspirations onto the most ancient of ideas. Of all the principal characters that in one way or another created the so-called psychedelic revolution of the last fifty years, I find Dr. Timothy Francis Leary (1920–1996) to be by far the most paradoxical and confounding.

The High Priest

As a scientist and a psychologist, Leary has a most impressive resume. In his early work in psychology he published a complex and respected interpersonal circumplex model that is still used in psychology today. The timing that led him to Mexico to ingest magic mushrooms in 1960 before he began his research assignment at Harvard could not have been more propitious to the nascent psychedelic movement. Leary's subsequent oft-quoted statement that he learned more about psychology in the five hours on those mushrooms than he did in fifteen years of research and studying, drew the battle lines for the future emergence of what I will now dub the "mystical sciences" paradigm.

The early work that he and Richard Alpert did at Harvard largely produced solid scientific results, and studies like their Concord Prison experiment had the opportunity to produce real change from within the American system. In the prison study Leary gave psilocybin to prisoners in an attempt to reduce prison recidivism: 20 percent of the study's test group returned to prison after release, a reverse of the normal 80 percent. (These reported results have since been characterized as inaccurate.) Walter Pahnke's "Good Friday experiment," however, investigating the entheogenic effect of psilocybin on religiously predisposed subjects (with Leary as his principal academic advisor), remains one of the most intriguing experiments in the scientific study of religion ever performed in an American university (and its findings were supported by a 2006 study at Johns Hopkins University). Walter Huston Clark, a prominent psychologist wrote, "There are no experiments known to me in the history of the scientific study of religion better designed or clearer in their conclusions than this one."[2]

Leary was a Harvard professor; he had climbed the walls of the Ivy Tower and he was in a unique position to guide the use of psychedelics in research and psychology to hitherto unexplored regions of the human psyche. But before long, the temptations of glory as "the High Priest" of the exploding youth movement of the sixties proved too much for him. He was fired from Harvard for (allegedly) not turning up to lecture. While Leary has been deified as a counterculture icon, I can't help but feel that ultimately his own personal desire for fame damaged the counterculture movement as much as he did it any good. By losing his status at Harvard, and then preaching to the youth of America the mindless psychedelic propaganda that they only needed to "Turn On, Tune In, [and] Drop Out," he more than anyone was responsible for ensuring that psychedelics *could not become* instruments of mainstream interest—by being one of the high-profile vehicles for their eventual criminalization; instead of protecting them like the scientist and high priest he proclaimed himself to be.

LSD and the Beheading of the New Left

What we have to contemplate nevertheless is the possibility that the great American acid trip, no matter how distinctive of the rebellion of the 1960s it came to appear, was in fact the result of a despicable government conspiracy . . . if U.S. intelligence bodies collaborated in an effort to drug an entire generation of Americans, then the reason they did so was to disorient it, sedate it, and de-politicize it.

Carl Oglesby, former head of the
Students for a Democratic Society

Leary's paradoxical transformation from a Harvard scientist to a counterculture caricature raises some interesting and unsettling questions about the introduction and subsequent widespread use of psychedelics (and LSD in particular) in the sixties and about the ensuing effect that this enthusiastic LSD usage had both on various individuals and on the nascent politics of the New Left itself.

Among today's counterculture (and much of the popular culture) LSD is regarded as being one of the main (if not *the* main) agents of social change in the sixties. It is seen as fuel for the fire of change that America's youth embraced during that period and the source of much of that generation's creativity. The continued popularity of the Grateful Dead and the sixties acid culture into the twenty-first century could be considered nostalgia for those "days of the good acid." Acid's effect on the counterculture of the sixties is universally considered to have been a good thing—despite the occasional burnout along the way.

People tend to forget that members of the socialist student movement (such as the SDS—Students for a Democratic Society) in the United States were integrally involved in the victories of the Civil Rights movement in the late fifties and early sixties in the south and emerged from those years as a highly organized, politically mature, and battle-tested organization that would become known as the New Left. By 1965, thanks to the Vietnam War, they had a new front on which to fight. Social change had already become a priority among a significant portion of the youth at American universities, even before psychedelics were introduced.

We know that LSD was introduced to the colleges in the United States by the CIA—this is established fact.[3]

The common counterculture view of this historically provable fact is that this was a mistake and that the CIA unwittingly let the genie out of the bottle by introducing LSD to the already disgruntled youth culture. Personally, I don't buy into that view. The OSS had been experimenting with "mind-control" drugs since at least 1942. When it later became the CIA, it created a program in 1953 called MK-ULTRA, which studied the effects of various mind-altering compounds on different groups of the population. The CIA initially tried to buy a staggering ten *kilograms* of LSD from Sandoz, the Swiss pharmaceutical company that was Dr. Albert Hofmann's employer and the original supplier of LSD. While this staggering amount would have been enough to manufacture some *100 million doses,* it turned out that Sandoz had only manufactured some 40 grams of the compound to this point. Sandoz agreed to manufacture 100 grams a week for the CIA, and although it will probably never be known exactly how much LSD the CIA purchased from Sandoz, it is generally believed that Sandoz was unable to fulfill this commitment due to the difficulties of manufacturing LSD by their method. So in 1953, apparently wanting a larger supply of the compound and not trusting the Swiss company, the CIA convinced the American pharmaceutical company Eli Lilly (now the manufacturers of Prozac) to break the patent held by Sandoz. Significantly, Eli Lilly did so by coming up with a complicated twelve- to fifteen-step method that created the precursor for LSD (lysergic acid monohydrate) from chemicals available on the open market, as opposed to Sandoz's original method, which started with cultivated ergot-fungus to create ergotamine tartrate, a time-consuming process that produced only small batches of LSD at a time. Eli Lilly's new method effectively opened up the possibility of the mass-production of LSD. (They reputedly informed the CIA that they could manufacture "tons" of this compound if required.)

During the period that Sandoz was supplying the CIA directly, and then later the FDA, the CIA were aware of—and approved all—LSD sales by Sandoz. Therefore it is not inaccurate to say that *virtually all* the LSD consumed between the early 1950s and 1965 (when Sandoz stopped manufacturing LSD)—whether it was by Al Hubbard, Tim Leary, Wavy Gravy, Ken Kesey, or anyone else who gained access to the drug—was in fact "CIA-approved acid." Considering the fact that the OSS-CIA had been studying the effects of "mind-control" compounds like LSD since the days of World War II, I believe that they had a pretty good idea of what would happen if they released several million hits of LSD into the country over eight years: that the political center of the student movement would fall apart. The CIA couldn't have predicted the "acid-tests," the Summer of Love, or Woodstock, but they certainly could have "modeled" the subsequent political collapse of the U.S. student anti-war movement.*

The effect of LSD on the ego has been likened to the effect of hard

*The American ghettos were similarly flooded with destructive and highly addictive drugs at the same time as radical black political groups like the Black Panthers appeared. As William S. Burroughs has pointed out, the U.S. government was involved in illegal wars in Indochina in the 1970s, when the ghettos were flooded with heroin, and then in illegal wars in Central and South America in the 1980s, when the ghettos were flooded with cocaine.

exercise on muscle. LSD shreds the ego, but—just as a muscle rebuilds larger and stronger after being "torn down" by hard exercise—so too can the ego actually *strengthen* after years of repetitive high-dosage LSD use. This would explain a lot about the egomaniacal blowouts of the apparent leadership of the "psychedelic movement"—Leary immediately leaps to mind, while Tom Wolfe also portrays the other great LSD advocate of the day, Ken Kesey, as something of a control freak in *The Electric Kool-Aid Acid Test.* Similar fallout was also documented among the leadership of the SDS, which by 1968 was splintering from a cohesive whole into numerous competing factions. This foreshadowed the total disintegration of the so-called youth movement, which by the start of the seventies was almost completely headless. In the wake of its subsequent collapse after the end of the Vietnam War, the major universities and their student bodies have been virtually apolitical ever since.

Leary and the CIA

This brings me back to the paradox of Dr. Timothy Leary, who was undoubtedly responsible for helping to significantly change American culture with his snappy acid propaganda, and who, ironically, may have been a pawn of the CIA and their own plans, whether he knew it or not. We will probably never know the extent of Tim Leary's knowledge of the CIA's involvement in the introduction of LSD into American society, but Leary's numerous relationships with individuals involved in the CIA raises a number of unsettling questions and possibilities.

In 1947, while acting as the California state delegation leader at the national convention of the American Veterans Committee (AVC), Leary met Cord Meyer, a man that Leary would later credit for "helping me understand my political-cultural role more clearly." By late 1950, Meyer was a full-blown member of the CIA and was soon put in charge of its International Relations Division, whose expressed purpose was to covertly finance, infiltrate, and encourage noncommunist liberal movements and institutions such as labor unions, creative-academic societies, and student groups (including the SDS). Over a decade later, Leary would continue to be involved with Meyer's ex-wife, Mary Meyer, who was having an affair with President John F. Kennedy at the time and whom Leary (and numerous others) believe introduced Kennedy to LSD.* In 1964 she would be shot to death, execution style, in a murder that was never solved. Cord Meyer himself, when asked six weeks before he died of cancer who had killed his ex-wife, hissed "the same bastards who killed Kennedy."

From the fifties onward, the CIA gave over $25 million dollars (through a front organization called The Society for Human Ecology) to Harvard and other universities to study the effects of psychedelic drugs.[4] In an interview about the chemist Nick Sand, Leary also makes mention of the fact that the OSS-CIA was distributing LSD to hospitals in the late fifties and early sixties.[5] So Leary clearly *did* know, at least in part, of the CIA's involvement in these psychedelic research programs—the question is *when* did he realize that.

Numerous other strange connections between Leary and the murky world of the CIA also exist. In the late sixties Leary would live for two years in the headquarters of an LSD-smuggling cartel called "the Brotherhood of Eternal Love" who distributed the notorious Orange Sunshine acid. This group was controlled by a mysterious character called Ronald Stark, who reputedly turned up at the Brotherhood of Eternal Love compound with a *kilogram* of pure LSD . . . an amount far in excess to what had been known to be produced in the world at that time. (The famous underground chemist Owsley Stanley, for example, is thought to have produced only a half-kilo of LSD in his entire career.) While the Brotherhood of Love chemists Nick Sand and Tim Scully would be responsible for the production of an estimated 3.9 million doses of LSD between 1965 and 1969, Stark was reputedly responsible for the importation of 80 to 200 *million* doses of acid from his labs in Europe![6] Stark, who had numerous connections with paramilitary groups around the world, including Italy's Red Brigade and the Palestinian Liberation Organization (PLO), would later be arrested in Italy and then released by the Italian High Court judge on the grounds that he had been a CIA agent since 1960. Leary himself says he never met Stark, who disappeared without a trace, but interestingly the Brotherhood of Eternal Love funds were channeled through Castle Bank in the Bahamas, which was a known CIA "proprietary." It

*The Kennedy family was no stranger to LSD. Robert Kennedy's wife Ethel had undergone LSD therapy for alcoholism.

also seems highly unlikely that *any* of the LSD chemists of this period—including Owsley, Nick Sand, Tim Scully, or Ronald Stark—would have been able to obtain the large amounts of lysergic acid monohydrate that was required for such large-scale operations without the CIA knowing about it, considering their historical interest in the production and supply of these chemicals.

In 1970, Leary would be imprisoned for marijuana, stemming from an earlier arrest in 1968. His initial sentencing was for thirty years (for a total of half an ounce between the two offences—his second "bust" was for two joints), and the publicity of his original trial in 1966 would lead to a widespread media campaign about the dangers of the out-of-control use of LSD among the youth of America. Leary was liberated from the minimum-security prison he was incarcerated in by members of the Weather Underground, the most radical of the groups of the American New Left, who had been paid to spring Leary by the Brotherhood of Eternal Love (with funds drawn from the same Castle Bank in the Bahamas). Leary would pledge solidarity to the group and release a provocative "POW statement" that declared (among other things) that "to shoot a genocidal robot policeman in the defense of life is a sacred act. . . . Total war is upon us"—further turning American opinion against the New Left (and the menace of LSD). Leary escaped to Algeria where he and his wife Rosemary would be held virtual hostages for the next three years by Eldridge Cleaver and the Black Panthers, who apparently did not trust him.

They escaped to Switzerland, where Leary would then spend two years living the life of a jet setter before being kidnapped in Afghanistan by U.S. agents. He was returned to the United States, where he was convicted on weapons charges and incarcerated in Folsom Prison. President Nixon had described Leary as "the world's most dangerous man," and bail was set at five million dollars—at that time the highest sum ever. Leary would then turn State's evidence against the Weathermen Underground, the very organization that had liberated him. After spending three years in jail, he would later be pardoned in 1976 by then California governor Jerry Brown.

Although Leary claims that he never provided the government with any significant information—a claim that members of the Weathermen themselves agree with—the fact that the FBI revealed him as a government informant, code-named Charlie Thrush, caused him to be publically condemned by the likes of Abbie Hoffman, Allen Ginsberg, and Jerry Rubin. (Rubin called Leary's press conference after his release "the death of the sixties.") Others such as William S. Burroughs, Ken Kesey, and John Sinclair, the leader of the White Panther Party, would conclude that Leary had been involved in a CIA plot to discredit the New Left through the distribution of LSD all along. Upon his release he faced numerous death threats and then found himself ironically placed under police protection through the Witness Protection Program for a number of years.

By the end of the seventies, with the movement fading into memory, Leary would distance himself from the government and his old associates, his counterculture reputation now in tatters. A reputation that only suffered when early in the Reagan years he "debated" G. Gordon Liddy, the Watergate burglar who had once busted him at Millbrook, on a highly publicized nation-wide tour.* By the end of the eighties, with cocaine the main drug of choice among the "Greed Generation" and LSD now regarded (along with marijuana) as a hippie-throwback for burn-outs and losers, Leary seemed like a desperate publicity seeker and political lightweight whose star had long since faded.

To this day Leary's ties with the CIA continue to be vigorously debated, with numerous sites in the Internet dedicated to the possibilities. Leary's friends and supporters claim that he deliberately misled interviewers for his own amusement (such as in the notorious 1978 *High Times* interview) and that such accusations are absurd, while others point to the numerous close connections and say where there is smoke, there must be fire. Leary himself issued various contradictory statements, from saying that the CIA "never gave him a dime"[7] to claiming that "the liberal CIA are the best mafia you can deal with in the twentieth century."[8] There can be no doubt however that Leary was undoubtedly an elitist, and his infatuation with the intelligentsia within the fifties and sixties intelligence community is obvious, and

*As a side note, Leary's former associate Cord Meyer is one of the prime suspects for the identity of the infamous Deep Throat, *Washington Post* reporter Bob Woodward's key "intelligence community" source. Ben Bradlee, who was Cord Meyer's brother-in-law, and the person who identified Mary Meyer's dead body, was the editor of the *Washington Post.*

no more so than in the following statement from a speech that Leary gave at a meeting of the American Psychological Association in Los Angeles, August 15, 1994, at a symposium titled "Interpersonal Theory and the Interpersonal Circumplex: Tim Leary's Legacy."[9]

In this commentary, Leary begins by noting some of the people who influenced him and says, "And now let us toast Harry Murray, a founding father of the OSS-CIA, by the way," and then, "Another delightful thing about many of these Harvard people, particularly Harry Murray, was their cultural scholarship and aesthetic sensitivity—their interest in the psychology of art and literature. No question about it, Harry Murray was much more interested in Herman Melville than in the Wechsler-Bellevue. Over his office-house on Divinity Avenue he mounted the figure of a white whale."

Considering the high regard Leary clearly held for Harvard men like Harry Murray—and considering the fact that in the fifties and sixties both the CIA and the British Secret Service conducted most of their recruiting from the top universities—it certainly would not seem to be an outlandish stretch of the imagination to believe that Leary at least came to the attention of these same "spook" recruiters in those tumultuous days. And there is no doubt that in becoming the ego-maniacal Captain Ahab of his generation, Leary turned LSD into the twentieth century's own version of the legendary white whale.

Tim Leary's Redemption: The High Scientist Returns

Leary was always a futurist of note. In the sixties he attempted to create a new "typewriter" tool that could be used in real-time to describe the DMT experience,[10] while in the eighties he was on the vanguard of trying to recreate the psychedelic experience through sound-and-light shows, using the latest in electronic gear. He was a huge advocate of computer technology and a disciple of the idea that the human race was destined to go into outer space—so much so, he actually ridiculed the ecology movement that LSD itself undoubtedly helped to create. With the advent of the Internet, which Leary called the LSD of the nineties, Tim Leary was presented with an opportunity for redemption, an opportunity that he characteristically, and very publically, grabbed with both hands. He had one of the first websites on the World Wide Web and was an early proponent of virtual reality; a generation that read *WIRED* instead of *Rolling Stone* would come to know him as one of the pioneers of a new technological age.

As the era of Reagan/Bush was put to rest, and a former sixties draft-dodger who admitted he had tried to smoke weed but didn't inhale became the next president, nostalgia for the hippie era became fashionable. With the publication of his memoirs titled *Flashbacks,* the always media-savvy Leary found himself back in the public eye. As his stock rose with the tide of nostalgia, and he once again became something of an icon, Leary rubbed shoulders with much younger movie stars in his home in the Hollywood Hills and surrounded himself with computer-savvy Gen X'ers who had barely been born when he had advocated that their parents "Turn On, Tune In," and "Drop Out." Only now his message and philosophy was taken from William Gibson rather than Aldous Huxley, and the Internet was the New Revolution.

It is said that time mellows nearly everyone, and while some luminaries like Hunter S. Thompson and Owsley continued to disparage Leary's contribution to the psychedelic era, most of his contemporaries forgot and forgave, remembering only the best of what he had done. When Leary announced a few months after the death of legendary Grateful Dead guitarist Jerry Garcia in 1995 that he had been diagnosed with cancer, he received a worldwide show of support and attention; and when he died the following year, it was regarded as the end of an era, the likes of which will probably never be seen again. Ever the showman, Leary had long claimed that he wished to be stored cryogenically when he died; but he changed his mind about this in his last days, and later seven grams of his ashes were shot into outer space in a rocket (along with *Star Trek* creator Gene Roddenberry). With that final act, Timothy Leary's reputation and his place in history were effectively deified in a manner that he would have undoubtedly found immensely satisfying.

Leary and the Tibetan Book of the Dead

Apart from his immortal acid-propaganda, Timothy Leary's enduring contribution to the entheogenic world will undoubtedly be his book (with Richard Alpert and Ralph Metzner) *The Psychedelic Experience: A Manual Based on the Tibetan Book of the Dead,* which is the most notable attempt at establishing a "psychedelic religious philosophy" from that period. I personally find it somewhat paradoxical that a futurist like Leary looked to the past and the Tibetans—metaphysically passing the buck, so to speak—rather than seizing on the unique technological opportunity that LSD represented and carefully developing an effective way of exploring its transformative potential from within our own sciences.

However, I must note that I *agree* with Dr. Leary's assessment that *The Tibetan Book of the Dead* can be an effective metaphor for understanding the psychedelic experience. What I find strange is that a man as brilliant and innovative as Dr. Leary effectively turned his back on seeking parallels to the emerging psychedelic experience in the newly emerging sciences of the day (especially consciousness research and the new physics). As an innovative and well-published psychologist, Leary more than anyone was heir to the respect and interest that Aldous Huxley's reputation had (at that point) generated for psychedelics among the academic world; and by being in the employ of Harvard, he should have been introducing the psychedelic experience to the curiosity of these same new sciences and thus transforming the scientific community from within. But by opening the door to a mimicry of established mystical practices, he turned psychedelics into the first of the New Age cults. Thanks to the flaws of his own personality and the power of his own egomania, he was largely responsible for ensuring that LSD has not been studied in a scientific manner since he was fired from the very institution that was capable of integrating LSD into the core of our spirituality, science, and society.

That first modern entheogenic generation was thus encouraged by its self-proclaimed "High Priest" to go looking for answers in the past and in other cultures instead of confronting the future head on; soon Allen Ginsberg, the Beatles, and countless others were following Leary's lead, unleashing a plethora of fake gurus and false hopes upon the Western world. This fascination with ancient Eastern philosophies would cause a significant percentage of the Western youth to question the flaws of the Judeo-Christian society and ultimately would change the nature of American culture in ways that could never have been imagined only a decade before. But a thoroughly modern opportunity for the integration of entheogens into our society slipped away. Psychedelics were made illegal and banished from further study, forcibly sent underground and criminalized. By the time Leary was imprisoned, escaped the country, was extradited, reimprisoned, and ultimately pardoned and disgraced, LSD's day in the sun was over. For the wealth-obsessed generation that followed, its use was derided as nothing more than a hippy throw-back, while its epiphanies were reduced to the status of merely "tripping," nothing more than a brief escape from reality. In the brutal years that followed the demise of the hopes and dreams of the sixties, the counterculture would turn toward the destructive allure of amphetamines, cocaine, opiates, and benzodiazepines—any "feel good" or "feel nothing" drug, which was preferred over an opening of the mind.

Nevertheless, the shockwave of that entheogenic injection reverberated through the human consciousness, and it would affect the emerging technologies of mass-produced sound and visuals in a manner that could have never been predicted. Some folks believe that this shockwave can ultimately be credited with the seeds of inspiration that grew into the creation of the Internet, which many now believe will end up being the most revolutionarily transformative technology in human history.[11]

The roots of every multicolored psychedelic image you see printed or broadcast each day and each weird electronic sound you hear are embedded in the use of LSD (or something similar), even if the person who created that image or sound has never touched a visionary drug. Psychedelic lingo has even penetrated contemporary vernacular, with the descriptive word "trippy" now in common use by people who have never touched an illegal drug of any kind; while today's youth generation attempt to describe the visual effects of smoking DMT by making reference to acid-inspired video games and computer animation.

Entheogens (or psychedelics, to be more historically correct) have now been recognized as the mother of our Western ecology and conservation movements, as well as the entire field of transpersonal psychology and our apparent desire to return to some firsthand spiritual and/or mystical understanding of G/d (rather than blindly accepting traditional religious dogma without an experiential basis). As a modern agent of societal transformation, the obvious effectiveness of LSD can no longer be denied. Yet now, more than forty years after the Summer of Love and even though Leary himself abandoned much of what he preached in the sixties for the "new acid" of the Internet, still we are overrun with antique gurus and New Age philosophies. And what remains of the so-called counterculture seems obsessed with them. Everyone knows all about astrology, tantra, crystals, and the tarot, but far fewer people seem interested in quantum physics, DNA, or particle-accelerators, which were born out of the same Western sciences that invented LSD. How many hours have you spent speculating about the Mayan calendar's "end of time?" And when was the last time you and your friends discussed the latest findings of the Hubble Space Telescope over a joint? You get the point.

Science versus Speculation

Thanks to the construction of incredible instruments like space-based telescopes and particle accelerators over the past two decades, cutting-edge science is providing a plethora of factual discoveries that are as fascinating and potentially mind-blowing as the wildest speculations of any mystic or madman. These inventions have provided us with proven and exhaustively verified discoveries that should be at the center of our conversations about the nature of our universe and our reality. But thanks to the schism between the universities and the "New-Age" counterculture that occurred during the social fall-out of the sixties, it frequently seems that scientific achievements are viewed either with a certain skepticism or with total disinterest by the New Age movement; whereas often ridiculous speculation gets bandied around like hard evidence throughout our popular culture. I find this situation extremely perplexing and can only assume that it has something to do with the way the two types of information—science and speculation—are presented. It seems to me that a lot of people took Tim Leary's advice—Turn On, Tune In, Drop Out—as some kind of reasoning to turn their backs on the findings of *all* modern science, which is highly ironic if you consider the fact that science has now entered the most fascinating and mystical paradigm that it has ever encountered.

Take, as an example, the current search for the presence of pressure waves in the cosmic vacuum (the zero-point field). Astronomers in NASA's Chandra X-ray Observatory recently found such a wave generated by the supermassive black hole in the Perseus cluster of galaxies, some 250 million light years from earth. What is incredible to me is that this vacuum-pressure wave translates into the musical note B-flat.[12] This is a very real note that has been traveling through space for the past 2.5 billion years. Our ears cannot perceive it, since its frequency is 57 octaves below middle C—more than a million billion (!) times deeper than the limits of human hearing—but it is a proven fact that this wave exists, and I cannot help but wonder if those scientists have not accidentally found Aum, the original note of creation.

Personally I find speculation about this very real discovery a lot more interesting than, let's say, the counterculture's current fascination with December 21, 2012—but how many of you out there have even heard about this modern scientific discovery? How many of you are willing to read enough to try and understand it, instead of speculating, without any proof or shred of evidence, on the Mayan calendar, or psychic transmissions from Pleiades, the lost tribes of Atlantis, or some other popular science-fiction fantasy? It seems to me that these days our attention spans are so short that we fear anything that requires intellectual complexity or the necessity of verifying the accuracy of our information. Speculation has its place—and there is plenty of it in this book—but it should be understood to be just that—speculation—and not confused with hard facts that have earned the right to represent the truth. This is a lesson that can be applied not only to science, but many other arenas (i.e., politics) in our lives as well, since we only have to look at the mess that the Bush administration made of the world by preferring speculation rather than the facts when making its decisions. As George Clinton so succinctly put it, "You can't afford free speech, so you might as well pay attention."

I believe that this is the enduring legacy of Dr. Timothy Leary. This so-called High Priest was also supposed to be our High Scientist; he more than anyone was in a unique position to integrate entheogens into our society as an instrument of change and discovery, but he fumbled that responsibility. His folly resulted in the relegation of these sacraments to the status of cultish intoxicants and unleashed a culture of pseudo-science and pseudo-religion as people search for the same chance at meaning that entheogens briefly provided them in the sixties. Now, in this burgeoning New Age—this age of deliberately enticing *mis-information*—any ridiculous conspiracy or theory is happily circulated.

If we are ever going to come up with a modern philosophy of life that is practical, makes sense, and embraces the uses of entheogens, it has to have its basis in the solid discoveries of *our* time. We can look at other cultures, other mythologies, and we can learn, but we also have to incorporate the incredible knowledge that contemporary culture is generating at an astonishing rate about the nature of the universe and this mystery we call "reality."

A modern entheogenic philosophy needs to be a syncretic one. It can use the lessons in ancient texts and the timeless truths that they reveal, but it must build on that inherited knowledge with new perspectives and new discoveries. We cannot do this by burying ourselves in the past, or by solely following another culture's traditional practices—or even worse, the watered down "New Age" interpretations of those practices. The parallels between modern scientific views and ancient wisdoms are well documented, but no single scientist, shaman, or rock 'n' roll Rinpoche is going to save us. If there is a new doctrine to be written, then *we* must write it, based on current experiences.

That which has been lost to Western civilization—the mysteries of kykeon, Soma, and other sacraments that disappeared into the mists of time and the inspiration they offered their cultures and philosophies—must be rebuilt. But they must be rebuilt in an image reflective of today's times and used as a tool in our search for a spirituality fused with our science and cosmology. As a result of my own explorations, I now believe that the quantum viewpoint of the world is as important to our hopes for a better, more peaceful existence as the Buddhist viewpoint. Particle-accelerators and quantum computers can prove to be just as revelatory of the mystical experience as entheogens are, and our future spirituality must embrace *all* knowledge that leads us toward a greater understanding of reality. For while our society's infatuation with science has undoubtedly gotten us into much of the mess that humanity now finds itself in, the way out does not lie by solely looking back to the past. There are no gurus anymore, and those who claimed to be gurus failed us. We would be wise to recognize this, since we are the ones who will have to save ourselves.

ELEVEN

The Zero-Point Field and the 5MDE

A Quantum Explanation

The evidence that surfaces, surprising as it may be, indicates that our brain is not limited to the neural processes that go on . . . within our cranium—it is a wide-band receiver and high-powered processor of information. This information it receives originates not only in our own body, but comes from all over the world. The brain's ten billion neurons, with 10,000 connections each, constitute the most complex system of electronic organization in the known universe. This system, which operates at the edge of chaos, receives and transforms information from our own body, as well as the electromagnetic, acoustic, and other wave fields in our environment. It also receives and decodes information from more subtle fields, including the vacuum's zero-point holofield. Potentially, our brain connects us with the wide reaches of the cosmos.

As mystics, prophets, and people of insight and sensitivity intuited through the ages, our brain is an integral part of the universe, and our mind is a potentially open window on it. It is up to us to throw open that window, to the full extent of our remarkable, but hitherto largely unexploited, physical and mental capacities.

Ervin Laszlo, *3rd Millennium: The Challenge and the Vision—The Club of Budapest Report on Creative Paths of Human Evolution,* 1997

It is within the the theories regarding this "inexhaustible energy sea," which scientists now call the zero-point field, that I have been able to find some potential answers to the puzzling questions I posed at the beginning of chapter five. I will now examine each of these questions individually and attempt a "quantum explanation" for each particular aspect of the 5-MeO-DMT experience.

1. What Is the Source of the Brilliant Laser-like Light That I Encounter?

"Instead of an absolute space and time filled with an ether that sustains the epiphenomenon of light, light becomes the fundamental thing whose propagation determines the flow of time and the measure of distance. We can almost say that light creates space-time. I suggest here that light, in the form of a universal electromagnetic zero-point field, also creates and sustains the world of matter that fills space-time. Thus the words, "Let there be light," may express more than a poetic mythology after all.

BERNARD HAISCH, *THE GOD THEORY*, 2006

"With all your science can you tell how it is, and whence it is, that light comes into the soul?"

HENRY DAVID THOREAU, *JOURNAL*, JULY 16, 1851

Numerous modern writers, such as Thom Hartmann in *The Last Hours of Ancient Sunlight: The Fate of the World and What We Can Do Before It's Too Late,* have pointed out that we are in fact made up of light: every atom in our body (and our world) originated in the last gasp of a dying star, which threw the remains of its energy out into the galaxy in a cloud of rare elements. Our own sun creates and sustains life on this planet through its daily bombardment of solar energy. The energy from the food we eat is essentially stored sunlight, while the fossil fuels that we've tapped to create the Industrial Revolution and our consumer society are the culmination of millions of years of sunlight stored in the Earth (a vast sea of irreplaceable stored energy, which soon we will have managed to exhaust—taking only a little over two hundred years to do so).

We are beings of light, created and sustained by a star. Every culture has intuitively recognized this and credited that light as the source of our own divine nature. Creation mythology, common through much of humankind's history, credits the birth of material reality out of a void or darkness, from which a divine spark of light leapt forth. The ancient Egyptians (c. 3000 BCE) believed that a person possessed a body of flesh and a body of light. Each body needed the other in order to function as a human, with the body of light animating and "correcting" the physical body. The Tibetans assert that in the bardos—the intermediary states between dying and rebirth—we possess a body of light with which we can cross time and space as fast as a thought.

Mystics since the beginning of time have attributed an understanding of the Divine to knowledge of that light, and the two have become inexorably entwined. References to the divine nature of light are especially prevalent in the esoteric Eastern philosophies of Hindu and Buddhist teachings, but there are also numerous examples to be found within the Jewish Kabbalah, Greek Hermeticism, Gnosticism, Islamic Sufism, and in the New Testament. The following teachings attributed to Jesus himself clearly express that this was his belief: ". . . God, the blessed and only Ruler, the King of kings and Lord of lords, who alone is immortal and who lives in unapproachable light, whom no one has seen or can see" (Timothy 6). The gospel of John states Christ's philosophy irrevocably, "This is the message we have heard from him and declare to you: God is light; in him there is no darkness at all (1 John 1:5).

My experiences with 5-MeO-DMT have led me to believe that when our consciousness is freed of the constraints of matter and mass, it spontaneously returns to the universal ground state of light, where it ultimately recognizes the true nature of reality as union with that light: union with G/d. According to Stanislav Grof, the premier researcher of transpersonal states, this experience of recognition of the divine nature of light is not unusual among entheogen users. He asserts that in his experience (now of over fifty years) of administering LSD or holotropic breathing sessions:

> Time after time, people compared the Absolute to a radiant source of light of unimaginable intensity, though they emphasized that it also differed in some significant aspects from any forms of light that we

> know in the material world. To describe the Absolute as light entirely misses some of its essential characteristics, particularly the fact that it also is an immense and unfathomable field of consciousness endowed with infinite intelligence and creative power.[1]

Interestingly enough, this idea is consistent with some of the discoveries being made about the zero-point field in relation to one of the great mysteries of biology—the level of communication that must exist almost simultaneously between individual genes and cells to allow them to operate in unison, along with the process by which the DNA instructs the construction of a living entity.

According to Lynne McTaggart, "Each cell undergoes, on average, some 100,000 chemical reactions per second—a process that repeats itself simultaneously across every cell in the body. At any given second, billions of chemical reactions of one sort or another occur. Timing must be exquisite, for if any one of the individual chemical processes in all the millions of cells in the body is off by a fraction, humans would blow themselves up in a matter of seconds."[2] But we don't.

In the seventies, German physicist Fritz-Albert Popp discovered an extraordinary thing: all life-forms emit a weak light. There is some evidence that the source of this light, which Popp called biophoton emission, may be generated from the DNA in all living cells. Popp believes that this light exhibits the highest level of order, quantum coherence, which allows subatomic particles to cooperate and communicate with each other. By resonating in harmony through their shared electromagnetic waves, they begin acting like a single larger wave and a single larger subatomic particle. The greater the coherence, the greater the communication between the individual particles, which virtually cease to be individual particles at all, since they are now all in synch with each other.

Popp proposed that this organization occurs at the quantum level by means of the biophotons resonating in coherence with the zero-point field. According to him, "each molecule in the universe [has] a unique frequency and the language it [uses] to speak to the world [is] a resonating wave."[3] This means that it isn't the physical matter of the body (i.e., the chemicals) that causes a reaction; rather, it is the unique low frequency electromagnetic waves of subatomic particles resonating with the zero-point field that causes a reaction. This is the medium that allows all the molecules in the body (and the universe) to communicate nonlocally with each other, virtually instantaneously.

The mechanism within the body by which this is theorized to be possible is called "superradiance." This theory about the nature of human consciousness postulates that biophoton light "pulses" through the body via microtubules (the scaffolding of the cells), which resonate in coherence with each other, thus allowing the cells in the body to communicate instantaneously. These microtubules represent

> the Internet of the body. Every neuron of the brain [can] log on at the same time and speak to every other neuron simultaneously via the quantum processes within. . . . [Superradiance] would provide an explanation for the instantaneous operation of our brains, which occurs at between one ten-thousandth and one-thousandth of a second, requiring that information be transmitted at 100–1000 metres per second . . .[4]

Popp believes that, at the quantum level, the subatomic particles in our bodies (particularly the particles in our DNA) are acting with such singular unity that we actually emit a weak coherent light. Jeremy Narby has suggested that the images seen while under the influence of ayahuasca are the result of this biophotonic light emission from our DNA, which makes it possible for shamans to access a vast library of common planetary knowledge being shared between all living things in this Gaian web of biophoton emissions. As Narby points out, a laser uses this same sort of coherence to achieve its brilliance of light and color—the strength of the source itself is not important. Biophoton emission within our own bodies is thus a logical possibility as the source of the laser-like light I regularly encounter. But it wouldn't necessarily help to explain the similarities between the 5MDE and the near-death experience, with their common "tunnel of light" and the feeling of crossing through a gate into a new locality. However, further examination of quantum biophotonic coherence with consideration of the zero-point field opens the door to some deeper possibilities.

From the amount that I have read about the current emerging scientific views, I think it is safe to say that we are entering a new paradigm in which the isolated mechanical universe of Newton, Descartes, and Darwin is about to be replaced by the interconnected "enchanted" cosmos hinted at by Nicola Tesla and Albert Einstein, predicted by David Bohm, and now being realized by Hal Puthoff, Bernard Haisch, Ervin Laszlo and others. At the center of this shift is the experiential evidence amassing for the phenomena of coherence, which is evident throughout the universe at every level, from the very great to the very small. In the following passage Ervin Laszlo explains the special properties of this new form of coherence:

> The findings of coherence at various scales of size and complexity in nature, from quanta, the smallest identifiable units of the physical world, to galactic macrostructures, the largest units, is not the finding of the standard form of coherence. The standard form is observed in optical interference experiments. Ordinary light sources are coherent—show an interference pattern—over a distance of a few meters, since the phase coherence of radiation from the same source lasts only 10 nanoseconds. Lasers, microwaves, and other technological light sources remain coherent for considerably longer and hence over greater distances. But the kind of coherence now coming to light is more complex and remarkable than the standard form, even if in this form, too, phase relationships remain constant and processes and rhythms are harmonized. The pertinent kind of coherence shows a quasi-instant correlation of the parts or elements of a system in space as well as time. All parts of a system of this coherence are correlated in such a way that what happens in and to one of the system's parts also happens in and to all its other parts, and hence it happens in and to the system as a whole. In consequence the parts respond to the "rest of the world" as a whole, maintain themselves as a whole, and change and evolve as a whole. This kind of coherence also obtains in the sphere of the mind. It is recognized in quantum physics but has no realistic explanation, and it is mainly anomalous at the macroscopic level: the current paradigm of local action and interaction cannot account for it.[5]

According to Laszlo, more than anything it is the surprising discovery of this new form of coherence that is challenging the existing scientific paradigm:

> For the pertinent findings speak of a hitherto unsuspected form and level of coherence in nature. . . . Such connections seem to obtain over all finite distances and finite times, and they suggest that the "nonlocality" discovered in the microscopic domain of the quantum may extend into the macroscopic domains of life, mind, and cosmos. Nature, it appears, is made up as a nested hierarchy of nonlocally connected coherent systems.[6]

The most interesting thing to me, in relation to the 5MDE, is the fact that the light present in biophoton emission and superradiance is assumed to originate *from within the zero-point field.* Coherence with the zero-point field posits an explanation for the amazing coherence of the *body,* where trillions of cells (far more than the number of stars in the Milky Way) and millions of antibodies, "coexist at [any] given time [to] produce thousands of biochemical reactions in the body each and every second, and they are all precisely and almost instantly coordinated so that they maintain the dynamic order of the whole organism."[7] It could explain the amazing coherence of the *universe,* where even its basic parameters, "[the] mass of elementary particles, the number of particles, and the forces that exist between them are all adjusted to favor specific harmonic ratios (such as the ration 10^{40}) that recur over and over again."[8] Most importantly for my search, coherence with the zero-point field may explain the amazing coherence of the *mind,* with consciousness itself being a result of the highest possible form of coherence—a "Bose–Einstein condensate"—present in the neural matter of our brain.

A Bose–Einstein condensate is a singular quantum state first predicted by physicist Satyendra Nath Bose, with Albert Einstein, in which bosons (identical particles that share quantum states) confined in an external potential and cooled to temperatures very near to absolute zero collapse (or "condense") into the lowest accessible quantum state, resulting in a new form of matter. (The best way of understanding this is to imagine these bosons as millions upon millions of compass needles circling individually around and around, each with an independent magnetic north. A Bose–Einstein condensate forms when *all* the compass needles suddenly find the same position, and *all* point in the same direction. When this happens, each compass [boson] essentially no longer retains its own identity or individuality, and *all* the compass needles [bosons] can effectively be regarded as being *one.*)

In her pioneering work, *The Quantum Self: Human Nature and Consciousness Defined by the New Physics,* Danah Zohar (with the collaboration of her husband, I. N. Marshall) develops the hypothesis that consciousness is the result of a quantum-level coherence between the neural matter of the brain and the zero-point field (which she refers to by the early term "quantum vacuum"). In searching for a way to explain the mystery of the "unbroken wholeness" of human consciousness (i.e., the way we can perceive dozens of different thoughts and inputs, yet integrate them seemingly instantaneously into a singular "I" experience), Zohar identifies the unique capabilities of materials that are in "condensed phase." Being in "condensed phase" means that all the fields and atoms in the material "line-up" and act as one, which could be a possible mechanism for the brain's ability to achieve a similar coherence of thought. Materials in a condensed phase include such things as super-conductors, super-fluids, laser light, electric current in metals, and sound waves in crystals.

One problem with this idea is that super-fluids and super-conductors only work at temperatures around absolute zero. So how could such a system exist in the substantially warmer environment of a living biological system? According to Zohar, there is one system known to exist in biological systems, "the pumped system" first described by Professor Herbert Fröhlich in the seventies, which seems to satisfy the necessary criteria. Zohar writes:

> Fröhlich's pumped system is simply a system of vibrating, electrically charged molecules (dipoles—positive at one end and negative at the other) into which energy is pumped. As they jiggle, the vibrating dipoles (molecules in the cell walls of living tissue) emit electromagnetic vibrations [virtual photons], just like so many miniature radio transmitters. Fröhlich demonstrated that beyond a certain threshold, any additional energy pumped into the system causes its molecules to vibrate in unison. They do so increasingly until they pull themselves into the most ordered form of condensed phase possible—a Bose–Einstein condensate.
>
> The crucial distinguishing feature of Bose–Einstein condensates is that the many parts that go to make up an ordered system not only *behave* as a whole, they *become* whole; their identities merge or overlap in such a way that they lose their individuality entirely.[9]

Zohar points out that Fröhlich-type systems are found only in biological tissue, although no one has the slightest clue why. According to Ervin Laszlo: "Living tissue is a 'Bose–Einstein condensate': a form of matter in which quantum-type processes, hitherto believed to be limited to the microscopic domain, occur at macroscopic scales. That they do has been verified in 1995, in experiments for which the physicists Eric A. Cornell, Wolfgang Ketterle, and Carl E. Wieman received the 2001 Nobel Prize. The experiments show that under certain conditions, seemingly separate particles and atoms interpenetrate as waves."[10]

Zohar tells us that it has been hypothesized "that one of the fields within the [zero-point field] is thought to be a coherent Bose–Einstein condensate, that is, a condensate with the same physics as the ground state of human consciousness."[11] Another way of saying this is to say that the coherence of the waves of the zero-point field is thought to operate under the same principles as human consciousness: "Further, excitations (fluctuations) of this coherent vacuum condensate appear to have the same mathematics as the excitations of our own Fröhlich-style Bose–Einstein condensate."[12] So our atoms are resonating with the vibration of the quantum vacuum.

Thus the quantum mechanism of consciousness is hypothesized to operate something like this: quantum particles present in the neural cell walls of the brain "fire" in coherence with the zero-point field. There are over 100 billion neurons in the human brain, now all firing in coherence as one. This is how we are fed information from the zero-point field (in the form of electromagnetic waves), and this is how we organize it. This mechanism—called a Fröhlich-style Bose–Einstein condensate in the brain—is what Fritz-Albert Popp believes is present in biophoton emissions.

The implications of this are mind-blowing! The atoms of our "reality" are thought to be held together and given form by their interaction with the zero-point field, such that all matter is essentially a construct of this field. All biological and biochemical systems regulating the "program of life" appear to be modulated at the quantum level by the zero-point field (which occurs at such a level of organization that they can exhibit negative entropy, in defiance of the second law of thermodynamics). And now it is proposed that our very consciousness itself is the result of an interaction of extreme coherence between the subatomic particles (fermions) in the neural tissue of our brains and the waves (bosons) of this same zero-point field.

This model for consciousness, and the concept of resonant coherence, opens up an interesting possibility: that smoking 5-MeO-DMT (or DMT) briefly *increases* the coherence in the brain's Bose–Einstein condensate, causing all the neurons in the brain to fire simultaneously, which in turn "lifts the veil" from this reality by increasing the brain's resonant coherence with the Bose–Einstein condensate of the zero-point field. Then it is possible to experience the ground state of the zero-point field as a conscious entity of pure light; if consciousness is truly a bosonic phenomenon, then it is essentially light and it would resonate with the zero-point field as light.

We are like a radio tuned in to the zero-point field, resonating with the vacuum energy. Every atom in our body is quivering with that energy and literally bringing that energy across, as light, into material existence, very much like the ancient Egyptians postulated. This is the light I believe I encounter during a 5-MeO-DMT experience: a highly coherent light emitted via the neurons in my brain and my DNA, which originates from the other side, from the quantum vacuum, the void. It is the light of both creation and consciousness—a pure stream of coherent photons in resonant harmony with the emptiness of the "vacuum energy" of the zero-point field.

I believe this is the Tibetan light of Rigpa, "the true nature of mind that manifests spontaneously and blazes out as energy and light,"[13] and the same tunnel of light that people report from near-death experiences. This is the ultimate light, the light of creation, of mysticism, of religion, of information. As my consciousness leaves the confines of the physical world during a 5MDE and resonates in reunion with its original source, I briefly cease to exist except as that light. In that moment—in the classical mystical sense—the light and I are *one.*

2. How Can I Feel as If I Am Occupying a Reality Outside of Time?

Since light travels at the speed of light, let's imagine a disembodied observer (pure mind with no mass) traveling at the speed of light. Einstein's equations would predict that, from light's own point of view, it travels no distance and takes zero time to do so. This points toward something very strange indeed about the light. Whatever light is, it seems to exist in a realm where there is no before and no after. There is only now.

PETER RUSSELL, *FROM SCIENCE TO GOD: A PHYSICIST'S JOURNEY INTO THE MYSTERY OF CONSCIOUSNESS*, 2005

The trigger for the flood of ideas that presented themselves to me about the nature of mind and light when I was riding on the train at the end of my time in India came from a passage in an Indian newspaper (attributed to Krishna) in which he states, "Nothing in the universe is faster than mind." For the first time, I found myself considering whether this might be a real possibility, instead of how Western civilization had taught me to view it, as a metaphor. What if consciousness actually *is* capable of moving at speeds faster than light?

The commonly accepted special theory of relativity assumes that nothing can travel faster than light (186,000 miles per second), but this assumption lies in the belief that all "things" in our universe are comprised of matter and thus must have mass. Yet we intuitively know that the universe possesses real "quantities" that cannot be measured and which have *no* mass, entities that we label with names like consciousness, thoughts, soul, pain, joy, fear, courage, love, hate, dreams, mythology, poetry, language, knowledge, art, memory—even the varieties of tryptamine experience. They undeniably exist and have had a direct and profound effect upon our human society, which in turn has affected the life on this planet in all its various physical forms.

While Newtonian science and material reductionism have no place for quantities that cannot be divided or measured, quantum mechanics assumes the existence of anti-particles and virtual particles—all which cannot be measured. (Only their effect on other particles can be measured.) And at the quantum level, time is assumed not to exist within the unidirectional constraints of our reality: it can move forward or backward with equal ease. Einstein's theory that nothing can travel faster than light is now called into question by our realization of the existence of an underlying field that is the basis for reality and the medium through which information can travel at speeds greater than light. Lynne McTaggart explains:

> Pure energy as it exists at the quantum level does not have time or space, but exists as a vast continuum of fluctuating charge. We, in a sense, are time and space. When we bring energy to conscious awareness through the act of perception, we create separate objects that exist in space through a measured continuum. By creating time and space, we create our own separateness.
>
> This suggests a model not unlike the implicate order of [the American-born] British physicist David Bohm, who theorized that everything in the world is enfolded in this "implicate" state, until made explicit—a configuration, he imagined, of zero-point fluctuations.[14]

As we have seen, consciousness may well be an effect created by the interaction of the zero-point energy with the matter of our physical body, in which a miniature replica of the infinite Bose–Einstein condensate of the zero-point field is formed within our own physical body/brain. (Bringing to mind the perennial Heremetic intuition attributed to Hermes Trismegistus, "*As above, so below.*") Time and space as we experience them would thus be phenomena created by this essential interaction. The perverse dependence of our brain's Bose–Einstein condensate upon the finite nature of our body's physical lifetime causes our consciousness to recognize the physical nature of what we know of as time, and hence our own peculiar mortality. (This is, however, a condition to which the Bose–Einstein condensate of the zero-point field is presumably immune.)

My theory is that during a 5-MeO-DMT experience, my consciousness is freed of the linear three-dimensional limitations of its physical matter—this mortal knot in space-time we call life—and it is able to resonate in coherence with the zero-point field as a form of light, because it effectively "returns" to this "sea of potential." It is based on seeing light and omniscient Mind as linked entities. By "linked entities" I mean that light provides the energy and substance for all physical existence, while the "enfoldment" of Mind (out of the quantitatively immeasurable dimension of the zero-point field) provides organization (sub-molecular, molecular, biological, DNA, and so on). I propose that the purpose of matter (which is light moving at slower than light speed) is to slow Mind (in the form of light) down—by giving it mass or inertia—and in doing so, creating time, the physical universe, and (in the more organized forms in this evolution of matter) the apparatus of consciousness (mind with a small "m") to realize this creation. This mind with a small "m" is actually only a finite and restricted form of Mind—a filter of sorts, for what Haisch described as the "creation by subtraction" of our reality from the white light of infinite potential.

Thus: matter + Mind = consciousness (m)

While Space (S) and Time (T) = light (c) moving slower than the speed (V) of (c)

ST = c < Vc

In its purest, unhindered form, light and Mind are one and the same—the potential for everything. The "slowing of light" due to the creation of the mass of matter also creates both time and space, with human consciousness (m) having evolved as the filter mechanism for the perception of both of those "quantifiable" entities (time and space/matter). Conversely, when Mind is free of its interface with matter, it has the capacity to move *faster* than the physical speed of light. According to the special theory of relativity, if something could move at the speed of light and had no mass, then time and space (as we experience them) would no longer exist. Esoterically, this idea has been expressed in the belief expounded upon in the *Tibetan Book of the Dead* that in the bardos one possesses a body of light that is capable of crossing into universes existing in far-away dimensions at the speed of thought. 5-MeO-DMT is a powerful chemical "vehicle" that I feel is capable of temporarily erasing this interface between Mind and matter. When our consciousness (m) is momentarily freed of all mass, it "returns" to Mind as light. Smoking 5-MeO-DMT allows an evolved "finite" consciousness (m) to briefly recognize itself as the infinite Mind (M) from which it "enfolds." This allows us to experience a greater reality, where time does not exist. It is these glimpses of this greater reality that we bring back as fragments from an experience that is—in its entirety—a reunification with wholeness.

3. How Can This Dimension Outside of Time Seem to Contain All Possible Permutations and Information?

The quantum vacuum is a kind of neo-ether through which all matter and energy evolves in continuous nonhertzian communication. The neo-ether model posits that the vacuum state has the same properties as a dynamic holography crystal: it infinitely stores the diffraction patterns of matter-energy in a nontemporal and nonlocal fashion analogous to holographic information storage throughout the recording material. Due to quasi-infinite superposition possibilities, the quantum vacuum is the source of all possible matter-energy states and parallel universes. Individual states can be selected using a fundamental form of a holographic, self-referencing, phase-conjugate mirror-like process. This process accounts for the nonlocality observed in biological organisms as well as in consciousness.

MICHAEL J. COYLE, FROM ERVIN LASZLO,
THE CONNECTIVITY HYPOTHESES: FOUNDATIONS OF AN INTEGRAL SCIENCE OF QUANTUM, COSMOS, LIFE, AND CONSCIOUSNESS, 2003

"A growing storehouse of evidence indicates that when the brain functions coherently, consciousness is not limited to the signals conveyed by the senses."[15] So writes Ervin Laszlo, whose descriptions of the interactions between quantum coherence, brain functioning, and consciousness are impressive. Since the ideas that he presents are central to my speculations about the 5MDE, I have quoted extensively from him below.

> A series of experiments carried out by Italian physician and brain researcher Nitamo Montecucco provides impressive testimony to the kind and level of coherence that can obtain between the minds of different individuals. The experiments show that as people enter an altered state of consciousness—in deep meditation or prayer—the electrical activity of the left and right frontal hemispheres of their brain becomes synchronized. Still more remarkably, the electroencephalograph (EEG) patterns of the left and right brain hemispheres of an entire group of persons can become synchronized with one another. . . .
>
> Dr. Montecucco summed up the results of his research by distinguishing four states of brain coherence. The lowest state is the "state of disgregation" where coherence is absent. This is a state of no-consciousness, typical of severe bodily degeneration, cerebral death, or deep coma. The next state is the "state of fragmentation," hallmarked by some coherence, but of a low level. This is typical of low awareness, depression,

> disease, and psychic crisis. The third state is the "state of integration" characterized by a significant level of coherence. It is correlated with high awareness, integrated knowing and experiencing, and psychophysical well-being. The fourth state is the "state of unity." Here the EEG patterns produced by the brain exhibit harmonic relations: frontal hemispheres of the brain are fully synchronized and move in unison. According to Montecucco this state of the brain and of the consciousness that accompanies it is the state in which great evolutionary leaps occur, in the cognitive, social, as well as spiritual domains.[16]

It is this fourth state of coherence that I believe applies to the 5-MeO-DMT experience; this evidence of transpersonal coherence best explains how the 5MDE can incorporate dimensions of existence far beyond anything you have ever experienced. Laszlo notes the link between this kind of coherence and the explanation sought by Carl Jung, "in terms of what he called the unus mundi, a higher or deeper reality that would lie behind both psyche and physical and connect human minds with each other as well as with nature." Laszlo continues:

> [Jung] compared unconscious processes in individuals with the myths, legends, and folktales of a variety of cultures at various periods of history and found that the individual's recollections and the collective material had common elements. According to Jung, these elements make up humankind's "collective unconscious."
>
> The collective unconscious has both a historical aspect and an archetypal aspect. The historical aspect consists of experiences accumulated by human beings throughout history: these experiences have entered, and are conserved in, the collective unconscious of humankind. Archetypes are the dynamic principles that organize their manifold elements. They are irrepresentable in themselves, but have effects that make visualizations possible. Archetypal ideas do not merely repose in the historical dimension of the collective unconscious, but can become part of the waking consciousness of individuals.
>
> The collective unconscious, the same as other transpersonal phenomena, is evidence that our mind is not an isolated entity but is con-

> stantly in touch with other minds as well as with the world around us. We are never entirely detached from the outside world; never entirely enclosed within our skin. Our mind and our body resonate with our environment, including other people in our environment. Our mind is coherent with the world, and when we do not repress the intuitions that link us with other people and with nature, we can become aware of our oneness with the universe.[17]

A "mechanism" by which transpersonal coherence of this nature might be possible is suggested within Hal Puthoff's theories regarding the constant interaction of all subatomic matter with the zero-point field. He posits that the subatomic waves of the ZPF are constantly imprinting a record of the shape of everything through wave interference. As Lynne McTaggart explains it, when two waves collide, "each wave contains information, in the form of energy coding, about the other, including all the other information it contains. Interference patterns amount to a constant accumulation of information, and waves have a virtually infinite capacity for storage. . . . As the harbinger and imprinter of all wave-lengths and all frequencies, the Zero Point Field is a kind of shadow of the universe for all time, a mirror image and record of everything that ever was."[18]

If we consider the underlying structure of the universe to be "disturbances" caused by electromagnetic waves emitted by fluctuations in the zero-point field, then all possible permutations and information would be contained within the zero-point field (since it contains all possible waves). The amount of information that the zero-point field is calculated to be able to contain through the mechanism of wave-interference is virtually infinite, effectively making it the repository of all knowledge and the greatest "supercomputer" imaginable.

Every biological entity that has ever lived and created a Bose–Einstein condensate of its own (by the coherent firing of neurons born of the DNA and biological tissue of its existence) "feeds" the Bose–Einstein condensate of the zero-point field with the information of its own temporary experience. Such information exchanges may not be limited to biological systems, since other, *nonorganic* Bose–Einstein condensates are presumed to exist within the zero-point field. All of this information is then "captured" and contained within the zero-point field itself. This information (and all its permutations) would theoretically be instantaneously and simultaneously available. If the 5MDE does allow me to experience the zero-point field as a base-reality, then the overwhelming impression would be of a totality of knowledge and information.

4. How Can I Exist as Consciousness without Ego or Identity, and Yet Clearly Still Be Me?

Whoever has been parted from his source
Yearns always for the moment of reunion.

JALAL AD-DIN RUMI, *THE SONG OF THE REED*

Once again, the concept of the Bose–Einstein condensate is essential to understanding how smoking 5-MeO-DMT might affect consciousness. Zohar notes that "one physicist suggests that the purpose of the microwave-producing vibrations in living cells might be related to the way living systems, as opposed to nonliving ones, create order out of Nature's chaos and confusion." She continues: "When cell membranes vibrate sufficiently to pull themselves into a Bose–Einstein condensate, they are creating the most coherent form of order possible in Nature, the order of unbroken wholeness. . . . *I think that the same Bose–Einstein condensation among neuron constituents is what distinguishes the conscious from the nonconscious. I think it is the physical basis of consciousness.*"[19] (Emphasis in original.)

According to her, this quantum coherence of neurons in the brain gives us "the unity of consciousness." She asserts that

> without the ordered, Bose–Einstein orchestration of photons (or other bosons), there would be no sense of self and world; but equally, without the material components of the neural tissue, there would be no Bose–Einstein condensate. The two, quantum coherence (the ground state of consciousness), and neural tissue (matter), in relationship to each other, give the brain its conscious functioning capacity. This capacity is linked to all the neural networks that process data from the environment.
>
> So at the level of consciousness found in ourselves and higher animals, the creative dialogue between matter and consciousness is obvi-

> ous and crucial—neither is reducible to the other, and yet neither could function without the other.
>
> Equally, and at a more basic level, this same ordered quantum coherence is thought to be present in all biological tissue, right down to the level of DNA itself.[20]

Her explanation of the concept of quantum consciousness, and how the mechanism of the Bose–Einstein condensate can resolve any number of long-unanswered questions about the nature of consciousness (and indeed, the nature of humanity), is well considered and persuasive. By identifying mind with the wave aspect of reality and body (or matter) as the particle aspect, Zohar asserts that there is no duality at all—the two combine to create the "unbroken wholeness" of our consciousness. She eloquently states:

> Thus by understanding the quantum mechanical nature of human consciousness—seeing consciousness as a quantum wave phenomena—we are able to trace the origin of . . . our mental life right back to its roots in particle physics, just as has always been possible when seeking the origin of our physical being. The mind/body (mind/brain) duality in man is a reflection of the wave/particle duality, which underlies all that is. In this way, human being is a microcosm of cosmic being.
>
> We are, in our essential makeup, composed of the same stuff and held together by the same dynamics as those which account for everything else in the universe. And equally—which brings out the enormity of this realization—the universe is made of the same stuff and held together by the same dynamics as those which account for us.[21]

In a 5MDE my consciousness may be realizing the quantum reality of the zero-point field by achieving coherence with its standing Bose–Einstein condensate. There would then be no difference, in a quantum sense, between the two Bose–Einstein condensates ("mine" and that of the ZPF), and there would be no sense in saying that I exist any longer at all, as I would no longer be able to experience ego or identity other than as an infinite wholeness. In a very real sense, my consciousness and the zero-point field would then have become *One*.

TWELVE

A Quantum God

We are not human beings having a spiritual experience. We are spiritual beings having a human experience.

TEILHARD DE CHARDIN, *THE PHENOMENA OF MAN*, 1959

God is the unexcelled seed of all knowledge.

PATANJALI, *THE YOGA SUTRAS*

Question Five: Why do I so firmly believe that this experience is a recognition and subsequent realization of both the true nature of G/d, and of myself?

Because this question is the real reason that this book was ever written or that I ever needed to begin this quest for answers in the first place, it now warrants a chapter entirely of its own. To begin to answer this "Question of Questions," we must start again with the tangled web of possibilities that the Heisenberg uncertainty principle unleashed upon the world.

As I pointed out in my introduction to the quantum world, the implications inherent in Heisenberg's uncertainty principle, and this new quantum view of the universe, have ironically put humanity back in the center of existence, since it appears that some form of consciousness needs to be here for reality to exist at a fundamental level. For as the cosmologist Sir James Jeans wrote in *The Mysterious Universe* in 1930, "the universe begins to look more like a great thought than a great machine."[1]

The intuition that smoking 5-MeO-DMT gives me—that consciousness can exist free of any physical realm and that matter, the stuff of our reality, is effectively an illusion—could one day be proven by quantum physics to be fundamentally correct. Matter could simply be an illusion created by our consciousness in response to the blizzard of information the zero-point field of the universe bombards us with each day: a collective hallucination that we must decipher in order to progress toward realms of higher understanding. Or as Lynne McTaggart explains it: "At the lowest level of mind and matter, each of us creates the world." According to the quantum physicists, "We are the world." Their findings suggest that the material world may be a mechanism of consciousness. Danah Zohar's investigation of the wave/particle duality (as fermions and bosons) in the nature of life led her to the conclusion that

> [b]osons are, essentially, "particles of relationship." They are the fundamental building blocks of all Nature's forces—the strong and weak nuclear, the electromagnetic, and the gravitational. They are the most primary antecedents of consciousness, but they also bind together the material world.
>
> The fundamental building blocks of the material world itself are fermions (for instance, electrons and protons), those "antisocial" particles that prefer to keep to themselves. Without bosons, fermions would seldom get together and build anything; without fermions, bosons would have nothing to draw into relationship and thus nothing with which to order and structure their own more complex coherence. From the very beginning, then, from the most primary level of what later becomes the material world and the world of consciousness, the building blocks of matter (fermions) and the building blocks of consciousness (bosons) are necessarily involved in a mutually creative dialogue.
>
> That which, in a far more complex form, later becomes us, is part and parcel of the basic dynamic through which the universe unfolds. With this understanding of the origins of consciousness—that it begins wherever two bosons meet—it may not be too wild to speculate that a gradual evolution of consciousness is the driving force behind that

> unfolding. This is not quite as strong as saying that Mind created the world, but it is suggesting that the elementary building blocks of Mind (bosons) were there from the beginning, and were necessary partners in that creation. In creating themselves (fulfilling their nature as "relationship"), they evoke the world.[2]

Then, near the conclusion of *The Quantum Self,* she states:

> Understanding this might well lead us to conclude that the physics which gives us human consciousness is one of the basic potentialities within the quantum vacuum, the fundament of all reality. It might even give us some grounds to speculate that the vacuum itself (and hence the universe) is "conscious"—that is, that it is poised towards a basic sense of direction, towards a further and greater ordered coherence. *If we were looking for something that we could conceive of as God within the universe of the new physics, this ground-state coherent quantum vacuum might be a good place to start.* [Italics mine.][3]

This quantum view of consciousness, coupled with my own revelations from smoking 5-MeO-DMT, has allowed my view of the world to expand considerably. As the Jains and Buddhists have espoused, as well as the Gnostics in more modern times, I now believe that we are all unrealized gods, trapped in the illusion of mortality.

In one of my first solo 5-MeO-DMT experiences, I had a vision of the world as a fractal, with each moment in time branching off into millions of possible permutations—worlds upon worlds upon worlds, like those commonly depicted in Tibetan *thangka* paintings. Parallels to this vision—which I consider to be a visualization of the Hindu concept of emanation—appear throughout the quantum model, such as the "Many Worlds" hypothesis of theoretical physicist Hugh Everett. At every given instant, through our subconscious intent and interaction with the zero-point field, we create our world from the fractal web of future possibilities.

Visualize a dark road and you will walk down it; visualize the light and it will take you up. I have always somehow believed this, and I have joked with my friends about how "life is a self-fulfilling prophecy," but now I believe I understand the implications of that viewpoint more correctly. We can make the world as we want it to be. It is only the mechanistic folly of Newtonian science that has left so much of humanity without hope or direction; a lifeless universe has left no room for G/d. We have bulldozed our way down a blind alley "where the dead men lost their bones,"[4] and now—relegated to being mere powerless creatures of chance—we listlessly await our inevitable oblivion.

But after being lost on a short, sharp road that has led humanity to the brink of destruction, science is now ironically beginning to bring us back on course. The quantum physicists are listening, and they cannot believe the universe's song. This same song is singing everywhere, with the strongest voice right inside of us, in every cell, through every strand of our DNA. Our consciousness is not the mystery. Our consciousness is the *answer.* "You knew it all along! We knew it all along!"

The world of matter, of birth and rebirth, of wars, genocides, and starvations—every one of us is creating that. We are reality. And we are, ultimately, part of G/d. Our identities are merely the clothes that our consciousnesses wear during this burst of "reality," this projection into the video game of matter caused by fluctuations of possibility in the zero-point field. When you smoke 5-MeO-DMT, you are stripped of your body and its ego as you approach the world of the boson, the realm of the entelechy, and become a being of pure light. That's how you can exist as consciousness without knowledge of self, because that's what you *really* are.

Ervin Laszlo and the Akashic Field

Akasha (ā • kā • sha) is a Sanskrit word meaning "ether": all-pervasive space. Originally signifying "radiation" or "brilliance," in Indian philosophy akasha *was considered the first and most fundamental of the five elements—the others being* vata *(air),* agni *(fire),* ap *(water), and* prithivi *(earth). Akasha embraces the properties of all five elements: it is the womb from which everything we perceive with our senses has emerged and into which everything will ultimately re-descend.* The Akashic Record *(also called* The Akashic Chronicle*) is the enduring record of all that happens, and has ever happened, in space and time.*

Ervin Laszlo, *Science and the Akashic Field: An Integral Theory of Everything,* 2004

While virtually all of the information that I have presented on the zero-point field is less than thirty years old, the actual realization of the ZPF's existence has only really begun as we enter the twenty-first century, and most of its implications certainly aren't being taught at universities today. The worldview it implies is too staggering, too incredible, and our schools and our society are not moving anywhere near as quickly as our technology. This is a very important fact: everything I was taught at university less than twenty years ago could now be considered obsolete. The amount of technological knowledge being generated in the world today is so staggering that if a student is doing a four-year technical degree at the moment, the information they learn in their first two years is obsolete by their fourth year. Even worse, kids today are still being fed ideas from an obsolete paradigm that cutting-edge science no longer believes to be true. As cosmologist Ervin Laszlo puts it, "A field that transports light (that is, waves of photons) and density-pressure waves, and replenishes the energy lost by atoms and solar systems, is not an abstract theoretical entity. No wonder that more and more physicists speak of the quantum vacuum as a physically real cosmic *plenum*."[5]

The physicists have become true mystics, and they are on the verge of lifting the veil covering reality once and for all. But they, themselves, are mostly still products of the Newtonian paradigm: they were born in it, trained in it, and they represent the pinnacle of its methods; they are the high priests of the specific and the singular—they are specialists. There are very few Renaissance men anymore, thinkers who straddle numerous fields. But Ervin Laszlo is a prominent exception, having worked at universities as a professor of philosophy, music, futures studies, systems science, peace studies, and evolutionary studies. Laszlo deserves further mention at this point for two reasons: first, his background has allowed him to be uniquely qualified to address this area of study; and second, it is in his continuing work that the idea of the Bose–Einstein condensate in the zero-point field (or the Akashic Field, as he calls it) being the *literal* "mind of God" has found its most mystical and eloquent expression.

Hungarian–born, Laszlo was a successful concert pianist until he was thirty-eight, when an epiphany around the birth of his son caused him to seriously question the root of human existence, and he found himself enraptured with the sheer mystery of it all. He went back to university to study physics in search of a "universal theory" that would connect the mysteries of the quantum, the cosmos, life, and consciousness—his quest in the second forty years of his life. With an ability to cross disciplines that is rarely seen, Laszlo has written around seventy-five books (his words have been translated into at least seventeen different languages), and he has contributed to over four hundred papers. He is widely considered the father of systems philosophy and general evolution theory, and because of his systems knowledge he has worked as an advisor to the Director-General of the United Nations Educational, Scientific, and Cultural Organization. Oh, and he was nominated for the Nobel Peace Prize in both 2004 and 2005. The list of his accomplishments goes on and on, but you get the point.

Laszlo is considered one of the foremost thinkers and scientists of our age, maybe the greatest mind since Einstein. And he's all about the zero-point field for basically the same reason that I am*—because it can explain so many difficult things. In the end, it relates to everything, since it *is* the fundamental underlying basis for reality. When discussing what importance further investigations into the zero-point field will hold for the twenty-first century, Laszlo writes: "The sustained investigation of the cosmic plenum as the basis for the entire realm of manifest phenomena, including mass, energy, and information, will highlight the role of fields not only in physics and cosmology, but throughout the range of observed phenomena, *including the phenomena of mind.*"[6]

Naming Hal Puthoff, Roger Penrose, Fritz-Albert Popp, and a handful of others as "front-line investigators," Laszlo quotes Puthoff who says of the new scientific paradigm:

> [What] would emerge would be an increased understanding that all of us are immersed, both as living and physical beings, in an overall interpenetrating and interdependent field in ecological balance with the cosmos as a whole, and that even the boundary lines between the physical and "metaphysical" would dissolve into a unitary viewpoint of the universe as a fluid, changing, energetic/informational cosmological unity.[7]

---

*Well, not *exactly* the same reason—he doesn't smoke tryptamines, as far as I know. But increasingly, it wouldn't surprise me if he has.

This is very similar to how I might describe the view of reality invoked by a "full-release" 5MDE. Then, in discussing the metaphysical implications of the identification of the zero-point field, Laszlo specifically notes the fact that it can contain an infinite number of "waves" of information:

> This conception corresponds to a perennial intuition also articulated in Hindu cosmology. There the almost infinitely varied things and forms of the manifest world are united in an essential oneness at a deeper level. At the fundamental level of reality the forms of existing things dissolve into formlessness, living organisms exist in a state of pure potentiality, and dynamic functions condense into static stillness. All attributes of the manifest world merge into a state beyond attributes. Time, space, and causality are transcended in a state of pure being: the state of Brahman. Absolute reality is the reality of Brahman; the manifest world enjoys but a derived, secondary reality—mistaking it for the real is the illusion of maya.[8]

Laszlo's view of the history of the universe is of a series of universes that rise and fall, but are each "in-formed" by the existence of the previous one. In Laszlo's mind, the universe is becoming more and more in-formed, and within the physical universe, matter (which is the crystallization of intersecting pressure waves moving through the zero-point field) is becoming increasingly in-formed and evolving toward higher forms of consciousness and realization.

> A comparatively evolved system, such as the human, has a comparatively evolved brain and thus a correspondingly articulated mental potential. This endows the human brain with a highly evolved capacity for receiving sensory signals from the manifest domain, and nonsensory in-formation from the virtual domain [i.e., the zero-point field]. In regard to the latter, the brain is generally in-formed by the wave function of the universe and specifically in-formed by the wave function of the social and ecological systems in which the individual participates. Sensory information constitutes the familiar contents of everyday experience, whereas nonsensory information, in modern societies generally repressed, comes to light mainly in the form of intuitions,

> images, archetypes, and *the seemingly anomalous contents of altered-state experience.* [Italics mine.][9]

And so it appears that Ervin Laszlo (one of the greatest thinkers of our time, a man who has dedicated half of his life to the search for a theory that can unite the mysteries of the physical universe and consciousness) and my humble self (a seeker who has spent the last few years searching for some insight into the 5MDE) share at least one thing in common: Laszlo has (in this last passage) identified (as have I) the zero-point field as being the very source of the "altered-state experience." I find this extraordinary. When I began my search, I did not really think I would find any answers. But in this case—unlike dozens of investigators who have come before me—it would appear that I have found some relatively concrete scientific ground to stand on. And it turns out that "altered-state" or "transpersonal" experiences are something that Ervin Laszlo has focused considerable attention on as well. He states that

> [t]he altered-state interconnection of human consciousness with the world at large is of crucial importance for our times. It exhibits a fact that both mainstream science and mainstream public opinion has long disregarded: that our mind is spontaneously linked with other minds, and even with the cosmos as a whole.[10]

In both *The Connectivity Hypothesis* and *Science and the Akashic Field,* Laszlo points to the work of Stanislav Grof and states that when subjects are having the "experience of dual unity" (whether due to mind-altering substances or due to holotropic breathwork) that some people experience "a loosening and melting of the boundaries of the body ego and a sense of merging with another person in unity and oneness," while others achieve a sense of "complete identification to the point of losing the awareness of his or her own identity. In still deeper altered states, some individuals can expand their consciousness to an extent where it encompasses the totality of life on the planet, then seems to extend outward into the cosmos."[11]

So, in a series of books about an emerging field of new physics, I find descriptions of my own mystical experiences, with the apparent explanation being that my consciousness is somehow able to "identify with" the "nonsensory in-formation" of the zero-point field, the underlying reality of the universe.

Pretty heavy stuff indeed. But this still does not answer my final question: why do I subsequently *identify* the source of that "in-formation" as being G/d (or at least G/d as much as I am capable of knowing G/d), especially given that I didn't believe in *any* form of God prior to smoking 5-MeO-DMT?

I suspect that Ervin Laszlo would find that question simple to explain to me, for as scientific and encyclopedic as his works are, his conclusions are ultimately mystical. In his expanded concept of the zero-point field as the Akashic field, a modern quantum equivalent of the Hindu "Akashic Record," Laszlo ultimately appears to realize his own G/d in his evolved vision of the field. To Laszlo, the Akashic field began as a "primordial cosmic plenum," a blank sheet of virtual energy possibility, but no form. "Excitations" within the plenum (much like thoughts arising in our mind) caused the universe to emerge from the field as a fireball that created all the matter that occupies space-time in the first milliseconds of its existence. This universe is in-formed by the primordial (and less-coherent) universes that have preceded it that also in-form the cosmic plenum (the zero-point field), which replicates the information in the form of waves (inscribing the Akashic record). Each subsequent universe is therefore in-formed with the total knowledge of all the preceding universes, which is the process that guides evolution. Laszlo writes:

> Evolution, we should note, realizes a twofold potential in the cosmos: a physical potential for the progressive, although intermittent and nonlinear, complexification of manifest entities; and a mental potential for the intermittent yet progressive evolution of consciousness. These potentials were encoded in the primordial virtual-energy domain. In the maximum concept that domain constitutes *the primordial nature of God.*
>
> Upon the termination of the evolutionary process—following the "evaporation" of the last remnants of supergalactic structures in the space and time of the last universe—the potentials encoded in the primordial virtual domain achieve final realization. For the maximum concept the completely in-formed virtual-energy domain constitutes *the consequent nature of God.*[12]

Which is to say that everything—the countless number of possible universes, the existence of every cosmological, chemical, quantum, and biological system, even consciousness itself—is G/d in-forming itself in an evolution toward G/d's own ultimate realization. Every single Bose–Einstein condensate that has ever been formed through the interaction between wave and particle systems has imprinted itself on the "blank" plenum of the zero-point field, in the same way that the "blank" ground state of our own quantum consciousness is imprinted by our life's thoughts and experiences. The millions and billions and incalculable trillions of Bose–Einstein condensates of experience of this universe, and all the universes that have preceded it and all that will come after it, all act in coherence within the quantum, wave-like nature of the Akashic Field, so that they become *One*. Until finally, as Laszlo mystically envisages it:

> In the course of innumerable universes, the pulsating Metaverse realizes all that the primeval plenum held in potential. The plenum is no longer formless: its surface is of unimaginable complexity and coherence; its depth is fully informed. The cosmic proto-consciousness that endowed the primeval plenum with its universe-creative potentials becomes a fully articulated cosmic consciousness—it *becomes,* and thenceforth eternally *is, the self-realized mind of God.*[13]

Resonating with the Mind of G/d

Direct experience is the highest of all ways of gaining knowledge. All other means are only fragments. In the path of self-realization, purity, one-pointedness, and control of the mind are essentials. An impure mind hallucinates and creates obstructions but an orderly mind is an instrument for direct experiences.

Swami Rama, *Living with the Himalayan Masters,* 1980

Back in chapter 1, I described the basic progression of the 5MDE as moving from a dissolution into fractals upon exhalation to a rapid acceleration into pure white light, followed by the recognition of the unity of all and that love is the organizing principle behind the universe. Then, finally, I reach complete dissolution—from my ego, my identity, and any concept of time—into resonant consciousness with the Mind of G/d—Absolute Consciousness.

This is what the 5MDE is all about: total dissolution into the light radiation of the zero-point field, with the accompanying realization of the true nature of Mind and reality. That allows for an understanding that I am only capable of deifying. It's an expression of the atman-Brahman—a dissolution back into the coherent cogent standing wave that is the universe: the realm of pure potential from which this actuality has arisen. It is a world of nonlocality and coherence, a vacuum of quantum energy and information beyond human description that forms the basis for both ancient mystical experiences and the modern 5-MeO-DMT experience.

Bernard Haish and *The God Theory*

Earlier I mentioned Bernard Haisch's ideas on "creation by subtraction" and the creation of mass by light. Haisch is an astrophysicist whose professional positions have included Staff Scientist at the Lockheed Martin Solar and Astrophysics Laboratory, Deputy Director of the Center for Extreme Ultraviolet Astrophysics at the University of California, Berkeley, and Visiting Fellow at the Max-Planck Institute for Extraterrestrial Physics in Garching, Germany. His work has led to a close involvement with NASA; he is the author over 130 scientific papers; and was the scientific editor of the *Astrophysical Journal* for nine years, as well as the editor in chief of the *Journal of Scientific Exploration.* With solid qualifications like these and a lifetime of studying suns and stars, we can assume he knows a thing or two about the nature of light. And apparently he has given a great deal of thought to the nature of G/d as well, which he presents in his recent and remarkable book, *The God Theory.*

> If you think of white light as a metaphor of infinite, formless potential, the colors on a slide or frame of film become a structured reality grounded in the polarity that comes about through intelligent subtraction from that absolute formless potential. It results from the limitation of the unlimited. I contend that this metaphor provides a comprehensible theory for the creation of a manifest reality (our universe) from the selective limitation of infinite potential (God). . . .
>
> If there exists an absolute realm that consists of infinite potential out

> of which a created realm of polarity emerges, is there any sensible reason not to call this "God"? Or to put it frankly, if the Absolute is not God, what is it? For our purposes here, I will identify the Absolute with God. More precisely, I will call the Absolute the Godhead. Applying this new terminology to the optics analogy, we can conclude that our physical universe comes about when the Godhead selectively limits itself, taking on the role of Creator and manifesting a realm of space and time and, within that realm, filtering out some of its own infinite potential. . . .
>
> Viewed this way, the process of creation is the exact opposite of making something out of nothing. It is, on the contrary, a filtering process that makes something out of everything. Creation is not capricious or random addition; it is intelligent and selective subtraction. The implications of this are profound. If the Absolute is the Godhead, and if creation is the process by which the Godhead filters out parts of its own infinite potential to manifest a physical reality that supports experience, then the stuff that is left over, the residue of this process, is our physical universe, and ourselves included. We are nothing less than a part of that Godhead—quite literally.[14]

In his summation of The God Theory he offers an answer to the question posed by the physicist Paul Davies in *The Mind of God:* "Why should human beings have the ability to discover and understand the principles on which the universe runs?" According to Haisch the answer is simple: "We understand the rules because we made them up—not in the state we currently find ourselves as human beings, of course, but back when we were literally one with God, before God decided to temporarily become us."[15]

G/d is in everything. G/d *is* everything. You just have to have the veil lifted from your eyes to see G/d, to realize that you are a part of G/d also. Somehow, to my amazement, smoking 5-MeO-DMT has cleared my view, and just as William Blake famously stated,* everything does indeed look infinite.

---

*William Blake remarked, "If the doors of perception were cleansed every thing would appear to man as it is, infinite." This quote was, of course, the inspiration for the title of Aldous Huxley's book.

The mind produces a powerful illusion, that of existing in this body which we consider to be our own.

KALU RINPOCHE

Science does not need mysticism and mysticism does not need science, but men and women need both.

FRITJOF CAPRA, *THE TAO OF PHYSICS: AN EXPLORATION OF THE PARALLELS BETWEEN MODERN PHYSICS AND EASTERN MYSTICISM*, 1975

Six years of study, experimentation, and contemplation have led me to realize that it is easy to be seduced by powerful and exotic ideas, and much harder to discern the truth distilled within ourselves. But considering how much more I now know about a dozen fields of human research and philosophy, and considering how hard I have grappled with complex concepts generated from deep within my own "soul," I consider myself fortunate to have been able to undertake this intellectual adventure. The following are some of the conclusions and speculations I have come to in forming the foundation of my new expanded worldview.

Human consciousness is a bosonic coherence phenomenon: a complex interaction between the matter (fermions) in our brains and the waves (bosons) of the zero-point field, caused by an extreme form of neuron coherence called a "Bose–Einstein condensate." Time and space as we experience them are phenomena created by this essential wave/particle interaction.

Another (less scientific) name for the Bose–Einstein condensate within living beings could be the *soul*.

Mass and matter—the quantities by which we claim to define our physical reality—are caused by the "slowing down" of light, caused by inertia as it is "pushed" through the super dense medium of the zero-point field, and the stability of our physical universe is maintained and informed by the constant interaction of virtual particles (photons of light) from this same zero-point field. The zero-point field, this "quantum vacuum that is a plenum" that has been identified by mystics throughout the ages, and is now being rediscovered by our physicists and cosmologists, is the true underlying reality of our universe. The Akashic Record and the aether field, concepts that were intuited centuries ago and then dispelled by a wave of scientific determinism, are now being rediscovered.

The zero-point field is capable of containing all knowledge and information provided by the Bose–Einstein condensates of every entity and every particle throughout eternity; thus the function of our individual existences (in this universe) is to add to the collective in-formation of the zero-point field by way of our own temporal experience. Within the zero-point field there is a Bose–Einstein condensate that is identical (in its physics) to the Bose–Einstein condensate in our brain. This mirrors both the Hindu realization of atman–Brahman and the classical Hermetic intuition "As above, so below."

Another (less scientific) name for the Bose–Einstein condensate of the zero-point field could be *the Mind of G/d.* Smoking the correct dose of 5-MeO-DMT affects the coherence of the neurons in the brain, thus increasing the coherence of the Bose–Einstein condensate of our brain (our soul or consciousness) so that it achieves greater coherence with the Bose–Einstein condensate of the zero-point field (the mind of G/d). This allows a temporary "escape" from the dimension of matter, into a transpersonal, egoless mode of quantum consciousness that is a resonant glimpse of the coherent conscious existence of the Akashic Field itself. As consciousness of pure light, the smoker exists in a dimension of pure in-formation, where time and space no longer apply.

Interpreted in a linear Newtonian manner, the 5MDE makes no sense, but it makes perfect sense as a quantum event. Coherent nonlocal resonance with the standing ground-wave of all reality—the zero-point field—would give access to all knowledge in the universe, at once. And from this comes the recognition of self as a microcosm and reflection of the ultimate coherent state of the zero-point field—the Akashic Field—the conscious wave that we all came out of, and the wave to which we will all return. The 5MDE can be seen therefore as both a *mystical* experience and a *quantum* experience. And it can be recognized that the zero-point field is, in fact, the origin of the entheogenic experience.

All knowledge implicit in this coherent resonance is inherently untranslatable. It can only be experienced, but not explained. Once the tryptamine has been metabolized, our "normal," matter-bound Bose–Einstein condensate (our ego) begins to reestablish itself. This is the point where we wonder who we are and how it was possible for us to have just experienced the full omniscient power of Absolute Consciousness. We are left with the *mysterium tremendum et fascinans* of touching the mind of G/d.

Experientially, the state induced from smoking 5-MeO-DMT closely resembles the near-death experience. The 5MDE is also phenomenologicaly similar to aspects of the Tibetan Buddhist concept of Rigpa—the realization of the true nature of mind. The most recent major expressions of the realms that smoking 5-MeO-DMT can allow access to are alluded to by Carl Jung's concepts of archetypes, the *anima mundi,* and the collective unconscious. The 5MDE is also similar to certain mystical states common to virtually all creeds and religions since the beginning of time. The discovery of the 5-MeO-DMT experience is a modern continuation of the tradition of mystical experience, humanity's experiential connection to the numinous.

The greatest "proof" of the 5MDE being a genuine mystical experience is that it passes the basic test for all *true* religious conversions: it can result in intense self-examination and produce a tremendous sense of responsibility in the person who has had the experience. Ultimate knowledge causes ultimate gratitude-of-being; the sheer beauty of G/d revealed brings out the spontaneous joy of compassion. You move closer and closer to harmony and coherence with the world, a constant process that never ends and only grows more mysterious and beautiful as life deepens in content and purpose. If there is any true meaning in life, it is in our ability to wonder about, seek, and ultimately even know, the unknowable.

The path itself *is* the key to knowledge; we call that flowing river *life.* The mystical experience reveals the knowledge that more than just life as we know it exists. In a physical universe, replete with wonder, I believe that this mystery is the greatest gift of G/d to all creation.

If my identification of the Bose–Einstein condensate of the zero-point field as the Mind of G/d (or my belief that you can realize the Mind of G/d during a 5MDE) seems like a stretch, consider this astonishing passage from Ervin Laszlo's *Science and the Akashic Field.* Laszlo is discussing the fact that the zero-point field is essentially immeasurable by modern science:

> To begin with, even if we cannot directly observe consciousness in the vacuum, we could attempt an experiment. We could enter an altered

> state of consciousness and identify ourselves with the vacuum, the deepest and most fundamental level of reality. Assuming that we succeed (and psychotherapists tell us that in altered states people can identify with almost any part or aspects of the universe), would we experience a physical field of fluctuating energies? Or would we experience something like a cosmic field of consciousness? The latter is much more likely. We have already noted that when we experience anybody else's brain "from the outside," we do not experience his or her consciousness—at the most we experience gray matter consisting of complex sets of neurons firing in complex sequences. But we know that when we experience *our* brain "from the inside," we experience not neurons, but the qualitative features that make up our stream of consciousness: thoughts, images, volitions, colors, shapes, and sounds. Would not the same hold true when we project ourselves into a mystical union with the vacuum?[16]

Maybe Ervin Laszlo, universally regarded as one of the greatest scientists and philosophers of our time, knows something about smoking 5-MeO-DMT after all!

All phenomena I encounter on 5-MeO-DMT—in this white light of unlimited potential—are manifestations of the Universal Mind. Upon returning to this light, freed of mass, a suitably prepared consciousness is inexorably guided to the supreme realization of wholeness and Oneness that is at the center of existence, which I can only deify as G/d. This experience of Oneness is ineffable, since it occurs in a dimension that is devoid of time or mass, and is experientially infinite. When the fragment of that Oneness returns to this reality as our limited consciousness, it has no language to describe existing as Mind in a world without physical or temporal boundaries. It only has a series of fleeting glimpses of a greater reality that it struggles to understand and hold on to.

Although I continue to feel that ultimately this state of being is indescribable, in my humble opinion the closest our species has managed to approach describing a coherent resonance with this Wholeness is via the Sanskrit word/concept of Aum (or Om). The following explanation of the roots of the word comes from Joseph Campbell: "*Aum* is God. *Aum* is God as sound. We usually think of the divine as a form, as an image that we can visualize, but this is the sound aspect of the form that we are going to find when we meet God. It is the sound of God, the sound of the Lord of the World, out of whose thoughts, out of whose being, out of whose energy substance the world is a precipitation."[17]

After explaining how each letter in the word Aum is a syllable—associated with waking consciousness, dreaming consciousness, and deep, non-dreaming sleep—Campbell then asks: "What is the fourth syllable in the three-syllable word *aum*? It is the silence that is before and after *aum* is pronounced. That is the totality of the word and of the world now: you have the silence—that is to say non-being—and *aum*, which is being. Neither exists without the other. They are mutually interrelated. So this word when thought about contains in itself all the mysteries of the world."[18]

THIRTEEN

The Role of Light in Eastern Philosophy

Do not make the mistake of imagining that the nature of mind is exclusive to our mind only. It is in fact the nature of everything. It can never be said too often that to realize the nature of mind is to realize the nature of all things.

SOGYAL RINPOCHE, *THE TIBETAN BOOK OF LIVING AND DYING,* 2002

You do not really exist.

KALU RINPOCHE, WHEN ASKED TO EXPLAIN THE ESSENCE OF BUDDHISM IN AS FEW WORDS AS POSSIBLE, AS QUOTED IN *THE COSMIC GAME* BY STANISLAV GROF, 1998

It will undoubtedly seem contradictory for me to spend a chapter examining the role of light in Buddhist and Hindu philosophy after espousing the view that a modern mystic must firmly root his or her knowledge in the language and technology of the day. However, I have always espoused a Renaissance view toward life and believe that one must look for answers everywhere. We can find inspiration for our own personal mystical path in the esoteric Eastern philosophies that have mostly been lost to contemporary Western civilization (as Aldous Huxley, Baba Ram Das, Timothy Leary, and numerous nameless seekers have realized); we can also find fascinating parallels to our own speculative sciences.

I must confess that I have always been drawn to these fabulous Indian philosophies—and especially to the historical figure of Siddhartha Gautama, the Buddha. I am sure that if I had been incarnated as an English scholar a century ago, I would have been labeled an "Orientalist," since I have always loved the art, philosophy, and mythology of India, Tibet, China, and South-East Asia. It was this curiosity about Eastern philosophy (and especially Buddhism) that led me to briefly enroll in a university to study the phenomenology of religion. But while I was there my Eastern philosophy professor—a balding hippy philosopher who for twenty years had spent half the year teaching and the other half of the year in India "studying" —also told me that school was a waste of time for someone like me and that I should be "getting out in the world."

These were sage words of advice, which I obviously heeded. Yet, while I eschewed my formal education from this point, I never stopped reading. Over the course of many years, I read hundreds of books on Eastern philosophy, mythology, comparative religion, and shamanism. But—until I encountered 5-MeO-DMT—I just didn't get it. I read, and read, and read, and I came to know many things, but I did not understand.

This is one of the mysteries about smoking 5-MeO-DMT that is frustrating to try to convey: How the experience can change your life and your way of thinking so profoundly that you can look back on a lifetime of knowledge with a totally new understanding. How smoking a "drug" can change the foundation of your flesh-and-blood world so resoundingly that you can scarcely remember the human being you used to be, a person you can now only view as a child, full of facts, but devoid of any real knowledge.

When I returned to the great Eastern writings I had explored in my youth after smoking 5-MeO-DMT, I experienced a revelation about the world's religions that had never occurred to me before. As I re-read numerous passages from the esoteric traditions of Buddhism and Hinduism, which described specific states of altered consciousness in terms of light, I found that I could now easily relate to these descriptions from my own experience. After considering again Alfred North Whitehead's remark that the Hindu Vedanta is the most impressive metaphysics the human mind has conceived, I came to the startling conclusion that we have been getting it all wrong since the first day an Englishman learned to read Sanskrit. The occidental mind has insisted on reading these reports of light as a metaphor, while they are actually precise descriptions of accessible regions of the human mind, written by experienced travelers.

Before I examine this idea more closely, there is a tremendous irony here that I feel the need to briefly mention. How is it possible that occidental scholars have only been able to see Eastern philosophy (which may be experientially based) in metaphorical terms, while in our own forms of religion—Judaism, Christianity, and Islam—we have failed to separate obvious metaphor from historical fact, a failure that has resulted in the fanatical dogmatism of today's fundamentalist groups and the general intolerance that Christianity and Islam seem to breed?

According to the great contemporary mythologist Joseph Campbell, if you draw a line through ancient Persia at "sixty degrees east of Greenwich,"[1] this is the line between the Occident and the Orient, and this is where the split in human consciousness and our view of the Divine occurred. Campbell remarked:

> The fundamental thought in the Oriental philosophical world is that the mysterious, ultimate truth, that which you seek to know, is absolutely beyond all definition. All categories of thought, all modes of imaging fall short of it. When we ask, "Is God merciful, just, loving? Does he love me, does he love my people more than those? Are these not chosen, are those not rejected?" this from the Oriental standpoint is sheer kindergarten stuff. This is the projection of anthropomorphic forms of thought and feelings upon a mystery that transcends even the categories of being and nonbeing. The categories of logic, the forms of sensibilities of time and space—all of these are functions of human thought, and the mystery that you're seeking lies beyond it. This is taken seriously; the absolute is absolutely transcendent of all thought.
>
> In Occidental theology, the word *transcendent* is used to mean *outside of the world*. In the East, it means *outside of thought*. To imagine that your definitions of your God have anything to do with that ultimate mystery is a form of sheer idolatry from this standpoint. Your God is good enough for you and mine's good enough for me. A God,

> from this point of view, is merely a reflex of one's ability to conceive of God. Since people have various abilities of this sort, they have various powers of apprehending God.[2]

This fundamental difference in the way the oriental and the occidental view the essential nature of their gods—that one can be known, and that one cannot—is the reason why Eastern philosophy, in both its terminology and its construct, offers a much more copasetic understanding of the reality revealed by 5-MeO-DMT. In the East, where all forms of G/d are considered both possible and inadequate, everything that 5-MeO-DMT has taught me is known and assumed, while in the West, thanks to our rigid interpretation of dogma, we deny it and classify the experience as a "hallucination," or, even more frighteningly, "psychotic."

Campbell continues with an explanation so apt that, reading it, I felt that I could have saved myself a lot of trouble if I had just carried it around with me to explain my 5-MeO-DMT experiences. With all due respect to Aldous Huxley, Terence McKenna, and Alexander Shulgin, I can't think of a better description of the peak intensity of a true entheogenic experience, even though Campbell was not talking about entheogens, but instead expounding on the philosophical bedrock of the Eastern mind.

> In the East, however, this relationship is viewed slightly differently: that which is absolutely transcendent of all knowledge is the basis of your own being. It is you; it is immanent within you. This fundamental Oriental statement appears in the Chhāndogya Upaniṣad as early as the eighth century B.C.: *Tat tvam asi,* "thou art that." "You yourself are that which you would know." However, this "you" is not the you that you identify with, not this phenomenon in time and space that can be named, that can be identified, that can be described. That is not it, and so we have also come to the Sanskrit phrase, *Neti, neti*—"not this, not this!" Anything that you can name about yourself is not it. Therefore, when you have erased all that you can name and have broken through, then you have come to it. This is a very different sort of calculus. In this equation a is you and x is the mystery and $a = x$—you are that mystery, but not the "you" that you think you are. The you that you think you are is not it and the you that

> you can't even think about *is* it. This paradox, this absurdity, is the essential mystery of the East.[3]

In the introduction[4] to *Myths of Light: Eastern Metaphors of the Eternal* (a collection posthumously compiled from lecture transcripts archived by the Joseph Campbell Foundation), the great scholar has this to say about the state of religion in the West:

> Myths do not belong, properly, to the rational mind. Rather, they bubble up from deep in the wells of what Carl Jung called the collective unconscious.
>
> I think what happens in our mythology here in the West is that the mythological archetypal symbols have come to be interpreted as facts. Jesus *was* born of a virgin. Jesus *was* resurrected from the dead. Jesus *went* to heaven by ascension. Unfortunately, in our age of scientific skepticism we know that these things did not actually happen, and so the mythic forms are called falsehoods. The word *myth* now means falsehood, and so we have lost the symbols and that mysterious world of which they speak. . . .
>
> At present, our culture has rejected this world of symbology. It has gone into an economic and political phase, where spiritual principles are completely disregarded. You may have practical ethics and that kind of thing, but there is no spirituality in any aspect of our contemporary Western civilization. Our religious life is ethical, not mystical. The mystery has gone and society is disintegrating as a result.
>
> The question is whether or not there can ever be a recovery of the mythological, mystical realization of the miracle of life of which human beings are a manifestation.[5]

So spoke the greatest interpreter of mythos of our time—a man with his finger on the pulse of Western spirituality. The professor has declared us dead. But I don't believe that this *has* to be true. I believe that—here at the beginning of the twenty-first century—we can still create a meaningful spiritual experience that is structured around the wisdom of the great historical sages, supported by the scale of our current science and cosmology, and that includes the sacramental use of entheogens as a tool of realization. This experiential spiritual philosophy would be based on the recognition that the supreme realization is in our ability to transcend knowledge entirely, to find our own G/d. And it would presume that a transcendent experience was both valid and possible.

This amounts to a new mystical "tradition" that recognizes a variety of methods of exploring and mapping the human consciousness, based on the experientially recognizable but hard-to-grasp "fact" that the true state of reality is differentiated states of consciousness—one of which we currently occupy. This approach (which is the antithesis of the reigning Western viewpoint of material realism) is based on a philosophy called monistic idealism. In the words of Indian-born scientist Amit Goswami:

> In this philosophy, consciousness, not matter is fundamental. Both the world of matter and the world of mental phenomena, such as thought, are determined by consciousness. In addition to the material and mental spheres (which together form the immanent reality, or world of manifestation), idealism posits a transcendent, archetypal realm of ideas as the source of material and mental phenomena. It is important to recognize that monistic idealism is, as its name implies, a unitary philosophy; any subdivisions, such as the immanent and the transcendent, are within consciousness. Thus consciousness is the only ultimate reality.[6]

This philosophy of monistic idealism has been expressed in one form or another in virtually all the great religions and philosophical traditions, including the Judeo-Christian tradition. However, the most famous expression of the philosophy of monistic idealism in the West comes from *The Republic* and Plato's allegory of the cave:

> As hundreds of generations of philosophy students have learned, this allegory clearly illustrates the fundamental concepts of idealism. Plato imagines human beings sitting in a cave in a fixed position so they always face the wall. The great universe outside is a shadow show projected on the wall of the cave, and we humans are shadow watchers. We watch shadow-illusions that we mistake for reality. The real reality is behind us, in the light and archetypal forms that cast the shadows on the wall. In this allegory, the shadow shows are the unreal immanent manifestations

> in human experience of archetypal realities that belong to a transcendent world. In truth, light is the only reality, for light is all we see. In monistic idealism, consciousness is like the light in Plato's cave.[7]

The highest expression of monistic idealism cans be found among the assorted philosophies of Hinduism and Buddhism, as this has been a central tenet of these philosophies since their origins in the Indus Valley in pre-Aryan times, in an ancient yogic tradition (and philosophy) that appears to date back at least 3,000 years and remains at the heart of all Indian spiritual practices. It provided the philosophical bedrock for Hinduism after the invasion of the Aryans from where we now believe was Anatolia (now Turkey), who brought with them their colorful pantheon of Vedic gods. The ideas and practices of this yogic tradition were also later reinterpreted and enlarged in different forms by Mahavira, the founder of the Jain religion, and slightly later again in the teachings of Siddhartha Gautama, to subsequently develop into the various schools of Buddhism. Indian monistic idealism was succinctly expressed by the eighth century philosopher Shankara in this way: "This entire universe of which we speak and think is nothing but Brahman. Brahman dwells beyond the range of Maya [illusion]. There is nothing else."[8]

In light of the antiquity and sophistication of Indian philosophical thought and mystical expression, I looked more closely into Buddhist and Hindu concepts, finding that they provided great clarity in my quest to develop a model for the realms of consciousness experienced on tryptamines. What I found convinced me that a syncretic melding of the Western scientific viewpoint with certain ideas from Eastern philosophies can provide a possible basis for a modern form of experiential transcendental mysticism.

The outline of my 5-MeO-DMT experiences presented in chapter 1 provides a helpful framework in which to consider various descriptions of the realms and processes involving light, as detailed by Sogyal Rinpoche in *The Tibetan Book of Living and Dying.* These descriptions, taken from commentaries on the *Bardo Thodol,* are intended to guide a person through the actual process of dying. There is considerable debate among Buddhist scholars as to whether or not near-death experiences—let alone entheogenic experiences—can be considered relevant to the descriptions of the bardos, because, according to some, being near death doesn't actually mean that you have *experienced* death. Most Buddhist communities frown upon entheogen use. Dr. Rick Strassman, for example, received harsh criticism and was expelled from the Buddhist community that he was a member of because of his experiments with DMT on volunteer subjects.

It is my sincere hope that my comparison of some of Sogyal Rinpoche's beautiful descriptions of the bardo states to the 5-MeO-DMT experience does not offend serious practitioners of these ancient wisdoms. I do not wish to infer that smoking 5-MeO-DMT is in any way a "short-cut" substitute for years of meditation and practice. Yet I do believe that the ancient commentaries that the *Bardo Thodol* itself provides, which by tradition are accredited to Padmasambhava who was a Tibetan sage born in India, and which were originally written down by his primary student Yeshe Tsogyal in Sanskrit, are relevant to the 5-MeO-DMT experience. As well, the modern commentaries on the *Bardo Thodol* by Sogyal Rinpoche resonate so eerily with my own 5-MeO-DMT experiences that I find the comparisons remarkable. I also believe that the Sanskrit language itself is more etymologically open to the possibilities in the 5MDE, since its philosophic scaffolding was built around a monistic idealistic understanding of reality (consciousness is everything), as opposed to the West's narrow and mystically bigoted languages, which since the Greeks have been mostly built upon the foundations of material realism.

Although I feel that Timothy Leary missed a rare opportunity by overemphasizing Eastern traditions at the expense of incorporating Western science into the entheogenic model, he was nevertheless correct in his identification of the *Tibetan Book of the Dead* as a valuable resource for helping to understand the psychedelic experience. I also believe this is especially true when one is considering the phenomenology of the 5-MeO-DMT experience in particular.

Dissolution into Fractals upon Exhalation of the 5-MeO-DMT

This is the instantaneous eruption of Rigpa, the nature of mind. It is perhaps too subtle a state of consciousness to be really understood without years of dedicated meditation. The great Tibetan masters say that Rigpa can pass "in the snap of one's fingers" for some people, and last "the length of a meal" (about twenty minutes) for others.

Sogyal Rinpoche tells us, "As the Ground Luminosity dawns at death, an experienced practitioner will maintain full awareness and merge with it, thereby attaining liberation. But if we fail to recognize the Ground Luminosity, then we encounter the next bardo, the luminous bardo of dharmata."[9]

Every 5-MeO-DMT trip I have witnessed has been characterized by the complete immersion of the subject into the experience for the first few minutes. No one ever speaks; everyone lies down after exhaling, with his or her body often shaking from the incredible velocity that he or she seems to be encountering.

If the Tibetan philosophy is correct in its rigid adherence to the necessity of a lifetime of arduous study and training in order to have any chance of liberation at the moment of death, then none of the 5-MeO-DMT smokers I know (including myself) would have much of a chance of recognizing liberation anyway. So down we go . . .

Transportation via Rapid Acceleration into the White Light . . .

. . . into the luminous bardo of dharmata. This could also be the tunnel of light that people report from near-death experiences and the realm in which angels and protector-spirits may appear. Here is Sogyal Rinpoche again, this time with one of my favorite passages:

> In the bardo of dharmata, you take on a body of light. The first phase of this bardo is when "space dissolves into luminosity": Suddenly you become aware of a flowing vibrant world of sound, light, and color. All the ordinary features of our familiar environment have melted into an all-pervasive landscape of light. This is brilliantly clear and radiant, transparent and multicolored, unlimited by any kind of dimension or direction, shimmering and constantly in motion. The *Tibetan Book of the Dead* calls it "like a mirage on a plain in the heat of the summer." Its colors are the natural expression of the intrinsic elemental qualities of mind: space is perceived as blue light, water as white, earth as yellow, fire as red, and wind as green.[10]

The following description mirrors the paradoxical appearance of the white light of my 5-MeO-DMT experiences: "This white light—which blazes with the focused intensity of a laser and which is both whiter-than-white, yet also sparkling with brilliant color."[11] But then, as Sogyal Rinpoche explains:

> How stable these dazzling appearances of light are in the bardo of dharmata depends entirely upon what stability you have managed to attain in Tögal practice [a secret Tibetan meditation practice]. Only a real mastery of this practice will enable you to stabilize the experience and so use it to gain liberation. Otherwise the bardo of dharmata will simply flash by like a bolt of lightning; you will not even know that it has occurred. Let me stress again that only a practitioner of Tögal will be able to make the all-important recognition: that these radiant manifestations of light have no existence separate from the nature of mind.[12]

Which certainly leaves *me* out of liberation once again. Yet out of the light, the multitudes surround me and I begin the next stage.

The Recognition of the Unity of All, and That Love Is the Principle that Organizes the Universe

In the Tibetan bardo model, this is described as the second phase of dharmata known as "luminosity dissolving into union," which seems like a very precise description of stage three of a 5MDE to me. Since this is the phase of the bardos where you can see the various Buddhas or deities, this is probably about the point where I apparently get to my feet declaring, "It exist! It exists! I am there!" (Wherever *there* is.) And that I occasionally even utter the word "God."

Here is Sogyal Rinpoche's explanation of the concept of dharmata:

> The Sanskrit word *dharmata* . . . means the intrinsic nature of everything, the essence of things as they are. Dharmata is the naked, unconditional truth, the nature of reality, or the true nature of phenomenal existence. What we are discussing here is something fundamental to the whole understanding of the nature of mind and the nature of everything.
>
> The end of the dissolution process and the dawning of the Ground Luminosity has opened up an entirely new dimension, which now

> begins to unfold. One helpful way I have found to explain it is to compare it with the way night turns into day. . . . Now gradually the sun of dharmata begins to rise in all its splendor, illuminating the contours of the land in all directions. The natural radiance of Rigpa manifests spontaneously and blazes out as energy and light.[13]

Sogyal Rinpoche states that he finds it "extremely suggestive that modern physics has shown that when matter is investigated, it is revealed as an ocean of energy and light." He then quotes David Bohm, whose theory of wholeness and the implicate order has clearly resonated among the modern Tibetan scholars: "[. . . Matter], as it were, is condensed or frozen light . . . all matter is a condensation of light into patterns moving back and forth at average speeds which are less than the speed of light. . . . It's energy and it's also information—content, form and structure. It's the potential of everything."[14]

Complete Dissolution from Ego-identity and Any Concept of Time, As I Dissolve into Resonant Coherence with the Mind of G/d

Somehow, by recognizing the oneness of all creation and the true nature of the energy that manifests that creation, and by letting myself willingly dissolve into the conscious field of energy (that I call G/d), I can now resonate with that same omniscient field of energy as *One*. This state is an experience that is virtually beyond description—but historically some poets, artists, and mystics have tried.

My personal favorite description of the experience comes from a Sanskrit word for an ancient Indian concept, *Saccidānanda,* which roughly translates into three root words: existence, awareness, bliss. For me, that's the 5-MeO-DMT experience right there in a nutshell.

According to Stanislav Grof, "All we can say about this experience is that we are identified with a radiant, boundless, and dimensionless principle, or state of being, that seems to be endowed with infinite existence, has infinite awareness or wisdom, and experiences infinite bliss. It also possesses an infinite capacity to create forms and experiential worlds out of itself."[15]

Consider also this exquisite description of difference between the Sixth and Seventh chakras by Joseph Campbell, and how transcendence occurs when the *kundalini* ascends.

Nonetheless, at this level of the ascent of the kuṇḍalinī [at the sixth chakra], the soul and its beloved, the Lord, are still two. They are distinct.

At the sixth [chakra] everything is relationship—relationship of I to thee, of the soul to the beloved. Here we behold the divine aim of life, but it is as though there were a cellophane wall between the soul and the object, and perfect love requires that there should be no wall.

The ultimate goal is to transcend duality . . . and that is achieved only [when . . .] the dividing membrane is withdrawn from between the soul and its beloved, and both are gone. For there to be an object, there must be a subject of knowledge and a relationship between them. So, with the membrane withdrawn, both the soul and God are extinguished, joined beyond duality, beyond pairs of opposites.

There one finds what we, in our language, can only call identity. And yet it can't be called identity because it is beyond categories altogether . . . something impossible to think of takes place; namely, all phenomenology is transcended, and with that all subjectivity as well. Schopenhauer speaks of this in *The World as Will and Representation.* He says, "If we could only understand how it is that that which is one becomes many, how that which is no thing, becomes things." He calls this paradox the "world knot." If we could understand that, we would understand all, but it cannot be understood.[16]

Fear from Disorientation Caused by Transitioning Back into a Restricted Consciousness and the Return of My Ego

My exit from this state of resonant bliss seems to be precipitated by a sudden fear regarding how much knowledge I have achieved, and how omniscient I appear to have become. It is at this point that I begin to search wildly for identity, for a beginning, for something linear to grasp onto.

The last two phases of the bardo of dharmata are called "union dissolving into wisdom" and "wisdom dissolving into spontaneous presence." In the following passage, Sogyal Rinpoche elucidates on the final phase:

Now the whole of reality presents itself in one tremendous display. . . . The limitlessness of this vision is utterly beyond our ordinary imagination. Every possibility is presented: from wisdom and liberation to confusion and rebirth. At this point you will find yourself endowed with powers of clairvoyant perception and recollection. For example, with total clairvoyance and your senses unobstructed, you will know your past and future lives, see into others' minds, and have knowledge of all six realms of existence. In an instant you will vividly recall whatever teachings you have heard, and even teachings you have never heard will awaken in your mind.

The entire vision then dissolves back into its original essence, like a tent collapsing once its ropes are cut.[17]

As the Last of the 5-MeO-DMT Effects Fade Away, I Abruptly Repossess My Physical Body

This is analogous to "the bardo of becoming," or the *sipa bardo*. Sogyal Rinpoche explains that

> [w]ith our failure to recognize the Ground Luminosity and our failure to recognize the bardo of dharmata, the seeds of all our habitual tendencies are activated and reawakened.
>
> . . . The outstanding feature of the bardo of becoming is that *mind* takes on the predominant role, whereas the bardo of dharmata unfolded within the realm of Rigpa. So, in the bardo of dharmata we have a body of light, and in the bardo of becoming we have a mental body.[18]

A Period of Fading Resonance between Physical Consciousness and G/d Consciousness, as I Return Completely to My Normal "Baseline" State

This is the lingering resonance with the mystical union. And the beginning of the age-old struggle for words to try and explain the inexplicable experience.

These parallels between the ancient philosophies of Hinduism and Buddhism and the 5-MeO-DMT experience seem especially obvious if you read the accounts from the Eastern texts as literal events rather than as metaphor. Sogyal Rinpoche's detailed descriptions of the bardo realms surely could not be considered to be metaphorical. They contain descriptions of particular emanations of consciousness that are even more detailed than the ones I have quoted, including manifestations called *tiklé,* which are described as "simple rays and colors [that] begin to integrate and coalesce into points or balls of light of different sizes."[19] That sounds pretty specific to me, and is an accurate description of phenomena experienced while in an altered state of consciousness (or in this case, the *ultimate* state of altered consciousness: mind on its exit from material reality).

The same can be said for *The Yoga Sutras* of Patanjali (which detailed very specific realms of consciousness possibly as far back as three thousand years ago), and Sri Ramakrishna's descriptions of the ascent of the kundalini (corporeal energy). I am sure that countless other examples from Eastern philosophy, as well as many from our own mystical canon, can also be found. If these ancient mystics and philosophers were able to chart out the various regions of human consciousness so lucidly, then we should be able to do so also.

A New Model of Consciousness

The establishment of a foundation for a new understanding of human consciousness by a limited number of consciousness explorers has unquestionably already begun. Stanislav Grof has made extraordinary progress in mapping the frontiers of the modern psyche for more than fifty years now, and his contribution toward understanding the human subconscious mind may someday rank as great as Carl Jung's or Sigmund Freud's. From thousands of case studies, Grof describes vast realms of the mind that emerge in obvious patterns—and in far too great a detail for me to go into here.

Dr. Grof's focus these days is on accessing altered states of consciousness via the holotropic breathwork technique that he and his wife Christina invented. However, he first became aware of transpersonal states of consciousness through his clinical exposure to LSD, and there is no reason to think that he would have stopped working with entheogens if they hadn't been made illegal.

Interestingly enough, I found the following extraordinary description of consciousness expressed in terms of both the void and of light, not in a book on the effects of entheogens or in a book on Eastern philosophy, but in yet another book on quantum physics: Ervin Laszlo's popular 2006 offering,

Science and the Reenchantment of the Cosmos: The Rise of the Integral Vision of Reality. In a letter to Laszlo from Chris Bache, a professor of philosophy whom Laszlo mysteriously remarks has "carried out one of the most sustained and courageous explorations of deeply altered states ever attempted," Bache writes about Laszlo's ideas regarding the holographic retention of all things in the Akashic Field:

> I am receptive to your proposal both from theory and from my own transpersonal experience. As one "drops" into the vacuum layer by layer, structures that had appeared "real" from the perspective of space-time become transparent to the underlying ground. Not only ego but soul too, traditionally conceived, becomes permeable and fleeting, simply another intermediate organization of experience in an open, unbounded system of energy and information. All patterns of life including collective, archetypal, even cosmic structures can become transparent, sunyata, empty of self-existence.[20]

Bache, who states that, "from twenty years of exploring nonordinary states of consciousness, I have taken away a small number of fundamental convictions," later concludes his letter with this remarkable description:

> The universe relentlessly generates, collects, and integrates experience. In time, self-emergence yields systems strong enough to begin to form continuities across multiple incarnations. At first fragmented and disjointed, these lives eventually come together to form more integrated wholes. This process of accumulation and integration reaches a bifurcation point where something comes into being that had not previously existed. I experienced this birth as an explosion of brilliant, luminous, extremely dense, exquisitely clear, crystalline diamond light . . . [21]

While I have no clue how Chris Bache accesses his "transpersonal explorations," I think it is safe to assume after reading such an extraordinary passage that those realms of light and consciousness that mystics have been describing since the beginning of time have not closed their doors on the modern mind just yet. Science and spirituality are both languages of attempted understanding, since they both seek to find meaning out of the mystery of life. But words themselves are only symbols and metaphors; they are not the thing that they describe. I suspect that this is the dialogue that mystics and scientists have been having since the death of Pythagoras. And although the current parameters of mainstream science may have no need or desire to explain the 5MDE (or any other experiences outside of "provable" parameters), in my search to understand my own personal 5-MeO-DMT experiences, I found that science can be a powerful tool. Equally potent and revealing are the collective works of the great prophets and mystics. This is one of the reasons why I believe that the point where the tryptamine experience touches on both the great truths inherent in quantum physics and in all the philosophies that have come before it—is the place where G/d resides.

FOURTEEN

A Transcendent Future for Humanity?

Ought it to be assumed that in all men the mixture of religion with other elements should be identical? Ought it, indeed, to be assumed that the lives of all men should show identical religious elements? In other words, is the existence of so many religious types and sects and creeds regrettable?

To these questions I answer "No" emphatically. And my reason is that I do not see how it is possible that creatures in such different positions and with such different powers as human individuals are, should have exactly the same functions and the same duties. No two of us have identical difficulties, nor should we be expected to work out identical solutions. Each, from his peculiar angle of observation, takes in a certain sphere of fact and trouble, which each must deal with in a unique manner.

WILLIAM JAMES, *THE VARIETIES OF RELIGIOUS EXPERIENCE,* 1902

Experience is not what happens to a man: it is what a man does with what happens to him.

ALDOUS HUXLEY, *TEXTS AND PRETEXTS: AN ANTHOLOGY WITH COMMENTARIES,* 1932

Experience Is the Only Path to Understanding

Ironically, I have discovered that the greatest dilemma that my investigation has revealed is how to live with my conclusions. For I have come to believe that I am writing about one of the most difficult and controversial topics in the history of humankind: the existence of God and our own mortal ability to know, or directly experience, God's power. This newfound spirituality has clearly changed my own life, but as I have enthusiastically expounded my ideas over the last few years to those close to me, I have come to realize that the whole concept makes a lot of people uncomfortable, even hostile. The word *God* itself creates such immediate emotions, often negative in this modern age, and I can remember still how skeptical and derisive I would have been if I had been presented with the bulk of these ideas in my pre-5MDE days. "Direct experience is the highest of all ways of gaining knowledge," said Swami Rama, and I have to agree with him. Experience is the only path to understanding. Explanations just won't do.

Of course what I am presenting here are *my* views, and they relate to *my* 5-MeO-DMT experiences. Many people have bizarre and amazing experiences when they smoke 5-MeO-DMT, but don't necessarily realize G/d. In fact, *none* of the many people I have watched undergo a 5MDE has clearly identified his or her experience as definitively being a mystical "union with God," although Nathan's experience in Panama and some voyages I witnessed at Burning Man seemed to tread in the same territory. Smoking 5-MeO-DMT in the upper ranges is a powerful thing—it will blast any human being off into some very interesting realms—but apparently only a small percentage of those who do so feel that they have recognized the existence of an absolute consciousness that they *know* is God. You either believe you have made contact with G/d or you don't—there is no real in-between. Among my immediate circle of friends and enthusiasts, I am the only one who has come to such a definite conclusion, which was indelibly imprinted upon me from my first undeniable experience. To date, as far as I have *witnessed,* this has been my experience, and mine alone. Yet somehow the same experience happens virtually every time I smoke 5-MeO-DMT, with varying degrees of cosmic love and sheer power, while paradoxically I never get used to it.

References in the scant literature I have found definitely indicate that similar experiences *have* happened to other people on 5-MeO-DMT. And, after I gifted *Tryptamine Palace* on the playa in 2006 and 2007, I have now either met, or been contacted by, a handful of people who have had 5-MeO-DMT experiences that are virtually identical to mine. 5-MeO-DMT is universally regarded as one of the most powerful psychoactive compounds available, and as far as I am concerned, it is virtually in a class all of its own. However, I have also come to realize from my research—especially through the works of Alexander Shulgin and Stanislav Grof—that this same identification and "union with God" has happened to other people, and on other compounds, fairly regularly. Shulgin even has a category for the experience within his "rating system" that he explains in the introduction to *PIHKAL: A Chemical Love Story:*

> (++++) or Plus-four. This is a separate and very special category, in a class by itself. The four pluses do not imply in any way that it is more than, or comparable to, a plus-three. It is a serene and magical state which is largely independent of what drug is used—if any drug at all—and might be called a "peak experience," in the terminology of the psychiatrist, Abe Maslow. It cannot be repeated at will with a repetition of the experiment. Plus-four is that one-of-a-kind, mystical or even religious experience which will never be forgotten. It tends to bring about deep change of perspective or life-direction in the person who is graced with it.[1]

Thus 5-MeO-DMT is neither unique in its ability to cause a "genuine mystical experience" or "union with God," nor is it guaranteed to be able to do so. The mystical experience has been available to the human mind for centuries upon centuries, through a wide variety of means. 5-MeO-DMT just happens to be the one that arrived in a yellow envelope and unexpectedly worked for me.

A Healthy Dose of Skepticism?

Some of my friends (and undoubtedly some of my readers) say that I was looking for God all along and that the 5-MeO-DMT filled some deep inner need for me. They point at my brief university study of the phenomenology of religion, my continued interest in shamanism and mysticism, even my attraction to magic mushrooms and LSD, and say that unconsciously this is what I have been wanting all along. Though they don't come right out and say it, there is the definite implication that I am over-rationalizing while at the same time deluding myself. From that perspective, this book could be seen as the ultimate expression of that delusion. And they could be right. There is no way of proving any of this one way or the other. These are just my ideas and my experiences, and the "hypothesis that best fits the given evidence" for me. But the fact remains that before I smoked 5-MeO-DMT, I was a hard-core scientific-rationalist atheist who thought religion was an antiquated superstition for people with weak minds. I was personally happy, professionally content, and had no interest in the existence of God, until I came to believe that in the midst of the 5MDE I was granted classical mystical union with what historically has been called "a Higher Power."

In an effort to present a balanced view on the subject, I decided to seek out some books on skepticism. I tried reading Richard Dawkins' popular book *The God Delusion,* thinking that along with some interesting facts about genetics and Darwin, I would find some grounded scientific rationalism that might make me reconsider at least a few of my newly found views. An author of a number of books on genetics and evolution, Dawkins held the position of Charles Simonyi Professor in the Public Understanding of Science at Oxford University in Great Britain until September of 2008. He is described on his book's cover as being a "preeminent scientist and outspoken atheist," and the book contains a host of glowing recommendations from prominent scientists and authors, who describe how revolutionary Dawkins' view of God is. Surely I was in the right territory, I figured; this book must be some kind of an atheist's Holy Grail. (No pun intended!)

Alas, *The God Delusion* sorely disappointed me. From the beginning, Dawkins makes it clear that what he is debunking is the idea of God we have inherited from the Judeo-Christian religion. I have been disheartened to find that this is the approach that several other authors have also taken. I have yet to read a book that "debunks" the existence of any form of G/d other than this monotheistic and jealous "tribal god" we have inherited from the peoples of what we now call "the Middle East." Dawkins takes great offense at the use of the word *God* in the writings of scientists like Albert Einstein and Stephen Hawking. He argues that they don't really *mean* God, since they are talking about their *own* concept of God, not the Old Testament God with a white beard sitting up in heaven on a throne. He then pointedly describes the disastrous effects of religion, without ever really examining the concept of God in any detail.

Since Dawkins is a celebrated Darwinian, he sets about proving that natural selection can account for everything and that it is simply the illogical and unscientific mindset of the "great unwashed masses" that doesn't allow us to realize that God doesn't exist. He has an annoying habit of repeating the idea that understanding the concept of natural selection has given him "a raised consciousness," allowing him to see the truth in nature, while most of the rest of us remain superstitious and deluded.

Dawkins avoids examining the variety of concepts of God in any detail. There is virtually no mention of spiritual ideas from Eastern religions, excepting at the point where he dismisses them from the discussion: ". . . I shall not be concerned at all with other religions such as Buddhism or Confucianism. Indeed, there is something to be said for treating these not as religions at all but as ethical systems or philosophies of life."[2] With an off-handed rejection of more than half the world's religions just like that, it's not surprising that mysticism doesn't warrant *any* mention, and there's only a scant dismissal of the ideas from new physics, when Dawkins decrees that, "Our imaginations are not yet tooled-up to penetrate the neighbourhood of the quantum."[3] Adhering to a rigid dogmatism as bad as any of a religious nature (only with Darwin as the new God), Dawkins feels that the theory of evolution by natural selection is the ultimate scientific consciousness raiser, stating: "It is impossible to exaggerate the magnitude of the problem that Darwin and Wallace solved."[4] So strong is his faith in Darwin that the rather pompous Dawkins seems entirely unable to consider anybody else's viewpoint at all.

Take, for example, the following from chapter three, "Arguments for God's Existence," under the heading "The Argument from 'Personal Experience'":

> One of the cleverer and more mature of my undergraduate contemporaries, who was deeply religious, went camping in the Scottish isles. In the middle of the night he and his girlfriend were woken in their tent by the voice of the devil—Satan himself; there could be no possible doubt: the voice was in every sense diabolical. My friend would never forget that horrifying experience, and it was one of the factors that later

> drove him to be ordained. My youthful self was impressed by his story, and I recounted it to a gathering of zoologists relaxing in the Rose and Crown Inn, Oxford. Two of them happened to be experienced ornithologists, and they roared with laughter. "Manx Shearwater!" they shouted in delighted chorus. One of them added that the diabolical shrieks and cackles of this species have earned it, in various parts of the world and various languages, the local nickname "Devil Bird."[5]

This is the best ammunition against being able to personally experience G/d that the world's most prominent atheist has to offer? A friend of his, who was already "deeply religious," is scared by a noisy bird into becoming a priest. In the rest of the chapter, Dawkins alludes to the brain's ability to trick itself into believing in things that don't exist, and he claims that the "formidable power of the brain's simulation software . . . is well capable of constructing 'visions' and 'visitations' of the utmost veridical power." Dawkins insists that, "Constructing models is something the human brain is very good at. When we are asleep it is called dreaming; when we are awake we call it imagination or, when it is exceptionally vivid, hallucination."[6]

Dawkins takes a few stabs at the gullibility of mass Catholic visions, and falls back on the old idea that anything that doesn't have some kind of tangible physical reality is either imaginary or a form of psychosis—material reductionism at its finest. But this "paradigm" is crumbling with the discovery of biological quantum interactions with the zero-point field. Dawkin's book is filled with blind faith in the veracity of the "laws" of random mutation and natural selection, yet according to Ervin Laszlo, these ideas will have to be radically amended if it turns out that the structure of the genome is affected by the energy and/or information it receives from the zero-point field.

The Immutable Genome

The central pillar of modern Darwinism is that—with regard to the genome (your DNA) and phenome (the physical construction of that DNA, that is, you)—only the phenome is adaptable, while the genome is immutable. According to the current "synthetic theory" of modern Darwinism, the information contained in the genetic code is presumed to be immune to outside conditions, and is therefore always passed on unchanged between generations. The genome is said to mutate randomly, unaffected by the conditions that affect the phenome. However, statistical evidence is increasingly pointing to the conclusion that pure blind "random mutation" would lead to too many evolutionary "dead ends," and that the "search space" of possible genetic rearrangements within the genome is so enormous that random processes are unlikely to produce viable species. The laws of natural selection also cannot explain the relatively short (in geological terms) periods of intense diversity (that represent radical "jumps" in evolution) that are contained within the fossil record.

Stephen Jay Gould (then of Harvard) and Niles Eldredge postulated that new species do not arise through a stepwise modification of existing species—they appear almost at once. In this "macro-revolutionary theory," new species arise in a time span of no more than five to ten thousand years, which translates in geological time as an instant. This explains the mystery of the "missing links" in the fossil record that have puzzled biologists for years—there are no *missing* links, since they don't exist. Ongoing laboratory experiments appear to indicate the probability of coherence between the phenome and the genome, in the form of mechanical, chemical, biochemical, and field-transmitted connections.[7] This is perhaps one of the most exciting developments in biology today. If this turns out to be true, then it is Darwinists like Richard Dawkins who may have to evolve to realize that nothing can really ever be said to have been "proven"—it can only be said to have provided us with the best "minimum hypothesis" for the time being.

Dawkins is so clearly dogmatic in his faith in Darwin's ideas that he comes off just as bigoted and narrow-minded as any religious fanatic. But for me, the most immediately obvious thing wrong with Richard Dawkins' attempts to prove that God does not exist is that he is setting out to disprove the God of the Old Testament, which is clearly a God manifested out of the antiquated regional mythology of the Middle East, although Dawkins could just as easily be raging against Zeus, Ganesha, or Odin or any other tribal metaphor of the transcendental Godhead. The very use of the word *God* seems to incense Dawkins, who can only see a white-bearded heavenly "father" and won't even consider the possibility of the transcendental. He has no interest in examining a God greater than the most antiquated one that he has inherited from his society; nor, apparently, does he have any interest in redefining the existence of God with metaphors sufficient for the modern age. For Dawkins, the supernatural cannot exist—he simply won't allow it, like Niels Bohr "forbidding" the collapse of the electron in an atom. When Dawkins talks about Einstein's "regrettable" use of the word God, he goes as far as to say:

> I wish that physicists would refrain from using the word God in their special metaphorical sense. The metaphorical or pantheistic God of the physicists is light years away from the interventionist, miracle-wrecking, thought-reading, sin-punishing, prayer-answering God of the Bible, of priests, mullahs, and rabbis, and of ordinary language. Deliberately to confuse the two is, in my opinion, an act of intellectual high treason.[8]

Albert Einstein doesn't have the right to redefine humanity's understanding of the word *God*? It's all right to radically redefine our reality through mathematics and physics, but don't you dare mess with spirituality? I find such a narrow-minded viewpoint bizarre. Perhaps Dawkins had some rough days as a choirboy. He certainly comes across as a rabid God-hater, and when he states that the wonder of nature is enough for him (but that this should in no way be considered religious), I cannot help but laugh and remember Joseph Campbell's assertion: "The term *nature religions* has become the object of rejection and abuse. But what else are you going to worship? Some figment of your imagination that you have put up in the clouds? A strange thing has happened. It is so extreme that if you don't believe in a figure, you don't have any worship. Now everything is lost!"[9]

This is where our modern civilization has gone so radically wrong over the last three hundred years—we have mostly stopped developing our vision of God. We have become so allergic to the very word that its use immediately creates suspicion, linked, as it is, to archaic dogmas forcing rigid adherence to concepts of God that are hundreds, if not thousands, of years old. Richard Dawkins' book is really about (Western) monotheistic religion and the historic and political grip that this institution has held on the terminology of God in our culture—and it has precious little to do with whether or not God can exist. While Western thinkers as recent as Einstein, Heisenberg, and Sir Arthur Eddington had a decidedly mystical bent, it seems that since World War II (and the advent of the atomic bomb) our modern scientific culture has clearly stopped developing this idea—an idea that may be older than our branch of humanity itself, as it is increasingly accepted that the Neanderthals practiced a form of religion. Without such a development of our vision of God, we are left with only the tottering and archaic systems of our Euro-Christianity, or the countless schools of New Age and/or Eastern synthesis that have arrived on our shores since a generation momentarily blasted its third eye open with an ocean of LSD.

New Visions of God

> *I belong to a group of scientists who do not subscribe to a conventional religion but nevertheless deny that the universe is a purposeless accident. Through my scientific work I have come to believe more and more strongly that the physical universe is put together with an ingenuity so astonishing that I cannot accept it merely as a brute fact. There must, it seems to me, be a deeper explanation. Furthermore, I have come to the point of view that mind—i.e., conscious awareness of the world—is not a meaningless and incidental quirk of nature, but an absolutely fundamental facet of reality.*
>
> PAUL DAVIES, *THE MIND OF GOD: THE SCIENTIFIC BASIS FOR A RATIONAL WORLD*, 1992[10]

This situation in our society does however appear to be changing, with new visions of the nature of God emerging from some intelligent and prominent thinkers. I find it very telling that in the same year (2006) that Dawkins released *The God Delusion* to considerable success and acclaim, the astrophysicist Bernard Haisch quietly released his book *The God Theory* into the collective consciousness of the world. Here is Haisch's take on the current dilemma of the opposing views of science and spirituality, which he lays out in his introduction:

> If we are nothing but physical beings originating by chance in a random universe, then there really can be no ultimate purpose in our lives. This is not only bad news for us individually, it undermines the ethical and moral underpinnings of society and civilization.

> I propose a theory in this book that does provide a purpose for our lives while at the same time being completely consistent with everything we have discovered about the universe and about life on earth, in particular the Big Bang, a 4.6 billion-year-old earth, and, of course, evolution. The single difference between the theory I propose and the ideas current in modern astrophysics is that I assume that an infinite conscious intelligence preexists. You cannot get away from the preexistence of something, and whether that is an ensemble of physical laws generating infinite random universes or an infinite conscious intelligence is something present-day science cannot resolve, and indeed one view is no more rational than the other.
>
> One might argue that one view is supported by evidence and the other is not. I would agree one hundred percent. The evidence for the existence of an infinite conscious intelligence is abundant in the accounts of the mystics and the meditative, prayerful, and sometimes spontaneous exceptional experiences of human beings throughout history. The evidence for random universes is precisely zero. Most scientists reject the former type of evidence as merely subjective, but that simply reduces the contest of views to a draw: zero on both sides.[11]

With that last statement, I believe that Haisch identifies the problem exactly: since current science *can't* prove the existence of G/d, it feels *compelled* to deny it. But history is full of accounts of people who claim to have experienced G/d, with plenty of scientists and scholars included among them. The problem these days is that as soon as you mention the word *God,* you get dragged into a theological discussion about which dogma-attached version of God you are talking about—even if you profess to be attached to no particular religion or philosophy. Discussing the existence of God often degenerates into a historical–political debate rather than a spiritual–philosophical one.

Fading Metaphors and a Transcendental Remedy

Toward the end of his remarkable life, Joseph Campbell delivered a series of lectures at the University of California, Berkeley, based on the theme that humankind's future mythology would have to incorporate the new scale of the universe that it was discovering. *The Inner Reaches of Outer Space* was the name of a symposium he gave (with astronaut Rusty Schweickart) and is the name of a book based on these lectures, reissued by the Joseph Campbell Foundation in 2002.

In this series of lectures, Joseph Campbell argues that our society has totally lost the ability to understand metaphor in myth or religion, and that Western religions' dogged insistence on regarding spiritual metaphors (such as the Virgin Birth, that Jesus physically ascended to heaven, and so on) as actual facts that are clearly now in opposition to the established science of the day only reduces their argument's credibility. You can accept them as "miracles" or "articles of faith," but something like Ezekiel ascending to heaven in a chariot ends up being pretty hard to swallow. Metaphors that were inspirational and mystical 2,000 years ago now appear either dated or inconsequential when compared to our modern cosmology, or clearly impossible when examined by our current sciences. It is the loss of power in these metaphors, along with the dogged insistence of the clerical authorities that they actually occurred, in addition to the abuses that these same authorities have committed in the names of their various Gods, that has resulted in a complete split from spirituality for large chunks of our population. Now having lost the power to inspire many of us, when we are forced to try and rationalize these "scientific" impossibilities, the result is a form of societal split-psychosis, with either atheism or fundamentalism as the most tenable positions available.

According to Campbell, universal metaphors should be timeless and transcendental vehicles to greater truths.

> "Have you not heard," asked Nietzsche, already in the introduction to his *Thus Spake Zarathustra* (1883–84): "Have you not heard that God is dead?"—the god in point, of course, being the named and defined creator-god of the historically limited Bible. For the conditions, not only of life, but of thought also, have considerably changed since the centuries of the composition of that guide to truth and virtue, which by its deliberately restricted and restricting ethnocentric horizon and tribal "jealous God" (Exodus 20:5) is culture specific . . .
>
> The first step to mystical realization is the leaving of such a defined god for an experience of transcendence, disengaging the ethnic from

> the elementary idea,* *for any god who is not transparent to transcendence is an idol, and its worship is idolatry.* Also, the first step to participation in the destiny of humanity today, which is neither of this folk or of that, but of the whole population of this globe, is to recognize every such local image of a god as but one of many thousands, millions, even perhaps billions, of locally useful symbolizations of that same mystery beyond sight or thought which our teachers have taught us to seek in their god alone. Black Elk's phrase, *"The center is everywhere"* is matched by a statement from a hermetic, early medieval text, *The Book of Twenty-four Philosophers (Liber XXIV philosophorum):* "God is an infinite sphere, whose center is everywhere and circumference nowhere."[12]

5-MeO-DMT and the Potential for Transcendental Realization

My desire to see our societal vision of God recreated to a stature fitting of our current cosmology leaves me with the unenviable task of proposing a remedy that is quasi-illegal and that many will consider scientifically illogical. But I was once just as terminally unaffected by the presence of the sacred as most of the Western world is. I had accepted without question the same hopeless inherited worldview that much of my generation has accepted—a worldview where we are told to lose ourselves in the pursuit of sex, money, possessions, and entertainment. And I know that I have now experienced a radical transformation of my own spirituality.

If 5-MeO-DMT has allowed me the classic experience of mystical realization, then there is no reason why it can't work for others too. I have no qualifications for tasting enlightenment, other than a disdain for the contemporary model of society. If I can turn my tribe on, and you can turn yours on, and they can turn theirs on . . . then we just might start to inject some experiential mystical spirituality back into the fading memory of the Western soul.

---

*Joseph Campbell is referring here to terminology coined by Adolf Bastian (1826–1905), the German ethnologist of the nineteenth century, to define certain reoccurring mythic motifs common to all the religious traditions of the world. Bastian identified "folk ideas," *Volkergedanken,* as localized representations and applications of the universal or "elementary ideas," *Elementargedanken.* Carl Jung (1875–1961) would later redefine these mythical motifs as "*the collective unconscious.*"

Those who have never experienced 5-MeO-DMT may be skeptical. Be reassured that I would have been too. The effect that smoking 5-MeO-DMT has had on my life has been without parallel. I was a hardheaded motherfucker—they didn't call me "Rock" for nothing. But smoking 5-MeO-DMT dissolved a lot of that hardheadedness away in just over a half-an-hour, more effectively than a lifetime of reading and enough psychedelics to imprison a small nation. 5-MeO-DMT hit me like Zen lightning. I was totally ignorant and unprepared. And if the reason 5-MeO-DMT succeeded with me was because it caught me off-guard, with all my belief systems and defenses down, then my apologies: because if you have read this far, I have probably ruined the impact of surprise for you.

Various friends who have read my manuscript have suggested jokingly (and maybe not so jokingly) that I am interested in starting some kind of a cult. But they miss the point entirely. I am only interested in *personally experiencing* G/d. I believe that this experience is open to *all* of us and through a variety of means, not just by smoking 5-MeO-DMT. Transcendence, as Joseph Campbell points out, is a distinctly human phenomenon. And we have all experienced it in one form or another, even if we have never experienced the *totality* of G/d.

Music has always been an integral part of religion and has been considered sacred by virtually every human society because of its capacity to evoke transcendence. And it is the most common vehicle of transcendence in our current society. Most of us have "lost ourselves" in music at one time or another, while the popularity of the current dance (rave) culture is a clear example of how music and dance can enable us to transcend our normal consciousness.

This is not surprising, since music is based on scales and harmony that are in themselves a product of our natural world, despite what instruments we may invent to recreate them. Those same notes, scales, and harmonic values appear throughout both the inanimate universe (as shown by the B-flat vacuum-pressure wave discovered traveling through the zero-point field) and the world of biology. For example, the coherent whole-system behavior of the cells, organs, and organ systems of an organism has been compared to "a good jazz band" by experimental biophysicist Mae-Wan Ho. The "music" of a higher organism ranges over more than seventy octaves.[13] These scales and harmonies undoubtedly have a cosmic origin. One interpretation of the zero-point field is the idea that all matter has a signal, so it's the signal (or note) that causes reality, not the actual particles and atoms themselves.

Matter as the concretization of sound is also an idea that appears in many spiritual philosophies. In a fascinating lecture about the Sanskrit language presented at the World Psychedelic Conference (Basel, 2008) by Baba Rampuri—an American who became the first non-Indian to be initiated as a *Naga baba saddhu* (a "holy-man" from a Shiva sect known for its extreme austerities) after living in India for more than twenty-five years—remarked repeatedly that we paid too much attention to the written form of the word, or the meaning of the word, while it is the actual *sound* of the word that is the road to a deeper understanding.

Other forms of transcendence also clearly exist. Parents often talk of a type of transcendence when they experience the birth of a child, or watch with wonder the faculties of their children develop over time: the wonder of the first step, the first word. Meditation, prayer, art, sport, and even sex can also be transcendent; and countless other forms of transcendence clearly exist. Yet thanks to our society's rigid fascination with "material-reductionism," we tend to discount these very accessible realms of transcendence as being of little "practical" value. Advanced technologies for inducing transcendence have existed throughout the ages. Most notably kundalini yoga from India, which Joseph Campbell tells us "is not a game of 'as if' and make-believe, but an actual experience of psychological absorption in a metaphysical ground of some kind, a morphogenetic field that has not yet, as far as I know, been scientifically recognized in the West except by C. G. Jung and lately, by the [biologist] Rupert Sheldrake, whose works, according to one concerned scientific reviewer, ought to be burned."[14] In the West, the last great school of transcendence appears to have been the Greek mysteries of Eleusis, whose adepts used the entheogenic preparation called kykeon to carry them beyond the realms of their immediate consciousness, a methodology that was so successful it lasted 2,000 years.

The modern use of entheogens, and particularly the widespread use of LSD in the sixties, would seem to indicate a deep-rooted desire within our own society to reacquire knowledge of these transcendental realms. The subsequent prohibition of these same entheogens—and the apparent willingness of our governments to traffic decidedly non-transcendental inebriants like alcohol, heroin, and cocaine upon the peoples of the world—makes it apparent that the *individual* pursuit of transcendence is considered dangerous and undesirable to those institutions of mass *societal* control that currently run our world. Aldous Huxley had great foresight when, writing in 1954, he said:

> Systematic reasoning is something we could not, as a species or as individuals, possibly do without. But neither, if we are to remain sane, can we possibly do without direct perception, the more unsystematic the better, of the inner and outer worlds into which we have been born. This given reality is an infinite which passes all understanding and yet admits of being directly and in some sort totally apprehended. It is a transcendence belonging to another order than the human, and yet it may be present to us as a felt immanence, an experienced participation. To be enlightened is to be aware, always, of total reality in its immanent otherness—to be aware of it and yet to remain in a condition to survive as an animal, to think and feel as a human being, to resort whenever expedient to systematic reasoning. Our goal is to discover that we have always been where we ought to be. Unhappily we make the task exceedingly difficult for ourselves. Meanwhile, however, there are gratuitous graces in the form of partial and fleeting realizations. Under a more realistic, a less exclusively verbal system of education than ours, every Angel (in Blake's sense of that word) would be permitted as a sabbatical treat, would be urged and even, if necessary, compelled to take an occasional trip through some chemical Door in the Wall into the world of transcendental experience. If it terrified him, it would be unfortunate but probably salutary. If it brought him a brief but timeless illumination, so much the better.
>
> In either case . . . the man who comes back through the Door in the Wall will never be quite the same as the man who went out. He will be wiser but less cocksure, happier but less self-satisfied, humbler in acknowledging his ignorance yet better equipped to understand the relationship of words to things, of systematic reasoning to the unfathomable Mystery which it tries, forever vainly, to comprehend.[15]

Myself, having now experienced this transcendental gnosis at its sublime fullest, I have little interest in anything else. I still survive in the world the same as anyone else does. I still need air, and water, and food. I still love my wife, listen to music, travel, and enjoy the many other pleasures of my life—perhaps even more than I did previously. But I now consider my moments of knowing G/d within the 5-MeO-DMT experience to be the most important and fulfilling experiences that I have managed to achieve as a human being. These transcendental moments outside of space and time have both created a certain agitation and allowed a certain peace of mind.

I suspect that the rest of my life, with or without 5-MeO-DMT, will be spent developing my own personal viewpoint of and relationship with my G/d. I have recently realized *how much* time I now spend thinking about G/d and the meaning of our human existence, and I try to remember what I used to spend all that time thinking about! My interest in extreme sports, which dominated more than a quarter of my life, has clearly dropped, as has my interest in making money. When I look around, I realize that most other people are not spending their time thinking about the kind of things that I'm thinking about! If *The God Delusion* is the best argument against my experiences that the world's most prominent atheist has to offer me, then I'm going back to reading the likes of Joseph Campbell and Aldous Huxley for inspiration instead.

Even though Huxley's grandfather, Thomas Henry Huxley, coined the term *agnostic,* and Aldous Huxley's most famous book, *Brave New World,* reflected his youthful radical agnosticism, Huxley renounced his agnostic viewpoint after having his own first-hand experiences. He continued to develop his personal spirituality all the way until his dying breath (his wife gave him two 100 μg injections of LSD during his last hours).[16] He realized that there can be no denying the history of mystical experiences, and the words of the great mystics ring strikingly similar to Huxley's "perennial philosophy," no matter what their cult or creed.

Synthetic 5-MeO-DMT is a recent vehicle of mystical realization discovered by the ingenuity and curiosity of the human imagination, just as mescaline and LSD were for Huxley's generation. Throughout this book, I have presented my surprising discovery that under certain conditions you can experience union with G/d, while making a clumsy attempt at distancing my personal G/d from the gods of all known religions. But ultimately, as Huxley expounds with his "perennial philosophy," I know that all these gods are one and the same. They are atman-Brahman. The ineffable, indescribable, but paradoxically not un-knowable, nature of God, of which we are all but drops from the same infinite cosmic ocean.

My adventures and immersions—in other authors' psychedelic writings, in Buddhism, Hinduism, alchemy, mysticism, quantum physics, and in the startling implications of the zero-point field—these are all brush strokes on a masterpiece that had already been painted. I needed them to regain my balance in this world after I first smoked 5-MeO-DMT, because I needed to understand how I could have experienced what I now believe to be the undeniable existence of G/d, a God I did not believe in, in any form, prior to my first 5MDE, a God that I saw no need in believing in, since I was as staunch an atheist as Richard Dawkins.

I believed in the natural good and beauty in the world. I embraced the concept of karma as a good way to live, if not actually being a supernatural force. I believed in myself, and that was about it. The cynical, educated, over-intellectualized twentieth-century product that I was, I firmly believed that while material reality might not be all that there was to existence, it was all that we *could* know, and the belief in anything that was consciously *more* than that was merely "ignorant" superstition.

While I had been enthusiastic about various entheogenic drugs over the years, I had viewed them as doors into my own consciousness, and had gradually lost faith in them. I had eventually come to see "psychedelics" as being something fun to do (in low doses) for outdoor sporting activity, or when going out to dance and listen to music. I drink little alcohol and eschew powders. MDMA makes me cranky the next day, so I don't bother. My ayahuasca experiences in Ecuador and Peru had been weak, producing little more than vomiting and a few colors. Since all the good LSD had been drying up anyway, I generally just liked to puff chronic herb. But then along came the entirely different 5-MeO-DMT experience, and I realized that everything I had done up until that point was simply training-wheels.

In the days prior to my discovery of 5-MeO-DMT, I was more interested in self-knowledge through paths like yoga and meditation than I was in trying any new drug, since I no longer believed that any drug could teach me much more about myself than what I had already learned through my past history of psychedelic experiences. Hence my tremendous surprise at the experiential discovery (through the use of an entheogen) of that transcendent Other; my inner G/d revealed.

Early in a 5-MeO-DMT experience there comes a moment when you feel that everything in your life—everything that you have learned or have instinctively known—*everything* is about that single moment in time: "This is it." And then in you go. All the study, all the thinking, all the flying, and climbing, and acid, and mushrooms, all the good times, all the hard times, being washed in a bath as a child by my mother, bathing in the Ganges with millions of others at the Kumba Mela—all of those moments led to this *One* moment. Now, on the other side of that "black hole that is a white hole," nothing can ever quite be the same.

The Power of Absolute Consciousness

My discovery of G/d, and the peace this discovery has brought me, is undoubtedly the greatest spiritual and intellectual change in my inner being and is perhaps the greatest spiritual and intellectual revelation that any human *can* undergo. But the factor that has changed my life the most externally is the immense sense of responsibility that has accompanied this inner transformation: a sense of responsibility to myself, to my people, and to my planet. Other dedicated tryptamine smokers have expressed this same feeling of responsibility to me, just as many shamans and mystics have expressed it throughout history.

So where does this twin sense of purpose and responsibility come from? Reports of its existence are well documented in transpersonal experiences, and they are a significant aspect of the experience, which can inspire a genuine change in personality. Once again, this depends on what you believe the 5-MeO-DMT experience really is and how powerfully that belief takes hold of you. If you believe, as I do, that this experience can allow you to connect in coherent resonance with Absolute Consciousness, then it is pretty easy to understand where this sense of responsibility and purpose originates.

The source of mystical insight is considered at length in Ervin Laszlo's recent book, *Science and the Reenchantment of the Cosmos:*

> [The] most remarkable of altered-state experiences surfaces in individuals who are committed to the quest of apprehending the ultimate grounds of existence. When the seekers come close to attaining their

> goal, their descriptions of what they regard as supreme principle of existence are strikingly similar. They describe what they experience as an immense and unfathomable field of consciousness endowed with infinite intelligence and creative power. The field of cosmic consciousness they experience is a cosmic emptiness—a void. Yet, paradoxically, it is also an essential fullness. Although it does not feature anything in a concretely manifest form, it contains all of existence in potential. The void they experience is a fullness; the vacuum is a plenum. It is the ultimate source of existence, the cradle of all being. It is pregnant with the possibility of everything there is. The phenomenal world is its creation: the realization and concretization of its inherent potential.
>
> People who practice yoga and other forms of deep meditation report the same kind of experience. This was the basis in the Indian Vedic tradition for the affirmation that consciousness is not an emergent property that comes into existence through material structures such as the brain and the nervous system, but a vast field that constitutes the primary reality of the universe. In meditation, when the gross layers of the mind are stripped away, this field is experienced as unbounded and undivided by objects and individual experiences. Underlying the diversified and localized gross layers of ordinary consciousness there is a unified, nonlocalized, and subtle layer: "pure consciousness."
>
> There is a noteworthy parallel here between insights that have been present to the human mind for thousands of years and the implications of the latest findings of the sciences.[17]

The main—and blindingly obvious—parallel between the mystical (or transpersonal) experience and the latest findings in quantum science is the insight that we are all linked. We are a field of interdependent energies. We are all One. If you experientially realize that, then you become responsible for everything: for the entire planet, for all people, for every action, and every word. Experience your place in the universe outside of space and time, and you will feel the responsibility of resting in that love.

If the absolute consciousness that Ervin Laszlo and I are both describing is truly the essence of reality—the field of fields from which all other phenomena manifest—then the lesson that I am learning from resonating in harmony with this field is that it is motivated by the act of creation. Its intelligence and intention manifests in what I call the "complex creation principal."

As I have come to understand it, while Absolute Consciousness is an undisturbed field of all potentiality, we are actually the crystallization of the experience of creation. We have manifested into material "reality" as a knot of energy in time and space. We are no longer contained within the infinite sea of potential. We now exist as an *actuality*—potential be damned. We have *become* that "intense disturbance" in time and space. The Tibetans believe that we chose to be incarnated into these times. So, too, do I believe that the things that my consciousness is now motivated to search for in this physical universe are the same things that motivate the absolute consciousness in its own search for meaning. *"As above, so below."**

"Brahman, Existence-Knowledge-Bliss Absolute," Ramakrishna said, "is like a shoreless ocean. In the ocean visible blocks of ice are formed here and there by intense cold. Similarly, under the cooling influence, so to speak, of the devotion [*bhakti*] of its worshippers, the Infinite transforms Itself into the finite and appears before the worshipper as God with form. That is to say, God reveals Himself to His devotees as an embodied Person. Again, as, on the rising of the sun, the ice in the ocean melts away, so, on the awakening of Knowledge [*jñāna*], the embodied God melts back into the infinite and formless Brahman. . . . Therefore people compare the love of God to the cooling light of the moon, and knowledge to the burning rays of the sun."[18] And while Ramakrishna is talking in this passage about the appearance of God with form, this mechanism could just as equally apply to the appearance of our *own* form, pulled out of the sea of potential, just as the Gnostics surmised, as fallen G/ds unable to recognize our own divinity.

If all of this "reality" is indeed shades of differentiated consciousness, then most of the universe *is* in balance. It doesn't worry about being in existence—it simply *is*. Every physical thing in the universe is in harmony with its temporal existence, whether it is the sun shining in the sky or my

*Attributed to Hermes Trismegistus, the father of the magical and religious movement known as *Hermeticism*. Representing a congruence of the Egyptian God *Thoth* and the Greek *Hermes*, Trismegistus's Hellenistic Egyptian pseudepigraphical writings have heavily influenced the Western Esoteric Tradition. The Tarot card "The Magician" represents the Hermetic intuition expressed as, "As above, so below."

dog when he moves from sleeping to becoming instantly alert if he hears the slam of a truck door.

Everything in the universe—so far—except us. For as humanity has been infected with the Promethean knowledge of creation, so too have we been infected with the doubts and fears that come with that high knowledge. As the philosopher Martin Heidegger wrote: "Man alone of all existing things . . . experiences the wonder of all wonders: *that* there *is* being."[19] Just as I look around in the darkest turmoil of my 5-MeO-DMT visions and ask who am I and how did I come to be there, so too now does humankind look around in the universe and wonder how it all came to be, while attempting to understand our part in that plan. And somehow, through some weird quirk in human programming, our Western industrial civilization decided about four hundred years ago that we *are* Absolute Consciousness. We convinced ourselves that there is nothing in our heads but ourselves, and G/d went silent. Now look what a mess we have made of the world.

I am going to go out on a limb, and allow myself to be pigeon-holed as a nut-job by all the good atheists like Richard Dawkins (and myself, before I smoked 5-MeO-DMT), and say that while we have turned our backs on G/d and declared him (or her or them) dead, G/d has been quietly watching and waiting for enough of us to tune back in.

Nor am I alone; as I have mentioned previously, there are a number of scientists and philosophers who are also starting to say much the same thing that I am—that we have underestimated G/d and the possibilities that believing in G/d's existence could bring. In the first line of astrophysicist Bernie Haisch's book *The God Theory* he says: "Surely it is time for all of us scientists to consider returning to God?"[20] And while (according to Haisch) 93 percent of the members of the American Academy of Sciences reject the concept of God, in a subsequent review for *The Journal of Scientific Discovery,* Professor Richard Conn Henry has this to say about the book's key ideas.

> Let me quote a single sentence from his book, which I have chosen because it so perfectly encapsulates my own understanding: "It is not matter that creates an illusion of consciousness, but consciousness that creates an illusion of matter." That is correct physics: it is not controversial in the *slightest* degree that there is no reality; this has

> been demonstrated in both theory and experiment (Gröblacher et al., *Nature,* 446, 871, 2007).*
>
> And yet in how many physics classes today are students made aware of this most fundamental discovery? In all of my classes, I assure you; but I am confident that this is not common. The illusion of matter, which is to say the illusion of a really-existing world, is so strong, that I think most scientists are unable to overcome it. It took *me* decades to finally realize that this is not a joke, and that the universe is *purely* mental: that mind is fundamental; matter merely an illusion—and that this is physics, not philosophy (or religion).
>
> And how, out of this, does *God* appear? Well, the only mind I *know* exists is my own. My choice is solipsism or God. A leap of faith is required, yes—but it is an easy leap indeed! Haisch, too, says his is "a theory that looks promising, not scientific proof."[21]

At the conclusion of the review, Richard Conn Henry—a Professor in Physics and Astronomy at the prestigious John Hopkins University in Baltimore—has this to say:

> In his Introduction, Haisch says "I have arrived at a personal worldview that offers a satisfying and hopeful explanation of reality—a worldview that is not only possible, rational, and compatible with modern science, but compelling and capable of resolving some of the most intransigent moral issues facing us today. It embodies a way out of our global dilemma and so I offer it for your consideration." I endorse this offer.
>
> I am still personally uncomfortable mentioning God. When I made the transition (2004) I composed "Great omniscient Spirit" (GoS), to keep my notion pure, and free of the historical, often vicious, God. But I am coming to think that this is a mistake; that we scientists should be *in the lead* of the battle to reclaim God from the wrong-headed . . . I would like, please, *every* scientist, to give *consideration* to how much better off we would be, individually and collectively, if the God Theory could become, once again, just as it was

*The Gröblacher et al. citation appears in the original extract text and is not part of the Notes for this book.

for Newton, the working hypothesis of modern science. It beats hell out of reductionism![22]

If you can rationally *accept* the necessity for the existence of G/d within the science and philosophy of the day, then it should be much easier to actually *realize* that conclusion. And if proven entheogens are ritually used, a mystical realization can result in a release of tremendous personal energy and understanding.

Liberation Theology

Although a drug experience might seem "unearned," our evidence has suggested that preparation and expectation play an important part, not only in the type of experience attained, but in later fruits for life. Perhaps the hardest "work" comes after the experience which itself may only provide the motivation for future efforts to integrate and appreciate what has been learned.

WALTER NORMAN PAHNKE, *DRUGS AND MYSTICISM* (THESIS), 1963

I have recently come across a new movement in radical Christianity called "liberation theology,"[23] which I believe provides a good model for an effective modern entheogen-based mystical tradition. Liberation theology, which began in Latin America, focuses on the twin actions of mystical insight and pragmatic activism. It is now practiced in more than a million small communities worldwide, where its effectiveness among the most repressed and neglected of the planet's communities has earned it a reputation as being "*only* a theology of radical, and even revolutionary, social and political action."[24]

While I have mostly ignored the history of Christian mysticism throughout this book, it is important to mention that all over the planet there are on-going attempts by radical Christian groups to recover the core mystical precepts of early Christianity. I have also only briefly mentioned Islamic Sufism or the Jewish Kabbalah, two mystical movements that, like the Tibetan and Hindu esoteric traditions, are saturated with references to light and the twin ideas that both consciousness and God are primarily composed of light. Numerous further chapters could be written on the parallels in these traditions, but my knowledge of them is barely sufficient to scratch the surface. It is safe to say, however, that most mystical traditions share central concepts, such as the existence of God, the idea that our human consciousness is a part or reflection of God's consciousness, and of the primacy of light—rather than matter—in the universe, with the human soul/consciousness commonly being described in relation to that light.

We tend to forget that the origins of the Christian church are mystical. The historical figure Jesus of Nazareth was a Jew and possibly an Essene, a member of a Gnostic community that existed in Galilee. (John the Baptist is now believed to have been an Essene.) Jesus himself was apparently personally inspired by direct mystical experience of transpersonal realms and their revelations, as is clearly expressed in the statement attributed to Jesus in the Gospel of St. Thomas: *I am the light that is over all things. I am all: from me all came forth, and to me all attained.*

Religious scholars believe that Jesus disappeared out of the holy land for a number of years and then reappeared to teach his radical message for only two-and-a-half years before he was crucified (as were many other wandering prophets and revolutionaries of the day). It could be argued that the mystical content of Jesus' teachings are the basis that separated early Christianity from the multitude of competing philosophies that existed in those tumultuous days. There is no doubt that the accounts of the resurrection and the subsequent fanaticism of Jesus' followers (including the mystical conversion of Paul on the road to Damascus) greatly impressed the religious sensibilities of the time. What was the most revolutionary concept in early Christianity—the one that set it apart from competing ideologies of the time? It was that humanity could know God *personally;* that "the kingdom of God is within you" (Luke 17:21).

There has been some speculation that Jesus traveled to India in the years when he disappeared from Galilee, where he became exposed to powerful Indian philosophies such as karma and reincarnation, which he later incorporated into his radical view of Judaism. This then resulted in the idea of an afterlife and the early Christian values of compassion and charity, which represented a radical departure from the vengeful Jewish belief system of the day. In any case, Jesus expressed a pronounced mystical bent in his teachings; his followers may not have understood that he wasn't seeking a physical kingdom in this world but the realization of a "higher kingdom" in another realm. At that time in Judaism ideas like "heaven and hell" did not commonly exist. The idea that there could be an existence for the soul in another realm after the body dies was a radical departure from Jewish belief, whose interest in "an after-life" was minimal, as the covenant between Yahweh and the Nation during life was seen as more important.

The history of organized religion is of institutional dogma built upon the foundation of direct mystical revelation. To a certain extent, dogma is the inevitable mortification of the original sense of responsibility that the mystical experience produces. Or as Colin Wilson expressed it, "[All] religions begin like a mountain stream, and slowly turn into a rather muddy river."[25] The spontaneous act of inspiration ultimately results in rigid theocracies, passing the power of knowing God over to the priests. But the role of that initial energy of responsibility, the call to action that a powerful transpersonal experience can provoke, cannot be ignored. The following quotation neatly explains this phenomenon with regard to Christianity: "[T]here is a double composition to following Christ; the mystical and the political. There is not first the mystical and then the political. . . . The political is of the substance of the mystical."[26]

I agree wholeheartedly with this view. The feeling of responsibility that I emerge from a 5-MeO-DMT experience with is not a result of the awe-induced ecstasy of the experience—it is an essential component of realization. I believe that charity and compassion are not necessarily natural to humans, they are higher graces, and as our societies have grown more and more complex, they have, correspondingly, only been earned by contemplation as the mature psyche "develops." This is a very difficult concept for the greedy materialistic modern mind to even consider, let alone try to understand.

Once considered "virtues," acts like charity and compassion are characterized as weaknesses in today's result-driven capitalist society. The philosopher Jacob Needleman has pointed out that although we are both material and spiritual beings, our culture has largely excluded the rich experience of the sacred from systematic awareness. Since we have much more tangible material experiences, we find it difficult to maintain a balance between the spiritual and the material. Charity and compassion are therefore rarely seen as the reward of spiritual labor (unless it is in the eyes of the enlightened beholder).

The result of the responsibility that is generated through a spiritual epiphany is expressed in contemplative activism. The Reverend George Cairns explains that, "The contemplative experience leads one to deeply understand that the inner work and the outer work are fully intertwined." Cairns further remarks:

> In fact, contemplative activists are some of the most effective agents for encouraging the liberation of individuals and systems in all of human history. They are persons whose inner practice overflows into the public sphere in exceedingly effective and powerful ways. They heal the split and expose the great fallacy through their prayers and actions. Consider this short list of persons of action in the twentieth century who have a contemplative awareness: Gandhi, Martin Luther King, Jr., Thomas Merton, Mother Theresa, Thich Nhat Hanh, and the Dalai Lama are but a few. These people embody the contemplative potentialities of what it is to be human and to act effectively on these understandings.[27]

The realization that accompanies a spiritual awareness of the interconnectivity of all things is, first-and-foremost, experiential. You cannot explain it, but you cannot help but believe it. You *know* it. This is the kind of gnosis we will need to guide us through the storm of the oncoming years. If you accept the full implication of that gnosis, then you are no longer a creature of chance alone in a cold universe—you are an "in-formed" being, a creation of purpose. By accepting that you have purpose, you must then accept the responsibility (or choose to actively ignore what has been revealed to you—something that is difficult to do after a mystical experience).

Extinction Denial

I started by saying that one of the most fateful errors of our age is the belief that the problem of production has been solved. This illusion, I suggested, is mainly due to our inability to recognize that the modern industrial system, with all its intellectual sophistication, consumes the very basis on which it has been erected. To use the language of the economists, it lives on irreplaceable capital which it cheerfully treats as income. I specified three categories of such capital: fossil fuels, the tolerance margins of nature, and the human substance. Even if some readers should refuse to accept all three parts of my argument, I suggest that any one of them suffices to make my case.

E. F. SCHUMACHER, *SMALL IS BEAUTIFUL: ECONOMICS AS IF PEOPLE MATTERED*, 1973

Before I smoked 5-MeO-DMT, back when I was a cynical over-educated pseudo-intellectual, I used to joke about an idea of mine that I called "the ten billion" theory. Basically it went like this: Over the past two hundred years, we have caused the human population to swell from around one billion people to over seven billion, and the latest estimates suggest it will reach ten billion by the year 2075. With so many mouths to feed, life becomes increasingly about survival and less about a search for enlightenment, despite the optimistic promises of the Industrial Revolution. What's even worse, technological advances have allowed us to pass along an increasing number of traits that—in past environments—would have been considered to be inferior.

So to my (tongue-in-cheek) way of thinking, this means that if by some miracle the current human society continues on unimpeded until the year 2050, in ten percent of the human population (i.e., one billion) there will be the usual proportion of geniuses, journeymen, and imbeciles. The remaining nine billion will be genetically defective—the result of the accelerated reproduction of inferior genetic traits, since our technology has allowed us to bypass many of the tenets of natural selection. A society based on consumerism, informed by a steady diet of television (or the Internet), and sedated with a plethora of prescription drugs, only worsens the trend toward a dumber, more dysfunctional general population. Which is why I joked that around ninety percent of people these days are nothing more than standing "dead wood."

Look around. What proportion of the planet do you think are leading spiritually fulfilling lives? And how many people do you know who are plugged into the television and their jobs, pumped full of legal uppers and downers, just a couple of generations away from having microchips and feeding tubes surgically implanted? You only have to read a book written eighty to a hundred years ago to realize how much more intelligent people were then, how much they actually used their brains, could follow a chain of complex ideas, and questioned the status quo. The magazines and newspapers with the highest circulation today are written at a ninth-grade level (down from the twelfth-grade level in the late 1940s).[28] Harry Potter books are routinely passed off as great literature, since most adults are now only capable of reading children's books. Television programming targets the lowest common denominator in order to sell products to the largest number of people. The less-informed the population, the easier they are to manipulate. Fed a constant diet of "entertainment," sans any intellectual challenge, the mind stops growing and starts to wither. I spoke with the great jazz photographer Herman Leonard one evening about this phenomenon, and he was amazed that someone so young as me could see it. The legendary eighty-six-year-old photographer has been friends with Louis Armstrong, Marlon Brando, Miles Davis, and Duke Ellington, just to name a few. With friends like that—and as the creator of some of the most beautiful black-and-white images from the history of jazz—a viper like Herman seems as qualified as any to comment on the intellectual prowess of the last few generations. We agreed that this "dumbing down" of the general population has been ongoing since the end of World War II, and that the general citizen is much less intelligent or capable than he or she would have been even fifty years ago.

Now that the combined interests of industry and government have perfected the use of television (which has only been around for a little over seventy years) as an instrument of control and propaganda, we are producing a generation of morons—spiritually and intellectually impaired half-humans—who are nothing more than moldable little cogs for the ever-ravenous industrial-military machine. A population too ignorant to be able to recognize that our society is destroying our planet in a ravenous inebriated fog of what I have termed "extinction denial."

Abraham Maslow and Transcendence

Or at least, that was my theory. Sure it seems extreme, and admittedly one that was circulated with a degree of humor. But since I have become a fan of the British existentialist writer Colin Wilson and been introduced to the ideas of the American psychologist Abraham Maslow, I've become convinced that not only was I correct in my basic intuition, but in fact I wasn't extreme enough!

Maslow saw human existence as a pyramid, where the smallest number of the population (the tip of the pyramid) manages to escape the biological "fight for survival" and reach the ultimate human state of transcendence, a state he called "self-actualization." Maslow had a list of self-actualized people, which combined historic personages and people he knew; Aldous Huxley was included on his list. To Maslow, self-actualized persons were: "*reality centered,* which means they could differentiate between what was fake and dishonest from what is real and genuine. They were *problem-centered,* meaning they treated life's difficulties as problems demanding solutions, not as personal troubles to be railed at or surrendered to. And they had a *different perception of ends and means.* They felt that the ends don't necessarily justify the means, that the means could be ends themselves, and the means—the journey—was often more important than the ends."[29]

Self-actualized people are assumed to be rare in Maslow's model—five percent is the commonly used ratio (although Maslow himself said it was as little as two percent of the human population!). This five percent composes "the dominant majority" (not the ten percent that I allowed for!), which dictates the evolutionary direction of any species, while within that five percent there is a much smaller group—five percent of the five percent—that seek the highest of human experiences—the "peak experience."

> The two types of peak experiences are relative and absolute. Relative characterize those peak experiences in which there remains an awareness of subject and object, and which are extensions of the individual's own experiences. They are not true mystical experiences, but rather inspirations, ecstasies, and raptures. It is thought that probably the majority of peak experiences fall into this category. Absolute peak experiences are characteristic of mystical experiences, and are comparable to

> experiences of great mystics in history. They are timeless, spaceless, and characterized by unity, in which the subject and object become one.[30]

Maslow called the attainment of this "absolute peak experience" *transcendence,* and while he considered it the ultimate experience a human being could have, it was assumed to only occur among a very small portion of the people who had "peak experiences"—probably around five percent (that is, five percent of the five percent of the five percent). This description of the "absolute peak experience" seems as good as any other I have found in regard to my own 5-MeO-DMT experiences. Out of an adventurous life dedicated to the search for such "peak experiences," it is certainly the only "absolute experience" I have ever encountered. The "five per cent of five per cent of five percent" who experience an "absolute peak experience" could also correspond to the very small number of 5-MeO-DMT users who experience a mystical "union with God" while under the influence of this compound.

We are the sharpened point of the spearhead of humanity. We are the "penetrators," the "first-ones-into-the-unknown." And thus we must be the creators of our future, and we must lead our tribes back toward a transcendent dialogue with G/d before it is too late. This is not the tribal God of war, nor the God of industry that is exhorted from pulpits of propaganda and patriotism: I am talking about the self-realized G/d. The only real G/d. The G/d contained within each and every one of us.

A World in Crisis

Not long after I first smoked 5-MeO-DMT, I was looking in the mirror in a bathroom one day, and an idea jumped into my brain as loud as a shout or a command: *Find the tribe!* After some reflection, I took this as a sign to search for the enlightened society of 5-MeO-DMT-smokers that I believed existed (probably on the West Coast) who, for some unknown reason, had been keeping this revolutionary compound under wraps. This search led to my toading adventures with Yaron and to my return to Burning Man. But I eventually realized that this tribe probably didn't actually exist. At that point, the message seemed to change (or maybe I had had it wrong the whole time). The message became: *Find* your *tribe. Build* your *tribe. And quit pissing around and get started.*

Find your tribe? Build your tribe? Noah, go into the hills, and make an Ark! Sounds like "crazy people talk," right? The only problem is, if you take a long cold look at the state of the world, it might actually be the only sensible advice.

As we near the end of the petrochemical paradigm, we are beginning to witness the enormous pains that will accompany our civilization as it runs out of oil. Two hundred years of burning up the planet's nonrenewable resources have created an unprecedented explosion in the human population and its domestic species.* The human population on the planet doubled in the last forty years and it may nearly double again by 2075.[31] We are within half a century of completely using up that massive energy-bank, which took 3.8 *billion* of years to create. A recent article quoted British Petroleum as having said, "The world holds enough proved reserves for 40 years of supply . . . at current consumption rates."[32] This is not factoring in the rampant industrialized growth of India and China. And if you believe an *oil company's* take on how much is left, then I have some nice lakefront property in New Orleans you might be interested in. History, if our species continues to have such a thing, will undoubtedly consider this period of our civilization completely insane.

The United States is now perceived to be run by oil companies, with its military off on rogue oil-bearing land grabs, while nothing is being done on any discernible scale to move our culture toward alternative forms of energy. In the summer of 2001, when then White House Press Secretary Ari Fleisher was asked if Americans should think about altering their lifestyles to conserve gasoline, Fleisher declared that President Bush believed that the current (gas-guzzling) lifestyle was "the American way of life," and that "it should be the goal of policy makers to protect the American way of life—the American way of life is a blessed thing."[33] The United States has 5 percent of the world population, and yet consumes 23 percent of its

*People talk about the fact that there are now over 6.6 billion people in the world (www.census.gov/main/www/popclock.html); what about the fact that there are currently 1.5 billion cows! See wiki.answers.com/Q/How_many_cows_are_there in_the_world. Accessed January 28, 2009.

energy resources. And as Gandhi, E. F. Schumacher, and Ervin Laszlo have all pointed out, there are enough resources on the planet to support our nearly 7 billion people (if we could somehow halt our exponential population growth) with an adequate way of life—but the wealthy nations (i.e., North America, Europe, Japan, and Australia) would need to "voluntarily" cut back on their heavy consumption of the planet's resources. Judging by the above statement issued from the heart of the American government, this seems extremely unlikely—and in fact, the developed nations are pouring capital into China and India to encourage them to "catch-up" with our own rate of consumption!

An overall estimate for the year 2009 defense budget in the United States comes to a trillion dollars for that single year alone.[34] Meanwhile, every 2.5 seconds or so, someone on the planet (usually a child) dies of starvation; that's around 35,000 starvation deaths each day.[35] The standard of life is now materially poorer for a greater percentage of people on this planet than it ever has been and spiritually emptier for nearly all of us. It's an ever-worsening situation, due to overpopulation and a scarcity of resources, and one that we seemingly cannot solve. Politicians flip-flop between talking about the economy and conserving our environment, while nobody seems to realize that our economy *needs* to go into recession for the global community as we know it to have a chance of surviving. Meanwhile the gross domestic product of the entire planet continues to grow at close to 3 percent a year. That's a nearly 20 percent increase in the world's "production" for the first seven years of the twenty-first century over the *total* production of the twentieth—which means (in real terms) that we have consumed more of the world's resources since the year 2000 than we probably did in the first *60 years* of the twentieth century! As William S. Burroughs used to say, "Contact *that!* Identify *with that!*" Because the fact is, our species has used up vast stores of our planet's resources and released billions of years' worth of stored energy into our world civilization; and when it all runs out, the bill will come due.

If you have been out in the world and seen a few things, or if you have read any of the copious books written on the subject, or even if you only read the newspapers (which thes e days have become the worst kind of propaganda), it is easy to see that "the consumer society" can't go on much longer. So where are the theories about how the world's economy will change when we no longer have oil? What will we do when there are twice as many people on the planet (and very little else)? The fact that most of humanity is humming along as "good little consumers" and that our leaders of government and business rarely ask any tough questions about even the *very* near future, makes me believe that the modern mind has a built-in insanity that refuses to tally up the bill. As I have said before, our species is suffering from "*extinction denial.*" The blindness of contemporary society is without precedent, particularly since there are so many educated voices who are now shouting at the top of their lungs that Rome is about to fall.

James Lovelock, the scientist who proposed the Gaia hypothesis (that the Earth functions as a sort of "super-organism") has declared that he believes the damage humans have done to the ecosphere has reached a point where it is irreversible. A recent newspaper article (October, 2008: *Miami Herald International Edition*) reported that a review of the world's mammals by the International Union of Conservation of Nature had concluded that 1 in 4 mammalian species were in threat of extinction—somewhere in the region of 1,150 species of mammals in total. It also reported that 76 mammal species had *become* extinct since the year 1500. The IUCN's report listed 44,838 of the world's *total* species as "threatened"; with 16,928 listed as "threatened with extinction." This report was the largest investigation of its kind and took more than five years, involving more than 1,700 scientists around the world. The IUCN describes itself as the world's oldest and largest global environment network. It is made up of more than 1,000 government and nongovernment organizations and almost 11,000 volunteer scientists in more than 160 countries. The effects of global warming are now so undeniable that even the most conservative of groups (e.g., the Bush administration) no longer deny its effects, although they continue to argue about *why* it is happening! Even former politicians and actors, such as Al Gore and Leonardo DiCaprio, are using their fame to draw attention to the dangerous straits we are in.

Ervin Laszlo has written several books suggesting that the human species can bring about a change in consciousness in order to survive the oncoming crisis that we've created.[36] One of these is the 1999 book *The Consciousness Revolution: A Transatlantic Dialogue,* which is an edited transcript of conversations between Laszlo, scientist Peter Russell, and transpersonal psychiatrist Stanislav Grof. These three men's calm dialogue reveals a sobering (and terrifying) assessment of the depth and seriousness of humanity's dilemma. Yet Laszlo still maintained a positive outlook. Then in 2006, Laszlo released a book titled *The Chaos Point: The World at the Crossroads,* in which he appears to have reversed his previously positive assessment of our ability to pull ourselves out of this impending crisis. Laszlo now believes that unless humanity begins a massive shift in consumption and values within the next four years (by 2013), we will move past a tipping point and there will be no bringing our civilization back.[37]

So says "arguably [one of] the most profound thinkers alive today."[38] But if you are logical and you have been paying attention, using "all the available facts to form the best hypotheses," then you don't need to be a genius to see that there is no way out of this blind alley that the industrial revolution has led us down. Here is a random example of the wide variety of astonishing numbers that are readily available to demonstrate the exponential rate of increase of our expanding population's consumption of the planet's resources: a little over a century ago, the United States' leading automobile manufacturer produced six cars a day, while in 2007 alone the world produced 73 million automobiles and trucks. There are a staggering 251 million registered vehicles in the United States. China, whose production has been almost doubling each year, manufactured 8.8 million cars in 2007. While we junked *a billion* vehicles in the twentieth century, we will have produced nearly that many by the end of the first decade of the twenty-first. And under our current economic model, all production *must* increase . . .

The graph of our population growth (increasing dramatically) against our available energy supplies (decreasing significantly; at an *appalling* rate, if you consider the geological time scale they took to create) intersects between 2025 and 2030. Unless the human race has found abundant clean energy from either the zero-point field, hydrogen fusion (fairly unlikely), or some other source, then our society will hit its natural "ceiling"—known as an entropy watershed—and it will all be downhill from there.

It is easy to see that there is no discernible *decrease* in consumption, let alone any actual *conservation* of our rapidly extinguishing resources on a major scale. And if you can agree that the world has a finite amount of resources then you will come to a conclusion similar to mine: that in the not too distant future, the resources of the planet will begin to see such significant shortages (oil, water, top soil, wood, and so on) that we will not be able to sustain society at its required energy levels. Our society will hit its entropy watershed, and then our current style of civilization will completely unwind.*

Of course I knew a lot of this before I first smoked 5-MeO-DMT, and—like most modern intellectuals overburdened with information—I felt powerless to do anything to make a change. The 5MDE has changed that for me. As a modern mystic, I have considered these same conclusions and then found the strength and inspiration to try to take a stand. As I see it, our cancerous modern civilization *must* collapse; for if it does not, it will take down the entire ecosphere. As the majority of the nonrenewable resources on the planet run out—in about thirty years or so by my estimate—and in concert with the radical environmental crisis that our technology has created, there will be an upheaval of society that will be without parallel in human history. Out of the rubble of that society, over the centuries to come, survivors will emerge. You who have found strength from the transcendental G/d within must start taking steps to build your tribe and secure your future, to be part of the proactive 5 percent that will lead by surviving and not part of the 95 percent who are likely to be left behind. The future is dark, but it is clear to the enlightened. Now the task is to see if we can live up to that responsibility.

The First Shaman

The reduction of the human population by environmental pressures to small bands struggling to survive is not without precedent. The remarkable human genome project sponsored by *National Geographic* has revealed an incredible fact: that the human population was once a number of scattered tribes on the verge of extinction.[39]

---

*Terence McKenna came up with the end-date of December 21, 2012, which coincides with the culmination of the Mayan calendar. His proposal has aroused a great deal of speculation, and now other authors seeking popularity are running with it. Unless we get struck by a comet or an asteroid on that day (or someone goes mad on the nuclear trigger), then it strikes me as unlikely that any singular event on a specific day will precipitate a global collapse. In many ways this is irrelevant, since I do *agree* that we are clearly in the midst of a series of ongoing events, which have begun in the last century and will accelerate until our final societal collapse. We are within a shift between ages and paradigms, and the dramatic sort of change that will eventually come about would be difficult to achieve in a single day.

> What seems virtually certain now is that at a remarkably recent date—probably between 50,000 and 70,000 years ago—one small wavelet from Africa lapped up onto the shores of western Asia. All non-Africans share markers carried by those first emigrants, who may have numbered just a thousand people.
>
> Some archaeologists think the migration out of Africa marked a revolution in behavior that also included more sophisticated tools, wider social networks, and the first art and body ornaments. Perhaps some kind of neurological mutation had led to spoken language and made our ancestors fully modern, setting a small band of them on course to colonize the world.[40]

It appears that some new cerebral development occurred that spurred the next stage of human consciousness—apparently just when we needed it to survive. The discovery of art, body ornament, and indeed spoken language would all seem to require an inspiration beyond animal survival. Perhaps, as humanity reached its lowest population ever—a tribe in numbering in the thousands—we suddenly, inexplicably, discovered the voice inside our heads that we would come to call God. Subsequently—due to this newfound ability that apparently no other animal shares—we went on to become the dominant species on the planet in a little over 50,000 years.

Think about that original moment—the birth of the first word. As we have established, radical mutations seem to occur *spontaneously*—and I do not believe that language is an adaptation that was slowly acquired over time. So now if you will allow me a little poetic license, imagine if you will the lone hunter-gatherer, strayed away from his small family and tribe, foraging for something for them all to eat. The tribe's hunting grounds have grown smaller and smaller, and they have moved north and east, chased by the deteriorating environment, the hot wind, and ever-increasing sands of the growing desert seemingly always at their heels. The full moon is up and it is easier to hunt at night. But our early human gives no thanks to the moon, simply realizing its existence in an animal way, more interested in the immediate search for food than where that pale light might come from. He (or perhaps she) feels the pressure of hunger. The world is changing around the shrinking tribe, and somehow our hunter-gatherer poised right there on the dawn of *Homo sapiens sapiens* knows this in an intuitive way, but right now all he feels is a desperate hunger that roots him in the immediate. He rests on the trunk of a fallen tree, its underside rotting against the dark red earth. Seeing a large pile of dung mixed with the soft wood, he looks for beetles or grubs that might sustain him, as well as for traces of game, and he sees a form he has not seen before: a soft pliable fungus now growing upon the mixture of dung and wet wood, the moonlight clearly illuminating these popping pale nodes. Picking a handful, he examines these mushrooms by sniffing and finds no noxious odors, just a damp smell of the earth. His hunger forces him to throw any animal caution to the wind and he eats several handfuls of their abundance, filling his stomach, while gathering still more to take to his family.

On the way back down the hill he has climbed, he stops to drink from a small pond of water. Then, looking into it, he notices a most peculiar thing: the moon above him, reflected in the water, now looks down at him as a giant eye. Terrified, he looks up and sees that the moon is larger than he has ever noticed. It is growing and growing until it is larger than the world, a giant eye staring down at him and then eating him up in cold flames . . . until finally he sinks down in a daze and dies a death of light that takes him from this world, to worlds he could never have imagined before. Hours pass. But to our hunter-gatherer it makes no difference, for he has moved into a realm far beyond his animal senses of space and time . . . until finally he returns to his body, his new-consciousness infused with that light, with the memory of symbols attached to things and sounds attached to symbols. Once again he opens his eyes, and now he sees the sun rising ahead of him. After a night passed in ecstasy, full of the *mysterium tremendum et fascinans* that he has experienced and now seeing the light of lights rise, he opens his mouth, and he emits something more than a grunt, more than a howl, a sound that is now a symbol for meaning, a sound that tries to explain the power and wonder of what he has just experienced, a sound to express a new realization to the world. Opening his mouth to the universe, our hunter-gatherer, who has now become the first shaman, who will become the first *Human* breaks the silence of the world and shouts out the first spoken, screamed, awe-struck word: "*GOD!*" For what other word could have come first?

From that moment the direction and destiny of life on this planet was radically altered. Another connection between the world of matter and the world of in-formation had been made, a new higher interface. The first shaman, with a consciousness now sharpened like a knife and a voice inside his head to lead his tribe to safety, going on to decorate his body like the visions he saw, create tools out of the forms that appear in his mind, and marking the walls to honor the Gods he now sees. The greatest magic of the first shaman *must* have been the first word. And from that moment, language would have spread like an infection, bringing with it the radical new ability to store and transfer knowledge from generation to generation, an inexplicable learned technology that would transform the entire planet over the next 50,000 years.

A New Consciousness?

These days, having mostly lost that original ability to listen to G/d due to our own intellectual arrogance, we may soon face the threat of extinction again. Ironically, that may not be a bad thing for the future of the human species and definitely not for the planet as a whole.

Historically, the human race definitely would appear to have evolved through a series of evolutions of our consciousness, with the invention of language being one of the most radical. Our evolution as a species *is* our development of consciousness, for our physical body has remained essentially unchanged in forty thousand years. Numerous thinkers both ancient and modern—the Buddha, Sri Aurobindo, Teilhard de Chardin, Laszlo, and the modern spiritual teacher Eckhart Tolle, to name just a few—have espoused the view that humanity is destined to undergo an "ultimate" flowering of consciousness that will bring in a new understanding and a new age for humanity.

Now, I find it very difficult to believe that the billions and billions of people in the world will undergo a mass transformation of consciousness that will then allow us to fix the tremendous number of problems—social, political, and environmental—that overpopulation and the Industrial Revolution have managed to create. But I *do* find it credible that a humanity reduced to a series of small tribes on the verge of extinction could make that evolutionary leap—as it appears we did some 50,000 years ago. I also think that this transformation can begin *before* the inevitable collapse of our nonrenewable-energy driven society. Foresight alone may turn out to be the key to our evolutionary survival.

Thom Hartmann makes a convincing argument in the second half of his book *The Last Hours of the Ancient Sunlight* for the importance of building self-sufficient communities to prepare for the inevitable collapse that is on humanity's horizon. Burning Man should be considered an expression of the subconscious desire for such a future community—a place where we can be free and express ourselves without fear and to find our own G/d in our own manner. Historically, this type of community has a precursor in Gnosticism, a movement that appeared at several points during Western history, which caused numerous people to leave the cities of Europe to set up small, self-sufficient communities dedicated to the pursuit of directly experiencing God.

There is no doubt in my mind that if humanity is to become strong enough to survive the tests of the rest of the twenty-first century (and beyond), then we will need to create communities that are validated by direct spiritual experience. In the future society, we must regain the use of ritual, metaphor, and entheogens, as vehicles of transcendence and realize that the ultimate vision of G/d is formless, ensuring that the culturally bound manifestations of deities can no longer be used as instruments of war and control. Tryptamines may be the only sacraments strong enough to knock modern humans so totally out of our rationalist box that they guarantee a genuine "value experience," while for a small number of users 5-MeO-DMT would be able to conduit the ultimate human experience: the recognition of the true transcendental nature of G/d and the subsequent experience of that G/d within.

Within the entheogenic community, facets of this experiment in modern human spirituality have already begun. Within my own life, it is most obvious in my Burning Man tribe, where a loose-knit group of people with tenuous connections is steadily becoming more of a family. The intentional ritual use of 5-MeO-DMT has proven to be an integral part of our growth and identity. Inspired by the power of my own voyages, the experiences within my tribe, and from the knowledge that my research has steadily revealed, I have now adopted the cloak of the mystic-philosopher. This book can be considered the pinnacle of my delusion or the sum of my knowledge, depending on which position you take on my sanity and seriousness. It is my hope that more people will come to consider my ideas with interest, due to the intensity of their own direct experiences.

Thanks to my epiphany by using 5-MeO-DMT, I now possess the convictions of a man who believes he has experienced the intent of G/d, and who is willing to let that G/d guide him. The future of my life increasingly appears inexorably linked with the future community that I hope to help build. It is within my tribe, and within the greater Burning Man community, that I have the greatest hope of finding energized souls who carry irrevocable convictions similar to my own.

God Consciousness Is *Real*

> *The task of our generation, I have no doubt, is one of metaphysical reconstruction.*
>
> E. F. Schumacher, *Small Is Beautiful,* 1973

While this book is my act of radical self-expression, it is also my call to revolution. It declares the following manifesto: God consciousness is *real.* G/d is still there, waiting. There is the possibility of a positive future for the human race, or at least for that part of humanity that will survive the oncoming disaster of our own making. That is why there has been a rise in the entheogenic consciousness of the Western world; the telephone line is wired into our own DNA. As many of us as possible need to open ourselves back up to our own personally realized G/d and start listening again, before it's too late.

Our generation may not have had much in the way of spiritual or political leaders (and a good teacher is hard to find), but we do have rare scientists and authors like Sasha Shulgin and the late Aldous Huxley, who walked down this road before I was even born. Their words are guides for us, as sure as any Bible or scripture. Consider the following paragraphs from the introduction to the Shulgins' encyclopedic work *PIHKAL: A Chemical Love Story.* They perfectly express my own views on the value of entheogens, and especially 5-MeO-DMT, to our society.

> I have stated some of my reasons for holding the view that psychedelic drugs are treasures. There are others, and many of them are spun into the texture of this story. There is, for instance, the effect they have on

> my perception of colors, which is completely remarkable. Also, there is the deepening of my emotional rapport with another person, which can become an exquisitely beautiful experience, with eroticism of sublime intensity. I enjoy the enhancement of the senses of touch, smell and taste, and the fascinating changes in my perception of the flow of time.
>
> I deem myself blessed, in that I have experienced, however briefly, the existence of God. I have felt a sacred oneness with creation and its Creator, and—most precious of all—I have touched the core of my own soul.
>
> It is for these reasons that I have dedicated my life to this area of inquiry. Someday I may understand how these simple catalysts do what they do. In the meantime, I am forever in their debt. And I will forever be their champion.[41]

My personal faith in the reality of my experience has only grown as this investigation has proceeded. Evidence that my 5MDEs are true to the mystical experience now seem to litter the cosmos like Christmas lights, and I have no trouble believing in the veracity of my own experiences, even in times when I would rather not. Passages like this one from Joseph Campbell's *The Inner Reaches of Outer Space: Metaphor as Myth and as Religion,* where he is explaining the common origin of ancient metaphors and the sacred power that those metaphors can carry with them, only further that belief.

> Amongst the most widely known and (formerly) commonly understood symbolic signs inherited from Bronze Age times by the high civilizations of both the Occident and the Orient were the sun and the moon: the latter, the moon, which sheds its shadow to be born again, connoting the power of life, as here engaged in the field of time, to throw off death—which is to say, the power of life, as here embodied in each of us, to know itself as transcendent of carnality; with the sun, the light which is unshadowed, recognized as the light and energy of consciousness disengaged from this field of time, transcendent and eternal.
>
> In the context of these symbolic assignments, the cycle of a single

> lunar month has been compared, by analogy, to the term of a human lifetime, with the fifteenth night, which is of the moon becoming full, equated with the human adult's thirty-fifth year (in the reckoning of three-score years and ten as the human norm). On that very special evening there is a moment when the rising moon, having just emerged on the horizon, is directly faced across the world, from the opposite horizon, by the setting sun. Certain months of the year the two, at this perfectly balanced moment, are of equal light and the same size. By analogy, the confrontation *has been likened to that in the midmoment of a lifetime when the light of consciousness reflected in the mind may be recognized, either suddenly or gradually, as identical with that typified metaphorically as of the sun. Whereupon, if the witness is prepared, there ensues a transfer of self-identification from the temporal, reflecting body to the sunlike eviternal source, and one then knows oneself as consubstantial with what is of no time or place but universal and beyond death, yet incarnate in all beings everywhere and forever; so that as we again may read in the Upaniṣad:* tat tvam asi, *"thou art that."* [Italics mine.][42]

As universal, powerful, and ancient as this metaphor may be, still I was unaware of it when—in the last month of my thirty-fifth year—"the light of consciousness" exploded in my mind after I first smoked 5-MeO-DMT, and I came to recognize the timeless, sun-like, eviternal nature of its source: a light brighter than any sun. You can imagine the jolt of recognition that went through me like a lightning bolt when I first read this transcendental passage from our master mythologist. While science might not consider it a "proof" of any kind, I personally have no problem considering it solid evidence that my views and theories about the nature of the source of the 5-MeO-DMT experience have a historical basis and are far from entirely wrong.

Let me conclude this lengthy chapter with an anonymous quote I found one morning over breakfast from a spirituality column called "The Speaking Tree" in *The Times of India* newspaper. After several years of reading every Eastern philosophical text I could lay my hands on, as well as numerous volumes on quantum physics, mysticism, and transpersonal psychology, it remains the best phenomenological description I have yet found that mirrors my own 5-MeO-DMT experiences.

Then comes the state of dhyan, going back in time when there was nothing physical, but just pure consciousness. You will find that you are unable to draw boundaries to this fathomless space in front of you. There are so many human beings. This only indicates that at some level we all are one. . . . You do not achieve dhyan; you enter into the state of dhyan.

Finally comes the state of Samadhi. Samadhi is a state to be experienced and not discussed.

FIFTEEN

So Begin the Days of Strangeness

The answer is never the answer. What's really interesting is the mystery. If you seek the mystery instead of the answer, you'll always be seeking. I've never seen anybody really find the answer, but they think they have. So they stop thinking. But the job is to seek mystery, evoke mystery, plant a garden in which strange plants grow and mysteries bloom. The need for mystery is greater than the need for an answer.

KEN KESEY, "THE ART OF FICTION CXXXVI,"
THE PARIS REVIEW, 1994

The best things can't be told: the second best are misunderstood.

ATTRIBUTED TO HEINRICH ZIMMER (1890–1943) BY
JOSEPH CAMPBELL, *THE INNER REACHES OF OUTER SPACE: METAPHOR AS MYTH AND AS RELIGION,* 2002

I left India in December of 2004 and flew to Bangkok to meet my little sister and my girlfriend who would soon become my wife (I had bought her diamond engagement ring in India, but I had not yet proposed). I had never been so glad to leave a country in my life. India had totally exhausted me—beaten me to the ground—and the initial excitement of my discovery of 5-MeO-DMT had been well tempered by the harsh physical realities of those three hard months in Asia. But India had changed me in ways I did not know. It's one of those places you have to get away from before you can appreciate what happened to you while you were there. My mind was clear after the long weeks of unhurried reflection, and work on this book had already begun. Without really realizing it, I had started out on my road to knowledge.

The three of us spent Christmas together in Bangkok and met at the airport at 7:00 a.m. the next morning to fly to the islands off the east coast of Thailand. My girlfriend had a group of friends on a yacht in Krabi on the west coast that she wanted us to meet up with. She had left the travel arrangements to me, and I had uncharacteristically not followed up on them. This was partially because I had been trying to let my sister shape our trip in Thailand, since she had been there previously (and I had not), and I didn't want to seem like a bossy big brother. And it was partially because it just didn't seem like the direction we were supposed to go, based on a vague feeling that was still strong enough to cause my inertia every time I thought about booking our tickets to Krabi. Then all the seats got booked leading up to Christmas, resulting in our only being able to get tickets to the islands on Thailand's less popular east coast. My girlfriend wasn't particularly happy about it, and she was rather surprised since she was used to my being fairly efficient about such matters. But she didn't make a fuss, so we flew to Koh Samui early in the morning on Boxing Day, 2004.

We had barely found a room and made it to the beach when we first heard about the tsunami that had just struck the west coast of the country, only a hundred miles away. It seemed like paradise that morning on the beach where we were, and the news had a sense of unreality about it. At first I thought that there had been some kind of a terrorist attack, until—back at our bungalows—I watched reports on TV, and I slowly began to realize the magnitude of the event that had just occurred. Our initial concern was for my girlfriend's friends in Krabi (their boat was destroyed, but they all survived). Then I had a vision of the three of us arriving hung over with our luggage, looking for a room as the killer wave hit, and I instinctively felt that one of us would not have survived. One of the three of us, at the least—my little sister, my soon-to-be fiancée, or myself—would have been dead. We had just gotten very lucky indeed.

I later realized that the earthquake I had taken as a sign to smoke

5-MeO-DMT at that small temple in northern India a month earlier had been on the same fault line that stretched down into the Indian Ocean, and had in fact been a pretremor, a "warning shot" (if you like), of the massive 9.2 earthquake that caused the catastrophic tsunami. Another circle of understanding seemed to close.

The next couple of weeks in Thailand were sobering to say the least, as the country struggled to regain its balance after the cataclysmic event. Unfortunately, it seemed to set the tone for events to follow. Arriving back in New Orleans after many months, the first thing I did was go to the funeral of a friend who had drowned while having an epileptic fit in a hot tub. Four more years of Bush and Co. were upon us, and the mood of the country was bleak as the war in Iraq wore on. A personal slander of bizarre proportions then raised its head after seven years, only to burn out as quickly as it appeared. Mardi Gras was cold and quiet, brightened mostly by my own engagement (in full costume) on Mardi Gras day. My father had a cancer scare, and several of my friends' parents died. Captain Urquhart broke his back on a rope swing over the Mississippi river and was lucky not to be paralyzed. My best friend called to tell me that a mutual good friend, one of the most talented pilots I had ever known, had died in a tragic hang-gliding accident.

The blows just kept coming, and I kept my head down. Without having realized it while I had been there, my time in India had clarified a lot of things. I was reading constantly, and the discoveries on these pages were starting to take shape. But every time I tried to smoke 5-MeO-DMT, the power of it floored me and the message remained that I needed to take a break for a while. No more wandering around in the stratosphere for me. My feet were needed on the ground. This saddened me, since I wondered where the love-filled explorations of my early experiences had gone. But I (mostly) heeded the message and pressed on with writing this book. I went to my Caribbean home for the summer of 2005 and spent most of my time writing. I desperately wanted the book to be ready for Burning Man 2005. But as my intellectual explorations widened, I realized this would probably not be possible, so I went to the Man with a few unfinished drafts for friends instead.

When Captain Urquhart and I drove out of New Orleans a little more than a week before Burning Man in August of 2005, Hurricane Katrina was just another storm lurking in the Atlantic off the coast of Florida. By the time the weekend arrived, the storm had made its way into the Gulf and then undergone the rapid expansion that would make it one of the most powerful storms in recorded history. I was already in Black Rock City by then, setting up camp with members of our new tribe, and Sunday my wife-to-be caught the second-to-last flight out of New Orleans. (Southwest Airlines had the only planes that were still flying.) We had booked her flight months earlier, since Burning Man was to have been our unofficial honeymoon. (We ended up taking a while longer to actually *get* married—I think we took two honeymoons first!) She's a doctor with her own practice and gets very little free time—it had not been without considerable difficulty that she managed to take the time off. We had just gotten unbelievably lucky again.

The Monday that the hurricane struck New Orleans was the only windy day of the week at Burning Man. We sat inside our house-bus watching the dust storm pummeling the tents and domes, while wondering what the wind was doing to my wife's hometown. I was preaching the power of positive thought, since it seemed pointless to take any other approach, and I honestly believed that the storm would turn north and east at the last minute, sparing the city. I figured that the storm would move due to the difference in temperature between the warm waters at the mouth of the Mississippi and the cooler water of the Gulf of Mexico. But my wife, who had seen many hurricanes before, intuitively knew better. She told me that when she looked down on New Orleans as she had flown away in the airplane, leaving tens of thousands of less fortunate people behind on the ground, she knew that her home town would never be the same again. Unfortunately, we were both right.

The storm did turn, obliterating the area around the Bay of St. Louis in Mississippi like a nuclear bomb and leaving New Orleans with surprisingly little wind damage. It was the next day, when she called her father in New Orleans, that we discovered that the canals that led off the earthen levees had failed—not the levees themselves, as is often mistakenly thought—and the city we both loved was filling up like a soup bowl. The federal government likes to spin it another way, but the fact is that New Orleans *survived* Hurricane Katrina. It just didn't survive the shitty engineering of the U.S. Army Corps of Engineers.

Everybody with half a brain was over in Iraq, so nobody had a clue what to do when the shit hit the fan. There was one National Guard helicopter in the state—the rest were in Iraq. So were all the Louisiana National Guard's amphibious vehicles specially designed for the bayou, even though last time I looked, Iraq was a desert, since Hussein drained off all that country's swamps. I guess the U.S. military doesn't read *National Geographic.* After 9/11 and the ongoing disaster of the Afghanistan/Iraq occupation, the fallacy of American invincibility was over, once and for all.

For myself, 2005 will go down in history as a really tough year, but an eye-opening one, if nothing else. We pulled out of Black Rock City and quickly returned to New Orleans, and work on this book virtually stopped for the next nine months. America's most costly natural disaster: these words don't mean much until they're talking about your own hometown (or your wife's). I could write a whole other book about those first months in New Orleans, but the thoughts I have on that matter have no place in this volume. My wife's house had ten-and-a-half feet of water through it. She lost close to everything personal that she owned. A house that I owned took two feet of water in its downstairs apartment. But now, comparatively speaking, we consider our losses so minor that we barely bother talking about them. New Orleans was witness to devastation on a biblical scale, and we feel lucky to have come through it with the great majority of our friends and acquaintances still alive.

Suffice it to say that all the ideas I had been formulating about the necessity of preparing communities that will be able to withstand the tumultuous years to come, and all the intuitions I had about the importance of having a working tribe, proved to be far more prescient then I could have ever imagined. I have seen the response of normal people; I have seen the help that government (local, state, and federal) can offer us; and I have a far better idea of how quickly things can fall to pieces then I ever did when I began writing this book. I spent two months living by generator waiting for someone else to return, had every U.S. agency known to man stick a submachine gun in my face, and watched military hummers dumping their garbage in the parking lot of the retirement home behind my house. I sat there ignoring Hurricane Rita's "mandatory evacuation," when the city's civilian population was estimated at around 250 people, and my fiancé and I were two of the few who watched that fat yellow full moon rise over a city devoid of electricity, seeing it just like it must have looked two or three hundred years ago.

I feel that I have been granted a vision of how quickly our civilization will come apart, and how easily it can happen. I honestly believe that we don't have too much longer to go before this insane asylum we have built on the rewards of the Industrial Revolution hears the strains of music that signal the beginning of the last dance. In fact, the first chords of that tune may have already begun.

Through all the dirt and mold and grime and sweat and heat and mosquitoes the size of humming birds, through all the hard bitter months when I gutted my house and dragged what few possessions we could save from my wife's home, through all the weeks we gave shelter and support to shell-shocked friends as they returned to New Orleans to sift through the wreckage of their lives, I was glad that I had heeded the message of my later 5-MeO-DMT journeys and that I had "come back down to the ground." If there was ever a time in my life when I needed to have both of my feet firmly planted on the Mother Earth, it was during those months when most of the rest of the country seemed to have lost all common sense. While the rebuilding of New Orleans is a monumental task that will take years to realize, I can credit a lot of my "centeredness" during those critical first months to the new man I had become thanks to the wonders the 5-MeO-DMT experience had taught me. A man with faith in his heart truly can move mountains. This is one more lesson I have learned.

Five years have passed since I first discovered 5-MeO-DMT. This book has strayed far beyond the parameters I imagined for it that night walking the streets of Pushkar, when I first considered the idea of writing about my experience. There were several reasons why I wondered at that time if writing a book about 5-MeO-DMT was even a good idea at all.

The first (and main) doubt came from my recognition that writing a book dedicated to what was at the time still an easily available, unscheduled, powerful psychoactive tryptamine might draw unwanted attention from the authorities, resulting in the scheduling of 5-MeO-DMT and thereby impacting the ease with which it could be obtained. I suspect that many other users of non-scheduled tryptamines and phenethylamines felt the same way that I did, listening to that little voice in their heads that said, "Don't ruin a good thing." This may be the reason why there was a cloak of secrecy around the fact that you could obtain 5-MeO-DMT and other interesting "research chemicals" on the Internet around that time.

There is no mention of the legal status of 5-MeO-DMT in *TIHKAL,* which is the primary reliable source book on tryptamines that I have found. There is no mention of 5-MeO-DMT at all in the second edition (1992) of Shulgin's book *Controlled Substances: Chemical & Legal Guide to Federal Drug Laws,* which would lead one to believe that it was not illegal at the time that book was printed. Jonathan Ott's 1993 book *Pharmacotheon* (as well as the second edition in 1996) lists 5-MeO-DMT as "not controlled."

Daniel Pinchbeck, in his sophomoric take on "modern shamanism" titled *Breaking Open the Head* (2003) mentions a privileged group at Burning Man who called themselves "The Church of the Motherfuckers" who used a "white smokable powder" that provided "the white light of God"—which I was quite sure must have been 5-MeO-DMT, though Pinchbeck neither revealed the name of the compound nor mentioned actually trying it. When I engaged in a sustained investigation in an attempt to find out, it resulted in a lot of stonewalling by those in the know, who said that they had been sworn to secrecy. However when I asked Pinchbeck himself at a question-and-answer session at the World Psychedelic Conference in Basel, Switzerland in 2008, he confirmed that it was indeed 5-MeO-DMT, as I had long suspected. Maybe by then, since 5-MeO-DMT was no longer easily available on the Internet, he figured that it didn't matter anymore. But for the most part, in the late nineties and early years of this century, no one was mentioning, in the print media (in the U.S.) anyway, that 5-MeO-DMT was not illegal and readily available.

Websites were a different story however. Just prior to mid-2004, to discover any of multiple companies selling an assortment of nonscheduled "research chemicals," including 5-MeO-DMT, all you had to do was type the word "tryptamine" or "phenethylamine" into a search engine. The Internet was the real popularizer and distributor of unscheduled psychoactive chemicals, and the increased notoriety it provided eventually attracted government attention. In July of 2004 the DEA busted a number of vendors for violations of the Federal Controlled Substance Analogue Act. This action caused most of the remaining vendors to close up shop, and those companies selling research chemicals today have largely moved overseas or underground.

In October of 2007, a young man in Kansas City, Missouri was arrested on four drug-related charges, one of which was due to his possessing a toad "with the intent to extract the venom to smoke it." *Bufo alvarius* venom may contain trace amounts of bufotenine, a controlled substance, which could make it illegal. Apparently David S. Theiss was charged with three counts of possession of a controlled substance and one count of possessing drug paraphernalia; yes, the toad was considered as "paraphernalia."[1] This is the second toad-related arrest that I am aware of in the United States. The first one happened in 1994, when Robert and Connie Lin Shepard of Sonora, California were arrested on drug charges, including the possession of four toads. Despite the fact that 5-MeO-DMT is *not* technically illegal, the DEA has arrested vendors who sold it in the past. Practically speaking, this has made 5-MeO-DMT much more difficult to obtain in synthetic form today; hence, publication of this book is unlikely to have any impact on supply related issues. Strike reason number one not to write this book.

The second reason I considered not writing this book is obvious—for my own safety. I have chosen to write this book using a pseudonym in the hope of remaining anonymous, and in keeping with an approach that all today's psychonauts would be wise to embrace. The reality of this unfortunate situation was capably expressed by Hunter S. Thompson when writing about the "drug scene" in 1967:

> There is no shortage of documentation for the thesis that the current Haight-Ashbury scene is only the orgiastic tip of a great psychedelic iceberg that is already drifting in the sea lanes of the Great Society. Submerged and uncountable is the mass of intelligent, capable heads who want nothing so much as peaceful anonymity. In a nervous society where a man's image is frequently more important than his reality, the only people who can afford to advertise their drug menus are those with nothing to lose.[2]

My wish for anonymity is partially due to the draconian political atmosphere in most of the world today, but also because my identity is unimportant. In a world where the "cult of personality" has run amok, I would much rather have readers focus on the ideas I am presenting than on the person behind those ideas, a fate that H.S.T. himself came to intimately know. While I confess to a fondness for fiction, let me assure you that there is no fiction in this account. I have tried hard to avoid elaboration and just relate my experiences as they happened, which, when it comes to entheogens, is no easy task. But ultimately I decided that the information that I ended up gathering for this book was too important not to be shared.

The third reason I initially considered not writing this book was the fact that I have been writing for many years; and although I mention drugs frequently enough in my fiction writing, I did not want to be pigeonholed as a "drug writer." Since that time, I have had the opportunity to reacquaint myself with writers like Aldous Huxley, Ken Kesey, and Terence McKenna. I have also discovered other fine writers like the Shulgins, Jeremy Narby, and the great Peruvian novelist César Calvo. And I have also come to reconsider the role of William S. Burroughs—whom I consider one of the great writers of the twentieth century—within this pantheon. (See appendix 5 for my reflections on William S. Burroughs' role in the history of DMT.) Thus, I now consider it an honor to be able to participate in this particular branch of revolutionary Western literature.

In truth, the most obvious reason I considered not writing this book was because I wondered, "What's the point?" How could I hope to put into words the all-encompassing totality of the inexplicable power and mystery of the 5MDE? Or hope to rationally relate even a fraction of it? How can a man who had no discernible belief in God in his life explain how smoking a white powder caused him to realize—in his heart, soul, and finally mind—the undeniable existence of G/d? What skeptic would believe that a laboratory chemical had caused me to have a genuine mystical experience during which I believe I experienced a union with the Mind of G/d? From the outside, the whole idea is ridiculous. From the inside, its essence seems both sacred and untranslatable. Describing the ineffable is the same problem that mystics have been facing for thousands of years. So what new light could I hope to reflect in any book about 5-MeO-DMT?

I decided I should write this book from a "safe dosage" point of view, because many heads don't even know that there is a *difference* between 5-MeO-DMT and "normal" DMT. This is a dangerous simplification and should be avoided. Even extremely experienced, intelligent, largely well-read heads have accidentally smoked substantial overdoses of 5-MeO-DMT, due to the fact that they did not know that it was significantly more potent than DMT, and they based the amount that they took on the appropriate weight for DMT. There is also a definite phenomenological difference between the effects of these two tryptamine "cousins," particularly at lower doses. This book tries to address these differences and correct any misconceptions by providing factual information (as well as speculative theories) about 5-MeO-DMT and its safe use.

Ultimately there are really only two reasons for writing this book: me (the writer) and you (the reader). In that first year after smoking 5-MeO-DMT, I swam in a sea of radical ideas, and at times I felt like a drowning man, desperately looking for an island of firm ground to stand on. When the idea came to me to write this book, I resolved to write it for those people who had already fallen into "the intellectual black hole." Hence, this book is for the souls who have been out there swimming in post-5MDE seas without any form of guidance. If you are one of these people, and perhaps we have even met out on the playa, I pass this book along to you like a fully stocked life raft. Without this framework, and without the continuing effort and adventure of intellectual discovery that has built it, I would be like a fish attempting to swim in a washing machine—utterly overwhelmed by the rapid changes in direction and sudden shifts in equilibrium that the revelations of the 5MDE have created in what had previously seemed like a safe and familiar medium.

If you are a budding 5-MeO-DMT aficionado currently in the grip of a similar wave of discovery, then I hope that this book and my theories can in some small way provide you with a scaffolding coherent enough to allow you to construct your own elucidation. I suspect that you will be open to my ideas, and that many will resonate within you. Know that there are others who have already crossed this ocean before you, and who have found wonders on "the other side."

In keeping with one of the founding principles of Burning Man, this book is my gift of "radical self-expression" to the Burning Man community, to the countless artists and individuals whose annual inspiration has been a major fount of energy for the completion of this work. I offer it with all blessings and praises to G/d as the ultimate source of everything written here. This book and its creation has been a journey toward the center of myself and toward

G/d, and thus is one of the most important things that I have managed to accomplish with my life so far. I consider myself incredibly blessed to have been allowed the experience, and it is my sincere hope that others may enjoy the same transformation of mind and spirit that 5-MeO-DMT has allowed me. For those who have never tried 5-MeO-DMT, I present this work as an invigorating mental exercise, an attempt at the kind of synthesis of science and mysticism that I fear has mostly been abandoned since the death of Pythagoras. If you have made it this far, I thank you for reading it.

In closing I would like to share with you one last magical 5-MeO-DMT experience, which happened as I was completing the first Burning Man edition of this book. I came home to my house in the Caribbean after an afternoon of kite surfing and realized that instead of finishing the book like I was supposed to be doing, I actually felt like smoking some of the mystery-in-question instead. In the previous year-and-a-half I had smoked very little 5-MeO-DMT; it had become too powerful, and I had been heeding the clear message that I needed to stop for a while. And I had been up to my ears in disasters and hard work. But I had been back in my ivory tower in the islands for two months, getting strong and healthy again, and the memory of those anxious weeks after Hurricane Katrina were mercifully beginning to fade. So when I started to feel that it would be a good day to step through that door—without the nervousness that had accompanied my last few explorations—my excitement increased as I raced home determined to follow through on my intuition.

I decided that I would dip into my precious toad venom supply. Nearly two years had passed since I had gone down to Mexico on the bus, but incredibly I still had some of the crystallized venom in my freezer. Somehow I am never *really* sure what constitutes the appropriate time to break out my most precious treasure. But this day seemed to be the perfect day. I considered waiting for my best friend (who owns the downstairs apartment of our house) to return, so that we could both try the venom. But I realized once I opened the small plastic vial that I still had quite a bit left and that there would be plenty for my friend when he arrived.

With the inspiration upon me, I couldn't wait any longer. So I filled a glass pipe with a screen, a tiny bit of herb, and a solid layer of toad venom on top. As I packed the venom into the pipe, I noticed that it was no longer really a crystal anymore, but seemed almost like a matted fiber, soft to the touch. I realized that water vapor had somehow soaked into the crystallized toad venom, re-hydrating it, and I wondered if this might have spoiled the venom completely.

"Typical," I thought to myself, "You went through all the trouble of going to the desert and milking toads, and now you have let one of the rarest drugs known to man sit around and decompose, while all the time you're writing a book about how amazing a substance it is. Idiot."

But I packed the bowl anyway, figuring that I would see what would happen when I torched it. I made my way over to an easy chair, deciding to smoke in a completely relaxed position for a change, instead of the upright lotus position I generally like to adopt. I gave the bowl a good torching and tasted the flavor of the weed, but I also could taste the familiar 5-MeO-DMT taste, and smell its distinctive odor, so I knew that all the potency of the venom had not been lost. The three times prior that I had smoked the venom, I had never achieved the same kind of full out-of-body release that I achieved with synthetic 5-MeO-DMT. I thought this was probably due to dosage (since there was no way to tell how much 5-MeO-DMT the venom contained), so I did not expect such a release now. I held my breath as long as possible and was surprised to see that there was still smoke when I exhaled.

A billowing cloud of exquisite dark fractals flowed across my consciousness. As I took a couple of breaths, I felt the experience intensify while I tried to relax and let the visions flow. I was still aware of the fact that I was sitting in my armchair, but the essence of the wonder that is the 5MDE was also available to me, and I felt my connection to that mystery field solidify and increase in potency as it moved through me.

I had recently been reading Colin Wilson's novel *The Philosopher's Stone,* and I was struck by the similarities between the narrator's vision of the world after he had devised a simple operation that improved the power of his brain/imagination and my own rush of sensation that had accompanied those heady days after I first smoked 5-MeO-DMT. As far as I know, Colin Wilson is not interested in 5-MeO-DMT or any kind of mind drugs. He believes advanced mental capabilities are possible for all humans, but we generally don't exercise them. In his masterwork *The Occult,* he calls this underused capacity of the mind "Faculty X." With his assertion that the human brain has an inherent capability to tap into its unused potential in mind, I tried to use my strength of concentration to increase my own grip on the mysterious field I was entering. The results, while mild, seemed positive. I could feel a transpersonal connection with the universe and a deep sense of love—the effect was peaceful and healing.

Right then I heard the sound of my friend arriving on his bicycle, every creak of his spoke like a ringing bell, and I laughed at my own greediness: of course he would arrive at the peak of my experience! I had the urge to shout out for him to come up, but then a wave of images and sensations swept over me and I lay back in the chair, trying to hold on to the experience for as long as possible. Dislocated in time, I felt an overwhelming gratitude for being allowed the experience, for my best friend who was just outside, and for my wife who was a continent away. I was grateful for our love and our luck and the fact we had come through the last year intact and stronger. I felt grateful for every second of my life. I felt gratitude all the way down to my innermost core. The overall impression I got from the toad venom, just as I had from the other times I had smoked it, was healing—pure and simple healing. Toad is undoubtedly strong medicine.

Soaking that healing up as long as I could, I had only one problem: I felt like I needed to take a leak. So I got up and unsteadily made my way to the bathroom. Staring at myself in the mirror, I could see my physical reality flicker in and out of the field, and I realized that I was higher than I had thought. Relieving myself was difficult, as I knew I *needed* to go, but my brain just didn't seem capable of telling my plumbing to work. Finally I managed to pee and then made my way back to the easy chair, thinking that my friend would soon come upstairs to see what was going on.

Picking up the glass bowl and looking at its contents in curiosity, the scientist in me noticed that the venom had blackened and re-solidified in a hard layer across the top of the bowl. The hog in me saw that there was still plenty left. I felt so grateful for the experience I had just had that I wanted to share the venom with some people I loved; it seemed wrong to hold onto it all for myself. But I knew there was more in the freezer, and I rationalized that I had probably taken most of the 5-MeO-DMT in the venom with the first hit, so the second hit should inevitably be milder. Nevertheless, I was grinning when I raised the pipe back up to my lips, still high from the first pipe, and the little voice in my head said, "Greedy, greedy," as I sucked in with a strong and steady draw.

The effect was obvious immediately, even before I exhaled my breath in a short stunned gasp that contained no smoke. It was just like the 5-MeO-DMT trip report from *TIHKAL* that I quoted in the Introduction, which says, "The *entire universe* imploded through my consciousness." That is as good a way of describing it as any. Everything I have tried to say in this book (and an incalculable amount of other things) all happened simultaneously in a cosmic flash of pure insight. I went through all the different levels that I have described as *One,* moving through a timeless reality in a manner impossible to describe. I saw the teeming multitudes, I heard dogs barking and children playing, and I expanded out beyond the stars—all the while fearless and at peace, cocooned in a field of immeasurable love.

Pure love—there is no other way to describe it. It was the same love I had found my first time, the same love that had come when I asked it to name itself; it was the love that had been missing during my last few experiences, replaced by that awesome power. Yet I knew the love and the power were the same. Their tangled braid represented the creation principle of the universe and beyond, from the infinite emanation of forms, to the form-without-form that I can only call G/d. That mighty love drew me up and pulled me in. Lost in that moment outside of time, I knew that love was me, and my wife, and my friends, and my dog Koda who had died. Love was M.O.M.'s Ball and Burning Man. Love was this life we were all blessed with, this planet, this galaxy. Love created all of it, since love *is* the creation principle. Love *is* All. It makes everything possible and ultimately guides the universe in some mysterious unknowable way, and if the light is the energy of God, then the love is God's plan.

In the preface to Alex Grey's book *Sacred Mirrors,* Allyson Grey relates a shared psychedelic experience between the two artists that would shape both their personal and artistic futures.

> On June 3, 1976, we simultaneously shared the same psychedelic vision: an experience of the "Universal Mind-Lattice." Our shared consciousness, no longer identified with or limited by our physical bodies, was moving at tremendous speed through an inner universe of fantastic chains of imagery, infinitely multiplying in parallel mirrors. At a superorgasmic pitch of speed and bliss, we became individual fountains

> and drains of Light, interlocked with an infinite omni-directional network of fountains and drains, composed of and circulating a brilliant, iridescent love energy. We were the Light, and the Light was God.[4]

That light of love drew me up and made me understand what was happening, what I was *really* seeing, until the singular realization as bright as a burning star exploded in my mind brighter than the dawn of any day:

I exist! With G/d. This is real! This is reality.
G/d exists!

And for a single eternal moment outside of time, G/d and I were One: the Light of lights, the most sublime cosmic love and intelligence, Consciousness recognized as the beginning and the end of everything.

Two things made this toad venom experience unique: the "softness" of the experience (with an almost total lack of fear) and the fact that the entire time I was partially aware that I was still sitting in my armchair. My separate consciousness was somehow able to resonate with what I consider an "ultimate" 5-MeO-DMT experience (the union with G/d), and yet bizarrely at the same time still be cognizant of my physical existence. At the point when my mind actually fully opened up to union with G/d, I think I did lose contact with this physical reality (and more time passed than I realized, probably around ten minutes). At one point I remember abruptly coming out of the experience—without the usual disorientation that accompanies the come-down of a 5MDE—and seeing my hands on my knees and the surroundings around me. I was still dislocated in time and wondering what was going on, unable to recall any past. Then I realized exactly what had happened, as I tried to hold onto the last fleeting moments of the light and the love.

Three years after my initiation, this was undoubtedly the most beautiful 5-MeO-DMT experience that I have ever had. Laughing with the sheer exhilarating joy of it, I collapsed out of the chair and lay spread-eagle on the floor. At that moment nothing I have written in this book seemed relevant, not a single word came close to describing how I felt, and I laughed at the absurdity of attempting to describe it. Confounded by the sheer Zen nature of the 5MDE, I realized that I could have summed this whole book up in a couple of words: "Know G/d." Or even more simply in one word: "God." And still, no one without the experience would be able to understand. The revelation confirmed that I was G/d, that G/d was in me, and that G/d was in all of us. Like the Gnostics believed, our purpose in life is to bring ourselves closer to G/d, to improve ourselves in order to be more than we are, to fill ourselves up with that light. What possible use was my silly book compared to that? Then that voice came to me like it does, loud and clear inside my head: *"Don't you stop. Just keep going."*

And so I have. Giggling
like an excited child,
high on love.
Thinking
all the while,
That came out of a toad?!

Epilogue

What is this strange and bitter miracle of life? Is it to feel, when furious day is done, the evening hush, the sorrow of lost, fading light, far sounds and broken cries, and footsteps, voices, music, and all lost—and something murmurous, immense and mighty in the air?

THOMAS WOLFE, *OF TIME AND THE RIVER: A LEGEND OF MAN'S HUNGER IN HIS YOUTH*, 1935

A remembered truth is a dead thing.

WALLACE FORD MUHAMMAD

This is apparently the book that refuses to end, as one final strange event occurred that seems to demand inclusion.

A rather clueless Englishman recently built a large house next to mine in the Caribbean. After telling us that his house would be modest and not block any of our view, he then chose to build his two-story garage as close to my tower as he possibly could. He explained to me later that he hoped that I wasn't upset he had changed his mind about the layout of his house, because he had realized that I would "be able to look in his pool." While the proximity of this garage may seem like a petty complaint to many of you, the effect of a giant white wall within ten feet of you is rather shocking after you have been used to a view of mountains and a lush picket of native trees and palms (most of which he has now cut down). He owned a large piece of land, so the garage didn't need to be that close to our house. It was just an ignorant move on his part, and I had to struggle within myself not to be angry about my new neighbor.

Problem was, *everything* this guy did was backward. Just from watching the construction of his "dream home," I had a feeling that something was going to go wrong and that this house would end up a nightmare. I found out that he was a croupier at a big casino in Europe, and I thought that was typical; he had undoubtedly watched hundreds of people throw away their lives, so it was easy not to give a fuck about your new neighbors. I found it hard to believe that people could move through life so blind and uncaring about even the basic well being of the others around them, and I wondered how karma could allow someone like my new neighbor the outward trappings of success. Instinctively I knew that, as time went by, I would receive some illumination on my musings. But I had no idea how quickly my questions would be clarified.

On the Englishman's second night in his dream home, a group of armed men came to rob him. From a security point of view, his house was designed all wrong. It had a huge wall with an electric gate in the front of the house and a low wall in the back, which his assailants basically just hopped over. As it turned out, all that he had over his slatted wooden doors was insect screening, which the thieves simply sliced with a knife to gain entry. More than likely, the thieves knew all this and more, informed by either his ex-hooker girlfriend (who was alone in the house with him) or his builders, I suspect.

The thieves came to his side door at around 1:00 a.m. on a Sunday night. While they were getting into his house, they must have noticed that I had left both a metal gate and my screen door open—something that I usually never do. (We had smoked a little bubble-hash that night and promptly passed out.) Two of the thieves made their way through the hedge onto my property, went up the stairs to the second story of my tower, and then came in through an open door while my wife and I were asleep upstairs on the third floor. We had just come back from a few days in another town and had belongings scattered all over the second floor. The thieves stuffed a number of these into a small leather backpack of my wife's: jewelry, my expensive Canon camera, and—most shockingly—the laptop that contained the first complete draft of this book.

Satisfied with what they had found, the thieves left my house again, but as they came down the stairs, they woke my friend who occupies the first-floor apartment. Although he is usually the kind of person who would just rush right outside to see what was going on, he had the sense to quietly peer out the window first. When he saw two men hiding behind a large flax plant, he turned on the outside light, which sent them scattering back next door.

Two other men with guns had woken my neighbor out of a deep sleep, and he was being marched around his house while his girlfriend did all the talking (my guess is she knew the thieves), until he finally coughed up 6,000 euros in cash that he had at the house (a fortune in that country). Since the robbers now had what they were looking for, they made a move to tie up the Englishman and his girlfriend. Then, as one of the men put his pistol in his waistband and bent over to tie the Englishman's feet, the gun accidentally went off, and the intruder shot himself in the leg!

I had been sound asleep through the robbery of my own house. But the sound of a gunshot close to my tower, where I usually only hear crickets and cane toads, sent me flying out of bed. My friend from downstairs was out in the garden by now, trying to figure out what the hell was going on, and once I heard him shout that we had intruders, I had my pants on as quickly as possible and went down my bedroom stairs. It was then that I realized with a sickening certainty that we had been robbed, since one glance told me that my laptop computer and camera were gone.

Our hapless neighbor emerged from his house, announcing that he had just been robbed. Although my friend jumped on his dirt bike and went looking for the thieves, it was obvious that they had gotten away into the wilderness behind our houses. The Englishman was spooked and wanted someone to talk to, but I felt little compulsion to ask him in. He had shown us no reason to by this point, and now he had brought all this shit down on our heads. But really, I was mad at myself for leaving the gate and a door unlocked and for leaving my laptop downstairs. (I usually keep all the valuables on the third floor.) Then it slowly sunk in that my computer was gone and, with it, the years of work I had spent on this book.

My wife and my friend tried to console me, realizing the significance of the missing laptop straight away. Yet I felt strangely calm. Even if I could write it all again, there was no way that it would be ready by Burning Man, and so the whole purpose seemed somehow lost. The more I thought about it, the more I had to assume that this was one book that obviously didn't need to be written. My 5-MeO-DMT theories and experiences were clearly meant for my personal enrichment only. I must have had it wrong all along, I decided. There could be no other real answer.

We got up again at dawn and went looking for anything that the thieves might have dropped. We found a small bag of my wife's jewelry, a pair of jeans of my neighbor's, and the hole cut in the wire fence where the thieves had entered, but that was all. I went back to bed ruminating on all the time I had spent on my manuscript and decided that it was the *knowledge* that was important—all the new things that I had learned—and the book itself was just the manifestation of my over-active ego. My wife kept telling me how sorry she was, but after a year that had included a tsunami and a hurricane, I couldn't feel too sorry for the loss of a mere book. She also told me that I would have to write the book again, but I couldn't really see it. Another of life's lessons I kept telling myself. The next book I wrote I would make sure to back-up!

The following morning we were heading out for breakfast when I bumped into my friend on his bicycle at the bottom of the stairs, and he offered his condolences again on the stolen laptop. Having watched me write the book over the past few years he knew as much as anyone how much it meant to me. I replied with my philosophical "the world must be trying to teach me something" answer. He laughed, and commented on how much we had both changed since we had first smoked 5-MeO-DMT.

"The old you would have been crying for this guy's blood," he said with a grin and a nod to the neighbor's house. I had to admit it was true. The younger, less enlightened, version of myself would have wasted no opportunity in telling my neighbor exactly what I thought of him. Then I had to admit that I had fought the compulsion to verbally rip into the guy the previous night, after I had discovered that my laptop was gone.

"I'm just glad no one got hurt," I said. "None of us wanted to wake up and find our neighbor dead. I can't be angry with this guy, because he's so clueless. He believes himself as a victim in all this, I'm sure, not even realizing he brought it all down on his own head. The old me might have wanted to kill the guy, but now the new me is just struggling to decipher the messages that the world is giving. Like, why was I so stupid that I forget to close the gate?" I was struggling to understand how I could have got caught up in my neighbor's bad karma and lost the very thing I had spent the previous few years working on. Life could be strange, I knew that much—and sometimes quite cruel. But still this didn't seem *right.*

My friend cycled off on his cruiser, and my wife and I headed down the driveway toward the road, when my neighbor saw us and shouted out. "Hey guys, if you come over, I think I have got some good news for you."

We walked next door not really wanting to see the guy. I'd had enough by now and figured that he was going to tell me that the police had offered extra security, or something equally inane. (The police had been laughing their tits off when they left his house at three in the morning—I had seen them from the shadows of my balcony.) When we got onto his property he waved at us and held up my wife's leather backpack.

"I found this at the back wall," he explained, "It's got a camera and laptop in it, and I figured it was probably yours."

Which it was. And which is why you are able to read the final pages of this book right now—because the mighty, mighty, universe gave it back to me. The thieves had dropped the backpack getting their injured party over my neighbor's wall, and had apparently either not noticed, or decided not to go back over to recover it, since they already had 6,000 euros and a serious leg wound.

My wife got back virtually everything that was stolen from her. The only things I lost were my silver toad ring from the Great Frog in London and my silver "Om Mani Padme Hum" bracelet that I bought in Dharamsala—the two things that most represented my current view of the world and my G/d, two possessions that I prized and rarely took off, but that are ultimately only symbols of a much greater treasure that can never be taken from me. This is the greatest treasure that a man can ever discover—the secret treasure that he carries within.

Yet still, despite myself, despite all the universe has tried to teach me, there is a part of me that can't help but see in my mind: the hapless thief, with my bulging silver ring and wide stiff bracelet stuffed in the front pocket of his jeans, pistol in his waistband, and as he's bending down, the rounded head of my toad ring managing to push itself deeper and deeper into the inviting hole of the pistol's denim-covered trigger guard . . .

G/d moves in mysterious ways. Hare Om!

APPENDIX ONE

Resources

Erowid

www.erowid.org

Erowid's mission statement reads, "Erowid is a member-supported organization providing access to reliable, non-judgmental information about psychoactive plants, chemicals, and related issues. We work with academic, medical, and experiential experts to develop and publish new resources, as well as to improve and increase access to already existing resources. We also strive to ensure that these resources are maintained and preserved as a historical record for the future."

If you're looking for any kind of information about tryptamines (or any other psychoactive compound all the way down to tea and coffee), this Internet-based organization is the place to start. Each important compound has its own "vault" (such as the 5-MeO-DMT vault) that lists a bewildering amount of information on subjects like history, use, laws, and chemistry, along with a number of "personal experiences" that are well worth the visit alone. With quotations and analysis from the Shulgins' *PIHKAL* and *TIHKAL* and Jonathan Ott's *Pharmacotheon,* the information on tryptamines is as good as it gets. If you want to do something constructive to help fight government propaganda, then join Erowid at one of its many membership levels; it is quite simply the most important weapon we have.

www.erowid.org/archive/sonoran_desert_toad/almost.htm

Albert Most's *Bufo alvarius: The Psychedelic Toad of the Sonoran Desert* (1984).

The Lycaeum

www.lycaeum.org

This is another website that has a wealth of information about tryptamines.

The Schaffer Library of Drug Policy

www.druglibrary.org/schaffer

The Schaffer Library of Drug Policy has a section on "psychedelics."

Shroomery: Magic Mushrooms Demystified

www.shroomery.org

Although this site is primarily about magic mushrooms, it does have a great DMT forum with lots of information and extraction recipes.

Ayahuasca.com

www.ayahuasca.com

This website describes itself as the "homepage of the Amazonian Great Medicine" and has all the information on ayahuasca you could ever want.

Serendipity

www.serendipity.li

This site covers a wide variety of topics, which include an informative three-part DMT history.

www.serendipity.li/dmt/sacred.pdf

Moving Into the Sacred World of DMT

This article from *The Entheogenic Review* is (in my opinion) by far one of the best I have ever read about the more spiritual aspects of DMT use, by someone who has been around it for forty years. A must read.

Podomatic: The Entheogenic Evolution

www.entheogenic.podomatic.com

Martin Ball's entheogenic podcast based in Ashland, Oregon. Martin has a Ph.D. in Religion and Philosophy and has written books about magic mushrooms and *Salvia divinorum*. These days he is as big a convert to 5-MeO-DMT as I am! His podcast features information, speculation, and topical interviews, all set to groovy music. His unique contribution to the Burning Man community is a theme camp that houses something called the God Box. Check out both Martin's podcast and the God Box if you can.

www.5meodmt.net

The name pretty much says it all: a reference site for 5-MeO-DMT.

Web pages specific to *Bufo alvarius* (Sonoran Desert toad) include

www.erowid.org/animals/toads/toads.shtml
www.bouncingbearbotanicals.com/colorado-river-toad-p-368.html
www.herbalfire.com/toad.htm

The Entheogen Review

www.entheogenreview.com

The Entheogen Review was a (mostly) quarterly publication that—from 1992 through 2008—served as a clearinghouse for data about the use of visionary plants and drugs. Subscribers shared information about the cultivation, extraction, and use of entheogens. Over the years they published numerous recipes for ayahuasca analogues, as well as several techniques for extracting DMT and 5-MeO-DMT. Their Autumnal Equinox 2008 issue featured my article "Where is God in the Entheogenic Movement?" Although *The Entheogen Review* is no longer publishing, both print and electronic copies of their issues can be obtained via the website listed above.

APPENDIX TWO

Tryptamine-Containing Plants

Numerous plants contain psychoactive tryptamines, and—so far as I am aware—none of these plants are themselves specifically scheduled (except in Louisiana, when the intended use is consumption). Below I mention a few of the plants that contain higher amounts of DMT and 5-MeO-DMT, and I note the range of their content based on analyses reported in the literature. This information is from the 2007 compendium *Some Simple Tryptamines,* second edition, by Keeper of the Trout & Friends; citations for the primary sources reporting on tryptamine content are all provided in that book. Unless otherwise noted, all weight ranges listed refer to analysis of dried plant material. It is important to realize that natural products can vary dramatically with regard to potency, and in most cases there are not very many distinct analytical data points (from multiple researchers, reporting on multiple plant samples) to go on. If a single figure is given rather than a range, it is because no further quantitative analysis data was available. A plant's genetics and environment, as well as the time of year and even the time of day of harvesting, can all play a part in the concentration of its alkaloids. Hence, the range of figures provided below for each plant should only be seen as a "rough guide" related to chemical content. Also, some of these plants may contain other chemicals (psychoactive, nonactive, or toxic) along with the targeted tryptamines reported on here. Those considering performing extractions on any plant materials should further inform themselves of the entire chemical profile of a plant as well as of the laws in the country that they live in. Manufacture (including extraction), possession, or sale of a controlled substance is a crime in many countries, and can result in a lengthy prison term and significant fines.

Acacia maidenii: DMT in bark at 0.36%; 5-MeO-DMT in trace amounts
Acacia obtusifolia (= *A. intertexta*): DMT in bark at 0.1–0.7%; 5-MeO-DMT possibly present in trace amounts
Acacia phlebophylla: DMT in leaf at 0.3%
Acacia simplicifolia: DMT in bark at 0.81%
Anadenanthera peregrina: DMT in immature seeds at 0.16%; 5-MeO-DMT in roots 0.678%
Desmanthus illinoensis: DMT in root-bark at 0.34%
Diplopterys cabreana: DMT in leaf at 1.46%; 5-MeO-DMT in leaf and dried stem in trace amounts
Meliocope leptococca (= *Evodia leptococca*): 5-MeO-DMT in aerial parts 0.21%
Mimosa tenuiflora (= *M. hostilis*): DMT in root-bark at 0.31–11%
Phalaris aquatica: 5-MeO-DMT in leaf at 0.01–0.28%
Phalaris aquatica cv. AQ-1: DMT at 1+%; 5-MeO-DMT in trace amounts
Phalaris arundinacea P.I. 172442 Turkey (cv. Turkey Red): 5-MeO-DMT in leaf is the predominant alkaloid from a total *wet* weight alkaloid range of 0.0025–0.045%
Pilocarpus organensis: 5-MeO-DMT in leaf at 0.41% (Caution: Shulgin and Shulgin 1997 and Ott 1994 both pointed out that other species of *Pilocarpus* are known to contain the poisonous cholinergic chemical pilocarpine.)
Psychotria carthaginensis: DMT in leaf 0.0–0.65%
Psychotria viridis: DMT in leaf 0.1–0.34%
Virola calophylla: DMT in leaf at 0.15%; 5-MeO-DMT in bark at trace amounts
Virola rufula: DMT in bark at 0.19%; 5-MeO-DMT in bark at trace amounts
Virola theiodora: DMT in bark at 0.003–0.25%; DMT in flowering shoots at 0.44%; 5-MeO-DMT in bark at 0.11%

APPENDIX THREE

Serotonin, Melatonin, 5-MeO-DMT, and the Pineal Gland

In his book *DMT: The Spirit Molecule* Rick Strassman, M.D., proposes the convincing hypothesis that DMT is produced by the ancient and mystifying pineal gland, which lies nestled up against the base of our brain. Since the book was published in the year 2000, Strassman's hypothesis has increasingly been circulated, both within the entheogenic community and without, as a fact. But as it stands today, this hypothesis has remained unproven, and DMT *has not* been found in the pineal. Due to the lack of sustained ongoing research in this matter, it is unlikely that there will be any breakthroughs in this area in the future

What *is* a fact is that the pineal is a rich source of both serotonin and the methlytransferases enzymes that transform (methylate) serotonin, melatonin, and tryptamine into psychedelic compounds. The presence of these compounds in the pineal in such high quantities is the basis for Dr. Strassman's hypothesis that the pineal is the source of the endogenous DMT that has been found in the body. It would seem worthwhile to examine some of these naturally occurring compounds a little closer and to examine their relationship to 5-MeO-DMT, which, like DMT, is also an endogenous entheogen.

Serotonin (5-hydroxytryptamine or 5-HT*)* is a neurotransmitter that is produced throughout the brain and the gastrointestinal tract and seems to be responsible for higher functions of behavior such as planning and other time-related events.[1] Serotonin is found in all animals and some plants and is produced in the human body from dietary L-tryptophan, an essential amino acid. The fact that serotonin is a tryptamine is the reason that both DMT and 5-MeO-DMT are able to cross the blood brain barrier (BBB); their similar molecular shape allows them to "key in" to the receptor sites that are found on the end of neurons.

In addition to serving as a neurotransmitter (which is responsible for the communication between the nerves cells by relaying electric impulses from one cell to another), serotonin is also the metabolic precursor of melatonin. According to researcher Jace Callaway, "Serotonin's major function is basically one of inhibition within the complex neurochemical pathways of the central nervous system (CNS), as if to screen out spurious bits of data to allow one to better focus on the task at hand."[2] Many psychotropic compounds affect at least some aspect of serotonergic activity, and deficiencies in serotonin and tryptophan have been linked with mental disorders such as violent alcoholism, anxiety, depression, and suicide.

What is of interest to us here is the fact that serotonin can serve as a precursor in healthy humans for the production of 5-MeO-DMT and 5-hydroxy-DMT (bufotenine). From another metabolic route, DMT can be produced following the formation of an endogenous tryptamine.[3] Bufotenine has been found in human urine.[4] However, due to its polarity, it is generally thought to be unable to cross the BBB, and any psychoactivity from exogenous bufotenine has been speculated to be due to conversion to 5-MeO-DMT in the body.[5] There is some evidence from bioassay studies that this statement is not correct; however, *how* bufotenine could cross the BBB has not been explained.

Melatonin has also been linked to the production of entheogenic compounds within the human body. Melatonin production occurs at night or when the eyes are closed, such as during meditation.[6] Like serotonin, DMT, and 5-MeO-DMT, it is also a tryptamine (*N*-acetyl-5-methoxy-DMT). It is the primary pineal hormone and is present in primitive pineal glands.[7] According to R. A. Masters' book *Darkness Shining Wild: An Odyssey to the Heart of Hell & Beyond,* "Mantak Chia (2004), following Ananda Bosman, speculates that greatly increased melatonin levels, as induced through prolonged time in utter darkness, result not only in increased DMT and 5-MeO production, but also in other substances that inhibit the very enzymes that normally break down DMT and 5-MeO. Darkness retreats, featuring lengthy immersion in complete darkness, are perhaps best known in Tibetan Buddhism."[8] As mentioned earlier, Mantak Chia instruct his pupils in Thailand that this is what is happening during their month-long darkness retreats.[9]

Due to the pineal's role in producing endogenous tryptamines like serotonin and melatonin, I personally find Dr. Strassman's suggestion that the pineal gland might be the source of endogenous DMT production convincing, and others give it credence as well. In a May 1983 talk at a UCSB conference titled "Psychoactive Drugs Throughout Human History," Dr. Andrew Weil remarked that "dimethyltryptamine . . . is almost certainly made by the pineal gland in the brain." Nevertheless, others have expressed doubt about Strassman's theory. Keeper of the Trout, a writer with a background in chemistry, has stated that it seems unlikely to him that DMT could be created out of melatonin as the result of a simple enzymatic conversion, and he also feels it is even more improbable for such a thing to occur cyclically, which Strassman proposes as a possibility.[10] Trout has suggested that if a chemical with psychedelic activity actually exists in the pineal gland, a better candidate would be one of the 6-methoxylated beta-carbolines (the 6-substitution in a beta-carboline is in the same spot as the 5-substitution in a tryptamine). He states that these compounds are much more likely to cyclically be inter-converted with melatonin via an enzymatic reaction.[11]

Through psychonautic bioassays, Claudio Naranjo found both 6-methoxyharmalan (which has been produced in vitro from melatonin[12]) and 6-methoxytetrahydroharman to be "hallucinogenic," stating that the subjective effects for each became apparent with an oral dose of approximately 1.5 mg/kg. (This equates to doses around 100–150 mg according to Sasha Shulgin, who found no activity himself in bioassays of up to around 100 mg of 6-methoxytetrahydroharman.)[13] Naranjo described these two compounds as being "of a less hallucinogenic nature in the strict sense of the word, their effect being more akin to a state of inspiration and heightened introspection," (although perhaps higher doses might produce more psychedelic results).[14] There appear to be no further bioassays of these chemicals reported in the literature. Sasha Shulgin has described this area of human pharmacology as remaining as "a rich and promising virgin field for exploring."[15] It is somewhat odd that no one has done any further studies, considering that these chemicals aren't controlled in any way and they are relatively simple to synthesize.[16]

Someday, with further scientific investigation, it is possible that evidence for both pineal-produced DMT and 5-MeO-DMT may be discovered. However, it has been pointed out by Trout that testing for DMT in the pineal gland of a living human being would be hugely problematic. And since DMT is aggressively destroyed by oxidation and other means, there may not be any remaining in the pineal gland of a cadaver.[17] Strassman himself found no DMT present in the pineal glands he obtained from "about ten" human cadavers, and he noted that for such a test to obtain the most accurate results, the brains would have to be removed immediately at the time of death and placed into liquid nitrogen to halt any breakdown of the compound.[18]

APPENDIX FOUR

Is 5-MeO-DMT the Most Potent Entheogen Known to Humanity?

Although I have touched upon this topic within the main confines of this book, since my assertion that 5-MeO-DMT *is* the most potent entheogen known to humanity remains highly controversial (among non-5-MeO-DMT initiates!), I think I need to examine this subject a little further.

There are of course *two* ways to define the potency of any given entheogen—*physiologically* and *phenomenologically.* And herein lays the main confusion about the veracity of my claims. With a minimum effective dosage of approximately 5 mg when smoked, physiologically 5-MeO-DMT is most clearly *not* the most potent entheogen we know. (It is even less so if we accept the idea that at around 100 mg 5-MeO-DMT is active if eaten.) That honor would have to go to LSD, which is sold at the street level (these days) at around 50 mcg! The dose of "street acid" in the sixties and early seventies was *much* higher—frequently in the region of 300 to 500 mg—or 6 to 8 times the dose of today's acid! This tremendous potency of LSD has also given me cause to consider its tremendous *value* as a crystal. These days (so I was told at World Psychedelic Forum in Basel, Switzerland) a gram of pure LSD can fetch as much as $25,000 dollars (with its "street value" far eclipsing that). I would imagine this qualifies LSD for the title of "world's most valuable crystal!" LSD is physiologically *one of the most potent* substances known to humans. You could eat the same amount, 50 mcg, of cyanide, or even plutonium, and it would pass through your body without any noticeable effect.

Since LSD (and a number of other entheogens) are considerably more potent by weight than 5-MeO-DMT, it cannot be considered "the most potent" *physiologically.* However, *phenomenologically* this distinction becomes much more blurred. Numerous attempts have been made to establish a methodology for rating the phenomenological aspect of an experience—most notably Strassman's Hallucinogen Rating Scale and the system that chemist Alexander Shulgin uses to rate the various compounds he has invented. However, it does not appear that it is possible under any rating system to consider any compound *the most potent,* since these systems essentially rate the *experience* and not necessarily the compound itself. To determine the "most potent" entheogen phenomenologically, statistical analysis of experience reports would need to be undertaken, with a balanced number of user reports for each compound provided and with a high enough number of sample reports for there to be any validity. Unfortunately a study as extensive as this seems unlikely in the current political climate.

In the absence of such studies, to rate 5-MeO-DMT (or any entheogen for that matter) phenomenologically we can only examine the accounts of experiences of those individuals who have been able to try a wide variety of entheogens and see how they rate 5-MeO-DMT within the entheogenic pantheon. Terence McKenna clearly thought that 5-MeO-DMT was more "forceful" than "normal" DMT, and he preferred the more "magical" aspect of DMT. Robert Augustus Masters compared his single 5-MeO-DMT experience to ayahuasca by stating, "It resembled my ayahuasca journey at its most titanically wild and insane, sped up and intensified a hundredfold."[1] And in *TIKHAL,* there are a number of trip reports (including the one quoted at the beginning of this book) that seem to indicate the tremendous intensity of the experience, although Shulgin himself adds little to the discussion. While Daniel Pinchbeck broods on his DMT experiences at length in *Breaking Open the Head* and presumably had the opportunity to try 5-MeO-DMT with The Church of The Motherfuckers at Burning Man, he makes *no* mention of 5-MeO-DMT at all in that book. One would think that if Pinchbeck had indeed experienced 5-MeO-DMT, he would have found it worthy of inclusion in his own investigation aimed at "the heart of contemporary shamanism."

The greatest confirmation I have of the veracity of my claim comes from those individuals I have met who *have* experienced 5-MeO-DMT at the same transcendental level that I have. They all agree 100 percent that their 5-MeO-DMT experiences are in a league of their own, well beyond *any* other experiences they have had on *any* other entheogen. I probably get an e-mail once every couple of months from an individual who has read one of the initial versions of this book, and who is clearly glad that someone else has experienced the same transcendental knowledge of G/d that they have. This is all the more remarkable when you consider that there are only around 500 Burning Man copies of *Tryptamine Palace* out there, and the book has received close to no publicity as yet. In fact, apart from a couple of mentions in *The Entheogen Review,* the only prior publicity that I am aware of *Tryptamine Palace* ever having received was when it was discussed on Dr. Martin Ball's entheogenic podcast *before* he had ever had the opportunity to experience 5-MeO-DMT himself.

When I listened to that podcast, I could tell that Martin was undoubtedly comparing the experiences related in the book to experiences of his own (on other entheogens), and finding the claims within my book somewhat far-fetched. It is natural for humans, especially if they have spent years studying a certain subject, to believe that *their* experiences are as valid as anybody else's and to dismiss more "extreme" claims as hyperbole. Hence my personal pleasure and gratification upon receiving the e-mail I got from Martin the day after he had experienced a full 5MDE, quoted in chapter 3, "The Aftermath." Martin now fully agrees with me that 5-MeO-DMT is phenomenologically in a class of entheogens of its own, which he explains in the introduction to his latest book, *The Entheogenic Evolution: Psychedelics, Consciousness, and Awakening the Human Spirit.* Here Martin describes some of the history of his own interest in entheogens:

> In the years that followed, I continued to explore the shamanic and mystical states of consciousness that mushrooms opened up for me—what I considered to be my "personal" schooling as I made my way through my graduate program. After finishing graduate school, I discovered *Salvia divinorum,* and began working with that magical plant, eventually using those experiences as the basis for my book, *Sage Spirit: Salvia Divinorum and the Entheogenic Experience.*

> I spent over a decade working with mushrooms, and then later salvia, exploring shamanic consciousness and practice. I felt I had a fairly good understanding of how these two visionary medicines worked and what kinds of experiences they made possible, but through it all, I would never claim that I had experienced God in a direct sense. Certainly, I had many profound and deeply meaningful spiritual encounters, but there was never a moment where I felt secure enough to say that I had absolutely experienced a force that I would describe as God. In fact, if asked if I believed in God, I would give a fairly cogent Buddhist response about the impermanent and empty nature of existence and how all our concepts are relative, and how even in the Buddhist wheel of reincarnation gods are still conditioned by karma and not absolute. I had my intellectual and philosophical views, but no real experience to base those views on.[2]

He then goes on to describe how this situation was radically changed by his first successful "full-release" on a potent, high 5-MeO-DMT mixture of toad venom, *Phalaris* grass extract, and *Psychotria viridis* extract that was vaporized in a pressurized chamber of argon gas(!).

> Within the space of a few heartbeats, I had completely expanded into God. Eyes open in absolute awe and wonder, the room dissolved, my ego dissolved, my entire world dissolved. Everything I had ever known or thought or felt dissolved away into absolute pure nothingness. There was nothing to see, nothing to experience, nothing to perceive. Absolutely pure nothingness. And this nothingness was pure consciousness. And it was love. Infinite love and infinite perfection. . . . And this state was not a thing. It was not an object of perception. It was not a concept. It was not an emotion. It was not anything that I could describe in any way. In fact, when asked later, I vaguely described it as "living starlight," but even that was not accurate, for in truth, it was *nothing*.
>
> But that no-thing was *everything*.
>
> It was God.
>
> And it was my deepest nature.
>
> I was one with God.

Not my ego self. That was thoroughly obliterated through the impossibly fast 5-MeO-DMT expansion. It was not as though I identified my personal sense of self with God. Rather, the deepest core of my being, not my ego-identity, was identical with God. As a finite being in a body with a sense of self and identity, I was an expression of God. At my core, at the very deepest level, my nature as an incarnated being was one with that pure consciousness. I was one with that infinite love, that infinite source of creative energy in which all things exist in absolute and unquestionable perfection. In those few heartbeats, this beautiful and sacred medicine had opened me up to the All. I had accepted my own divinity.

"Thank you, God!" I called out as my hands reached up towards that infinite expanse of nothingness, a few moments after the hit of psychedelic medicine flowed out of my lungs. Eyes wide open, gaping in sheer awe at the *mysterium tremendum,* I embraced God, and the embrace was returned.

"Thank you," I said, over and over and over again, lasting the better part of an hour as the medicine expanded me out into the farthest reaches of cosmic consciousness and then gently brought me back to myself. I was so overwhelmed that I began crying and laughing at the same time. It was, beyond any doubt, the most beautiful, profound, and total experience of my life. Nothing in my psychedelic or spiritual history could have prepared me for this divine embrace. It was so total, so complete, so beyond any sense of doubt or wonder or skepticism. It was absolutely undeniable. I could hardly believe that it was true. I could hardly believe that I was saying that word: God.[3]

In this account, Martin Ball has clearly phenomenologically encountered the same experience as I have—union with God. (And was apparently as surprised by that as I was—even though he had read my book beforehand!) Similarly, *all* the people I know who have experienced 5-MeO-DMT at what I call at its "fullest" unanimously agree with me that 5-MeO-DMT's entheogenic effect—its ability to allow you to realize the existence of God—is without parallel. And that it *is* the most powerful entheogen that they have ever experienced, though clearly from a phenomenological point of view, and not a physiological one. But try to express this to someone who has not experienced 5-MeO-DMT at its fullest, but who has had "entheogenic" experiences of their own on other compounds. These people are the ones who will tell me that I cannot describe 5-MeO-DMT as "the most powerful entheogen known to humanity," even when they admit that their own "entheogenic" experiences have paradoxically fallen short of union with God.

From my side I have tried to remain open to the fact that there are other entheogens that can provide this same truly entheogenic effect of union with God, and have done so historically. Otherwise we would never have come up with the term *entheogen* in the first place, right? Compounds like ketamine, 2C-B, 2C-I, DOC, DOM, DIPT, LSD, DMT at high doses, even magic mushrooms have been known to produce "union with God" in individuals, and their accounts are readily available in the volumes of entheogenic literature and on Erowid (www.erowid.org). I find ketamine among the most interesting, since it seems to me that it works a lot like 5-MeO-DMT (phenomenologically) by basically anesthetizing the body into believing that it is dead, thus freeing the consciousness to return to the source. I have friends who believe they have approached "the face of God" on ketamine, and it is the only compound other than 5-MeO-DMT that I have had a true out-of-body experience on—somewhat bizarrely while sitting at a bar in Bangkok! But I can't say that I find the physical effects of that compound appealing.

But the one account I have always kept in the back of my mind as a reminder of the fact that other compounds are capable of providing the same entheogenic effect as 5-MeO-DMT is probably the most famous account in "LSD literature," after Dr. Hofmann's legendary bicycle ride itself. That is the account of Stanislav Grof, the noted LSD and transpersonal researcher, of his own first LSD experience.*

In the fall of 1956, after graduating as a clinical psychiatrist in Prague, Grof volunteered as a test subject for the clinical trials of LSD that were being conducted at his university. Grof had been working as an aide on

*Of course, Ken Kesey's account of being an "LSD guinea pig" in a psychiatric hospital in the early sixties (in the USA) probably rivals Dr. Grof's in the "fame" category, since it was immortalized in print by Tom Wolfe in *The Electric Kool-Aid Acid Test.* That account is undoubtedly better known by the general public, while Dr. Grof's account is probably the more often discussed among the so-called entheogenic community.

these trials, but could not apply to be a subject until he had graduated from the university. His initial LSD session appeared to be progressing normally. A few hours into the session, a lab assistant hooked Grof up to some EEG equipment and turned on a powerful stroboscope, as Grof had agreed to take part in an experiment studying how brainwaves might become entrained via flashing light while under the influence of LSD. Grof describes his experience:

> I was hit by a vision of light of incredible radiance and supernatural beauty. It made me think of the accounts of mystical experiences I had read about in spiritual literatures, in which the visions of divine light were compared with the incandescence of "millions of suns." It crossed my mind that this was what it must have been like at the epicenter of the atomic explosions in Hiroshima or Nagasaki. Today, I think it was more like Dharmakaya, or the Primary Clear Light, the luminosity of indescribable brilliance that, according to *The Tibetan Book of the Dead (Bardo Thödol),* appears to us at the moment of our death.
>
> I felt that a divine thunderbolt had catapulted my conscious self out of my body. I lost my awareness of the research assistant, the laboratory, the psychiatric clinic, Prague, and then the planet. My consciousness expanded at an inconceivable speed and reached cosmic dimensions. There were no more boundaries or difference[s] between me and the universe.[4]

This experience completely shattered Grof's paradigm, and set his course of lifelong study of the realms of human consciousness. He relocated to the United States where he eventually was hired as the Chief of Psychiatric Research at the Maryland Psychiatric Research Center. During his professional career, Grof has personally conducted over 4,000 clinical psychedelic sessions "with substances such as LSD, psilocybin, mescaline, DPT, and MDA"[5] and has had access to over 2,000 sessions from his colleagues. (His clinical trials on psychedelics lasted until 1974 and were the last approved studies in the United States until Rick Strassman's trials with DMT at the University of New Mexico in the nineties.) After LSD became illegal, and all work with psychedelics stopped, Grof and his wife Christina developed the technique of holotropic breathwork as a means to access transpersonal realms without the use of entheogens. They have since supervised over thirty thousand holotropic sessions. Grof is considered the "Father of Transpersonal Psychology," and he was the founding president of the International Transpersonal Association.

Stanislav Grof is obviously a heavyweight—perhaps the greatest authority on entheogens and consciousness in the world. Because his strobe-light experience on LSD seemed phenomenologically so similar to my 5-MeO-DMT experiences, I have always kept his account of that "initiation experience" in the back of my mind as evidence *against* describing 5-MeO-DMT as "the most powerful entheogen known to humanity." Clearly there are other entheogens—or combinations of entheogens and other psychological techniques—that will produce the same effect as smoking 5-MeO-DMT. I managed to mostly retain that mental position, until I read Grof's account of the first time *he* tried 5-MeO-DMT, from his recent book: *When the Impossible Happens: Adventures in Non-ordinary Realities.*

> The beginning of the experience was very sudden and dramatic. I was hit by a cosmic thunderbolt of immense power that instantly shattered and dissolved my everyday reality. I lost all contact with the surrounding world, which completely disappeared as if by magic. In the past, whenever I had taken a high dose of psychedelics, I liked to lie down and make myself comfortable. This time, any such concerns were irrelevant because I lost awareness of my body, as well as of the environment. After the session, I was told that after taking a couple of drags, I sat there for several minutes like a sculpture, holding the pipe near my mouth. . . .
>
> In all my previous sessions, I had always maintained basic orientation. I knew who I was, where I was, and why I was having unusual experiences. This time all this dissolved in a matter of seconds. The awareness of my everyday existence, my name, my whereabouts, and my life disappeared as if by magic. Stan Grof . . . California . . . United States . . . planet Earth . . . these concepts faintly echoed for a few moments like dreamlike images on the far periphery of my consciousness and then faded away altogether. I tried hard to remind myself of the existence of the realities I used to know, but they suddenly did not make any sense.

In all my previous psychedelic sessions there always had been some rich specific content. The experiences were related to my present lifetime—the story of my childhood, infancy, birth, and embryonal life—or to various themes from the transpersonal domain—my past life experiences, images from human history, archetypal visions of deities and demons, or visits to various mythological domains. This time, none of these dimensions even seemed to exist, let alone manifest. My only reality was a mass of radiant swirling energy of immense proportions that seemed to contain all existence in a condensed and entirely abstract form. I became Consciousness facing the Absolute.

It had the brightness of myriad suns, yet it was not on the same continuum with any light I knew from everyday life. It seemed to be pure consciousness, intelligence, and creative energy transcending all polarities. It was infinite and finite, divine and demonic, terrifying and ecstatic, creative and destructive—all that and much more. I had no concept, no categories for what I was witnessing. I could not maintain a sense of separate existence in the face of such a force. My ordinary identity was shattered and dissolved; I became one with the Source. In retrospect, I believe I must have experienced the Dharmakaya, the Primary Clear Light, which according to the *Tibetan Book of the Dead,* the *Bardo Thödol,* appears at the moment of our death. *It bore some resemblance to what I encountered in my first LSD session, but it was much more overwhelming and completely extinguished any sense of my separate identity.* [Italics mine][6]

So says one of the world's greatest authorities on entheogens and consciousness: a man who has either tried, or seen tried, virtually every class of consciousness-expanding compound there is. At the end of the day there is not much point arguing *which* entheogen is the most powerful—since a variety of entheogens *can* bring about the ultimate entheogenic realization. I can only really say what works as the strongest entheogen for *me,* and perhaps for Stan Grof and Martin Ball as well. I have stated my case for 5-MeO-DMT's place in that pantheon, and now I will leave it for the rest of you to decide.

APPENDIX FIVE

William S. Burroughs, the Godfather of DMT

There is no thing to fear . . . Your [ayahuasca] consciousness is more valid than "Normal Consciousness."

WILLIAM S. BURROUGHS, *THE YAGE LETTERS*

William S. Burroughs (1914–1997): The elder statesman of the Beat Generation, writer, poet, performance artist, social revolutionary, junkie, homosexual, weed-grower, fugitive, and the drunken assassin of his wife Joan in the most infamous modern case of "William Tell." Other writers more talented than I have written screeds about the life of this remarkable counterculture icon who managed to outlive all his contemporaries despite the tremendous odds of his own brutal existence. I have stated repeatedly that I think Burroughs is one of the most important writers of the twentieth century, but his role in the "entheogenic revolution" has always caused me problems. In my original draft I included Burroughs in my dedication to "the fathers of Western entheogenic literature." Then, before I sent the book to the printer for the first Burning Man edition, I took his name out. Now, nearly three years later, I have had to reinstate him into my pantheon of the greats, for I have come to realize that one of the least known aspects of William S. Burroughs' long life is that he was effectively the modern "Godfather of DMT."

Since Burroughs is primarily known for his opiate addiction, this may seem like an outlandish claim, but the evidence is there. I also believe that there is equal evidence—and I think this is an important point that has never been picked up by *any* of Burroughs critics or chroniclers—that Burroughs' early exposure to ayahuasca, and later to pure injectable DMT, had a critical effect on his life's work and was perhaps the *main* influence in the development of his unique and revolutionary style of writing. I also believe that many of Burroughs' apparently cryptic comments and life-long obsessions can attributed to his early ayahuasca and DMT explorations, and are better understood in that context. For example, his quote from the little-known *Ah Pook Is Here* (1979), "When I become death, death is the seed from which I grow," could be read as a classical description of the experience of the shamanic psychospiritual death and rebirth, something that Burroughs himself experienced as early as the 1950s on yagé, and one that countless entheogen users have since experienced. "All present, all past and all future can be contained in a single note of music" (*The Western Lands,* 1987) is something that many tryptamine initiates have reported, including this author, while his oft-quoted assertion that "language is a virus" is another common intuition among DMT users and a theme that Terence McKenna explored at length.

Burroughs and Ayahuasca

But I'm getting ahead of myself. The intersection between Burroughs and DMT began in 1953, when Burroughs journeyed to Colombia in search of the legendary (even then) South American shamans' DMT-rich brew that was known by either its Spanish name yagé or its (then) scientific name telepathine. Today, of course, we call yagé by a phonetic approximation of one of its many original names: ayahuasca. But even as recently as 1993, when I personally first had the opportunity to try ayahuasca on a trip to Ecuador, it was still commonly being called yagé. (Terence McKenna is probably the one who effectively changed that with the popularity of his book *Food of the Gods.*)

Burroughs was looking for a cure to his opiate addiction, and yagé had a reputation for being able to reform addicts. In Bogotá, he met the great plant explorer and ethnobotanist Richard Evans Schultes, who was a fellow Harvard alumnus and who had just recently named and classified *Banisteriopsis caapi*—the creeping ayahuasca vine that is the heart of the brew in question. Showing Burroughs samples of the vine, he told Burroughs that telepathine's reputation was all rubbish and that he himself had only seen "colors and squiggly lines" when he had taken yagé. But he informed Burroughs where he could find the *brujos*—the Spanish word for a male witch, as the local shamans were then called—who would prepare yagé for him; and then—in what must have been one of the strangest traveling combinations in history—actually journeyed with Burroughs to the Sibidnoy, a (then) remote region of the Colombian Amazon.

There Burroughs immersed himself in the consumption of yagé*:* a sometimes terrifying experience that he would describe to his friend Allen Ginsberg in surreal prose in a series of letters that became the basis for the publication of *The Yage Letters* more than a decade later, after Ginsberg had traveled to Colombia and tried yagé himself. If it were for no other reason than that sublime book, I would *have* to include Burroughs as one of the "fathers of Western entheogenic literature"—since it would be more than two decades later before the likes of the McKenna brothers would try to follow his path. While certainly there had been other Westerners who had taken yagé at that time or earlier, not all of them were anthropologists or botanists, and none of them wrote about their extraordinary experiences as did Burroughs. Therefore *The Yage Letters* is one of the earlier known examples of "Western entheogenic literature," while Burroughs' trip to Colombia could be considered the precursor for the current popularity of ayahuasca tourism that is all the rage in Peru and Ecuador. Thus Burroughs is "the Godfather of 'recreational' ayahuasca."

Burroughs and DMT

But Burroughs' links to the history of DMT use do not stop there. In the late 1950s and early 1960s, Burroughs was living in London, England. He was reputedly working on a theory of "neurological geography," with the idea that the cortical areas were divided into the heavenly and the diabolical. In the following passage, from *Ghost of a Chance,* Burroughs explains his take on the bicameral mind.

> A rift is built into the human organism, the rift or cleft between the two hemispheres, so any attempt at synthesis must remain unrealizable in human terms. I draw a parallel between this rift separating the two sides of the human body and the rift that divided Madagascar from the mainland of Africa. One side of the rift drifted into enchanted timeless innocence. The other moved inexorably toward language, time, tool use, weapon use, war, exploitation, and slavery.[1]

Due to his tremendous intellectual curiosity, Burroughs had learned about DMT and managed to obtain a supply of the pure compound from a chemist friend in London. His small circle of friends in London included a number of psychiatrists, and it was with them that Burroughs experimented with injecting DMT—presumably to test some of his theories. Timothy Leary recounts a story about Burroughs injecting one of his psychiatrist friends and then injecting himself, only to have his friend "freak out" during the trip and ask Burroughs to inject him with a sedative. Burroughs then prepared the necessary injection, only to discover that his friend had turned into "a wriggling bejeweled serpent on the floor," leaving Burroughs puzzled about how to find a vein in such a marvelous spectacle of a creature.

Burroughs reputedly stopped using the drug after having taken a massive 100 mg injection. He supposedly wrote Timothy Leary a letter warning him of the evils of the compound.

You can imagine, then, Burroughs' amusement a few years later when "the psychedelic sixties" broke out and LSD was all the rage. For someone who had taken both massive quantities of ayahuasca and had injected himself with 100 mg of pure DMT, I doubt that LSD really seemed like that big of a deal. Burroughs himself wrote little about LSD or mescaline, despite his relationship with Timothy Leary, Neal Cassady, and other counterculture figures. As a result, most reviewers of his life take the position that Burroughs thoroughly *disliked* psychoactive drugs. While this may have been the case *after* his overdose of DMT in London, it certainly seems unlikely during his decade-long progress from yagé to the intravenous injection of DMT. In any case, the reports of Burroughs' injecting DMT are once again among the earliest accounts of any kind of "non-sanctioned" DMT use that we have, so I crown him "the Godfather of recreational DMT." (It would not be until half a dozen years later that the chemist Nick Sand would discover that DMT was—thankfully—smokable.)

Was DMT an Influence on Burroughs' Writing?

In truth, Burroughs was always an outsider. He was not really a member of the Beat Generation; they were just boys compared to him. He never considered himself a "Beat writer," and his writing style is very different from that of the Beats like Jack Kerouac, Allen Ginsberg, or Gregory Corso. It was clearly he who influenced them and not the other way around—Burroughs seems to have had few influences other than history itself. But I believe that if there is one single influence that can be most clearly seen in his writing, it is the influence of DMT.

Queer and *Junkie,* Burroughs' first two published works, while daring in their content, show no indication of the radical experiment in the English language that Burroughs writing would later become. It is in the language and themes of *Naked Lunch,* his most famous book that was published in 1959 and written in Tangiers, Morocco, *after* his encounters with yagé in Colombia, that the grand experiment in writing begins that would create his reputation as a "literary outlaw." The linear progression of his earlier works ends here with this convulted visionary novel that takes place in a shadowy world called the "Interzone," which in itself could be a combination of Tangiers and the strange shifting worlds one encounters on ayahuasca. Both humans and non-humans occupy Interzone; it is the home of narcotic-fluid excreting creatures Burroughs calls *mugwumps,* which appear to have an alien nature. Since Burroughs was infamous for his heroin use, reviewers tend to treat all "drug references" in *Naked Lunch* as metaphors for opiate use. But heroin and opium are not known to produce visual hallucinations, and the novel is full of hallucinatory moments. Typewriters speak and turn into giant cockroaches that are "Agents of Interzone," alien-type creatures abound, and the whole novel seethes and writhes with hallucinatory imagery. This would seem to have been far more influenced by Burroughs' yagé experiences than due to any amount of opiate use. Transformation—of creatures into humans, humans into aliens, aliens into machines, and so on—is one of the main phenomena listed over and over again in many ayahuasca and DMT accounts. Burroughs' "talking-typewriters" themselves would seem to presage McKenna's "self-replicating transforming mechanical elves."

But for me, the most telling example in *Naked Lunch* of the influence of Burroughs tryptamine use is the state of mind of the protagonist of the novel, Bill Lee, who is obviously based on Burroughs himself. Lee is not writing a novel; he is writing a *report* for the Masters of Interzone, who are the Masters of the Universe. The idea that the point of human existence is to write a report for the "Masters of the Universe," or—as I have described it in this book, to create a record of experience in the zero-point field—is a common intuition among tryptamine users, and one that I often promote myself. (You are reading *my* report.)

Further evidence for the influence of tryptamines in William S. Burroughs' writing can be found in virtually any of his books that followed. Take this passage from the introduction to the little-known *Ah Pook Is Here* (1979).

> The Mayan codices are undoubtedly books of the dead; that is to say, directions for time travel. If you see reincarnation as a fact then the question arises: how to orient oneself with regard to future lives? Consider death as a dangerous journey in which all past mistakes will count against you. If you are not orienting yourself on sound factual data, you will not arrive at your destination, or in some cases you may arrive in fragments. What basic principles can be set forth? Perhaps the most important is relaxed alertness, and this is the point of the martial arts and other systems of spiritual training—to inculcate a psychic and physical stance of alert passivity and focused attention. Suspicion, fear, self-assertion, rigid preconceptions of right and wrong, shrinking and flinching from what may seem monstrous in human terms—such attitudes of mind and body are disastrous. See yourself as the pilot of an elaborate spacecraft in unfamiliar territory. If you freeze, tense up, refuse to look at what is in front of you, you will crack up the ship. On the other hand, credulity and uncritical receptivity are almost as dangerous.[2]

This passage includes a number of recurring themes in Burroughs' lifework: the Mayan codices, time travel, space travel, books of the dead. These are all themes that reappear in the work of both Timothy Leary and

Terence McKenna decades later. And yet this passage reads like an analogy of *being on* DMT—even if DMT is never mentioned. In his letters to Ginsberg, Burroughs describes yagé as both "time travel" and "a spaceship." And Burroughs' was something of an expert on the Mayan calendar—he reputedly did Ph.D. work on Mesoamerican civilizations and had a corresponding interest in the Mayan predictions for "an end in time" that once again predates Terence McKenna's interest by decades.

Numerous further examples can be found in Burroughs' work. But the most telling influence of the unique nature of the DMT experience that I can see is Burroughs' dedication to "the cut-up technique" that his friend Brion Gysin invented. Probably the most radical attempt at redesigning the format for the novel attempted during the twentieth century, Gysin's and Burroughs' technique involved "cutting up" pages of writing and then randomly reassembling them into a new form. Here is a description of how this technique worked.

> The book's field of vision takes in a full 360°. The main intention of Burroughs and Gysin has been to free the text from the page, to free the word from the surrounding matrix. Not actually, but by placing the text and graphics at the extreme limit of readability. Not so that these elements are unreadable in an absolute sense—in other words, so that they escape comprehension—but that, within the confines of the printed book, they reach a point indicative of unreadability.
>
> How in the final analysis is the book to be defined? It eludes definition just as it eludes itself; a prey to unfathomable anamorphosis, it rubs itself out and rewrites itself; it allows itself to be read, only to slip away. The Third Mind jumbles the linguistic network, simultaneously revealing and antagonizing it. It is a strategic device for confronting semiotic assaults. But for it to do so, it calls on a fourth author—yourself—to establish the operational field of another book, an invisible book that you can make visible.[3]

It seems obvious to me that what Burroughs was attempting to do with this technique is to recreate the distinctly tellurian and nonlinear world of the DMT experience in writing—"The Third Mind jumbles the linguistic network, simultaneously revealing and antagonizing it"—a place where what *happens* is more important than meaning. "An invisible book you can make visible," with the random rearrangement of text designed to decode its hidden meaning. Burroughs' randomness "is one with a very limited definition: the cut-up is random ONLY as far as [its] results are unintended." Tellingly Burroughs himself states, "From my point of view there is no such thing as a coincidence."[4] This sounds to me like his experiences with yagé and DMT had clearly revealed to him a world of extraordinary synchronicity.

My final piece of evidence for Burroughs' lifelong (but unnoticed) interest in matters regarding shamanism and DMT would seem to be confirmed by his friendship with the noted shamanist William S. Lyon. An account from *The Road to Interzone,* a book on Burroughs by Michael Stevens, describes one of Lyon's visits to Burroughs late in his life, with a surprising reference to a Terence McKenna book contained within it.

> After awhile another visitor showed up. Burroughs looked up and said, "It's Bill." Brad answered the door and I was introduced to William S. Lyon, the author of *Black Elk* and one of the contributors and editors of *Shaman's Drum* magazine. Lyon and Burroughs got along very well and it was a pleasure to have him there as Burroughs bounced off what I guess were real life routines. I had heard about it and I was now seeing it and hearing it with my own eyes and ears. . . . Lyon had a copy of *The Ticket That Exploded* that he wanted Burroughs to sign. As he went about it Burroughs talked about shamanism, healing, and that bull. . . .
>
> At one point Lyon asked Burroughs if he still had his copy of *True Hallucinations.* Burroughs said he didn't know where it was. Lyon said he needed it because another friend of his wanted to read the book. After batting it around for a little bit Burroughs animatedly scuttled around in and out of rooms without the wheelchair and without a cane looking for it. He finally came back to the living room while Lyon was in the kitchen, sat down next to me and said, "I can't find it . . . Scout's honor." I believed him until I saw the trace of a smirk on his lips.[5]

That is classic William S. Burroughs right there—holding his cards close to his chest. His influences were his own, and he mostly kept them to himself, preferring his work to do the talking. While my personal fascination with the life and work of Burroughs is undoubtedly evident in this book—for I am one of those writers who believe that Burroughs may be the *only* American writer that will still be read in the twenty-second century (if we make it there)—in this essay I believe I am the first person to clearly point out his links to the tryptamine realm and the influence that it had on his work. Virtually all of his biographers have somewhat paradoxically taken the point of view that Burroughs was actually *against* the use of psychoactive compounds and have relegated him to being the greatest "junkie" of all time; so it is my intention here to "set the record straight" and recognize William S. Burroughs, the most famous "literary outlaw" of the twentieth century, in his rightful role as "the Godfather of DMT."

APPENDIX SIX

Heaven and Hell—Potential Negative Effects of 5-MeO-DMT

I feel that it is both wise and necessary to end this book with an examination of the potentially negative effects of smoking 5-MeO-DMT. While I most definitely do not want to cause a negative mind-set or be the cause of paranoia for anyone who may be considering experimenting with 5-MeO-DMT, I realize that since I have only described the potentially liberating effects of 5-MeO-DMT in ecstatic terms, it is only correct that I also convey the seriousness of the potentially negative effects that—in a small number of cases—have been known to occur. These are very real and can be exceedingly powerful, adversely affecting the unfortunate user for days, weeks, months . . . and even years to follow. These potentially negative effects are not restricted, as some might think, to the novice initiate, or to users with little experience in entheogens. No matter how spiritually or psychologically prepared the user may think he or she is, 5-MeO-DMT opens up new realms of consciousness that have never been accessed before. There are well-documented cases of experienced entheogen users suffering from the unique terrors and pitfalls they behold there.

5-MeO-DMT gets mentioned a couple of times in the collection *Tripping: An Anthology of True-Life Psychedelic Adventures*[1] although none of the accounts are very appealing. In one, the user collapses immediately into a severe white hole, and when she finally returns to consciousness nearly half-an-hour later, her husband has dialed 911. She had barely been breathing and her vital signs were weak. This experience is similar to my own accidental overdose (related in chapter 4). Erowid also has a number of negative reports in its 5-MeO-DMT vault. The quarterly journal *The Entheogen Review* kindly has allowed me to reprint this article from issue 8(4): 136–37, which appeared under the heading: "5-MeO-DMT WARNING."

> I know someone who had a severe and prolonged response to a vaporized 20 mg dose of 5-MeO-DMT. This person had done all the usual entheogenic substances for some years and was careful and intelligent. She had done her research and when offered this dose by a good friend, she agreed to do it but questioned the amount, as she felt that it should be 5–10 mg. Her friend assured her that he had done it, and others too, many times without problem.
>
> Immediately on ingesting, she became unconscious for half-an-hour, then came 'round groggy and remembering nothing. The sitter encouraged her to walk and eat something, however this was difficult for her. From that time on she experienced difficulty in sleeping, fear upon closing her eyes, and three nights later awoke at 3:30 am in the grip of a very severe, intense, and frightening panic attack. These attacks continued nightly, with nausea, vertigo, and heart palpitations during the day. Ativan® (lorazepam) was prescribed and later Klonopin® (clonazepam). Her doctor did a full check and said that her blood pressure was elevated, but that she had no apparent physical problems.
>
> Her symptoms persisted for eight weeks. Normally this person has slight, intermittent asthmatic symptoms around cats and mold. On coming 'round from the 5-MeO-DMT overdose, and for the eight weeks following it, she experienced breathing difficulties that usually occurred at night and when having panic attacks. This person is not unduly sensitive, was taking no medications, and had not eaten or drunk anything untoward. In fact, she had fasted the day before. Acupuncture was useful in the latter part of the eight weeks, but the Klonopin® was essential in controlling the symptoms.
>
> I have read many things about this material and even spoke with Charles Grob, whom I know. No one had heard of such a prolonged reaction (until now) and it occurred to me that *The Entheogen Review*

might like to let readers know that great care should be taken with the dosage of 5-MeO-DMT. Dr. Grob did say that if the blood pressure goes up too much during the session, it could precipitate a stroke. My friend was a very healthy woman of 59. I do hope this may be of help to others; information and warnings should be made available, and I feel that this is a volatile and unpredictable material.—A. S., CA[2]

This account was followed by an editorial comment:

People do seem to have quite varied reactions to 5-MeO-DMT, from mild to severe, but this is the first time that we have heard of aftereffects lasting for eight weeks. When trying *any* new compound it is advisable to start with a low dose, and gradually work one's way up. In the case of very potent materials, such as 5-MeO-DMT, great care must be taken to make sure that the dose is accurately weighed, and this can be difficult if one doesn't own a scale that weighs with a 1–2 mg accuracy. 20 mg would definitely be an overdose for most people, and we agree that it is important to report the situation that you described as a warning to others to be extremely careful with dosing.[3]

There is also the following "trip-report" from *TIHKAL* (with an unknown but large amount smoked):

I observed the subject pass very quickly into an almost coma-like state. Within seconds his face became purple and his breathing stopped. I pounded his chest, and breathed for him, and he seemed to emerge in consciousness, with the comment, "This is absolute ecstasy." He stopped breathing a second time, and both heart massage and mouth-to-mouth resuscitation was provided. Again, he recovered and managed to maintain a continuing consciousness and achieve a partial recovery. In the awake condition he was increasingly lucid, but on closing his eyes he became possessed with what he called "The energy of terror." He could not sleep, as upon closing his eyes he felt threatened in a way he could not tolerate. Three days later, medical intervention with antipsychotic medication was provided, which allowed the recovery of an acceptable behavior pattern in a few more days.[4]

The slim record thus clearly shows that 5-MeO-DMT can be both extremely unpredictable and powerful without precedent. But undoubtedly the most compelling rendition of the perils of smoking 5-MeO-DMT that I have encountered comes from the book *Darkness Shining Wild: An Odyssey to the Heart of Hell & Beyond,* by Robert Augustus Masters, with the sobering subtitle *Meditations on Sanity, Suffering, Spirituality, and Liberation.* If you take the idea of Bernard Haisch and others on polarity with any seriousness—the idea that *all things* must have an opposite for reality to emerge—then this book is the antithesis of *Tryptamine Palace,* the literary yang to my own written yin. Thus I find it as fascinating as I do terrifying.

A psychotherapist since the late 1970s, Masters describes himself as "a group leader, and teacher of spiritually deepening practices." His essays have appeared in publications ranging from *Magical Blend* to the *Journal of Transpersonal Psychology.* He is also an apparently successful author of several "self-help" books, such as *The Way of the Lover* and *Love Must also Weep.* With speaking engagements all over the world, Masters had amassed a considerable following: a psychospiritually oriented community with multiple chapters in Canada, Australia, Europe, and a headquarters somewhere near San Luis Obispo. Masters was "leading" this community in early 1994, when (after an earlier experimentation with ayahuasca), he smoked 30 mg of 5-MeO-DMT on the "enthusiastic recommendation of several members" of that same community.

In his book Masters actually writes that he smoked 30 *grams* of 5-MeO-DMT, but this is clearly a mistake since it would be both lethal and impossible to consume, so I am assuming that this was a typo and the correct amount should be 30 mg. This amount is a full third higher than that noted in the warning from *The Entheogen Review,* and is approximately the same as my own *first* (uninformed) dose of 5-MeO-DMT. I must state again that I consider 30 mg dosages to be *definitely* too high, and obviously dangerous. Part of the reason I have written this book is so that other uninformed users will not be tempted to try such a large dosage as I did!

In his account of that fateful incident, Masters had to actually take *two* hits, which is rather strange in itself, and I can only assume that the 5-MeO-DMT melted down as it had when I overdosed. Here is Masters' description of what happened next.

What I saw in front of me—the pipebowl, the faces of Marcelo and Nancy, the room, the framed sunlight, *everything*—immediately shrank into a rapidly contracting circle, as if it all were being viewed through some quickly closing aperture of a camera. In less than ten seconds, I became completely—*completely*—unconscious of waking/physical reality, finding myself bodiless in a horizonless horror that was madly and monstrously pulsating, moving far too fast, in all directions at once.

It resembled my ayahuasca journey at its most titanically wild and insane, sped up and intensified a hundredfold. I knew that I was in very serious trouble; I was completely disconnected somatically, unable to locate or feel my body (as in sleep-dream), unable to locate myself—or *anything* else—*anywhere* in particular. I had no body, not even the slightest semblance of a dream-body or mental-body, and I had absolutely no sense of where I was. And *what* was *I* now? I was wide awake, but could not leave this domain, as I might leave a dream once I knew I was in a dream.

What remained of me was but a ghostly speck of awareness, an entombed locus of ricocheting attention in a completely unfamiliar locale, pervaded with a sickening despairing intuition that the "waking state" me was in grave danger, perhaps already dead.

If what "I" was immersed in possessed any discernible or translatable form, it was vaguely reptilian, full of scaly-headed waves that were both surface and depth, both organic and metallic, sliding in and out of form. No limits, no edges, no exit. It was timeless, boundless Chaos, continuously creating and consuming itself on every sort of scale with unimaginable power and ease and significance. . . .

In the shadowlands of the Unimaginable floated I, bodiless yet pinned. Terror and Awe locked in boundless embrace.[5]

According to Masters' account, "Twice in fifteen minutes or so, I almost died, suffering not only respiratory failure, but also apparently having seizures (of which I had no previous history). Again, I had no awareness of this—all I was conscious of was the madly pulsating, sentient Wonder-Horror that seemed to be the very bedrock and breath of reality, bereft of horizon, including itself in every form, every possibility, every alternative to itself."[6]

Masters' account of his "seizures" and apparent lack of breathing should not be disregarded—he had CPR performed on him while he was "locked as if in rigor mortis, purple-faced and unbreathing." Overdoses occupy a category all of their own. It seems clear from this account that his dosage was *way* too high. Thus the cause of his problems could be credited to a lack of information about the compound (5-MeO-DMT) involved and over-enthusiasm on the part of his "follower" who undoubtedly wanted to make sure that the good doctor "got off." As has been repeatedly stated throughout this book, if you are experimenting with an entheogen you have no previous experience with, start *low.* Alexander Shulgin's explanation of how he developed his bioassay system (in *PIHKAL*) for the new compounds he creates is essential reading for any would-be psychonaut.

Two Sides to Ego-Death

I in no way wish to degrade the life-threatening danger that Masters believes he was in (he describes it as his near-death experience throughout the book), but it seems clear to me that phenomenologically Masters and I actually experienced approximately the same psychological event—a psychospiritual ego-death—the *mysterium tremendum et fascians* of experiencing the full formless totality of existence. Yet while I regarded my 5-MeO-DMT experience as a paradisiacal liberation and the "recognition of recognitions," Masters only found horror in the experience—his terror clearly outweighing his awe. It seems that it was his psychospiritual ego-death that caused him to have ongoing problems—not the physical near-death he believes he nearly suffered. Consider this next passage describing his mental state in the weeks and months after his experience.

> Death, it seemed to me, was no escape at all, nor even the entry point into oblivion, but rather was the very process through which the whole cosmic drama could continue. The unrelenting, unboundaried Wonder and Horror and Mystery of it all—peering through me at me from all angles—made me tremble and want to totally disappear. It was so fucking inconceivably *real,* and I (and everything else) seemed so blatently dream-like, so conspicuously unreal—had I ever *really* existed? Had *anything?*
>
> And if manifest existence was but the Absolute "making an

> appearance" then *what* exactly was I? I did not dare pursue such questions too closely—and yet I could find no significant distance from them—for I felt incapable of bearing their "answers.[7]

Passages like these astound me, for I have felt the same things and considered the same questions, but all the time with a sense of joy and gratitude, for I believe that I have been presented a "key" for unlocking some of the greatest secrets of existence. 5-MeO-DMT paradoxically *confirmed* the reality of existence for me, the reality of *who and what I am*. All the things that Masters mentions above are the same forces that helped me to shape this book—but viewed from the absolutely polar point of view. How could it be that Masters and I could have arrived at such opposite destinations from the same pivotal event? Aldous Huxley's comments about the physical effects of psychedelics offer a helpful perspective:

> The negative visionary experience is often accompanied by bodily sensations of a very special and characteristic kind. Blissful visions are generally associated with a sense of separation from the body, a feeling of deindividualisation. . . . When the visionary experience is terrible and the world is transfigured for the worse, individualization is intensified and the negative visionary finds himself associated with a body that seems to grow progressively more dense, more tightly packed, until he finds himself at last reduced to being the agonized consciousness of an inspissated lump of matter, no bigger than a stone that can be held between the hands.[8]

In terms of the physical difficulties that some people encounter on 5-MeO-DMT, this presents the question of what came first, the horse or the cart? Or to put it more clearly, are the anxieties actually a *physical* reaction to the compound or are they a *mental* reaction to the apparent willingness of part of our consciousness to leave the bodily form? I tend to believe that the latter is true, and that because a full-5-MeO-DMT release so closely resembles a NDE, the "ego-mind" will put physical stresses upon the body in an effort to keep the mind grounded in this reality. The body tensing up during a 5MDE is generally the first sign of problems—while the deepest 5MDE journeys appear to be accompanied by an intense physical "calm"—so much so that witnesses are often concerned that the participant does not appear to be breathing.

It must be also noted, however, that Huxley linked negative effects to physical deficiencies in the body—and one has to wonder if these "negative effects" are not in some way related to a serotonin imbalance in the body (see appendix 4). Masters himself speculates on these possibilities in one of his footnotes (chapter 8) and notes that "[bufotenine] catalyzed life-threatening circulatory crises and cyanosis ('plum-colored face') when injected into unsuspecting(!) patients"—which sounds a lot like his own reaction to his second toke of 5-MeO-DMT. Masters wonders if some enzyme in his body caused 5-MeO-DMT to "de-methylate" into bufotenine (*O*-methyl transferase, the enzyme found in our old friend the *Bufo alvarius,* methylates bufotenine into 5-MeO-DMT). Judging by the severe physical reactions that a very small percentage of 5-MeO-DMT users suffer, it would seem like this could be a promising area of potential research.

In his essay *Heaven and Hell* (1955), Huxley examined what he called "the antipodes of the Mind," and offered this view on the subject.

> Like heaven, the visionary hell has its preternatural light and its preternatural significance. But the significance is intrinsically appalling and the light is "the smoky light" of the *Tibetan Book of the Dead,* the "darkness visible" of Milton. In the *Journal d'une Schizophrène* [by M.A. Sechehaye, Paris, 1950], the autobiographical record of a young girl's passage through madness, the world of the schizophrenic is called *le Pays d'Éclairement*—"the country of lit-upness." It is a name which a mystic might have used to denote his heaven. But for poor Renée, the schizophrenic, the illumination is infernal—an intense electric glare without a shadow, ubiquitous and implacable. Everything that, for healthy visionaries, is a source of bliss brings to Renée only fear and a nightmarish sense of unreality. The summer sunshine is malignant; the gleam of polished surfaces is suggestive not of gems, but of machinery and enameled tin; the intensity of existence which animates every object, when seen at close range and out of its utilitarian context, is felt as a menace.
>
> And then there is the horror of infinity. For the healthy visionary, the perception of the infinite in a finite particular is a revelation of divine immanence; for Renée, it was a revelation of what she calls "the

> System," the vast cosmic mechanism which exists only to grind out guilt and punishment, solitude and unreality.
>
> Sanity is a matter of degree, and there are plenty of visionaries, who see the world as Renée saw it, but contrive, nonetheless, to live outside the asylum. For them, as for the positive visionary, the universe is transfigured—but for the worse. Everything in it, from the stars in the sky to the dust under their feet, is unspeakably sinister or disgusting; every event is charged with a hateful significance; every object manifests the presence of an Indewelling Horror, infinite, all-powerful, eternal.[9]

Masters experienced that "Indwelling Horror" for months and years to come, the full account of which is contained in his remarkable book. (One reviewer states it is "as if Buddha had a terrifying psychotic episode.") He spent sixty-three consecutive nights after his 5MDE/NDE sitting in "terror and madness," either unable to sleep, or—more terrifyingly for him—falling back into the 5-MeO-DMT experience in his sleep. A single night's rest without fear followed—only for the sleepless terror to return. In his waking time, his own identity was threatened; the psychospiritual dissolution of his ego had challenged his view of himself so soundly he was no longer sure of who he *was.* His worldwide "psychospiritual community"—which he readily admits had clearly been held together by his apparently considerable ego—fell apart from internal divisions once the cult of his personality was insufficient to keep it together.

Feelings of intense dread would suddenly descend upon him without warning, nightmares continued to rule his nights, and he began to wonder if he was going insane from the constant terror—"terror" is a word he uses over and over again in his account. He ended up having to take Ativan (three times a day) to "stabilize" his daily life, his work falling apart around him. Then, ten years later, he delivered his remarkable book of "meditations on sanity, suffering, spirituality, and liberation." Mercifully, he emerged from this long ordeal with a new sense of spiritual awakening, with the view that his traumatic experience had been necessary for his spiritual development. (His book also presents some fascinating insights regarding the close links between madness and creativity.)

Unfortunately, due both to the laws of polarity and to the same logic that requires that only a very small percentage of 5-MeO-DMT users will ever be able to experience the ultimate liberating experience of Oneness with G/d, I think it is inevitable that a small percentage of 5-MeO-DMT users must experience the realms of hell. And that a *very* small percentage—the five percent of the five percent of the five percent of Abe Maslow's "ultimate peak experience" turned upside down—will undergo an experience equally as destroying as Masters'. However, the similar language of our books and apparently of our desires (he *already had* a psychospiritual Gnostic community, while I now hope to one day help create one), and the completely opposite initial psychic transformations—coupled with the extreme severity of Masters' reaction—forces me to wonder what was so different in his makeup and experience that he journeyed to hell, rather than to the heaven that some other users will experience?

Entheogenic Paradox

Apparently this is an essential paradox of the use of entheogens. The key that opens one man's door to heaven can equally easily open another man's door to hell, even if, outwardly, the two individuals involved may seem similar. Colin Wilson, the British existentialist writer, examines this bizarre anomaly and recounts the difference in the mescaline experiences of two great intellects and writers: Jean Paul Sartre, and Aldous Huxley.

> In the second volume of Mlle de Beauvoir's autobiography, *The Prime of Life,* she reveals that Sartre took mescaline. She describes Sartre's experience as this: "He had not exactly hallucinations, but the objects he looked at changed their appearances in a most horrifying manner; umbrellas had become vultures, shoes turned into skeletons, and faces acquired monstrous characteristics, while behind him, just past the corner of his eye, swarmed crabs and polyps and grimacing Things . . ."[10]

Colin Wilson notes this passage from Sartre's novel *Nausea,* which clearly seems to have been influenced by Sartre's mescaline experience, since it was written within the same year.

> And then all of a sudden, there it was, clear as day: existence had suddenly unveiled itself. It had lost the harmless look of an abstract

> category: it was the very paste of things, this root was kneaded into existence. Or rather the root, the park gates, the bench, the sparse grass, all that had vanished: the diversity of things, their individuality, were only an appearance, a veneer. This veneer had melted, leaving soft, monstrous masses, all in disorder—naked with a frightful, obscene nakedness.[11]

Colin Wilson then asks us to consider Huxley's account of *his* initial experience on the same compound.

> The word "naked" recalls Aldous Huxley's use of it in describing his own mescalin experiences in *Doors of Perception.* But there is a curious difference. What Huxley says was "what Adam saw on the morning of his first creation—the miracle, moment by moment, of naked existence." It would seem also that mescalin delivered Huxley from the world of inauthenticity . . . Huxley became aware that things existed in their own right, but the realization was entirely pleasant. Huxley uses the word *istigkeit* [coined by the Christian mystic Meister Eckhart] to describe it: "is-ness."
>
> . . . Huxley goes on to mention that mescalin may have one of two effects; it may plunge the drug-taker into heaven or hell, depending on his mind or nervous constitution. A man who feels a basic dislike or distrust of life will probably find himself in hell.[12]

The difference between the two men seems clear: according to Sartre's philosophy, the world has completely no meaning. Sartre expresses this most clearly in his most famous work, *Being and Nothingness* (1943). And if the world has no meaning, then there can be no *transcendence.* His own philosophy of the world closed Sartre off from the possibilities of the mescaline experience. (Interestingly enough, the passage from Sartre is very similar to many of Robert Augustus Masters' passages from *Darkness Shining Wild.*) Aldous Huxley, on the other hand, had already undergone a spiritual transformation from being one of the most famous agnostics of his generation to becoming arguably the West's most famous philosopher of mysticism, *even before he had taken mescaline.* Huxley could certainly be considered an authority on the subject of transcendence and had already had mystical experiences of his own; he was thus uniquely "primed" for the revelations of the mescaline experience.

It is because of who Huxley was *before* he took mescaline for the first time that makes *The Doors of Perception* the most important and influential book on entheogens that will ever be written. Huxley had spent half his lifetime studying spirituality and mysticism, and his knowledge was both highly respected and encyclopedic. So when he told the world that mescaline had opened up his soul and mind like no amount of meditation or contemplation before it, a lot of learned people took notice. *The Doors of Perception* itself is an amazing compendium of thoughts about art, religion, spirituality, schizophrenia, and the nature of existence. His theories about the Mind as a reducing valve, or "filter" for reality, and the comparison he makes between the mescaline experience terminology from Buddhism and Hinduism, and most specifically, the *Tibetan Book of the Dead*, laid the groundwork for the future discussion of "psychodelics" for years to come. There will probably never be another book like *The Doors of Perception,* because it is doubtful that there will ever again be the possibility of an unprejudiced, chance crossing of one of the world's greatest scientist-philosophers with an emerging technology for the mind like mescaline.

As Huxley readily admits, he was always a poor "visualizer," and the mescaline experience was not what he expected; he had thought he would be carried off into William Blake's world of fantastic visions. Instead he saw "the veil of reality lifted." 5-MeO-DMT is phenomenologically a lot different from mescaline, and one can only wonder what Huxley would have made of an experience as disorienting and all encompassing as the 5MDE. Robert Augustus Masters seems like a throwback to Huxley's age of philosophical search and discovery, and in the following passage from the introduction to *Darkness Shining Wild,* I think may have found a clue to the essential difference between our initial separate experiences.

> And yet here it is, apparently immune to meditative practice and cathartic discharge—breath awareness, awareness of body and mind, prayer and pranayama, Vipassana and Dzogchen, bodywork and yoga and running and relaxation practices, raw emotional release, psychospiritual insight, tears and tears and deeper tears, providing at best a sporadic, extremely fragile relief. Short-lived interruptions of terror.[13]

While Masters is describing the various ways he was trying to control his unabated terror, he is also running off a formidable list of esoteric techniques that he had learned over the decades. All of the techniques he mentions require a *focusing* of the mind, with the ultimate goal being the identification of Self with the Ground of Being. It seems very apparent that Masters has been on that hunt for more than twenty years. So when he took his hit of 5-MeO-DMT, I'm pretty sure he felt he would be able to "control" the experience once he was in there. Only there is no controlling 5-MeO-DMT. And in many ways I believe what you need to be able to do at the height of the experience is paradoxically the *opposite* of yogic techniques—you have to be able to de-focus and completely let go.

One of the extreme sports that I spent twenty years chasing offers a good analogy. In paragliding it is possible to turn within the circumference of a thermal and rise up from the ground at rates in excess of fifteen hundred feet per minute—I consider this one of the most thrilling experiences I have ever encountered. But if you have the misfortune to enter or exit this same thermal incorrectly, then the soft body of the paraglider (which doesn't have tubing like a hang glider and is inflated by constant air pressure) can collapse, sometimes entirely. This can then cause the glider to "ball up" behind you, and send you into a terrifying spin. My point is that you have to train yourself (or at least I did!) to do something quite extraordinary if this should happen: in the instant after the collapse, you have to do nothing—or to be accurate, you have to wait for the glider to reinflate, at which point you then "dampen" the ensuing surge. In the moment that all hell breaks loose, you have to have the confidence (or faith) to do nothing but wait. This can be a pretty damned hard thing to do, especially if you are nervously close to the ground. But if you *do* react and pull on a brake or do anything to try and alter the situation—as many beginner-intermediates do—then you actually *cause* the next collapse, and surge, and collapse, and spin. This results in a situation of increasingly violent action and reaction, which in paragliding we call *cascading.*

I have seen numerous people try to "control" or "come out" of their 5-MeO-DMT experience—something that is virtually impossible to do. These attempts at retaining their identity (and ego) seem to greatly increase the anguish of their situation, as they *cascade* from one egocentric internal dilemma to the next. The best thing you can do at the height of the experience when your whole life seems to have come to that one unbelievable moment outside of space and time is to do *nothing*—and, if you can, just let yourself go. Let yourself dissolve. Rid yourself of your "I" and go dance with the Supreme State of Being. Because you can't take your ego with you to the party.

Consider this following passage from Dr. Masters where he describes his constant fear of reentering his experience.

> If I indeed was—as I vainly hoped a few short-lived times—in the throes of actual ego-death, I was nonetheless apparently stuck in the passageway (no longer, so to speak, in an amniotic universe), despite my times of emergence. Proferred notions from well-meaning others—shamanistic crisis, spiritual emergency or just plain purification—were of no use to me. Conceptualizing did not, as it often had before, distance me from my feelings, but now only suffused them with a shiveringly creepy transpersonal paranoia. Never had I worked so hard at being present, and never could I remember being so scared.[14]

A passage from Joseph Campbell's *The Inner Reaches of Outer Space: Metaphor as Myth and as Religion* sheds an interesting light on this issue. He is discussing *pranayama,* the Tantric yoga breathing technique, in which the left nostril and breathing passage are said to embody our *lunar* (temporal) consciousness, while the right represents our *solar* (infinite) consciousness. He says:

> [It is] at *Yuktatriveṇī,* "The Meeting Place of Three Rivers," that the differentiated lunar and solar energies at last blend into a single fire, which then, like a blast, ascends with the awakened *kuṇḍalinī* into and along the central way. Until this fusion of the two breaths occurs, the central portal remains closed. The embodied *lunar* consciousness of the practicing individual must first, that is to say, be experienced as in fact the same as the universal *solar* consciousness by which all beings are energized and given light. Otherwise the mind will either remain locked in materiality, imagining the body and its experience to be of matter alone, or fly rapt away on some supernatural fancy, as though (the universe being of matter alone) soul or spirit should be sought somewhere else.[15]

This passage equally explains the fate of the unsuspecting 5-MeO-DMT initiate. To recognize the Ultimate Reality, you must *transcend* your ordinary reality—and in that process the "you" gets left behind. Or to clarify, the "you" has to let go of "yourself" because, essentially, "you" cannot go along for the ride—"you" can only release the part of "you" that is timeless to return to its ground of being. If you rigidly attempt to hold onto your "I-dentity," you will not be able to "dissolve" into the transcendental ground. So, if there is a fundamental difference in the ground of Masters' experience on 5-MeO-DMT and in my own, it is in the fact that I had no expectation attached to my first 5MDE (since I knew so little about the compound), nor, due to the overwhelming intensity of the experience once it began, do I recall any inclination or attempt to try to control it . . . from what I can remember I was simply swept away in a blissful tide of *being,* which was probably the best thing that could have happened to me. In Masters' case, on the other hand, a combination of fear, ego, and a mind trained in being able to focus on the ground of being actually may have *prevented* his consciousness from taking that final leap into the unknown.

When Masters contacted Stanislav Grof a few days after his experience to get his advice, Grof advised him to take no medicines and to try to achieve "full catharsis," even if it meant being held down by a number of his followers to do so. But by then Masters' overwhelming fear seemed to be way too far past the point of ever allowing him to "let go"—and he was not tempted to take Dr. Grof's advice.

In his book *The Cosmic Game,* Stanislav Grof has this to offer:

> [T]he ego death that immediately precedes rebirth is the death of our old concepts of who we are and what the world is like, which were forged by the traumatic imprint of birth.
>
> As we are purging these old programs from our psyche and our body by letting them emerge into consciousness, we are reducing their energetic charge and curtailing their destructive influence on our life. From a larger perspective, this process is actually very healing and transforming. And yet, as we are nearing its final resolution, we might paradoxically feel that, as the old imprints are leaving our system, we are dying with them. Sometimes, we not only experience the sense of personal annihilation, but also the destruction of the world as we know it.

> While only a small step separates us from the experience of radical liberation, we have a sense of all-pervading anxiety and impending catastrophe of enormous proportions. The impression of imminent doom can be very convincing and overwhelming. The predominant feeling is that we are losing all that we know and all that we are. At the same time, we have no idea what is on the other side, or even if there is anything there at all. This fear is the reason that at this stage many people desperately resist the process if they can. As a result, they can remain psychologically stuck in this problematic territory for an indefinite period of time.
>
> The encounter with the ego death is a stage of the spiritual journey when we might need much encouragement and psychological support. When we succeed in overcoming the metaphysical fear associated with this important juncture and decide to let things happen, we experience total annihilation on all imaginable levels. It involves physical destruction, emotional disaster, intellectual and philosophical defeat, ultimate moral failure, and even spiritual damnation. During this experience, all reference points, everything that is important and meaningful in our life, seems to be mercilessly destroyed.
>
> Immediately following the experience of total annihilation—"hitting cosmic bottom"—we are overwhelmed by visions of light that has a supernatural radiance and beauty and is usually perceived as sacred.[16]

It may be that Robert Augustus Masters was in fact moments away from "enlightenment," but the power and fear of his ego-mind was such that it would not let him undergo that final annihilation that would have allowed him to identify his own consciousness with the "cosmic consciousness" itself. The result was that he became "trapped" in his own "ego-hell," unable to identify with *anything* at all—even himself. Both his "lunar" (temporal) and "solar" (cosmic) consciousnesses presented themselves, but they were unable to take the final step and merge—leaving "the central portal" firmly closed.

This phenomenon of the "mind-being-at-large" on a 5MDE, while the tattered remains of your ego flop around with your "meat" on the floor, continues to affect me personally. It is one of the main reasons I prefer to smoke 5-MeO-DMT alone. For when I smoke 5-MeO-DMT in the company of others, I have found myself increasingly embarrassed by the behavior of my "meat and ego," or more specifically, my behavior as I *return* to my "skin-encapsulated ego" from a 5MDE. It seems that if there is any personal point of focus for my ego-mind to grab onto as it returns from the state of undifferentiated transcendence, I start babbling the most ridiculous egotistical inanities. For example, if I have a close friend from my paragliding days in front of me, I will latch onto him and start talking about how amazing our flights were together. Or I will recall old girlfriends, and openly discuss my sexual history in graphic, almost pornographic terms. I grab onto everyone in the circle and tell them how much I love them and how much they all mean to me. This very unenlightened behavior was really beginning to bother me, until I decided that this literally *was* my ego-mind, which I had transcended and left behind, but to which I ultimately had to return. (This obviously doesn't happen when I am alone, because my ego has nobody to latch onto.)

I have a ton of ego—way more than most, my wife constantly tells me—and yet it clearly can't come with me when I transcend it. But the ego still has to be *somewhere.* So it makes sense that it should remain behind with my matter-bound form. This is the reason why, when friends ask me if I would like them to film one of my 5MDEs so I can watch it later, I always tell them *"NO."* I have no interest in seeing what my meat is up to when I am gone; as far as I am concerned those actions are irrelevant. I am now actually trying to train my friends who witness my 5MDEs to tell my "ego-mind" to be quiet when it reappears and to try and get me to "lay back down" in the experience and let my deeper-self retain contact with the field. But with my eyes still shining wild from the light I have just encountered, I usually tell them that they are out of their minds, along with the now common instruction that if they loved me they would "bury that vial in the ground and never let me near it again!"

This phenomenon has also made me reconsider the idea of reincarnation and of escaping this wheel of form. I used to think that a higher reincarnation would be easy and obvious: wouldn't all sentient beings wish to climb the ladder of existence toward Buddhahood and enlightenment? Wouldn't everyone accept that option and take paradise? But if the next level of existence, the next dimension of being, cannot be experienced by this "form," then the "I" would have to be released, let go of for eternity . . . And in that moment you will be tempted by all the beautiful things you have experienced in this world, all the love, and wonder, and joy. And your ego will be offered the opportunity to either return back to everything you have known and loved, to all the things you have not yet done or mastered, or to transcend to a place "you" cannot know, and that your ego cannot go. "You" must give up both the world and your I-dentity for the Mystery. As someone who loves this planet, and loves this life, and still has lifetime after lifetime of things he would like to see and do, I can now appreciate what an awesomely difficult choice that will be.

Clearly this essay has wandered and threatens to become a book of its own! But in returning to the theme with a hope of closing, I will recount the very few negative encounters with 5MDE I have witnessed or encountered. As I mentioned in the Burning Man chapter, my good friend Captain Urquhart believes he suffered adverse effects from his Burning Man 5MDE some months after it occurred. He suffered from fainting fits, a general feeling of light-headedness, and an increased sensitivity to smoking weed. He has no interest in ever trying 5-MeO-DMT again.

Several people have vomited during their experience while I have been sitting with them. I deal with them all the same way: by rolling them into the recovery position, ideally *before* they vomit. Each time, their physical discomfort seemed obvious and also seemed to come from "fighting the experience," so to speak. Once they vomit, they generally calm right down, the psychological "blockage" they were encountering purged with their physical discharge.

My wife had a dark and violent first 5MDE, much darker and more violent than she actually verbalized to me. She remained silently fearful of the compound for some time, but living with me, I guess it was inevitable that she would try it again. Upon her second release she went to a remarkable "love zone"—a place where her body would suck in every iota of breath it could manage and then she would shout, "I love . . . I love . . . I love . . ." at the top of her voice, over and over again, for at least five minutes. She returned from her experience with this overwhelming sense of love, and she was amazed at the difference between her two polar-opposite experiences. She now goes to this very beautiful place when she (very) occasionally feels the desire to have a 5MDE.

I have watched numerous people experience apparent difficulties within their 5MDE who have absolutely no recollection of *any difficulty* once they return; in their minds they were in a place of love and joy, and they often have a hard time believing the accounts of their physical difficulties from concerned witnesses. No one that I have ever watched smoke 5-MeO-DMT has had any short or long-term psychological difficulties that I am aware of, nor has anyone required any form of antidepressant or any other form of medication. There is, however, one more experience that I witnessed that was followed by a tragedy, and while I have given this one experience more thought than any other single experience I have ever witnessed, I still have no answers. Like so many other facets of the 5MDE, it is, in its essence, as much of a mystery as the Mystery we are contemplating.

This experience occurred shortly after my own epiphany on 5-MeO-DMT, when I was still incredibly excited for *all* of my friends to try 5-MeO-DMT. It was only a couple of weeks after I had first smoked 5-MeO-DMT, and only the second time I tried it. I was in New Orleans for my thirty-sixth birthday, and when my wife (at that time my girlfriend) had asked me what I wanted to do, I told her I wanted to have a 5-MeO-DMT session with close friends, instead of any kind of a party. So she invited a few close friends over to her house, and that was what we did.

Now everyone had been hearing from me about how amazing and life-changing 5-MeO-DMT was, so they were obviously pretty curious to try it. The only problem was that when I had previously smoked it in Portland, we had imbibed it using the "chasing the dragon" technique off tin foil—a technique at which my friend in Portland was quite expert. But when I tried it with my friends at my wife's house, I couldn't get the hang of it all, and neither myself, my wife, or Captain Urquhart released using that method. Frustrated, I put a dose in a pipe on some weed, and managed some kind of a release, which was in itself apparently something to witness—I grabbed my wife quite hard by the forearms and shouted "Breathe, Breathe, Breathe!" as I managed to find my way back to that zone I had first encountered.

There was one other close friend there with us at this time. He was a great fan of psychedelics, and after he had witnessed my experience, he was all ready to be next in the psychonaut chair. Once I had gathered myself from my own experience, I packed him a bowl. My friend took a long steady hit on the pipe, obviously trying to fill his lungs up with the smoke as much as he could, and then he went into a very spooky 5MDE, obviously dark and discomforting. As he came out of it he was extremely disoriented and he kept apologizing for something over and over again, telling us to tell his wife and his kids that he was sorry, but for what he couldn't or wouldn't tell us. This apologizing and general disorientation went on for some time, along with him repeating that, "he never wanted to try that 5-MeO-DMT again." I was quite worried about him, since I had only previously witnessed two other real 5MDE releases and I had no reference upon which to base my friend's experience. He seemed so out-of-sorts that I was thinking I would have to drive him home, when he suddenly seemed to pull himself together, and within half an hour he seemed as if he was back to his normal self. We smoked a little weed and chilled out some more, and finally he said he was fine and drove himself home a little after midnight.

Still I was worried about him, and so the next day I called him up. He was laughing on the phone, saying that the experience hadn't been that bad, and even that he might like to try 5-MeO-DMT again sometime in the future, so I figured that he was all right. But when I asked him about the heavy "guilt" that he had obviously experienced, he had no recollection of it, nor of mentioning his wife or children. I found this very strange, but everything about 5-MeO-DMT seemed pretty strange at the time. And I had witnessed so few 5MDEs at that point that I had little to compare his experience with anyway (unlike now, when I have come to realize that it is probably the strangest reaction that I have ever seen). I was still processing my own experiences, so I didn't give his a lot more thought. That is, I didn't give it much more thought until I was back in my home in the Caribbean about a month later, and I received an email from Captain Urquhart telling me that this same friend had died in a tragic and unnecessary accident around his house, the details of which I don't need to go into here.

At first my fear was that this tragic accident had something to do with his state of mind after his 5MDE. But when I later talked to his wife she told me that his mental outlook had been great—they had just had a two-week holiday in the Caribbean without their kids and he had been tanned and happy and relaxed, with no mention of any lasting ill effects from his 5MDE. I was deep into my own ongoing experimentations with 5-MeO-DMT at the time, and it wasn't until later—when I really began to believe that the 5MDE was capable of taking my consciousness out of this physical realm and to a place outside of space and time—I began to wonder about what had happened during my now-dead friend's experience. So dark and heavy was his guilt upon returning from his 5MDE—with the numerous admonishments that we should tell his wife and kids that he was sorry—I began to wonder if he had not glimpsed his own senseless death that was just a few weeks away. The portal of time opened wide enough that the short remainder of his life was laid out like a page.

There is no answering a question like that—not in this life anyway—and only a disconcerting wonder that I am sure I will carry with me for the rest of my life. And if my friend *did* see his own death, he certainly did not remember it afterward. Nor apparently could he have avoided it. But no matter what you might think about my thoughts on this matter, one incontrovertible fact remains: 5-MeO-DMT opens the door to the Mystery of Mysteries, and when we smoke it we have no clue what we may discover once we pass through that door. So it is always best to prepare yourself the best you can for the Unknown you will encounter. For—as both I and Robert Augustus Masters would attest—if you smoke 5-MeO-DMT, you need to be prepared for the fact that your life may never be the same again.

The choice is always ours. Then, let me choose
The longest art, the hard Promethean way
Cherishingly to tend and feed and fan
That inward fire, whose small precarious flame,
Kindled or quenched, creates
The noble or the ignoble men we are,
The worlds we live in and the very fates,
Our bright or muddy star.

Aldous Huxley, "Orion," *The Cicadas and Other Poems*, 1931

Notes

Preface

1. Check out www.Burningman.com for more information.

Introduction. How This All Began

1. Condensed from a definition of material realism provided by Bernard Haisch, *The God Theory: Universes, Zero-Point Fields, and What's Behind It All* (York Beach, Maine: Red Wheel/Weiser, 2006).
2. Vladimir Nabakov, *Pale Fire* (New York: G.P. Putnam's Sons, 1962).
3. A. Huxley, from the Introduction to the Isherwood-Prabhavananda translation of the *Bhagavad-gita* (1944).

Chapter One. The 5-MeO-DMT Experience

1. This description of Stanislav Grof's fourth prenatal matrix (BPM IV) is found in S. Grof, *The Cosmic Game: Explorations of the Frontiers of Human Consciousness* (Albany: State University of New York Press, 1998).

Chapter Two. 5-MeO-DMT: Science, Discovery, and the History of Human Use

1. S. T. Christian et al., "Gas-Liquid Chromatographic Separation and Identification of Biologically Important Indolealkylamines from Human Cerebrospinal Fluid," *Biochemical Medicine* 14 (1975): 191–200.
2. J. Narby, *The Cosmic Serpent* (New York: Jeremy P. Tarcher/Putnam, 1998).
3. M. S. Fish, "*Piptadenia* Alkaloids. Indole Bases of *P. peregrina* (L.) Benth.

and Related Species" *Journal of the American Chemical Society* 77 (1955): 5892–95.

4. R. Strassman, *DMT: The Spirit Molecule: A Doctor's Revolutionary Research into the Biology of Near-Death and Mystical Experiences* (Rochester, Vt.: Park Street Press, 2001).
5. T. Hoshino and K. Shimodaira, "Über die Synthese des Bufotenin-Methyl-Äthers (5-Methoxy-*N*-Dimethyl-Tryptamin) und Bufotenins (Synthesen in der Indol-Gruppe. XV)," *Bulletin of the Chemical Society of Japan* 11 (3) (1936): 221–24.
6. I. J. Pachter et al., "Indole Alkaloids of *Acer saccharinum* (the Silver Maple), *Dictyoloma incanescens, Piptadenia colubrina,* and *Mimosa hostilis,*" *Journal of Organic Chemistry* 24 (1959): 1285–87.
7. G. Legler and R. Tschesche, "Die Isolierung von N-Methyltryptamin, 5-Methoxy-N-methyltryptamin und 5-Methoxy-N,N-dimethyltryptamin aus der Rinde von *Piptadenia peregrina* Benth," *Die Naturwissenschaften* 50 (3) (1963): 94–95.
8. J. Ott, *Pharmacotheon: Entheogenic Drugs, Their Plant Sources and History* (Kennewick, Wash.: Natural Products Co., 1993/1996).
9. V. Erspamer et al., "5-Methoxy- and 5-hydroxyindoles in the Skin of *Bufo alvarius,*" *Experientia* 21 (1965): 504.
10. D. R. Frost et al., "The Amphibian Tree of Life," *Bulletin of the American Museum of Natural History* 297 (2006): 1–370.
11. W. Davis and A. Weil, "Identity of a New World Psychoactive Toad," *Ancient Mesoamerica* 3 (1) (1992): 51–59. There are other candidates from the animal kingdom used in rites of passage and ritual—ants, scorpions, and poisonous snakes, to name a few—but they are none too safe or savory, and none produce an entheogen near as powerful as 5-MeO-DMT.
12. Bufotenine had been found a decade earlier in normal human blood and urine (see Fr. Franzen and H. Gross, "Tryptamine, *N, N* -Dimethyltryptamine, *N, N* -Dimethyl-5-hydroxytryptamine and 5-Methoxytryptamine in Human Blood and Urine," *Nature* 206 (1965): 1052). Around that time 6-methoxytetrahydro-harman—which in 1961 had been reported (under the name adrenoglomerulotropin) as a pineal gland hormone (see G. Farrel and W. M. McIsaac, "Adrenoglomerulotropin," *Arch Biochem Biophys* 94 (1961): 543–44)—was also characterized as a "hallucinogen" based on human bioassays (see C. Naranjo, "Psychotropic Properties of the Harmala Alkaloids," In: *Ethnopharmacologic Search for Psychoactive Drugs.* D. H. Efron, ed. Washington, D.C.: U.S. Government Printing Office, 1967).

13. S. T. Christian et al., "Gas-Liquid Chromatographic Separation and Identification of Biologically Important Indolealkylamines from Human Cerebrospinal Fluid," *Biochemical Medicine* 14 (1975): 191–200.
14. C. M. Torres and D. B. Repke, *Anadenanthera: Visionary Plant of Ancient South America* (Binghamton, N.Y.: Haworth Herbal Press, 2006).
15. A. Shulgin and A. Shulgin, *TIHKAL: The Continuation* (Berkeley, Calif.: Transform Press, 1997); and J. Ott, *Shamanic Snuffs or Entheogenic Errhines* (Solothurn, Switzerland: Entheobotanica, 2001).
16. R. E. Schultes and A. Hofmann, *The Botany and Chemistry of Hallucinogens,* second edition (Springfield, Ill.: Charles C. Thomas, 1980); and B. Holmstedt and J-E. Lindgren, "Chemical Constituents and Pharmacology of South American Snuffs" In: *Ethnopharmacologic Search for Psychoactive Drugs,* D. H. Efron, ed. (Washington, D.C.: U.S. Government Printing Office, 1967).
17. Mark Plotkin, private conversation, 1992.
18. A. Shulgin and A. Shulgin, *TIHKAL: The Continuation* (Berkeley, Calif.: Transform Press, 1997).
19. Anon, "Journal of a Voyage up the Amazon and Rio Negro by Richard Spruce, San Carlos del Rio Negro, June 27, 1853." From J. Ott, *Pharmacotheon: Entheogenic Drugs, Their Plant Sources and History* (Kennewick, Wash.: Natural Products Co., 1993/1996).
20. Jon Hanna, private communication, 2009.
21. *Legal Highs* presents a dose range for 5-MeO-DMT from 3.5 to 5 mg, an amount substantially lower than what I would consider "an effective dosage."
22. Jeremy Bigwood and Jonathan Ott, "DMT," *Head* (1977).
23. M. V. Smith, *Psychedelic Chemistry* (Port Townsend, Wash.: Loompanics Unlimited, 1981).
24. Jeremy Bigwood and Jonathan Ott, "DMT," *Head* (1977).
25. M. Aldrich, R. Ashley, and M. Horowitz, *High Times Encyclopedia of Recreational Drugs* (Ephraim, Wis.: Stonehill Publishing Company, 1978).
26. W. Beifuss and J. Hanna, "Jonathan Ott Speaks. . . ," *The Entheogen Review* 8 (1) (1999): 25.
27. For more information, see www.alternet.org/story/12393/. Accessed January 28, 2009.
28. J. Ott, *Shamanic Snuffs or Entheogenic Errhines* (Solothurn, Switzerland: Entheobotanica, 2001).
29. See www.universal-tao.com/dark_room/index.html.
30. Sogyal Rinpoche, *The Tibetan Book of Living and Dying,* revised and updated (San Francisco: HarperSanFrancisco, 2002).

31. C. M. Torres and D. B. Repke, *Anadenanthera: Visionary Plant of Ancient South America* (Binghamton, N.Y.: Haworth Herbal Press, 2006).
32. J. Ott, *Pharmacotheon: Entheogenic Drugs, Their Plant Sources and History* (Kennewick, Wash.: Natural Products Co., 1993/1996).
33. Ibid.
34. M. Eliade, *Shamanism: Archaic Techniques of Ecstasy* (London: Routledge & Kegan Paul, 1964).
35. R. Walsh and C. Grob, *Higher Wisdom: Eminent Elders Explore the Continuing Impact of Psychedelics* (Albany: State University of New York Press, 2005).
36. H. L. Bergson, *The Two Sources of Mortality and Religion* (Notre Dame, Ind.: University of Notre Dame Press, 1935), as cited in H. Smith, *Cleansing of the Doors of Perception: The Religious Significance of Entheogenic Plants and Chemicals* (New York: Jeremy P. Tarcher/Putnam 2000). Also see P. de Félice, *Poisons sacrés. Ivresses divines: Essai sur quelques formes inférieures de la mystique* (Paris: Albin Michel, 1936).
37. H. Smith, *Cleansing of the Doors of Perception: The Religious Significance of Entheogenic Plants and Chemicals* (New York: Jeremy P. Tarcher/Putnam, 2000).
38. Ibid.
39. Rig Veda 8:48.
40. Terence McKenna, *Food of the Gods: The Search for the Original Tree of Knowledge* (New York: Bantam Dell, 1992).
41. H. Smith, *Cleansing of the Doors of Perception: The Religious Significance of Entheogenic Plants and Chemicals* (New York: Jeremy P. Tarcher/Putnam, 2000).
42. Jon Hanna, personal communication, 2009.
43. R. Rodd, "Snuff Synergy: Preperation, Use, and Pharmacology of Yopo and *Banisteriopsis caapi* Among the Piaroa of Southern Venezuela," *Journal of Psychoactive Drugs* 34 (3) (2002): 273–79.
44. P.A.G.M. de Smet and L. Rivier, "Intoxicating Snuffs of the Venezuelan Piaroa Indians," *Journal of Psychoactive Drugs* 17(2) (1985): 93–103.
45. L. E. Luna, *Vegetalismo: Shamanism Among the Mestizo Population of the Peruvian Amazon* (Stockholm, Sweden: Almqvist and Wiksell International, 1986).

Chapter Three. The Aftermath

1. T. K. McKenna, *The Archaic Revival: Speculations on Psychedelic Mushrooms, the Amazon, Virtual Reality, UFOs, Evolution, Shamanism, the Rebirth of the Goddess, and the End of History* (San Francisco: HarperSanFrancisco, 1991).

2. Sogyal Rinpoche, *The Tibetan Book of Living and Dying,* revised and updated (San Francisco: HarperSanFrancisco, 2002).

Chapter Four. Welcome to the Power Zone

1. Aldous Huxley, *The Doors of Perception* (New York: Harper & Brothers, 1954).
2. Bernard Haisch, *The God Theory: Universes, Zero-Point Fields, and What's Behind It All* (York Beach, Maine: Red Wheel/Weiser, 2006).
3. A. W. Watts, *Psychotherapy East and West* (New York: Pantheon Books, Random House, 1961).
4. B. Haisch, *The God Theory: Universes, Zero-Point Fields, and What's Behind It All* (York Beach, Maine: Red Wheel/Weiser, 2006).
5. A. Huxley, *Heaven and Hell* (New York: Harper, 1956).
6. Rumi, "I See My Beauty in You," in *The Glance: Songs of Soul Meeting* (New York: Penguin, 1999).
7. W. Davis and A. Weil, "Identity of a New World Psychoactive Toad," *Ancient Mesoamerica* 3 (1) (1992): 51–59.
8. A. Shulgin and A. Shulgin, *TIHKAL: The Continuation* (Berkeley, Calif.: Transform Press, 1997).

Chapter Five. Into the Quantum Realm

1. Alvin Toffler, introduction to Ilya Prigogine's *Order Out of Chaos* (New York: Bantam, 1984).
2. Danah Zohar, *The Quantum Self: Human Nature and Consciousness Defined by the New Physics* (New York: Quill/William Morrow, 1990).
3. E. Laszlo, *The Connectivity Hypothesis: Foundations of an Integral Science of Quantum, Cosmos, Life, and Consciousness* (Albany: State University of New York Press, 2003).
4. T. Jennewein, G. Weihs, J-W. Pan, and A. Zeilinger, "Experimental Nonlocality Proof of Quantum Teleportation and Entanglement Swapping," *Physical Review Letters* 88 (2001).
5. E. Laszlo, *Science and the Akashic Field: An Integral Theory of Everything* (Rochester, Vt.: Inner Traditions, 2004).
6. Lynne McTaggart, *The Field: The Quest for the Secret Force of the Universe* (New York: Harper Perennial, 2003).
7. Check the latest version of "Did You Know?" on YouTube for more information on the exponential rate of increases that our society is currently experiencing.
8. Lynne McTaggart, *The Field: The Quest for the Secret Force of the Universe* (New York: Harper Perennial, 2003).

9. R. Weber, ed., *Dialogues with Scientists and Sages: The Search for Unity*. London and New York: Routledge & Kegan Paul, 1986; see "Bohm."
10. E. Laszlo, *Science and the Akashic Field: An Integral Theory of Everything* (Rochester, Vt.: Inner Traditions, 2004).

Chapter Six. Enter the Zero-Point Field

1. Diane Greco, *Ether and Field Theories*, 2002; www.victorianweb.org/science/ether.htm. Accessed January 28, 2009.
2. Ibid.
3. wikipedia.org; Aether theories.
4. Ibid.
5. wikipedia.org; Uncertainty principle.
6. L. McTaggart, *The Field: The Quest for the Secret Force of the Universe* (New York: Harper Perennial, 2003).
7. B. Haisch, *The God Theory: Universes, Zero-Point Fields, and What's Behind It All* (York Beach, Maine: Red Wheel/Weiser, 2006).
8. L. McTaggart, *The Field: The Quest for the Secret Force of the Universe* (New York: Harper Perennial, 2003).
9. Ibid.
10. Ibid.
11. Ibid.
12. Ibid.
13. Ibid.
14. Ibid.
15. B. Haisch, *The God Theory: Universes, Zero-Point Fields, and What's Behind It All* (York Beach, Maine: Red Wheel/Weiser, 2006).
16. Ibid.

Chapter Seven. Toading

1. T. Lyttle et al., "*Bufo* toads and Bufotenine: Fact and Fiction Surrounding an Alleged Psychedelic," *Journal of Psychoactive Drugs* 28 (3) (1996): 267–90.
2. A. B. Kennedy, "Ecce Bufo: The Toad in Nature and in Olmec Iconography," *Current Anthropology* 23 (3) (1982): 273–90.
3. W. Davis and A. Weil, "Identity of a New World Psychoactive Toad," *Ancient Mesoamerica* 3 (1) (1992): 51–59, citing Wasson, S. H. 1934.
4. T. Lyttle et al., "*Bufo* toads and Bufotenine: Fact and Fiction Surrounding an Alleged Psychedelic," *Journal of Psychoactive Drugs* 28 (3) (1996): 267–90.

5. W. Davis and A. Weil, "Identity of a New World Psychoactive Toad," *Ancient Mesoamerica* 3 (1) (1992): 51–59.
6. T. Lyttle et al., "*Bufo* toads and Bufotenine: Fact and Fiction Surrounding an Alleged Psychedelic," *Journal of Psychoactive Drugs* 28 (3) (1996): 267–90.
7. V. Deulofeu and E. A. Rúveda, "The Basic Constituents of Toad Venoms," in *Venomous Animals and Their Venoms* 2, W. Bücherl and E. Buckley, eds. (New York: Academic Press, 1971).
8. T. Lyttle et al., "*Bufo* toads and Bufotenine: Fact and Fiction Surrounding an Alleged Psychedelic," *Journal of Psychoactive Drugs* 28 (3) (1996): 267–90.
9. A. B. Kennedy, "Ecce Bufo: The Toad in Nature and in Olmec Iconography," *Current Anthropology* 23 (3) (1982): 273–90.
10. N. L. Hamblin, "The Magic Toads of Cozumel," *Mexicon* 3 (1) (1979): 10–14.
11. W. Davis and A. Weil, "Identity of a New World Psychoactive Toad," *Ancient Mesoamerica* 3 (1) (1992): 51–59.
12. A. B. Kennedy, "Ecce Bufo: The Toad in Nature and in Olmec Iconography," *Current Anthropology* 23 (3) (1982): 273–90.
13. Märki, F. et al., "Dehydrobufotenine, a Novel Type of Tricyclic Serotonin Metabolite from *Bufo marinus*," *Journal of the American Chemical Society* 83 (15) (1961): 3341.
14. J. Daly and B. Witkop, "Chemistry and Pharmacology of Frog Venoms," in *Venomous Animals and Their Venoms* 2, W. Bücherl and E. Buckley, eds. (New York: Academic Press, 1971).
15. Ibid.
16. K. Trout, *Some Simple Tryptamines*, second edition (Austin, Tex.: Mydriatic Productions, 2007).
17. A. Shulgin and A. Shulgin, *TIHKAL: The Continuation* (Berkeley, Calif.: Transform Press, 1997).
18. W. Davis and A. Weil, "Identity of a New World Psychoactive Toad," *Ancient Mesoamerica* 3 (1) (1992): 51–59.
19. Ibid.
20. A. Most, *Bufo alvarius: The Psychedelic Toad of the Sonoran Desert* (Denton, Tex.: Venom Press, 1983).
21. Ibid.
22. V. Erspamer et al., "5-Methoxy- and 5-hydroxyindoles in the Skin of *Bufo alvarius*," *Biochemical Pharmacology* 16 (7) (1967): 1149–64, as cited in W. Davis and A. Weil, "Identity of a New World Psychoactive Toad," *Ancient Mesoamerica* 3 (1) (1992): 51–59.

23. A. Most, *Bufo alvarius: The Psychedelic Toad of the Sonoran Desert* (Denton, Tex.: Venom Press, 1983).
24. W. Davis and A. Weil, "Identity of a New World Psychoactive Toad," *Ancient Mesoamerica* 3 (1) (1992): 51–59.
25. Ibid.
26. See http://en.wikipedia.org/wiki/Hohokam.
27. W. Davis and A. Weil, "Identity of a New World Psychoactive Toad," *Ancient Mesoamerica* 3 (1) (1992): 51–59.
28. P. Furst, *Hallucinogens and Culture* (Novato, Calif.: Chandler & Sharp Publishers, 1976).
29. Quote taken from T. Lyttle et al., "*Bufo* toads and Bufotenine: Fact and Fiction Surrounding an Alleged Psychedelic," *Journal of Psychoactive Drugs* 28 (3) (1996): 267–90.

Chapter Nine. India

1. From A. W. Watts, *The Joyous Cosmology: Adventures in the Chemistry of Consciousness* (New York: Pantheon Books, 1962/1965/1970); the quote is new to the 1965/1970 edition (page 26) and is not found in the original 1962 edition.
2. C. Calvo, *The Three Halves of Ino Moxo: Teachings of the Wizard of the Upper Amazon* (Rochester, Vt.: Inner Traditions, 1995).

Chapter Ten. The High Priest: Leary and the Legacies of the Psychedelic Age

1. A. Huxley, *Huxley and God: Essays on Religious Experience,* J. H. Bridgeman, ed. (San Francisco: HarperSanFrancisco, 1992).
2. Huston Clark, 1969; Taken from Rick Doblin, "Pahnke's Good Friday Follow-Up and Methodological Critique," *The Journal of Transpersonal Psychology* 23 (1) (1991). As seen in: *Psychoactive Sacramentals: Essays on Entheogens and Religion,* T. B. Roberts, ed. (San Francisco, Calif.: Council on Spiritual Practices, 2001).
3. Read *Acid Dreams: The CIA, LSD, and the Sixties Rebellion* by Martin A. Lee and Bruce Shlain (New York: Grove Press, 1985) for a comprehensive history of the CIA's interest and involvement in the American drug culture.
4. M. Riebling, "Was Timothy Leary a CIA Agent?" at http://home.dti.net/lawserv/leary.html. Accessed January 28, 2009.
5. "Timothy Leary on Nick Sand," www.serendipity.li/dmt/nsand/leary.htm. Accessed January 28, 2009.
6. Peter Stafford, *Psychedelic Encyclopedia,* third revised edition (Ronin Publishing, 1993).

7. Taken from the *Journal of Personality Assessment* 66 (2) (1996): 301–7.
8. "Was Timothy Leary a CIA Agent?" at http://home.dti.net/lawserv/leary.html. Accessed January 28, 2009.
9. J. Hanna, 2009, personal correspondence.
10. "Timothy Leary's Experiential Typewriter," http://everything2.com/index.pl?node_id=1399688. Accessed January 28, 2009.
11. For an evaluation of the role of psychedelics in the creation of Silicon Valley, see Ralph Abraham's introduction to chapter two: "Psychedelics, Computers, and Mathematics," in *The Evolutionary Mind: Trialogues at the Edge of the Unthinkable* (with Rupert Sheldrake and Terence McKenna (Rhinebeck, N.Y.: Monkfish Book Publishing, 1998); also see John Markoff, *What the Dormouse Said: How the 60s Counterculture Shaped the Personal Computer Industry* (New York: Viking Adult, 2005).
12. E. Laszlo, *Science and the Akashic Field: An Integral Theory of Everything* (Rochester, Vt.: Inner Traditions, 2004).

Chapter Eleven. The Zero-Point Field and the 5MDE: A Quantum Explanation

1. S. Grof, *The Cosmic Game: Explorations of the Frontiers of Human Consciousness* (Albany: State University of New York Press, 1998).
2. L. McTaggart, *The Field: The Quest for the Secret Force of the Universe* (New York: Harper Perennial, 2003).
3. Ibid.
4. Ibid.
5. E. Laszlo, *The Connectivity Hypothesis: Foundations of an Integral Science of Quantum, Cosmos, Life, and Consciousness* (Albany: State University of New York Press, 2003).
6. Ibid.
7. E. Laszlo, *Science and the Reenchantment of the Cosmos: The Rise of the Integral Vision of Reality* (Rochester, Vt.: Inner Traditions, 2006).
8. Ibid.
9. D. Zohar, *The Quantum Self: Human Nature and Consciousness Defined by the New Physics* (New York: Quill/William Morrow, 1990).
10. E. Laszlo, *Science and the Akashic Field: An Integral Theory of Everything* (Rochester, Vt.: Inner Traditions, 2004).
11. D. Zohar, *The Quantum Self: Human Nature and Consciousness Defined by the New Physics* (New York: Quill/William Morrow, 1990).
12. Ibid.

13. Sogyal Rinpoche, *The Tibetan Book of Living and Dying*, revised and updated (San Francisco: HarperSanFrancisco, 2002).
14. L. McTaggart, *The Field: The Quest for the Secret Force of the Universe* (New York: Harper Perennial, 2003).
15. E. Laszlo, *Science and the Reenchantment of the Cosmos: The Rise of the Integral Vision of Reality* (Rochester, Vt.: Inner Traditions, 2006).
16. Ibid.
17. Ibid.
18. L. McTaggart, *The Field: The Quest for the Secret Force of the Universe* (New York: Harper Perennial, 2003).
19. D. Zohar, *The Quantum Self: Human Nature and Consciousness Defined by the New Physics* (New York: Quill/William Morrow, 1990).
20. Ibid.
21. Ibid.

Chapter Twelve. A Quantum God

1. Sir J. Jeans, *The Mysterious Universe* (New York: Macmillan Co., 1930).
2. D. Zohar, *The Quantum Self: Human Nature and Consciousness Defined by the New Physics* (New York: Quill/William Morrow, 1990).
3. Ibid.
4. T. S. Elliot, *The Waste Land* (New York: Boni and Liveright, 1922).
5. E. Laszlo, *Science and the Akashic Field: An Integral Theory of Everything* (Rochester, Vt.: Inner Traditions, 2004).
6. E. Laszlo, *The Connectivity Hypothesis: Foundations of an Integral Science of Quantum, Cosmos, Life, and Consciousness* (Albany: State University of New York Press, 2003).
7. Puthoff, 2001, as quoted in E. Laszlo, *The Connectivity Hypothesis: Foundations of an Integral Science of Quantum, Cosmos, Life, and Consciousness* (Albany: State University of New York Press, 2003).
8. Ibid.
9. Ibid.
10. E. Laszlo, *3rd Millennium: The Challenge and the Vision* (London: Gaia Books Limited, 1997).
11. E. Laszlo, *Science and the Akashic Field: An Integral Theory of Everything* (Rochester, Vt.: Inner Traditions, 2004).
12. E. Laszlo, *The Connectivity Hypothesis: Foundations of an Integral Science of Quantum, Cosmos, Life, and Consciousness* (Albany, N.Y.: State University of New York Press, 2003).

13. E. Laszlo, *Science and the Akashic Field: An Integral Theory of Everything* (Rochester, Vt.: Inner Traditions, 2004).
14. B. Haisch, *The God Theory: Universes, Zero-Point Fields, and What's Behind It All* (York Beach, Maine: Red Wheel/Weiser, 2006).
15. Ibid.
16. E. Laszlo, *Science and the Akashic Field: An Integral Theory of Everything* (Rochester, Vt.: Inner Traditions, 2004).
17. J. Campbell, *Myths of Light: Eastern Metaphors of the Eternal,* D. Kudler, ed. (Novato, Calif.: New World Library, 2003).
18. Ibid.

Chapter Thirteen. The Role of Light in Eastern Philosophy

1. J. Campbell, *Myths of Light: Eastern Metaphors of the Eternal,* D. Kudler, ed. (Novato, Calif.: New World Library, 2003).
2. Ibid.
3. Ibid.
4. Drawn from the beginning of a lecture entitled "Transformation of Myth Through Time," delivered in Santa Fe, New Mexico on November 9, 1982.
5. J. Campbell, *Myths of Light: Eastern Metaphors of the Eternal,* D. Kudler, ed. (Novato, Calif.: New World Library, 2003).
6. A. Goswami, *The Self-Aware Universe: How Consciousness Creates the Material World* (New York: Jeremy P. Tarcher/Putnam, 1993).
7. Ibid.
8. Ibid.
9. Sogyal Rinpoche, *The Tibetan Book of Living and Dying,* revised and updated (San Francisco: HarperSanFrancisco, 2002).
10. Ibid.
11. Ibid.
12. Ibid.
13. Ibid.
14. Ibid., D. Bohm, as quoted in *Dialogues with Scientists and Sages: The Search for Unity*, R. Weber, ed. (London and New York: Routledge & Kegan Paul, 1986).
15. S. Grof, *The Cosmic Game: Explorations of the Frontiers of Human Consciousness* (Albany: State University of New York Press, 1998).
16. J. Campbell, *Myths of Light: Eastern Metaphors of the Eternal,* D. Kudler, ed. (Novato, Calif.: New World Library, 2003).
17. Sogyal Rinpoche, *The Tibetan Book of Living and Dying,* revised and updated (San Francisco: Harper San Francisco, 2002).

18. Ibid.
19. Ibid.
20. Personal correspondence between Chris Bache and Ervin Laszlo, July 2005, cited in E. Laszlo, *Science and the Reenchantment of the Cosmos: The Rise of the Integral Vision of Reality* (Rochester, Vt.: Inner Traditions International, 2006).
21. Ibid.

Chapter Fourteen. A Transcendent Future for Humanity?

1. A. Shulgin and A. Shulgin, *PIHKAL: A Chemical Love Story* (Berkeley, Calif.: Transform Press, 1991).
2. Richard Dawkins, *The God Delusion* (London: Bantam Press, 2006).
3. Ibid.
4. Ibid.
5. Ibid.
6. Ibid.
7. E. Laszlo, *Science and the Akashic Field: An Integral Theory of Everything* (Rochester, Vt.: Inner Traditions, 2004).
8. R. Dawkins, *The God Delusion* (London: Bantam Press, 2006).
9. J. Campbell, *Myths of Light: Eastern Metaphors of the Eternal*, D. Kudler, ed. (Novato, Calif.: New World Library, 2003).
10. Paul Davies, *The Mind of God: The Scientific Basis for a Rational World* (New York: Simon and Schuster, 1992). Taken from Bernard Haisch, *The God Theory: Universes, Zero-Point Fields, and What's Behind It All* (York Beach, Maine: Red Wheel/Weiser, 2006).
11. B. Haisch, *The God Theory* (San Francisco: Weiser Books, 2006).
12. J. Campbell, *The Inner Reaches of Outer Space: Metaphor as Myth and as Religion* (Novato, Calif.: New World Library, 2002 [Original edition 1986]).
13. E. Laszlo, *Science and the Akashic Field: An Integral Theory of Everything* (Rochester, Vt.: Inner Traditions, 2004).
14. J. Campbell, *The Inner Reaches of Outer Space: Metaphor as Myth and as Religion* (Novato, Calif.: New World Library, 2002 [Original edition 1986]).
15. A. Huxley, *The Doors of Perception* (New York: Harper & Brothers, 1954).
16. L. A. Huxley, "O Nobly Born!" in *Moksha: Aldous Huxley's Classic Writing on Psychedelics and the Visionary Experience*, M. Horowitz and C. Palmer, eds. (Rochester, Vt.: Park Street Press, 1977, 1999).
17. Ervin Laszlo, *Science and the Reenchantment of the Cosmos: The Rise of the Integral Vision of Reality* (Rochester, Vt.: Inner Traditions, 2006).

18. The Gospel of Sri Ramakrishna, translated by Swami Nikhilananda; taken from Joseph Campbell, *The Inner Reaches of Outer Space: Metaphor as Myth and as Religion* (Novato, Calif.: New World Library, 2002 [Original edition 1986]).
19. Martin Heidegger, *What is Metaphysics?* is the text of Heidegger's inaugural lecture at the University of Freiburg in 1929. An Afterword and Introduction were later added. The final line of this work concludes with the question, "Why are there beings at all, why not rather nothing?" (Published 1934).
20. B. Haisch, *The God Theory: Universes, Zero-Point Fields, and What's Behind It All* (York Beach, Maine: Red Wheel/Weiser, 2006).
21. Richard Conn Henry, "Review of *The God Theory,*" http://henry.pha.jhu.edu/haisch.html. Accessed January 28, 2009.
22. Ibid.
23. G. F. Cairns, "A Theology of Human Liberation and Entheogens: Reflections of a Contemplative Activist," in *Psychoactive Sacramentals: Essays on Entheogens and Religion,* T. B. Roberts, ed. (San Francisco, Calif.: Council on Spiritual Practices, 2001).
24. Ibid.
25. C. Wilson, *A Criminal History of Mankind* (London: Granada, 1984).
26. B. J. Lee and M. A. Cowan, *Dangerous Memories: House Churches and our American Story* (New York: Sheed & Ward, 1986). Taken from G. F. Cairns, "A Theology of Human Liberation and Entheogens: Reflections of a Contemplative Activist," In: *Psychoactive Sacramentals: Essays on Entheogens and Religion,* T. B. Roberts, ed. (San Francisco, Calif.: Council on Spiritual Practices, 2001).
27. G. F. Cairns, "A Theology of Human Liberation and Entheogens: Reflections of a Contemplative Activist," in *Psychoactive Sacramentals: Essays on Entheogens and Religion,* T. B. Roberts, ed. (San Francisco, Calif.: Council on Spiritual Practices, 2001).
28. "Victims of Fog Creep: What's With the Newspapers?" *Plain Language at Work Newsletter* (May 2, 2005). Online at www.impact-information.com/impactinfo/newsletter/plwork15.htm. Accessed January 28, 2009.
29. C. George Boeree, "Abraham Maslow," at http://webspace.ship.edu/cgboer/maslow.html. Accessed January 28, 2009.
30. See www.themystica.com/mystica/articles/p/peak_experiences.html. Accessed January 28, 2009.
31. See the Population Reference Bureau's web page at www.prb.org. Accessed January 28, 2009.
32. J. Vidal, "The End of Oil Is Closer Than You Think," *The Guardian,* April 21, 2005.

33. Frank Rich, *The Greatest Story Ever Sold: The Decline and Fall of Truth in Bush's America* (New York: Penguin, 2007).
34. T. Engelhardt, "A Global Arms Race Hidden in Plain Sight," *The Nation,* Blog: *The Notion* (2008), www.thenation.com/blogs/notion/284571/a_global_arms_race_hidden_in_plain_sight. Accessed Nov 19, 2008.
35. See www.starvation.net. Accessed January 28, 2009.
36. Some of Laszlo's titles in this arena include *Macroshift: Navigating the Transformation to a Sustainable World,* with Arthur C. Clarke and Kay Mikel (San Francisco: Berrett-Koehler, 2001); *You Can Change the World: The Global Citizen's Handbook for Living on Planet Earth* (New York: Select Books, 2003); and *Global Survival: The Challenge and Its Implications for Thinking and Acting,* with Peter Seidel (New York: Select Books, 2005).
37. E. Laszlo, *The Chaos Point: The World at the Crossroads* (Charlottesville, Va.: Hampton Roads Publishing, 2006).
38. Lady Montagu of Beaulieu, First Ambassador of the Club of Budapest.
39. See www.nationalgeographic.com/genographic/index.html. Accessed January 28, 2009.
40. James Shreeve, "The Greatest Journey Ever Told," *National Geographic,* March 2006; http://ngm.nationalgeographic.com/2006/03/human-journey/shreeve-text.html. Accessed January 28, 2009.
41. A. Shulgin and A. Shulgin, *PIHKAL: A Chemical Love Story* (Berkeley, Calif.: Transform Press, 1991).
42. J. Campbell, *The Inner Reaches of Outer Space: Metaphor as Myth and as Religion* (Novato, Calif.: New World Library, 2002 [Original edition 1986]).

Chapter Fifteen. So Begin the Days of Strangeness

1. G. E. Rice, "Leapin' Lizards! The Things People Will Do to Get High," *The Kansas City Star,* 2 Dec. 2007, sec. B1.
2. Hunter S. Thompson, "The 'Hashbury' Is the Capital of the Hippies." *The New York Times Magazine* (1967). Taken from *The Proud Highway: Saga of a Desperate Southern Gentleman. 1955–1967. The Fear and Loathing Letters, Vol. One.* Douglas Brinkley, ed. (New York: Ballantine Books, 1997).
3. B. Haisch, *The God Theory: Universes, Zero-Point Fields, and What's Behind It All* (York Beach, Maine: Red Wheel/Weiser, 2006).
4. Alex Grey, *Sacred Mirrors: The Visionary Art of Alex Grey* (Rochester, Vt.: Inner Traditions, 1990).

Appendix 3. Serotonin, Melatonin, 5-MeO-DMT, and the Pineal Gland

1. Jace C. Callaway, "Phytochemistry and Neuropharmacology of Ayahuasca," in *Ayahuasca: Hallucinogens, Consciousness, and the Spirit of Nature,* Ralph Metzner, ed. (New York: Thunder's Mouth Press, 1999).
2. Ibid.
3. Ibid.
4. Karkkainen and Raisanen, 1992, found within J. C. Callaway, *Phytochemistry and Neuropharmacology of Ayahuasca.* Taken from *Ayahuasca: Hallucinogens, Consciousness, and the Spirit of Nature,* Ralph Metzner, ed. (New York: Thunder's Mouth Press, 1999).
5. J. C. Callaway et al., 1995, found within J. C. Callaway, "Phytochemistry and Neuropharmacology of Ayahuasca." Taken from *Ayahuasca: Hallucinogens, Consciousness, and the Spirit of Nature,* Ralph Metzner, ed. (New York: Thunder's Mouth Press, 1999).
6. J. C. Callaway, "Phytochemistry and Neuropharmacology of Ayahuasca," 1999, found within *Ayahuasca: Hallucinogens, Consciousness, and the Spirit of Nature,* Ralph Metzner, ed. (New York: Thunder's Mouth Press, 1999.)
7. R. Strassman, *DMT: The Spirit Molecule: A Doctor's Revolutionary Research into the Biology of Near-Death and Mystical Experiences* (Rochester, Vt.: Park Street Press, 2001).
8. R. A. Masters, *Darkness Shining Wild: An Odyssey to the Heart of Hell & Beyond* (Tehmenos Press, 2005).
9. SoulLab, personal correspondence, 2007. See www.universal-tao.com/dark_room/index.html. Accessed January 28, 2009.
10. J. Hanna, 2007, personal correspondence with Keeper of the Trout.
11. J. Hanna, 2008, personal correspondence with Keeper of the Trout.
12. W. M. McIsaac et al., "10-Methoxyharmalan, a Potent Serotonin Antagonist which Affects Conditioned Behavior," *Science* 134 (1961): 674–75.
13. A. Shulgin and A. Shulgin, *TIHKAL: The Continuation* (Berkeley, Calif.: Transform Press, 1997).
14. C. Naranjo, "Psychotropic Properties of the Harmala Alkaloids," in *Ethnopharmacologic Search for Psychoactive Drugs,* D. H. Efron, ed. (Washington, D.C.: U.S. Government Printing Office, 1967).
15. A. Shulgin and A. Shulgin, *TIHKAL: The Continuation* (Berkeley, Calif.: Transform Press, 1997).
16. J. Hanna, 2008.
17. Ibid.

18. R. Strassman, *DMT: The Spirit Molecule: A Doctor's Revolutionary Research into the Biology of Near-Death and Mystical Experiences* (Rochester, Vt.: Park Street Press, 2001).

Appendix 4. Is 5-MeO-DMT the Most Potent Entheogen Known to Humanity?

1. R. A. Masters, *Darkness Shining Wild: An Odyssey to the Heart of Hell & Beyond* (Tehmenos Press, 2005).
2. Martin Ball, *The Entheogenic Evolution: Psychedelics, Consciousness, and Awakening the Human Spirit* (Kyandara Publishing, 2008).
3. Ibid.
4. S. Grof, *When the Impossible Happens: Adventures in Non-ordinary Realities* (Boulder, Colo.: Sounds True, Inc., 2006).
5. S. Grof, *The Cosmic Game: Explorations of the Frontiers of Human Consciousness* (Albany: State University of New York Press, 1998).
6. S. Grof, *When the Impossible Happens: Adventures in Non-ordinary Realities* (Boulder, Colo.: Sounds True, Inc., 2006).

Appendix 5. William S. Burroughs, the Godfather of DMT

1. W. S. Burroughs, *Ghost of a Chance* (London: Serpent's Tail Books, 1995).
2. W. S. Burroughs, *Ah Pook Is Here* (New York.: Calder Press, 1979).
3. From "23 Stitches Taken" by Gérard-Georges Lemaire, a foreword to Gysin's and Burroughs' *The Third Mind* (Viking Press, 1978).
4. See www.socialfiction.org/?tag=burroughs. Accessed January 28, 2009.
5. Michael Stevens, *The Road to Interzone,* http://home.swbell.net/felix23/. Accessed January 28, 2009.

Appendix 6. Heaven and Hell: Potential Negative Effects of 5-MeO-DMT

1. *Tripping: An Anthology of True-Life Psychedelic Adventures,* Charles Hayes, ed. (New York: Penguin, 2000).
2. "5-MeO-DMT Warning," *The Entheogen Review* 8 (4) (1999): 136–37.
3. Ibid.
4. A. Shulgin and A. Shulgin, *TIHKAL: The Continuation* (Berkeley, Calif.: Transform Press, 1997).
5. R. A. Masters, *Darkness Shining Wild: An Odyssey to the Heart of Hell and Beyond* (Tehmenos Press, 2005).
6. Ibid.

7. Ibid.
8. A. Huxley, *Heaven and Hell* (New York: Harper & Brothers, 1955).
9. Ibid.
10. Colin Wilson, *Beyond the Outsider* (London: A Barker, 1965).
11. Jean-Paul Sartre, *Nausea* (New York: New Directions, 1959).
12. Colin Wilson, *Beyond the Outsider* (London: A Barker, 1965).
13. R. A. Masters, *Darkness Shining Wild: An Odyssey to the Heart of Hell & Beyond* (Tenemos Press, 2005).
14. Ibid.
15. J. Campbell, *The Inner Reaches of Outer Space: Metaphor as Myth and as Religion* (Novato, Calif.: New World Library, 2002 [Original edition 1986]).
16. S. Grof, *The Cosmic Game: Explorations of the Frontiers of Human Consciousness* (Albany: State University of New York Press, 1998).

Bibliography

Aanstoos, C. M. "Life as a Symphony." In *Narrative Identities: Psychologists Engaged In Self-Construction,* G. Yancy and S. Hadley, eds. London: Jessica Kingsley Publishers, 2005.

Bergson, H. L. *The Two Sources of Mortality and Religion.* Notre Dame, In.: University of Notre Dame Press, 1935.

Beifuss, W., and J. Hanna. "Jonathan Ott Speaks . . ." *The Entheogen Review* 8 (1) (1999): 25–34.

Bohm, D. *Wholeness and the Implicate Order.* London and Boston: Routledge & Kegan Paul, 1980.

Bohm, D. As quoted in *Dialogues with Scientists and Sages: The Search for Unity,* R. Weber, ed. London and New York: Routledge & Kegan Paul, 1986.

Burroughs, W. S. *Ah Pook Is Here.* New York: Calder Press, 1979.

———. *The Western Lands.* New York: Viking Adult, 1987.

Burroughs, W. S., and A. Ginsberg. *The Yage Letters.* San Francisco: City Lights Books, 1963.

Burroughs, W. S., and B. Gysin. *The Third Mind.* New York: Viking Press, 1978.

Cairns, G. F. "A Theology of Human Liberation and Entheogens: Reflections of a Contemplative Activist." In *Psychoactive Sacramentals: Essays on Entheogens and Religion,* T. B. Roberts, ed. San Francisco: Council on Spiritual Practices, 2001.

California Department of Fish and Game. *Amphibian and Reptile Species of Special Concern in California: Colorado River Toad.* Rancho Cordova, Calif.: CDFG, 1994.

Calvo, C. *The Three Halves of Ino Moxo: Teachings of the Wizard of the Upper Amazon*. Rochester, Vt.: Inner Traditions, 1995.

Campbell, J. *The Inner Reaches of Outer Space: Metaphor as Myth and as Religion.* Novato, Calif.: New World Library, 2002.

———. *Myths of Light: Eastern Metaphors of the Eternal,* D. Kudler, ed. Novato, Calif.: New World Library, 2003.

Christian, S. T., et al. "Gas-Liquid Chromatographic Separation and Identification of Biologically Important Indolealkylamines from Human Cerebrospinal Fluid." *Biochemical Medicine* 14 (1975): 191–200.

Copeland, N. G., et al. "GENOMICS: Enhanced: Mmu 16—Comparative Genomic Highlights." *Science* 296 (5573) (2002): 1617–18.

Daly, J., and B. Witkop. "Chemistry and Pharmacology of Frog Venoms." In *Venomous Animals and Their Venoms* 2, W. Bücherl and E. Buckley, eds. New York: Academic Press, 1971.

Davis, W., and A. Weil. "Identity of a New World Psychoactive Toad." *Ancient Mesoamerica* 3 (1) (1992): 51–59.

Dawkins, R. *The God Delusion.* London: Bantam Press, 2006.

Deulofeu, V., and E. A. Rúveda. "The Basic Constituents of Toad Venoms." In *Venomous Animals and Their Venoms* 2, W. Bücherl and E. Buckley, eds.. New York: Academic Press, 1971.

Eliade, M. *Shamanism: Archaic Techniques of Ecstasy.* London: Routledge & Kegan Paul, 1964.

Elliot, T. S. *The Waste Land.* New York: Boni and Liveright, 1922.

Engelhardt, T. "A Global Arms Race Hidden in Plain Sight." *The Nation,* blog: *The Notion* (2008; Feb 13), www.thenation.com/blogs/notion/284571/a_global_arms_race_hidden_in_plain_sight. Accessed Nov 19, 2008.

Erspamer, V., et al. "5-Methoxy- and 5-hydroxyindoles in the Skin of *Bufo alvarius.*" *Biochemical Pharmacology* 16 (7) (1967): 1149–64.

Farrel, G., and W. M. McIsaac. "Adrenoglomerulotropin." *Arch Biochem Biophys* 94 (1961): 543–44.

de Félice, P. *Poisons sacrés. Ivresses divines: Essai sur quelques formes inférieures de la mystique.* Paris: Albin Michel, 1936.

Fish, M. S., et al. "*Piptadenia* Alkaloids. Indole Bases of *P. peregrina* (L.) Benth. and Related Species." *Journal of the American Chemical Society* 77 (1955): 5892–95.

Franzen, Fr., and H. Gross. "Tryptamine, *N, N*-Dimethyltryptamine, *N, N*-Dimethyl-5-hydroxytryptamine and 5-Methoxytryptamine in Human Blood and Urine." *Nature* 206 (1965): 1052.

Frost, D. R., et al. "The Amphibian Tree of Life." *Bulletin of the American Museum of Natural History* 297 (2006): 1–370.

Furst, P. *Hallucinogens and Culture.* Novato, Calif.: Chandler & Sharp Publishers, 1976.

Goswami, A. *The Self-Aware Universe: How Consciousness Creates the Material World.* New York: Jeremy P. Tarcher/Putnam, 1993.

Grey, A. *Sacred Mirrors: The Visionary Art of Alex Grey.* Rochester, Vt.: Inner Traditions, 1990.

Grof, S. *The Cosmic Game: Explorations of the Frontiers of Human Consciousness.* Albany: State University of New York Press, 1998.

———. *Psychology of the Future: Lessons from Modern Consciousness Research.* Albany: State University of New York Press, 2000.

———. *When the Impossible Happens: Adventures in Non-ordinary Realities.* Boulder, Colo.: Sounds True, Inc., 2006.

Haisch, B. *The God Theory: Universes, Zero-Point Fields, and What's Behind It All.* York Beach, Me.: Red Wheel/Weiser, 2006.

Hamblin, N. L. "The Magic Toads of Cozumel." *Mexicon* 3 (1) (1979): 10–14.

Hammerson, G., and G. Santos-Barrera. "*Bufo alvarius.*" In *IUCN Red List of Threatened Species.* Gland, Switzerland: International Union for Conservation of Nature, 2007.

Hanna, J. 2007. Personal correspondence with Keeper of the Trout.

Hanna, J. 2008. Personal correspondence with Keeper of the Trout.

Hartmann, T. *The Last Hours of Ancient Sunlight: The Fate of the World and What We Can Do Before It's Too Late.* New York: Three Rivers Press, 1998.

Holmstedt, B., and J-E. Lindgren. "Chemical Constituents and Pharmacology of South American Snuffs" In: *Ethnopharmacologic Search for Psychoactive Drugs.* D. H. Efron, ed. Washington, D.C.: U.S. Government Printing Office, 1967.

Horowitz, M., and C. Palmer. *Moksha: Aldous Huxley's Classic Writing on Psychedelics and the Visionary Experience.* Rochester, Vt.: Park Street Press, 1977/1999.

Hoshino, T., and K. Shimodaira. "Über die Synthese des Bufotenin-Methyl-Äthers (5-Methoxy-*N*-Dimethyl-Tryptamin) und Bufotenins (Synthesen in der Indol-Gruppe. XV)." *Bulletin of the Chemical Society of Japan* 11 (3) (1936): 221–24.

Huxley, A. *The Doors of Perception.* New York: Harper & Brothers, Publishers, 1954.

———. *Heaven and Hell.* New York: Harper & Brothers, Publishers, 1955.

———. *Island.* London: Chatto & Windus, 1962.

———. *Huxley and God: Essays on Religious Experience*. J. H. Bridgeman, ed. San Francisco, Calif.: HarperSanFrancisco, 1992.

Huxley, L. A. "O Nobly Born!" In *Moksha: Aldous Huxley's Classic Writing on Psychedelics and the Visionary Experience*. M. Horowitz and C. Palmer, eds. Rochester, Vt.: Park Street Press, 1977, 1999.

Impact. "Victims of Fog Creep: What's With the Newspapers?" *Plain Language at Work Newsletter* (May 2, 2005), www.impact-information.com/impactinfo/newsletter/plwork15.htm (accessed Nov 19, 2008).

Iyengar, B. K. S. *Light on the Yoga Sūtras of Patañjali*. Ottawa, Ontario: Educa Books, 1993.

Kaplan, J., et al. "Blood and Urine Levels of *N,N*-Dimethyltryptamine Following Administration of Psychoactive Dosages to Human Subjects." *Psychopharmacologica* 38 (1974): 239–45.

Kennedy, A. B. "Ecce Bufo: The Toad in Nature and in Olmec Iconography," *Current Anthropology* 23 (3) (1982): 273–90.

Kesey, K. "The Art of Fiction CXXXVI," *The Paris Review* 36 (120) (1994): 58–94.

Kump, L. R., and M. E. Barley. "Increased Subaerial Volcanism and the Rise of Atmospheric Oxygen 2.5 Billion Years Ago." *Nature* 448 (2007): 1033–36.

Lacarrière, J. *The Gnostics*. San Francisco, Calif.: City Lights Books, 1989.

Laszlo, E. *3rd Millennium: The Challenge and the Vision*. London: Gaia Books Limited, 1997.

———. *The Connectivity Hypothesis: Foundations of an Integral Science of Quantum, Cosmos, Life, and Consciousness*. Albany, N.Y.: State University of New York Press, 2003.

———. *Science and the Akashic Field: An Integral Theory of Everything*. Rochester, Vt.: Inner Traditions, 2004.

———. *Science and the Reenchantment of the Cosmos: The Rise of the Integral Vision of Reality*. Rochester, Vt.: Inner Traditions, 2006.

Lee, B. J., and M. A. Cowan. *Dangerous Memories: House Churches and our American Story*. New York: Sheed & Ward, 1986.

Legler, G., and R. Tschesche. "Die Isolierung von N-Methyltryptamin, 5-Methoxy-N-methyltryptamin und 5-Methoxy-N,N-dimethyltryptamin aus der Rinde von *Piptadenia peregrina* Benth." *Die Naturwissenschaften* 50 (3) (1963): 94–95.

Luna, L. E. *Vegetalismo: Shamanism Among the Mestizo Population of the Peruvian Amazon*. Stockholm, Sweden: Almqvist and Wiksell International, 1986.

Lyttle, T., et al. "*Bufo* toads and Bufotenine: Fact and Fiction Surrounding an Alleged Psychedelic." *Journal of Psychoactive Drugs* 28 (3) (1996): 267–90.

Manske, R. H. F. "A Synthesis of the Methyltryptamines and Some Derivatives." *Canadian Journal of Research* 5 (1931): 592–600.

Märki, F., et al. "Dehydrobufotenine, a Novel Type of Tricyclic Serotonin Metabolite from *Bufo marinus*." *Journal of the American Chemical Society* 83 (15) (1961): 3341.

Masters, R. A. *Darkness Shining Wild: An Odyssey to the Heart of Hell & Beyond.* Tehmenos Press, 2005.

McIsaac, W. M., et al. "10-Methoxyharmalan, a Potent Serotonin Antagonist which Affects Conditioned Behavior." *Science* 134 (1961): 674–75.

McKenna, T. K. *The Archaic Revival: Speculations on Psychedelic Mushrooms, the Amazon, Virtual Reality, UFOs, Evolution, Shamanism, the Rebirth of the Goddess, and the End of History.* San Francisco: HarperSanFrancisco, 1991.

McTaggart, L. *The Field: The Quest for the Secret Force of the Universe.* New York: Harper Perennial, 2003.

Metzner, R., ed. *Sacred Vine of Spirits: Ayahuasca.* Rochester, Vt.: Park Street Press, 2005.

Meyer, K., and H. Linde. "Collection of Toad Venoms and Chemistry of the Toad Venom Steroids." In *Venomous Animals and Their Venoms* 2. W. Bücherl and E. Buckley, eds. New York: Academic Press, 1971.

Most, A. *Bufo alvarius: The Psychedelic Toad of the Sonoran Desert.* Denton, Tex.: Venom Press, 1984.

Naranjo, C. "Psychotropic Properties of the Harmala Alkaloids." In *Ethnopharmacologic Search for Psychoactive Drugs.* D. H. Efron, ed. Washington, D.C.: U.S. Government Printing Office, 1967.

Narby, J. *The Cosmic Serpent: DNA and the Origins of Knowledge.* New York: Jeremy P. Tarcher/Putnam, 1998.

New Mexico Department of Fish and Game. *Natural Resources and Protected Species List of Threatened and Endangered Species,* Title 19, Chapter 33, Part 6, 1996.

Ott, J. *Pharmacotheon: Entheogenic Drugs, Their Plant Sources and History.* Kennewick, Wash.: Natural Products Co., 1993/1996.

———. *Shamanic Snuffs or Entheogenic Errhines.* Solothurn, Switzerland: Entheobotanica, 2001.

Pachter, I. J., et al. "Indole Alkaloids of *Acer saccharinum* (the Silver Maple), *Dictyoloma incanescens, Piptadenia colubrina,* and *Mimosa hostilis.*" *Journal of Organic Chemistry* 24 (1959): 1285–87.

Pahnke, W. N. *Drugs and Mysticism* (thesis), 1963.

Plotkin, M. Private conversation at an Audubon Society–sponsored slideshow in New Orleans, 1992.

Popp, F-A. "Coupling of Fröhlich-Modes as a Basis of Biological Regulation." In *Herbert Fröhlich, FRS: A Physicist Ahead of his Time: A Centennial Celebration of his Life and Work*. G. J. Hyland and P. Rowlands, eds. Liverpool, England: The University of Liverpool, 2005.

Rice, G. E. "Leapin' Lizards! The Things People Will Do to Get High." *The Kansas City Star*, (Dec 2, 2007): B1.

Roberts, T. B., ed. *Psychoactive Sacramentals: Essays on Entheogens and Religion*. San Francisco, Calif: Council of Spiritual Practices, 2001.

Sartre, J-P. *Nausea*. New York: New Directions, 1959.

Schopenhauer, A. *The World as Will and Representation (Die Welt als Wille und Vorstellung)*, translated by E. F. J. Payne. New York: Dover Publications, 1967.

Schultes, R. E., and A. Hofmann. *The Botany and Chemistry of Hallucinogens*, 2nd edition. Springfield, Ill.: Charles C. Thomas, 1980.

Schumacher, E. F. *Small Is Beautiful: Economics as if People Mattered*. New York: Harper Torchbooks, 1973.

Shankara, Swami. *Shankara's Crest-Jewel of Discrimination: Timeless Teachings on Nonduality* by Viveka-Chudamani. Hollywood, Calif.: Vedanta Press, 1975.

Shulgin, A., and A. Shulgin. *PIHKAL: A Chemical Love Story*. Berkeley, Calif.: Transform Press, 1991.

———. *TIHKAL: The Continuation*. Berkeley, Calif.: Transform Press, 1997.

Smith, H. *Cleansing of the Doors of Perception: The Religious Significance of Entheogenic Plants and Chemicals*. New York: Jeremy P. Tarcher/Putnam, 2000.

Smith, M. V. *Psychedelic Chemistry*. Port Townsend, Wash.: Loompanics Unlimited, 1981.

Sogyal, R. *The Tibetan Book of Living and Dying*, revised and updated. San Francisco: HarperSanFrancisco, 2002.

Strassman, R. *DMT: The Spirit Molecule: A Doctor's Revolutionary Research into the Biology of Near-Death and Mystical Experiences*. Rochester, Vt.: Park Street Press, 2001.

Torres, C. M., and D. B. Repke. *Anadenanthera: Visionary Plant of Ancient South America*. Binghamton, N.Y.: Haworth Herbal Press, 2006.

Trout, K. *Some Simple Tryptamines*, second edition. Austin, Tex.: Mydriatic-Productions, 2007.

USDA:APHIS:VS. *The Reptile and Amphibian Communities in the United States*. Fort Collins, Colo.: Centers for Epidemiology and Animal Health, 2001.

Vidal, J. "The End of Oil Is Closer Than You Think." *The Guardian* (April 21, 2005).

Vogel, N. "Couple Leap at Chance to Fight Toad-drug Charge." *The Sacramento Bee* (March 2, 1994): B1.

Walsh, R., and C. Grob. *Higher Wisdom: Eminent Elders Explore The Continuing Impact of Psychedelics*. Albany: State University of New York Press, 2005.

Wassén, S. H. "The Frog-Motif among South American Indians." *Anthropos* 29 (1934): 319–70.

———. "The Frog in Indian Mythology and Imaginative World." *Anthropos* 29 (1934): 613–58.

Wasson. R. G., et al. *The Road to Eleusis: Unveiling the Secret of the Mysteries*. Ethnomycological Studies No. 4. New York: Harcourt Brace Jovanovich, 1978.

Watts, A. W. 1961. *Psychotherapy East and West*. New York: Pantheon Books, 1961.

———. *The Joyous Cosmology: Adventures in the Chemistry of Consciousness*. New York: Pantheon Books, 1962/1965/1970.

Weber, R., ed. *Dialogues with Scientists and Sages: The Search for Unity*. London and New York: Routledge & Kegan Paul, 1986.

Wilson, C. *Beyond the Outsider*. London: A. Barker, 1965.

———. *The Philosopher's Stone: A Novel*. Los Angeles: Jeremey P. Tarcher, 1969.

———. *A Criminal History of Mankind*. London: Granada, 1984.

Wolfe, T. *Of Time and the River: A Legend of Man's Hunger in His Youth*. New York: Grosset and Dunlap, 1935.

Zohar, D. *The Quantum Self: Human Nature and Consciousness Defined by the New Physics*. New York: Quill/William Morrow, 1990.

Acknowledgments

I would like to first and foremost give thanks to my wife, the "Large Laser" and my shining light, for supporting me unconditionally throughout all of my adventures; to Rob for listening to hours and hours of my ideas as they slowly emerged; to Y. for taking me toading; to Kelly N. for being a role model of a truly open intellect; and of course to J. for turning me on in the first place—I love you my mad toad brother.

Through my gifting of copies at Burning Man, an early draft of *Tryptamine Palace* ended up in the hands of Jon Hanna, who I ultimately hired to edit the book for what I thought would be self-publication. Jon has played an important part in challenging me to really understand my own ideas as well as providing me with a wealth of information and references. His support has been invaluable, his intellectual antagonism stimulating, and I must thank him for his dogmatic insistence that those wiggly little things called "facts" really do exist. His efforts to wake me up from my complacency resulted in a much better book.

I would also like to thank specifically Goody for all the times he had to take care of the practicalities while my head was still in the clouds; Flashy for her unwavering enthusiasm; and Ronnie for lighting up when he read this book and for letting me know. Also my Burning Man tribemates, past and present, for always making me think that this work was important—with special thanks to Brother Dance, Jeff, and Uncle Andy for their invaluable support and trust. Love to King Weep, sorely missed. I would like to thank

Lorenzo Hagerty for giving me the opportunity to speak at the Palenque Norte dome at Burning Man in 2007; Love and appreciation to the Burning Man organization, the DPW, and the entire Burning Man community for all the hard work that is accomplished each year to make Black Rock City a reality. Finally, I would like to thank my editors, Chanc VanWinkle and Nancy Yeilding, for their hard work and invaluable help in clarifying my views and thus making this a much better book, and I would like to thank Jon Graham from Inner Traditions for allowing my voice to lift off the playa and out into the greater world.

True liberation is in our hearts and in our minds.
Namaste, peace, love, and light.

The author can be contacted at TryptaminePalace@hotmail.com.

Remember these teachings,
remember the clear light,
the pure bright shining white light
of your own nature.
It is deathless.

Attributed to *The Tibetan Book of the Dead*

Index

Page numbers followed by n indicate notes and those followed by f indicate figures.

BOOKS OF RELATED INTEREST

BOOKS OF RELATED INTEREST

DMT: The Spirit Molecule
A Doctor's Revolutionary Research into
the Biology of Near-Death and Mystical Experiences
by Rick Strassman, M.D.

DMT and the Soul of Prophecy
A New Science of Spiritual Revelation in the Hebrew Bible
by Rick Strassman, M.D.

Inner Paths to Outer Space
Journeys to Alien Worlds through Psychedelics
and Other Spiritual Technologies
by Rick Strassman, M.D., Slawek Wojtowicz, M.D.,
Luis Eduardo Luna, Ph.D., and Ede Frecska, M.D.

The Psychedelic Explorer's Guide
Safe, Therapeutic, and Sacred Journeys
by James Fadiman, Ph.D.

Dreaming While Awake
Techniques for 24-Hour Lucid Dreaming
by Arnold Mindell

Psychedelic Healing
The Promise of Entheogens for Psychotherapy and Spiritual Development
by Neal M. Goldsmith, Ph.D.

Plants of the Gods
Their Sacred, Healing, and Hallucinogenic Powers
by Richard Evans Schultes, Albert Hofmann, and Christian Rätsch

LSD: Doorway to the Numinous
The Groundbreaking Psychedelic Research into
Realms of the Human Unconscious
by Stanislav Grof, M.D.